ECCLESIASTICAL AUTHORITY
AND SPIRITUAL POWER

IN THE CHURCH OF
THE FIRST THREE CENTURIES

ECCLESIASTICAL AUTHORITY AND SPIRITUAL POWER

IN THE CHURCH OF THE FIRST THREE CENTURIES

HANS von CAMPENHAUSEN, D.D.

PROFESSOR OF ECCLESIASTICAL HISTORY
IN THE UNIVERSITY OF HEIDELBERG

TRANSLATED BY J. A. BAKER

STANFORD UNIVERSITY PRESS
STANFORD, CALIFORNIA

From the German
Kirchliches Amt und geistliche Vollmacht
© J. C. B. Mohr (Paul Siebeck), Tübingen, 1953

Stanford University Press
Stanford, California
© 1969 by A. and C. Black Ltd
Originating publisher: A. and C. Black Ltd, London, 1969
Stanford edition printed in the United States of America
ISBN 0-8047-0665-4
Last figure below indicates year of this printing:
86 85 84 83 82 81 80 79 78 77

CONTENTS

v

FOREWORD

MANY YEARS of work, and even more of preparation, have gone to the writing of this book. Its beginnings date in fact from the time when I first became a lecturer in the Faculty of Theology at Göttingen, to whom I now dedicate it. In doing so my mind goes back in gratitude to teachers who are no longer members of that Faculty as well as to those others who took their places. I have also received constant help and advice from my colleagues at Heidelberg, especially from Heinrich Greeven, now at Bethel, and Edmund Schlink, who has read every chapter, and whose criticisms have been of great benefit. My warmest thanks go also to Dr. Heinz Kraft for his help in reading the proofs.

As a man finds with his children, that the joy they bring is not unmixed, because they bear within them traces of one's own frailties, so it has been with this book. Moreover, it is never easy to convey to others one's own most cherished thoughts and experiences. My hope is that life will enable the reader to supply what is lacking, and that the work will prove of some use.

H. VON CAMPENHAUSEN

ABBREVIATIONS

ARW	Archiv für Religionswissenschaft
BM	Benediktiner Monatsschrift
BZTS	Bonner Zeitschrift für Theologie und Seelsorge
CSEL	Corpus Scriptorum Ecclesiasticorum Latinorum
DTC	Dictionnaire de théologie catholique
GCS	Griechische christliche Schriftsteller
HE	Historia Ecclesiastica
HTR	Harvard Theological Review
JBL	Journal of Biblical Literature
JEH	Journal of Ecclesiastical History
JTS	Journal of Theological Studies
LZ	Liturgische Zeitschrift
MGWJ	Monatsschrift für Geschichte und Wissenschaft des Judentums
NF	Neue Folge
NS	New Series
PRE	Protestantische Realenzyklopädie für Theologie und Kirche
RAC	Reallexikon für Antike und Christentum
RB	Revue biblique
RevHR	Revue de l'histoire des religions
RGG	Religion in Geschichte und Gegenwart
RHE	Revue de l'histoire ecclésiastique
RHPR	Revue d'histoire et de philosophie religieuses
RSR	Recherches de science religieuse
RTAM	Recherches et Bulletin de théologie ancienne et médiévale
SBA	Sitzungsberichte der berlinischen Akademie
SEÅ	Svensk exegetisk Årsbok
TLZ	Theologische Literaturzeitung
TQ	Theologische Quartalschrift
TR	Theologische Rundschau
TSK	Theologische Studien und Kritiken
TWNT	Theologisches Wörterbuch zum Neuen Testament
TZ	Theologische Zeitschrift
VC	Vigiliae Christianae
ZAM	Zeitschrift für Aszese und Mystik
ZKG	Zeitschrift für Kirchengeschichte
ZKT	Zeitschrift für katholische Theologie
(B)ZNW	(Beiträge zur) Zeitschrift für die neutestamentliche Wissenschaft
ZRG	Zeitschrift für Rechtsgeschichte
ZRGG	Zeitschrift für Religions- und Geistesgeschichte
ZST	Zeitschrift für systematische Theologie
ZTK	Zeitschrift für Theologie und Kirche
ZWT	Zeitschrift für wissenschaftliche Theologie

CHAPTER I

The Authority of Jesus

IN EVERY culture and in all ages human society has known the tension between the position assigned to a man and the ability which the man's own inner resources allow him to display. The former endues all that he does with the force of law and of the commission which stands behind him; the latter bestows on him as a person immediate credibility, and is the convincing justification of his claims. Only rarely are these two things entirely divorced. The man with gifts claims a position commensurate with those gifts; the man with position is obliged to try to fill it. A disproportionate emphasis on one of these elements at the expense of the other usually indicates a disturbed and strained situation on the verge of conflict, and threatened from within either by revolution or by equally drastic reaction. It is a serious symptom—especially in societies where high value is attached to office—when there is nothing more by way of authority to which appeal can be made than the givenness of the office as an institution, and when the office-holder (to borrow a phrase from Lichtenberg) invests his office with dignity only to the extent to which he himself is invested with the dignities of office. But even the man with particular 'gifts', and in that sense a special 'vocation', must acknowledge the prevailing order, or at least *some* higher order and norm, and be willing to serve it, if he is to win men's confidence and not merely to cause upheaval and destruction. The authority of office and the validity of personal endowment can become a danger to one another; but they also exercise mutual attraction and support.[1]

This twofold law applies also in the sphere of religion. Here, too, we find the familiar conflicts, painted for the most part in much too emphatic blacks and whites, between the functionary and the charismatic types of authority, between the priests and the prophets, between the champions of the sacral system and the witnesses to direct religious

[1] Some thoughts on the concept of organisational and charismatic structures are to be found in the works of Max Weber; cf. esp. the section, 'Grundformen der Herrschaft', in *Wirtschaft und Gesellschaft*, 1925². But the categories are developed in too schematic a manner to be useful as they stand for throwing light on early Christian situations.

experience. The only reason, however, why such conflicts can in fact be fruitful and instructive is that it is impossible to define the relation between these two types simply as one of pure contrast. Particularly when religious development has reached a fairly high level, the functionary must of necessity do his best to have some significance as a person, and to be holy in himself, since it is his task to sanctify others. Nor can the saint who acts without official authority have as his sole intention that of merely negating and dissolving spiritual discipline and order. In the real life of history each has his allotted place in relation to the other, and each must affirm the other; indeed, to a certain extent each assimilates to the other. That is why there has never been any lack of attempts to combine the various preconditions of religious authority, either by making the receiving of a spiritual endowment from God a prerequisite of investiture with office, or conversely by regarding appointment to office as the source of the appropriate spiritual capacity, which automatically results from it. In fact, however, it simply is not possible to base one form of authority on the other in this way. The two types cannot be thus amalgamated. If one is derived from the other, then it tends to dissolve, and to be deprived of its distinctive quality. Each must maintain its independence, if it is to survive.[2]

To a certain extent this sociological and religio-historical law of tension can be applied to Christianity also. But the order of things to which Christianity aspires has a distinctive character, and unfolds into a more elaborate and complex entity, calling for a broader interpretation. In the Christian context two presuppositions are decisive for the status both of official and of free authority, and from the outset make it difficult to place them either in straightforward mutual opposition or in conjunction. All considerations of office and authority, of organising tradition and quickening spirit aside, the Christian community is at all times determined first and foremost by faith on the one hand in Christ and on the other in the reality of his Church. The true 'High Priest' and 'Holy One of God' is never a mere human being, but Jesus Christ himself. Christ's congregation is constituted solely by faith in him; but as his congregation it then also has a real share in his authority and his spirit. This 'trinitarian' character of the order of the Christian community derives from the trinitarian form of the Christian revelation, and from the very beginning decisively and fundamentally shapes—and shatters—the salient concepts of special divine commissioning and special divine endowment. So long as it is not forgotten, it makes it equally impossible to treat office and charisma as absolutes either in opposition or in conjunction. The purpose of the present work

---

[2] On these issues cf. G. van der Leeuw, *Phänomenologie der Religion*, 1933, 'Heilige Menschen', pp. 173ff., and 'Stifter', pp. 618ff.

is to set out the historical evidence which enables us to recognise the mutual relationships of these various factors, and their basic importance, during the period from the beginnings of primitive Christianity to the threshold of the new developments which produced the phenomenon of the state church. In the course of these three centuries the ideal to which Christianity had originally been committed was impaired in various ways: not only do we find rigidities of attitude, curtailment of aspiration, distortion of insight, but also in every department—an indisputable trivialisation. On the other hand, there were also gains: a broader approach to the issues involved, and an extension of the material considered relevant. Nevertheless, however varied the development may have been, the starting-point is unquestionably to be found in Jesus himself. Our first and all-important concern must therefore be to grasp the distinctive character of his public ministry, and the nature of his claim to authority.

The difficulties of such an undertaking are great, even though for our present purposes no more is demanded than a sketch, drawn in a few bold strokes, but accurate enough to make later developments stand out in contrast. We know Jesus only as he was seen by the young Christian Church with the eyes of faith. Even where tradition seems to have preserved the particular, near eastern setting of the master's earthly life, this has not, for the most part, been done without specific theological intent or emphasis. Any attempt, therefore, to reconstruct Jesus's individual self-consciousness is hopeless from the start. On the other hand, the story of Jesus in the Gospels is, on the whole, comprehensible only as a revision and reshaping of quite definite living impressions and traditions, and in no sense as a work of pure theological fiction or speculation. Behind the Gospels, especially the Synoptics, stands Jesus himself. It is true that we can no longer come at him or apprehend him directly; but provided certain definite—and for our purposes essential—questions are pursued with vigour, answers are to be had which are remarkably clear, coherent, and original, and which cannot be explained as either the accidental by-product of theological composition or the result of cross-fertilisation from different theological treatments. Hence, at the very least, we stand in close proximity to the original Jesus, even if the genuineness of any one feature of the portrait may still be questionable or controvertible. Assuming then that we are willing to work on these lines, what does the synoptic material have to say in answer to our question about Jesus himself?

Jesus comes on the scene neither as one demonstrably endowed with a particular charisma nor as the holder of an office within his nation. He tells of no call; but neither does he pursue a calling. He has no title which might bestow upon his person a precise rank or station. The equivocal designation 'prophet' is bestowed upon him by others, but they are unable to confine him to this category alone.[3] The form of address 'Rabbi', 'Teacher', seems to accord with his teaching activity and with his position at the centre of a circle of disciples, but it does not make him a member of a particular profession,[4] with established rights and well-founded authority. Again and again the only discernible backing for his words and actions is himself and his own decision; and for this there seems to be no appropriate name nor standard of comparison. But for all that, Jesus comes before men with complete assurance and resolute authority. He teaches directly, without seeking to cover himself; he acts as the moment demands, not by precedent. Like a king he summons men to follow him; and he challenges the scribes to combat as if he himself had absolutely no need of rabbinic instruction. For Jesus there is no 'formal principle' of theology,[5] and no institutional public position either to confine or to support him. He acts with complete freedom as the person he is, and thus, in this comprehensive sense, 'with authority'.

In the environment of Jewish religious belief it goes without saying that Jesus was not, on the strength of this, regarded as, for example, a demi-god or a superman. On the contrary, the tradition emphasises the human traits in his portrait, or, at all events does nothing to suppress them.[6] Jesus is hungry and eats, is tired and sleeps. He expressly conforms with the structures of human life: he is subject to his parents, he allows himself to be baptised, he has God above for his heavenly Father, to whom he gives thanks and makes his petitions, and to whom he still submits in obedience, even when he believes himself abandoned. But for all that, the concept of 'authority' does give his mission and nature a supra-terrestrial reference.[7] The word ἐξουσία originally has a legal significance, and means the freedom which a person either receives or possesses to do a particular thing or exercise a particular

---

[3] Cf. Mt. 21:11, 46; Mk. 6:15 par.; 8:28 par.; Lk. 7:26; 24:19; Joh. 4:19; 9:17. Cf. R. Meyer, Der Prophet aus Galiläa. Studien zum Jesusbild der drei ersten Evangelien, 1940, pp. 10ff., 120ff. The present writer finds it impossible to accept the positive interpretation of Jesus's sense of his own calling and mission given in this exhaustive study. For a critique of Meyer's views cf. M. Veit, Die Auffassung von der Person Jesu im Urchristentum (Diss. theol. Marburg), 1941, pp. 104ff.

[4] Cf. K. H. Rengstorf, art. διδάσκαλος, TWNT 2, 1935, pp. 154ff.; art. μαθητής, TWNT 4, 1942, pp. 447ff.

[5] In TLZ 44, 1919, p. 220, M. Dibelius, reviewing D. A. Frövig, Das Selbstbewusstsein Jesu, 1918, writes: 'The thing which distinguishes Jesus from the Rabbis I too consider to be the absence of the formal principle, as we would describe it'.

[6] On what follows cf. W. Förster, art. ἐξουσία, etc., TWNT 2, 1935, pp. 559ff.

[7] Is this change an innovation made as a result of the confrontation with secular hellenism? Förster, op. cit., did not ask this question, and consequently took no notice of the shifts in emphasis.

jurisdiction. In Judaism it is used particularly of the omnipotence of God as unlimited 'authority', without precise definition of the sphere in which that authority holds.[8] In the same unrestricted way it is now asserted of Jesus that he taught and acted 'with authority'. This concept is a special favourite of Matthew.[9] In this usage it is very closely linked with the related concept—also employed in an absolute sense— of 'power' (δύναμις) as the miraculous, supernatural, and superhuman capability which expresses itself in 'works of power (δυνάμεις).[10] The meaning, however, undergoes a marked shift away from the naturalistic and physical in the direction of the legal and personal.[11] 'Authority' signifies the capacity to carry through his actions, both spiritually and physically, in such a way that resistance to them can never prevail. In this sense Jesus is seen to be exalted as 'sovereign' over all authorities which stand in his way, the Lord of every situation in which he finds himself. For the Evangelists this invincible lordship is the expression of his mysterious nature and power, and accordingly evokes astonishment and awe, enthusiasm or terror, as appropriate in each situation, but in every case a deep emotion and agitation in face of the new, unwanted, and unheard-of thing which makes itself known and present in his person.[12]

The impact of Jesus's authority should not be restricted to a merely 'moral' effect within the sphere of the human psyche. It is shown most directly precisely in the non-human, 'demonic' realm. Jesus possesses 'authority' over the demons,[13] which as incarnations of the power that is alienated from God create sickness and corruption in the unredeemed world. These beings have a demonic 'nose' for what Jesus is, and want

[8] Cf. W. Grundmann, *TWNT* 2, 1935, p. 302. In the Latin Bible ἐξουσία is consistently rendered by *potestas*.

[9] Cf. M. Dibelius, 'Gethsemane', *The Crozer Quarterly* 12, 1935, pp. 254ff.

[10] Cf. W. Grundmann, *Der Begriff der Kraft in der neutestamentlichen Gedankenwelt*, 1932, and artt. δύναμαι, etc., *TWNT* 2, 1935, pp. 286ff.

[11] Cf. K. L. Schmidt, 'Die Natur- und Geistkräfte im paulinischen Erkennen und Glauben', *Eranos-Jahrbuch* 14, 1946, p. 135, on the question 'how ἐξουσία and δύναμις may and must be distinguished. In keeping with the usage of the verb ἔξεστιν, the reference of ἐξουσία tends to be to the delegated right to power, whereas δύναμις, without any such theorisings, is concerned with the fact of power as such. Hence I am inclined to translate ἐξουσία as "right to power", and δύναμις as "expression of power".'

[12] The use of phrases with ἐκπλήσσειν, ἐξιστάναι, θαμβεῖσθαι, θαυμάζειν, is already conventional in the New Testament, and is generally typical of other comparable literature of the period: cf. R. Bultmann, *Die Geschichte der synoptischen Tradition*[2], 1931, pp. 247, 371 n. 2. A significant feature of the stories is the way in which men do not dare to challenge Jesus or address him directly: cf. Mt. 22:46; Mk. 9:32 *par.*; 12:34; Lk. 20:40.

[13] Mt. 10:1: ἐξουσία πνευμάτων; Mk. 6:7: ἐξουσία τῶν πνευμάτων τῶν ἀκαθάρτων = Lk. 9:1: ἐξουσία ἐπὶ πάντα τὰ δαιμόνια; cf. Mk. 1:27 *par.*; Lk. 10:19.

to have nothing to do with him. But when he threatens them, they are obliged to acknowledge his superiority, to accept his orders, and to come out of their victims in his presence.[14] There can be no doubt that the large number of miraculous healings of sick and possessed people, even if adorned in detail with legendary material, yet belong on the whole to the historically most certain elements of the traditions which have come down to us about Jesus. By the testimony of the demons, and afterwards of the sick who have been healed, the gaze of the people even against their will is constantly directed toward him.[15] The uncanny force of his psychic power simply cannot be disregarded. In the opinion of his enemies Jesus is in league with the Evil One,[16] and his own relatives are inclined to believe that he is mad.[17] Equally, however, his power to heal and to work miracles is not unlimited—as it becomes in later dogmatic christology.[18] Miracles which overthrow the laws of inanimate Nature are exceptional in the Jesus tradition, and in most cases can in fact be recognised as later additions.[19] Special psychological and parapsychological traits and capacities, which belong to the typical endowment of the contemporary hellenistic wonder-workers, likewise play no great part in the picture of Jesus.[20]

It is clear, however, that the true focal point of Jesus's activity and authority is not to be found in his miracles and deeds of power as such, but in his work as a teacher and preacher; it is this for which he has been 'sent'.[21] He preached 'as one that had authority, and not as the

[14] Mk. 1:27 par.; 3:11 par.; 3:22 par.; 5:2ff. par.; 9:25 par.

[15] On the problem of the command to the demons not to make him known which there is no need to discuss here, cf. esp. the exposition of H. J. Ebeling, Das Messiasgeheimnis und die Botschaft des Marcus-Evangelisten, 1939, pp. 115ff.

[16] Mk. 3:22 par.; 3:30; Mt. 10:25.

[17] Mk. 3:21.

[18] Mk. 6:5 par.; cf. Lk. 5:17. The difference in this respect between Jesus and God is stressed in Mk. 10:18 par.; 10:10 par.; 13:32 par. '. . . The "man having authority" is thus a pre-dogmatic interpretation of Jesus, which directly reflects the impact of his presence and activity': H. Windisch, 'Jesus und der Geist nach synoptischer Überlieferung,' Studies in Early Christianity (ed. S. J. Case), 1928, p. 226.

[19] Cf. the story of the withered fig-tree (Mk. 11:13ff. par.) and of the coin in the fish's mouth (Mt. 17:24ff.). The issue is less simple in the case of the stilling of the storm (Mk. 4:35ff. par.) and of the various raisings of the dead.

[20] Cf. L. Bieler, ΘΕΙΟΣ ΑΝΗΡ. Das Bild des 'göttlichen Menschen' in Spätantike und Frühchristentum, 1935, pp. 93f.; R. Meyer, Der Prophet aus Galiläa, pp. 10f. These features were given one-sided emphasis by R. Otto, The Kingdom of God and the Son of Man, 1943, pp. 333ff. Mk. 14:13ff. is, however, perhaps relevant here, though the locus classicus for charismatic insight in the case of Jesus remains Joh. 1:47.

[21] Lk. 4:43 par.; cf. 11:29 par. On the strictly traditio-historical interrelation of the words and miracles—the latter being for the most part effected by the spoken word—of Jesus, cf. O. Perels, Die Wunderüberlieferung der Synoptiker in ihrem Verhältnis zur Wortüberlieferung, 1934; on the meaning of the miracles

scribes'.[22] With this assertion Mark opens his account of Jesus's appearance at Capernaum, and the astonishment which it occasioned. The teaching of Jesus strikes men as new and 'authoritative'.[23] In Matthew the words corresponding to the latter verse have been moved, with great effect, to the end of the Sermon on the Mount.[24] In reading statements of this kind one should, of course, think primarily not of the outward form of Jesus's utterances, of the radical character and the freshness which may have distinguished them from the customary scribal instruction, nor even of the repartee and the vigour with which he was able in direct debate with his opponents to knock them down and 'stop their mouths'. Rather was it the actual content of what he said, in so far as this was peculiar to him and to him alone, which had this shattering and terrifying effect. In the preaching of Jesus the whole legal system which had obtained hitherto is finished and done with; it has no further part to play. The eternal, holy will of God, as he sets it before his hearers, cuts to pieces terrifyingly and uncompromisingly all the dilutions and falsifications, all the reservations and reassurances with which the exposition of the Torah sought to parry and restrict it. Man sees himself set naked and defenceless in the presence of the coming judgment; unless his righteousness is far better than that of the theologians and the pious—indeed, of the most pious people in the land—he will never enter the kingdom of God. But this threat is not to be separated from the promise, of which it is the reverse side, the promise that draws men with the new and boundless possibilities which are simultaneously made known and opened up in the acts of Jesus: 'The blind receive their sight, the lame walk, the lepers are cleansed, the deaf hear, the dead are raised up, and the poor have the gospel preached to them.'[25] 'Repent! for the kingdom of heaven is at hand.'[26]

The end of the old world has come, judgment and the sovereignty of God stand at the door—that is the message which Jesus brings; and it is in this perspective that we are to see the new and unprecedented element in his authority. In his works the demons are compelled to experience 'before the time'[27] that their power is broken, that the Holy One of God has come, the one with whom the new world begins.[28] For men, however, the decisive question is this: whether they 'hearken' to him, or instead stumble, are 'offended' at him,[29] that is to say, whether or not they are willing to affirm not only the preaching, which comes

---

as promises of the messianic age cf. Hoskyns and Davey, *The Riddle of the New Testament*[3], 1947, pp. 119ff.

[22] Mk. 1:22.
[23] Mk. 1:27: διδαχὴ καινὴ κατ' ἐξουσίαν = Lk. 4:36: ἐν ἐξουσίᾳ καὶ δυνάμει ἐπιτάσσει τοῖς ἀκαθάρτοις πνεύμασιν.
[24] Mt. 7:29. [25] Lk. 7:22 *par.* [26] Mt. 4:17 *par.*
[27] Mt. 8:29. [28] Mk. 1:24 *par.* [29] Lk. 7:23 *par.*

with no guarantees of any kind, but also the new authority of the preacher who brings it. The two things go together; it is a double offence. By demanding faith in his message Jesus sets up a claim which cannot be concealed by his appearing in the lowliness of humanity; and because he brings the 'gospel' in conjunction with his own person, the divine action that he proclaims possesses a 'humanness' which is precisely the thing that offends and enrages the most pious of his compatriots. For Jesus's call to conversion applies to everyone, and throws open the gates of the kingdom of heaven without distinction to all who will listen to him, not simply to the devout and the 'righteous', but also and particularly to those who are the objects of their rejection and reproach, the transgressors of the Law, the utterly lost, the sinners.[30] In the light of the coming kingdom of God not only have the detailed legal prescriptions and the 'fences round the Law' become pointless but also the very principle of drawing moral and religious gradations and distinctions between man and man. Sin too, as well as the power of the demons, is stripped of its consequence and importance; and again this disabling is accomplished in Jesus's own action, and there becomes visible for the first time. Jesus eats in company with tax-collectors and prostitutes,[31] and dares to announce explicitly to individual men and women the forgiveness of their sins.[32] The latter represents the extreme point beyond which a decision concerning the rightness or otherwise both of the 'gospel' and of the authority of Jesus himself can no longer be postponed. For by forgiving sins Jesus not only sets himself against the prevailing Law, which demands instead that the sinner be punished, but steps straight into the very place where, as the Jews believed and knew, only God can stand. The man who is not prepared to 'believe' in Jesus in deadly earnest is obliged to see his behaviour as a blasphemy —for 'who can forgive sins but God only?'[33]

It is this underlying theme which has determined the shape of the pericope about the paralytic. Here Jesus is made, in opposition to the critical challenge of the 'scribes', to provide a practical demonstration that 'the Son of Man has power on earth to forgive sins'.[34] The allusion, however, to the status of the 'Son of Man' as an eschatological, super-human figure patently derives from the standpoint of the evangelist, and is not original.[35] Jesus himself is precisely the one who does not

[30] Mk. 2:17 par.; Lk. 19:10, etc.
[31] Mk. 2:16 par.; Mt. 11:19 par.; Lk. 19:7.
[32] Mk. 2:5 par.; Lk. 7:48; Joh. 8:11.
[33] Mk. 2:7 par.; Lk. 7:49.   [34] Mk. 2:10 par.
[35] It may originally have arisen as the result of a mistranslation of the idiom 'son of man' meaning 'child of man', i.e., human being. The present explanation, which is that of Wellhausen, would not then be necessary: cf. E. Klostermann, *Das Markusevangelium*[3], 1936, pp. 23f.; E. Hirsch, *Frühgeschichte des Evangeliums* I, 1941, p. 10. For R. Bultmann, *op. cit.*, pp. 12f., as for W. Wrede earlier,

need a justification of his authority in terms, so to speak, of an official position, for this authority is vindicated by his action, that is to say, it is demonstrated. That is why the deeply agitated crowd gives the praise for this act not to him but simply to God, 'who has given such authority to men'.[36] A similar comment could be made about the story in which Jesus's disciples rub the ears of corn on the sabbath. Here, according to the testimony of the evangelist, Jesus proclaims the Son of Man, that is, himself, as lord of the sabbath, and thus sets aside the prescriptions of Jewish legalism; but a second, more original answer attributed to him is not restricted to his own person, but makes a quite general assertion about the fundamental human position as such: 'The sabbath was made for man, not man for the sabbath.'[37] This double reference to the eternal and the exceptional, to that which has been from the beginning and that which is sheerly once-for-all, permeates the whole of Jesus's preaching, and demarcates the mystery of his person. There can be no *simpliste* resolution of this mystery by distributing all the relevant material among different strata of the tradition. It is true not only of his moral commands, which autocratically declare the Law invalid, and in its place seek to put nothing other than a confirmation of the ancient and primal will of God, the earlier revelation of which ought properly to have sufficed mankind;[38] it is equally manifest in the distinctive character of faith as Jesus demands it. Where Jesus is ready to help and to heal, men have to believe that he can do what is necessary for their hopes to be fulfilled.[39] But in that case faith is directed yet again quite simply and directly to God himself, and to the possibilities which he now bestows; if the disciples only had faith 'as a grain of mustard seed', then they too would heal the sick, drive out demons,[40] even move trees and mountains[41]— for 'all things are possible to him that believes'.[42]

Of his own faith, however, Jesus never speaks.[43] Hidden behind the

---

the whole debate in vv. 5b–10 is an interpolation; for a criticism of this view cf. M. Dibelius, in *Theologische Rundschau* NF 1, 1929, p. 211.

[36] So Mt. 9:8. According to A. Schlatter, *Der Evangelist Matthäus*, 1929, p. 311, with whom R. Bultmann, *op. cit.*, p. 14, is in agreement, the use of the plural τοῖς ἀνθρώποις already indicates the conviction that 'Jesus's authority to forgive sins has become the possession of the community'.

[37] Mk. 2:27f. *par.*

[38] Mk. 10:6 *par.*; Lk. 16:29; cf. also the juxtaposition of Mt. 5:17ff. with 5:22, etc.

[39] Mt. 9:28, on which cf. Bultmann, *op. cit.*, pp. 234f.

[40] Mt. 17:20 *par.*   [41] Mk. 11:23 *par.*

[42] Mk. 9:23. For a most impressive discussion of this double perspective and its inner unity cf. A. Schlatter, *Der Glaube im Neuen Testament*[3], 1905, pp. 132ff. His solution in terms of Jesus's filial consciousness is, however, somewhat dogmatic.

[43] Even on the subject of his prayer life virtually nothing can be discovered.

veil of his own silence he remains in the end the one man who already stands on the far side of the old nature,[44] not merely proclaiming the coming of the kingdom and the holiness of a renewed humanity, but also exhibiting and incarnating them. He himself is the great 'sign' of the coming and irruption of the kingdom of God, and it is clear that behind him, the man, stands the glory of this kingdom and of God himself.[45] In Jesus we see a freedom, a serenity, and a power of human nature which point to the future, and which before him had been unheard of.[46] Jesus has no official status, but he has a mission; he is at the same time the one who is sent and the one who from the start and in his inmost self matches the demands of that mission. He does not, like an ordinary prophet, need to receive God's spirit and endowment; he stands completely on God's side. Nor is he the holder of any office in the customary sense, he appeals to no official commissioning; for commission and office are combined in his person. Hence there are no ready-made categories under which the distinctive quality of his authority, as this is to be seen in the Gospels, can be subsumed. Seemingly the only effective reality is the demand and promise which stem from God alone, to which Jesus bears witness, and behind which he vanishes in an anonymous humanity. But precisely because of this it is through him that God's demand and promise are made present directly and 'in power'; and only because they are present in him do they insist on being heard. In whatever way we approach the subject, therefore, we come up against the same question, and one which, for all that it is a concealed question, cannot be evaded: the problem of the nature of the person of Jesus. In his own lifetime, at any rate in public, Jesus never supplied an unequivocal answer.[47] It is obvious that in his own day, which was one of tense messianic eschatological expectations of many kinds, many different interpretations were put upon him. Both friend and enemy puzzled over the enigma of his person.[48] Some had

---

If we set aside the Gethsemane legend, the doubtful words from the Cross, and certain edifying elaborations in Luke, then all that is left is that Jesus said a grace at mealtime for those who were with him, which is something we could take for granted.

[44] 'As is well known, Jesus never simply groups himself with the rest of mankind': M. Kähler, *Der sogenannte historische Jesus und der geschichtliche, biblische Christus*[2], 1896, p. 81 n. 3.

[45] Mt. 12:38ff.; Lk. 17:21.

[46] Mt. 11:11 *par.*

[47] A personal public attestation of what he was (leaving aside the doubtful case of the confession before the Sanhedrin) would never have fallen into oblivion. Cf. M. Dibelius, *Jesus*[2], 1947, p. 91: 'This above all is clear, and clear beyond a peradventure, that Jesus during his active ministry did not accord prominence to the messianic question.' Cf. further A. Fridrichsen, 'The Messiah and the Church', in G. Aulen *et al.*, *The Root of the Vine*, 1952.

[48] Mt. 11:3 *par.*; 12:23; Mk. 6:2f. *par.*; 6:14–16 *par.*; 8:27f. *par.*; Lk. 4:41

their suspicions (at which they shuddered with horror); many expected him to bring in the eschaton. But even the latter never found an attitude toward him to which they could commit themselves irrevocably, and so they were still not truly bound to him. 'Those who are with me have not understood me'.[49] Even his most loyal disciples abandon him every one in the end, and Jesus dies alone.

Only the resurrection enables men to transcend this situation, and it does so in a twofold way. First of all, the 'name' of Jesus is now made known without disguise or concealment to every man as that of the Messiah and Redeemer, the Son of God and Lord of the world and of its future.[50] The riddle of his person is solved, and confession takes the place of conjecture and doubt. But with confession a new humanity, or rather a new 'people', is founded, which affirms the new Name, and takes it upon itself in baptism. The distinctive nature and the holiness which Jesus possessed do not become things of the past, nor do they remain restricted to his own person. This means that the problem of Jesus's authority is posed in a new way: the fact that this authority continues to exist as a present reality, and the way in which this is brought about, are decisive for the nature of his community. In the first instance, however, the question does not arise in this general form, but as a question about the authority and commission of certain quite definite persons within the community, namely the 'apostles'.

---

par.; 5:21. In John this stimulating incomprehensibility of Jesus's person has been made into a separate theme of conscious theological reflection.

[49] *Actus Petri cum Simone* 10; cf. J. Jeremias, *Unbekannte Jesusworte,* 1951, p. 73. The emphasis on the 'strangeness' of Jesus in the eyes of his followers is a gnosticising trait.

[50] From the very beginning, when it is a matter of giving special content to the Name, a variety of roles are predicated of Jesus and allowed to stand side by side; but the idea of revelation and fulfilment is common to them all. There is therefore no need to discuss here their emergence, origins, and meaning.

CHAPTER II

The Apostles

THE HISTORICAL problems in the way of any attempt to grasp the spiritual ethos and organisational tendencies of the primitive community in Jerusalem are no less than those which confronted us in the case of Jesus himself. We possess hardly one word which can, in its present form, be ascribed with certainty to their circle; though even so there are various sources from which conclusions can be drawn—the Synoptic Gospels, the picture in Acts, and above all the Pauline Epistles—in addition to scattered hints in other and later traditions. First and foremost, however, one thing is quite incontestable, namely that the primitive community was the point from which the whole succeeding development began. It was in no sense a mere episode in the story of early Christianity, but the centre from which the new movement radiated, the fountainhead of its entire history. Paul had already acknowledged its significance in this respect, and later generations were to follow his lead. Those who came after interpreted the tradition they received, and in so doing they naturally from the very first also transformed it, and in numerous ways placed it in a different light; but they did not invent it, and therefore their evidence concerning it can still be of use to us.

Above all, it was from the primitive community that there came the decisive witness on which the whole of Christendom was built, the witness to the Resurrection. The encounters in which various men, and perhaps women too, of the earliest circle of disciples had, as they did not doubt, really and truly met with their risen Master were the fixed starting-point of the Christian movement. Nor may we doubt that this was a datum of their experience, however difficult it may be today either to introduce any critical order into the luxuriant confusion of mutually contradictory individual traditions or to throw light on their psychological character.[1] For the primitive community Jesus *had* risen; and with this sign of the imminent consummation of the age a twofold reality had become a certainty for their faith. On the one hand, the riddle of his person is now resolved by God himself; Jesus is the living

[1] A fresh attempt to do this can be found in my own study: *Ablauf der Osterereignisse und das leere Grab*, 1952.

Lord and Redeemer, Messiah and Son of Man,[2] soon to return on the clouds of heaven. On the other, the revelation of this truth simultaneously brought with it the conviction that the gathering and renewal of Israel, the eschatological people of God, must now begin.[3] In Jewish expectation the one could not be separated from the other; and the enthusiastic spirit of holiness, which in fulfilment of the ancient prophecies was poured out on all who believed in and were baptised into the 'Name' of Jesus, made the realisation of the promise a matter of direct experience. Hence the message of Jesus's resurrection must be made known and proclaimed to 'all the world'. The community does not keep itself to itself, but at once turns outward on its work of preaching; and even though the little group does not succeed in winning the whole, or even the greater part, of the Jewish people for Christ, yet it does not therefore allow itself to be silenced, but spreads abroad with explosive force in all directions.

There was, then, in the first Christians a living enthusiasm which was through and through something historically conditioned and determined.[4] For this reason alone it would be perverse to try to describe the nature and self-consciousness of the group on the model of modern 'spiritual' sects, which are concerned only with seeking direct religious experience 'in the spirit', and consequently never attain any firm organisational shape or structure. The young Church starts from the historical message of the Resurrection, and as a result is assigned a particular place and task in the history of salvation. Hence from the very first, for all the intensity of its life and experience, it is marked by a shape and structure which differentiate between its members and give each an individual role. In the primitive community freedom reigns, but not equality. At no time is there a lack of outstanding personalities with their own particular vocation and authority; and these distinctions are not the product of the merely fortuitous diversity of individual natures and their endowments, nor do they arise 'organically' out of the practical requirements of community life—though it is true that the latter call for attention at an early stage, and do lead to particular forms of organisation. Instead they make their appearance simultaneously with the Church itself, and are an integral part of the story of its origin. The 'Apostles' are earlier than the Church, earlier even than the Church in the limited sense of a sociologically definable entity; and the later

[2] The problem, when were these various titles first used, and whence did they derive, need not, as already remarked (cf. p. 11, n. 50 above), be discussed here.

[3] On this subject cf. esp. N. A. Dahl, *Das Volk Gottes. Eine Untersuchung zum Kirchenbewusstsein des Urchristentums*, 1941, and A. Oepke, *Das neue Gottesvolk in Schrifttum, Schauspiel, bildender Kunst und Weltgestaltung*, 1950.

[4] Cf. A. Fridrichsen, 'Die neutestamentliche Gemeinde', in G. Aulen *et al.*, *Ein Buch von der Kirche*, 1950, pp. 51ff. and esp. 57ff.

view of them in Church history and law is justified to the extent that theirs was an antecedent authority by which the Church itself was established and defined. Nevertheless, the dogmatic conception of the apostle and of the apostolic authority has drastically over-simplified the real situation in the primitive period, and given it a coherence it did not in fact possess. If we wish to recover the true circumstances in all their living, complex reality, we must set aside the rigid formulas and concepts of a later age, and start by breaking down or at least teasing out the community into the individuals and groups which the records show to have been the leading elements within it, and which may then be examined separately. Only when this has been done can we go on to determine the common factor in their positions of power and authority, and hope to throw light on whatever may have been the unique status which they all shared.[5]

A present-day Christian, when the apostles are mentioned, thinks first and foremost of the 'twelve Apostles'.[6] Now it is in fact true that 'the Twelve' are the oldest and most venerable group within the primitive community; but it was precisely as 'the Twelve', and originally hardly at all as apostles, that they enjoyed their corporate status. It was only at a later stage that they were made first into apostles and then finally into the only apostles. It is probable—despite all the doubts that have been raised—that their appointment really does go back, as the tradition would have it, to Jesus himself; and that at a particular point in the course of his earthly ministry he did, as Mark puts it, 'make' the Twelve,[7] calling and commissioning them. On any other hypothesis it is difficult to explain when or where the circle of the Twelve must have been formed. Nevertheless, the conception which, thanks to Luke, became the dominant one, namely that the Twelve were the real leaders and governors of the primitive community, is untenable. Even as early as the Epistle to the Galatians there is no longer any mention of the Twelve as such when Paul speaks of the 'men of repute' in Jerusalem, and gives their names.[8] The widely disseminated second-century legends of the missionary journeys, which they are supposed to have made to every part of the world after years of ruling the Church from Jerusalem, are entirely without historical value; and the same applies to the many differing accounts of their martyrdoms. Except for Peter and the shadowy figures of James and John, the sons of Zebedee—and of course, though in a legendary and stylised manner, Judas Is-

---

[5] For a more detailed presentation of the evidence on which the brief sketch which follows is based cf. H. Von Campenhausen, 'Der urchristliche Apostelbegriff', *Stud. Theol.* I, 1948, pp. 96ff.

[6] On this subject cf. K. H. Rengstorf, art. δώδεκα, *TWNT* II, 1935, pp. 325ff.; also E. Lichtenstein, 'Die älteste christliche Glaubensformel', *ZKG* 63, 1950–52, pp. 53f.

[7] Mk. 3:14.   [8] Gal. 1:18ff.; 2.2.

cariot—the Twelve are merely names to us, lacking all personal or biographical detail. The most probable hypothesis, therefore, is that these men, the ones chosen by Jesus himself, though undoubtedly present when the primitive community first came into being, and naturally held in a certain respect by its members, nevertheless as a group played no vital part in its life, and may even before very long have been broken up and disbanded by death and other circumstances.

What then can Jesus have had in mind, and what significance did he attach to the Twelve, when he chose them, and raised them from the rank and file of his other 'disciples' to their special position? Our Gospels picture them as his personal companions, who on occasion acted also as his plenipotentiary messengers and preachers to the people. Jesus had already sent them out on one such mission before his death; and after the Resurrection he commissioned them afresh for this work. It may well be that these narratives have been influenced by the concept of apostleship, which has been retrojected on to the Twelve; for in fact, apart from Peter, none of the Twelve figures later as a missionary. Even if, however, the tradition is accepted as correct, this cannot have been the unique and distinguishing characteristic which would explain why Jesus selected them. The preaching mission to Israel was no narrowly restricted privilege. Luke, for example, records a parallel sending out of 'another' seventy, or seventy-two, disciples,[9] who have been likewise assimilated to 'apostles' by subsequent tradition. This much at any rate is correct, namely that there is some connection between the number of the Twelve and 'Israel', the nation of the twelve tribes, and that this is the reason for the choice of this particular number. The Israel in mind, however, may in fact not be the Jewish people as objects of the Christian mission, but rather the new, Christian Israel, which is to triumph at the day of Christ's return, when the kingdom of God breaks into world-history. It is this Israel which is represented by the Twelve.

This is borne out by the tradition that the circle of the Twelve had to be made good after it had been broken by the removal of the traitor. Luke makes use of this tradition as an introduction to the book of Acts,[10] and it can hardly be without any kernel of historical truth. According to the story the decision to appoint Matthias was made by casting lots after invoking the Lord; in other words, the intention was that the calling of this new member to make up the number should, like the earlier vocations, be entirely the work of Jesus himself. Much

[9] Lk. 10:1.

[10] *Acts* 1:15ff.; in support of the genuiness of this account cf. the not entirely satisfying argument of J. Renié, 'L'Élection de Mathias (Act. 1, 15–26)—authenticité du récit', *RB* 55, 1948, pp. 43ff., and more recently E. Stauffer, 'Jüdisches Erbe im vorchristlichen Kirchenrecht', *TLZ* 77, 1952, pp. 201ff.

more important, however, is the fact that an act of this kind was performed on this one occasion only, in order to provide a substitute for
the 'son of perdition'[11] who had been eternally lost. By contrast, no
such procedure was felt to be necessary after the martyrdom of James.[12]
This can only mean that the real and imperishable significance of
the Twelve was not connected with the contemporary life of the community at all. Their function was not that of an ecclesiastical magistracy
or permanently constituted court of appeal, where the loss of a member
means that a replacement must be elected at once; their importance
as a group was of a very different, once for all, nature. The Twelve
were formed in view of the coming kingdom of God, and they enter on
their real duties only at the Last Day, when they are to 'sit on twelve
thrones, judging the twelve tribes of Israel'.[13] It is in expectation of
this hour, which is to exalt them to the supreme honour, that they
regard it as their prime duty 'not to depart from Jerusalem'.[14] They
remain in the holy city of the chosen people as a sign proclaiming and
representing the coming order and sovereignty of God.

It was, therefore, natural enough that at a later stage—and perhaps
not only later—the twelve should have been regarded as already ful-
filling this function of supreme judges and rulers in the primitive
community itself. Their actual importance for the Church, however,
was the product less of this eschatological promise than of the historical
part which they had played in the story of its origins. For the Twelve
were among the primary witnesses to the Resurrection of Christ. The
risen Jesus had in very truth appeared to their assembled company, and
thus had made them his witnesses both to the body of believers and to
the whole world. Paul himself had already received this historical statement from the primitive community as a major element in the Gospel
tradition, and in his turn had handed it on to the Gentile congregations:
Christ 'was raised on the third day in accordance with the scriptures,
and . . . appeared to Cephas, then to the Twelve'.[15] Likewise, at the end
of the century John the Divine sees in a vision the Twelve as the foundation-stones of the eternal city of God; the twelve gates of the city
bear the names of the twelve tribes of Israel, and the foundation-
stones on which they are erected are inscribed with 'the twelve names of

---

[11] Joh. 17:12.   [12] Acts 12:2.

[13] Mt. 19:28 par.; that this hope was not, however, limited to the day of
judgment is indicated by the request of the sons of Zebedee (Mk. 10:37 par.),
and the expansion of the Lord's promise in Lk. 22:30.

[14] Apollonius, quoted in Eusebius, HE V, 18, 14. The limiting of this command to the period before Pentecost (Acts 1:4) will then be a later modification;
the original permanent instruction may underlie Acts 8:1: cf. Goguel, L'église
primitive, 1947, pp. 28ff.

[15] I Cor. 15:4f. Cf. E. Lichtenstein, op. cit., pp. 1ff.; H. von Campenhausen,
Der Ablauf der Osterereignisse, pp. 8ff.; also p. 35 n. 25 below.

the twelve apostles of the Lamb'.[16] As witnesses to Jesus the Twelve have become the 'foundation' of the Church,[17] and this significance, which they had acquired for the very first generation of Christians, they retain to all eternity, corporately providing the solid base on which the whole structure rests.

Nevertheless, this function of being witnesses to Jesus and the Resurrection was not originally exclusive to the Twelve. It will have been remarked that in the ancient formula just quoted the name of one particular individual occurs before the mention of the Twelve as a group, a man who is indeed a member of their circle, but whose importance far transcends that bestowed by this membership, someone who, so far as we can discover, was from the very first a man of quite peculiar weight: the apostle Peter.[18] As with the Twelve, the beginnings of his personal distinction seem to go back to the time before the first Easter and to Jesus himself. It must have been Jesus who described him as the 'Rock-man' by giving him the nickname Cephas, though the sense in which this designation was meant must remain an open question. It is conceivable that the sobriquet was intended only to characterise his personal qualities, in the same way presumably as James and John were dubbed 'Sons of thunder'. Probably, however, the reference was to something more than this, to a special promise pointing to a future eschatological position or function.[19] It is hardly possible now to make any definite conjectures as to the content of this promise. The famous saying that the whole Church is to be built on Peter is simply inconceivable in the mouth of Jesus, and in all probability reflects a situation in which expansion has already gone beyond the ambit of the primitive community.[20] In the present context, therefore, it must be left out of account. Moreover, Peter acquired his most vital significance primarily as a witness to the risen Christ, and in this capacity, as we have seen, originally took precedence even over the Twelve. Peter was the first to whom Jesus appeared after his Resurrection. This tradition is not only explicitly recorded by Paul, but the resurrection narratives in the Gospels also still show traces of it,[21] so that it must in fact be in accord

---

[16] Rev. 21:14.   [17] Cf. pp. 19f., 130f. below.

[18] On this subject cf. E. Fascher, art. 'Petrus', PRE XIX. 2, 1938, cols. 13335ff.; H. Strathmann, 'Die Stellung des Petrus in der Urkirche; zur Frühgeschichte des Wortes- an Petrus Matth. 16. 17–19', ZST 20, 1943, pp. 223ff.; E. Stauffer, 'Zur Vor- und Frühgeschichte des Primatus Petri', ZKG 62, 1943–4, pp. 3ff.; J. L. Klink, Het Petrustype in het N.T. en de oudchristelijke letterkunde (Diss. Leiden 1947); and more recently O. Cullmann, Peter: Disciple, Apostle, Martyr, 2nd edn. 1962.

[19] Cf. Strathmann, op. cit., pp. 227, 251; Stauffer, op. cit., pp. 9f.; also A. Schlatter, Der Evangelist Matthäus, 1929, pp. 507f., where, however, the argument assumes the genuineness of Mt. 16:17ff.

[20] Cf. pp. 129f. below. The same applies to Lk. 22:31f.; Joh. 21:15ff.

[21] I Cor. 15:5; Lk. 5:1ff.; 24:34; Joh. 21:1ff.; Gosp. Pet. 59f.

with the original historical state of affairs. This means that it was with Peter that the Easter faith in the Risen Christ began,[22] and therefore the history of the Christian Church as a whole.[23] Moreover, it is precisely in Peter's case that the first encounter with Christ is at the same time very clearly his vocation and commissioning: Peter is made a missionary by a call to become a 'fisher of men' which is prior to the call of the other Apostles.[24] Now it is not inconceivable that he did in fact come to the fore in Jesus's lifetime as his emissary, and that the relevant promises, albeit now in legendary form, do not simply represent later retrojections from the post-Easter period into the time of the ministry. The more probable interpretation, however, is that for Peter as for the rest it was the encounter with the risen Christ which provided the decisive impetus, the starting-point of his true vocation and genuinely 'apostolic' activity. It was therefore as the risen Lord that Christ gave Peter, as he was later to give Paul, both a particular charge, in this case to preach the gospel to all the circumcised, and also the power to carry out this command.[25] It may also be that the restriction, mentioned nowhere else, of this mission charge, confining it to the Jewish world, is no more than a detail added by Paul from his own special standpoint. For Peter it may at first have been simply something taken for granted that his mission was to the Jews; but in proportion as the scope of his operations spread farther and farther afield, beyond Palestine to Syria, and then possibly to Asia Minor, it must have become impossible in practice for him to confine himself exclusively to Jews and proselytes. It is unquestionable that there were Gentile congregations which venerated Peter as their apostle, and Acts stresses the particular importance of his mission for the Gentile world.[26] Indeed, his historical importance must have consisted not least in the fact that he gave the support of his personal approval to the changeover from a

[22] He must also have been the one who collected the eleven and led them to Galilee so that Christ could appear to them as a group: cf. Campenhausen, *Osterereignisse*, pp. 44f.

[23] F. Kattenbusch ('Die Vorzugsstellung des Petrus und der Charakter der Urgemeinde zu Jerusalem,' *Festgabe K. Müller*, 1922, pp. 324ff.) has raised objections on this point to the view of K. Holl (cf. p. 20 n. 39 below), butt hese have rightly been rejected. Cf. further K. G. Goetz, *Petrus als Gründer und Oberhaupt der Kirche*, 1927, pp. 3ff.; E. Seeberg, 'Wer war Petrus?', *ZKG* 53, 1934, pp. 571ff. O. Linton (*Das Problem der Urkirche in der neueren Forschung*, 1932, pp. 180f.) gives a more balanced account of the state of the question than Seeberg. More recently cf. also N. Hufman, 'Emmaus among the Resurrection Narratives,' *JBL* 64, 1945, pp. 205ff. (and the comments thereon of W. G. Kümmel, *TR* 18, 1950, pp. 23f.); Lichtenstein, *op. cit.*, pp. 46ff., and Cullmann, *op. cit.*, pp. 58ff.

[24] Lk. 5:10.

[25] Gal. 2:7f.; on this subject cf. A. Fridrichsen, *The Apostle and his Message*, 1947, pp. 6ff.

[26] Acts 8:14ff.; 10:1ff.; 15:7ff.

Jewish to a universal mission, and managed to secure for the latter a certain degree of recognition even in Jerusalem.[27]

Primarily, however, Peter is a figure of authority within the Jerusalem community itself. It is round him that the rest of the apostles group themselves,[28] and his testimony, his 'faith', gives stability to the congregation.[29] Hence, too, his judgment is of supreme importance in every problem of the community's life. It is no accident that the book of Acts portrays Peter as the permanent spokesman and leader of the Twelve, and makes him the one who gives the ruling in difficult cases.[30] Every stratum of the New Testament, and even more emphatically the apocryphal literature, through all the variety of viewpoint and presenttion indicates Peter as an outstanding and decisive figure in primitive Christianity. It would, nevertheless, be quite wrong to suggest that Peter was already playing the part of a spiritual monarch, a first Pope, or Bishop of Jerusalem. It is true that Paul undertook his first journey to Jerusalem in order to 'make the acquaintance of Cephas';[31] but Peter is not thought of here as the leader of the apostolic circle. The context seems rather to call for a rendering to the effect that Paul journeyed to Jerusalem simply and solely to make the acquaintance of Peter as an individual—and not of the definitive apostolic body as a whole and in its official capacity. On this occasion, indeed, apart from Peter, he also conferred with James, the Lord's brother.[32] In connection with his later visit Paul speaks of the circles of those who 'were reputed to be something', and observes that James, Cephas and John (listed in that order) were 'reputed to be pillars,'[33] that is to say, personalities who 'carried' the Church, and on whom its structure rested.[34] Later Peter left Jerusalem altogether,[35] and in all probability met a

---

[27] On this subject cf. the exposition (which can indeed be disputed on points of detail) by W. Grundmann, 'Die Apostel zwischen Jerusalem und Antiochia', ZNW 39, 1940, esp. pp. 128ff.

[28] They are described in the variant reading at Mk. 16:8–9, and in Ignatius, Smyrn. 3:2, as οἱ περὶ Πέτρον.

[29] Lk. 22:31f.   [30] Acts 1:15ff.; 5:1ff.; 15:7ff., etc.

[31] ἱστορῆσαι: Gal. 1:18. Paul may well have had a special interest in Peter, because the latter was the apostle most involved with the missionary work of the Church.

[32] Gal. 1:19.

[33] Gal. 2:9. The στῦλοι may well have formed an inner group within the δοκοῦντες: cf. H. Schlier, Der Galaterbrief, 1949, pp. 35f.

[34] Schlier, op. cit., p. 45, rightly emphasises that the imagery behind the expression is of the same type as the characterisation of the apostles as 'foundation-stones'. It is, however, much more of a commonplace or cliché, and therefore more suitable as the designation of a group of 'aristocrats' whose preeminence was a practical rather than a dogmatic affair. On the meaning of the imagery cf. H. G. Ewers, Tod., Macht und Raum, 1939, p. 99.

[35] Acts 12:17.

martyr's death as a missionary in Rome.[36] And with these few scraps of information we must perforce be satisfied.

In Jerusalem itself it seems that in course of time James took the direction of the congregation more and more into his own hands. In this way the primitive community acquired as its leader yet another personality who was *sui generis*.[37] James, the full brother of Jesus, was not a member of the Twelve, nor indeed in Jesus's lifetime was he even numbered among his disciples; he seems rather, like all Jesus's relatives, to have taken a hostile attitude to his work.[38] James, too, however, during the crucial days when the community was being established, was granted an appearance of the risen Christ,[39] and this may therefore in his case—as was to happen later in that of Paul—have acquired the simultaneous significance of a conversion. This event also immediately established his position and authority, as Paul testifies; for in the ancient list of witnesses to the resurrection, which he records, James's name follows that of Peter and of the Twelve.[40] In Antioch Peter yields to the emissaries of James,[41] and Acts portrays him as in the end the sole figure at the centre of the elders and congregation of the Jerusalem church.[42] The growth in his influence to which this appears to point must be linked with the disappearance of the hellenistic elements in the primitive community; for James was a representative of a markedly Judaistic Christianity.[43] Needless to say, neither was James the 'first Bishop' of Jerusalem, for all that the second century wished to make him such. In the older legends, however, he survives much more as the ascetic 'righteous man', the martyr, and the last priestly witness to the truth, whose work lay among his own people, but who found no successor to follow in his steps.[44]

It is interesting that other relatives of Jesus in addition to James played some part. At the beginning of Acts Luke mentions Mary and Jesus's brothers as forming with the apostles the nucleus of the earliest

---

[36] Despite all the objections that have been raised, this can be regarded as virtually certain: cf. esp. H. Lietzmann, *Petrus römischer Märtyrer*, 1936. A recent argument to the contrary is that of K. Heussi, 'Galater 2 und der Lebensausgang der jerusalemischen Urapostel,' *TLZ* 77, 1952, pp. 67ff., which is based on a by no means unqualifiedly convincing exegesis of Gal. 2:6. On his interpretation of the verb ἦσαν, the στῦλοι in this passage ought to be regarded as already dead (and James, despite Gal. 1:12, as the son of Zebedee). A sounder interpretation may be found in Schlier, *op. cit.*, pp. 42f.

[37] On what follows cf. H. Von Campenhausen, 'Die Nachfolge des Jakobus', *ZKG* 63, 1950–52, pp. 133ff., and the literature there listed.

[38] Mk. 3:21, 31 *par.*; 6:3 *par.*; Joh. 7:5, 10.

[39] I. Cor. 15:7; Gosp. Hebr., quoted by Jerome, *De vir. ill.* 2; cf. K. Holl, 'Der Kirchenbegriff des Paulus im Verhältnis zu dem der Urgemeinde', *Gesammelte Aufsätze* I, 1928, pp. 48f.

[40] I. Cor. 15:7.   [41] Gal. 2:12.   [42] Acts 15:13; 21:18; cf. 12:17.

[43] Gal. 2:12.   [44] Cf. Hegesippus, quoted in Eusebius, *HE* II, 23, 5f.

congregation.[45] Paul attests the fact that the Lord's brothers, like Peter, undertook missionary journeys, on which the congregations where they worked were required to support them and their wives;[46] and similar statements are made about even later members of Jesus's family from Galilee.[47] It must indeed have been there, and not in Jerusalem, that they were principally active and enjoyed relatively their greatest influence.[48]   In the Lukan version of the history of the primitive Church, and in Paul, they play no further part. The unique circumstance of their physical kinship with the Lord must have given them a certain importance, especially on their home ground;[49] in general they should not be put on the same level as the men whom the risen Christ himself called, and appointed as his witnesses.[50]

It remains now to consider the last, and by far the most important, group of notables in the primitive Christian community, namely the genuine apostles in the narrow and original meaning of the word.[51] It is to some extent impossible to draw hard and fast dividing-lines between these men and the leaders of other groups who at a later stage were also in many cases categorised as 'apostles'. On Luke's view, indeed, the Twelve alone are reckoned to be true apostles, and as a result of the influence of his own book, the Acts, this conception was to become in the end almost universal. Such a systematisation, however, does not correspond to the historical facts. Of the Twelve only Peter unquestionably also ranked as an apostle, whereas of others Paul undoubtedly and James the Lord's brother possibly were counted among the apostles;[52] and it is demonstrable that the original apostolic group must have been much larger. A striking feature of the group is the wide range of variation in importance and human status between its various members. Alongside the leading personalities of the primitive com-

[45] Acts 1:14.   [46] I Cor. 9:5.
[47] Cf. Julius Africanus in Eusebius, HE I, 7, 14.
[48] Cf. the information handed down by Hegesippus concerning the δεσπόσυνοι; also E. Lohmeyer, Galiläa und Jerusalem, 1936, pp. 53f., 57.
[49] This point has been brought out, with a great deal of evidence, by E. Stauffer, 'Zum Kalifat des Jakobus', ZRGG 4, 1952,, pp.1 ff. The parallels which he cites, however, cannot establish the validity of a 'dynastic' interpretation in the case of James himself; they merely indicate that one is possible.
[50] Against any over-valuation of their authority cf. also G. Kittel, 'Der geschichtliche Ort des Jakobusbriefes', ZNW 41, 1942, pp. 73f.
[51] On what follows cf. H. Von Campenhausen, 'Der urchristliche Apostelbegriff', Stud. Theol. I, 1948, pp. 96 ff.; K. H. Rengstorf, art. ἀπόστολος, TWNT I, 1933, pp. 406ff.
[52] It is well known that the Pauline statement in Gal. 1:19 is not unambiguous on this point. H. Schlier, Galaterbrief, 1949, p. 31, in agreement with Zahn, decides against James's being an apostle. On the other hand, H. J. Schoeps, 'Jakobus ὁ δίκαιος καὶ ὠβλιάς und Paulus', Aus frühchristlicher Zeit, 1950, pp. 120ff., infers, with the help of Hegesippus (Eusebius, HE II, 23, 7), that James bore the title שליח, the Jewish equivalent of ἀπόστολος.

munity we find virtual ciphers, such as the Jewish Christians Andronicus and Junias at Rome, of whom we would know absolutely nothing, were it not that Paul had felt it necessary to commit them to the special care of the congregation in that place, and to commend them as 'men of note among the apostles'.[53]

In what then did the distinctive character and activity of an apostle consist? In every case the apostles are missionaries, and to that extent the popular conception of the apostolate and of 'apostolic ministry' is entirely correct. Preaching is of the essence of the apostolate; no apostles are known to us who are not at the same time missionaries. But the modern concept of a missionary is not wide enough to characterise fully the status and weight of apostolic authority. For the apostles are quite plainly vested with the direct power and dignity of their Lord himself. The very word 'apostle' is nothing other than a literal translation of a Jewish legal term with a definite meaning, namely *shaliach*, which denotes the person of a plenipotentiary representative, whose task it is to conduct business independently and responsibly for the one who has assigned him these powers for a particular service. The apostles are thus the plenipotentiaries of their heavenly Lord; and their authority, therefore, does not derive from any human call or contingent developments, but is based in all probability on a call by the Risen Christ himself, who, we are told, appeared to Cephas, to the Twelve, to James, and also 'to all the apostles'.[54] As a result of their encounter with him the disciples are called to be apostles, and know themselves sent at his command into all the world[55] in order by teaching and baptising to make disciples of 'all nations'.[56] This means that they are not simply preachers and teachers, but also founders of Christian communities, and as such know themselves, as Paul at least clearly indicates, to be permanently responsible for their congregations. As witnesses, messengers, and personal representatives of Christ the apostles are the principal and most eminent figures in the whole primitive Christian Church,[57] and in Jerusalem and among the Gentile congregations alike theirs is the supreme authority.

This brings to an end our survey of the most important groups and individuals within the primitive community. We can, therefore, no longer evade the task of attempting a general assessment of the distinctive character of their position and authority. One thing at any rate has become clear from what has been said so far: the emergence within the

---

[53] Rom. 16:7.   [54] I Cor. 15:7.

[55] This connection between the apostolate and the resurrection experience seems to me today even more certain than it did at the time of my essay, 'Der urchristliche Apostelbegriff'.

[56] Matt. 28:19, where the commission is confined to the eleven apostles.

[57] I Cor. 12:28.

primitive Church of major determinative figures, described indiscriminately in later times as 'apostolic', derives without exception so far as we can judge from the experience of the Resurrection, or at the very least stands in a close historical and spiritual connection with that experience. It is true that the rise to prominence of particular men owed something to their natural gifts and capacities; and to some extent the circumstance of having in earlier days been associated with the Master in his earthly life comes into consideration. Nevertheless, again and again the decisive factor is the encounter with the Risen Lord, which was frequently both experienced and understood as a special call or commission. The number of eye-witnesses who had seen the Risen Christ ran into hundreds;[58] but the 'apostolic' men of the primitive community had not merely seen him, they had also been constituted by him public witnesses to his resurrection and person. Ringed with the iron of their testimony, the Church's faith in Christ could never be shattered. To this extent not only Peter and the Twelve, but also James and 'all the apostles', right through to Paul, the last apostle, are in fact part of the 'gospel'. With their testimony, therefore, they are in truth earlier than the Church, which is based on that testimony, and must continually renew its relationship with it. They are, indeed, the inaugurators and foundation-stones of the Church, despite the fact that their importance, their position, and their personal quality vary considerably in other respects, and that not even their number can be established with certainty.

Directly implicit in this once-for-all character of their function is the fact that the rank and authority of the apostolate are restricted to the first 'apostolic' generation, and can be neither continued nor renewed once this has come to an end. The Resurrection is a unique event set in historical time, the certainty of which is not (as might be quite conceivable in the abstract) confirmed and kept alive by constantly repeated manifestations of Christ. Instead, once experienced and attested, it has simply to be handed on, 'safeguarded' and 'believed'. It is true that the temptation to extend the apostolate beyond the apostolic generation was not entirely avoided; here and there attempts were made to turn the title of 'apostle' into a kind of professional designation for missionaries and for ascetic men of the Spirit.[59] In the long run, however, all these attempts proved abortive. The holders of the 'apostolic' office of bishop, who ultimately secured the government of the Church, did not describe themselves as apostles; they are simply the successors, or at most the representatives, of the apostles, and as such they too remain bound by the original apostolic word and witness, which finds its

[58] I Cor. 15:6.
[59] Rev. 2:2; Did. 11:3–6; Hermas, Sim. IX, 15:4; Hom. Clem. 11, 35; on this subject cf. Campenhausen, 'Apostelbegriff', pp. 109f.

definitive form in the New Testament canon. It was the latter which
in a certain sense became the real heir of the apostles' authority.

First of all, however, we have still to deal with the real apostles,
whose importance is not exhausted by their being 'historical witnesses,'
mere handers-on and guarantors of a tradition. This would in no way
be a full and sufficient account of their place, for witness to Christ is
a 'word' in the most living and comprehensive sense. It is no mere
neutral act of communication, but of its very nature has a significance
which speaks directly to the individual, convicts, imposes obligations,
renews. It has to be expounded, applied, made relevant, and so attested
and presented in a topical and forceful way.[60] It is for this that the
apostles, as living persons, are called, and for this that they receive
'power from on high',[61] the Spirit which abides upon them. Hence their
testimony works with superhuman power, and bestows upon them a
freedom and a joyfulness which does not fail them, even when faced
with powerful and seemingly overwhelming opposition, but is still
triumphant even in death.[62] But it is not just a matter of proclaiming
the word with a confidence of manner which was incomprehensible
by human standards. Exactly as Jesus himself had done, the apostles
use deeds to reinforce the word, the miraculous signs of exorcism,
healing, raising the dead, and similar 'works of power'. There is a
clearly defined concept of the miracles that are 'the signs of a true
apostle.'[63] To this extent everything which has been said earlier about
the authority of Jesus also applies precisely to the authority of his
apostles. The only question is: when were these parallels, which existed
from the very first, clearly discerned and emphasised as such? For
Luke the answer is, 'throughout'. He portrays the apostles' miracles,
the effect of their preaching, the sufferings and fortunes of their persons, in a way which corresponds point for point to the picture of
Jesus and which exhibits the fulfilment of the latter's earlier predictions.[64] In John we further find constant reflection on the basic theo-

---

[60] Cf. R. Asting, *Die Verkündigung des Wortes im Urchristentum*, 1939 *passim*.

[61] Lk. 24:49.

[62] In addition to the Pauline passages on this subject quoted in the next
chapter, cf. Mk. 13:11 *par.*; and the following incidents from Acts: 1:4, 8;
2:22, 43; 4:30, 33; 5:12; 6:8; 8:6, 13, 19; 13:10f.; 19:11f.; 28:8f.

[63] II Cor. 12:12, cf. Rom. 15:19; also p. 39 n. 57 below.

[64] Lk. 21:12ff.; 10:16. The tendency to 'model the disciples on the Master'
is especially apparent in the accounts of healing miracles: W. Grundmann,
op. cit., p. 131. A. M. Farrer, 'The ministry in the New Testament', *The Apostolic Ministry* (ed. Kirk), 1946, p. 134, sees in Luke nothing less than 'a most
emphatic typologist', because he makes not only the career of the apostles
parallel that of Jesus but also that of Paul parallel that of Peter. We should,
however, be careful to bear in mind here the more general rule that duplication
and parallelism are a feature of every aspect of Luke's writing: R. Morgenthaler,
Die lukanische Geschichtsschreibung als Zeugnis. Gestalt und Gehalt der Kunst des

logical concept that the word and operation of Christ are directly continued in the word and work of his disciples, in their 'testimony', and thus that for the world the two have the same significance. Indeed, the capabilities of the disciples in certain respects even go beyond Jesus's own acts during his earthly ministry, because in his victory the overcoming of the world has already been achieved, and the Spirit which glorified him has been given to his disciples: 'Truly, truly, I say to you, he who believes in me will also do the works that I do; and greater works than these will he do, because I go to the Father'.[65]

In the case of the disciples, therefore, just as in that of Jesus himself, word and action, claim and person, manifestly coincide. But throughout the New Testament there is also a decisive difference between the Lord and his followers which should not be overlooked. True though it may be that the authority and the power to act are here and there the same, and possess an equal 'judging' and saving meaning for men, yet only Jesus had this authority 'in himself'. By contrast, the disciples receive it 'in his Name', and only in his Name and in the power of the Spirit given by him can they remain what they have become; or, to put it another way, it is Jesus himself who takes them into his service, works in them, abides with them, and employs them in his cause. In this way the authority of the disciples is clearly distinguished from the unique authority of Jesus, and is subordinated to it in accordance with God's will. In the case of Jesus it is not possible to draw a line of demarcation between his person and his commissioning; by contrast, the apostles are much more closely akin to the Old Testament prophets who received and took upon themselves word and spirit, the prophetic commission and the prophetic capabilities, at a particular point in their lives, except that now this calling and witness in all its immediacy has a single historical starting-point, the person of the Risen Jesus, which can never pass away, but remains in some sense effectual and contemporary for all Christians and for all the world. Moreover, his Spirit is effective in a more comprehensive, more then merely prophetic, sense inasmuch as it is the spirit of the eschaton, and as such permeates, sanctifies, and re-creates every aspect of the Christian's life.[66]

Lukas I, 1946. Another detailed point of comparison is the effect on the astonished multitude (Acts 2:12,43; 8:13; 9:21; 13:12) and their divided reactions (2:12f.; 28:24f.). The question put to the apostles about their authority (Acts 4:7) corresponds to Lk. 20:2.

[65] Joh. 14:12.

[66] G. von Rad has pointed out to me that even the Old Testment prophet did not give his testimony as a completely isolated act, but was at all times involved in the existing relationship between God and people and with God's law; and that furthermore, in the development of prophecy from Amos to Deutero-Isaiah, the prophetic commission more and more seizes and takes over

Every action of the apostles, therefore, refers back to the person and authority of the one whose Name they bear. They are no more than his 'plenipotentiaries' and representatives; and it is of the essence of a true emissary that all his significance relates to his master, and none at all attaches to his own person: 'He who hears you, hears me.'[67] Again and again this dialectic of the apostolic life is expressed as clearly as anyone could wish. The apostles are described as attaching great importance to the fact that men, in the very moment when they are amazed by their miracles, nevertheless ascribe none of all this to the apostles themselves, but understand that their only purpose is to bear witness to another, and that 'by their own power or piety' they would never have accomplished such things.[68] The apostles are in no way supermen or heroes; on the contrary, it is vital for a right understanding of their character and calling to make it clear that they are by nature nothing more than weak, frail creatures, helpless and witless; in other words simply 'men', and that it is only as instruments of the Spirit and of divine election that they have been endowed with superhuman capacity. They have God's treasure, as Paul emphasises, in earthen vessels;[69] without Christ, as John says, they 'can do nothing'.[70] Even in Mark, however, we already find an unmistakable picture of the lack or discernment, the despondency, the worldly outlook, and the concern with self-assertion which dominate the disciples in the very presence of their master.[71] Even Peter, who was the first to confess his faith in him 'thinks not God's thoughts, but men's'. He tries to follow Jesus, but through doubt sinks into the waves; he swears to remain faithful, and betrays him before the cock crows. In the end all the disciples abandon Jesus. Such pieces of information are not there simply as literal historical truth; it is a dogmatic purpose which makes the oldest tradition keep such cruel hold on the disciples' failure, and lay such stress upon it. Matthew and Luke, it is true, attempt to mitigate this picture of weakness and shame at some points. Luke in particular portrays the apostles in Acts as also models of holiness for their congregations. Nevertheless, the crucial features of human frailty and guilt are nowhere completely effaced, and are still brought out even in later tradition—sometimes with quite surprising sharpness.[72]

---

the whole personal life of the prophet. This, however, does not alter the fact that with Christianity there is a change in fundamental principle.

[67] Lk. 10:16 par.

[68] Acts 3:12, cf. also 9:34, where Peter expressly states that it is Christ who heals through his miracle.

[69] II Cor. 4:7; cf. pp. 40f. below.   [70] Joh. 15:5.

[71] On what follows cf. Strathmann, op. cit., pp. 226ff.

[72] The most extreme example of this (though with a rather different didactic point in mind) is Barn. 5:9: 'When he chose as his own apostles to preach his gospel men [so] lawless [that they had gone] beyond every sin, in order to show that he "came not to call the righteous, but sinners..."'

For all the common human failings, however, inherent in the apostles as in every man, nothing can alter the fact that they were chosen and called by Jesus Christ, and filled with the power to bear living witness to him. In this consists the permanent value which is theirs within the Church as well as outside it. This value is based not merely on the actual abilities which they may share with other Spirit-filled and prophetic men, but on the central fact of their being appointed by Christ as witnesses. To this extent the apostolic status is not only 'authority', but also has a value resembling that of an assigned office. Yet such a description does not completely fit the case; it is no accident that in the New Testament the explicit concept of an 'apostolic office' is absent. Paul terms his calling a divine ordinance, a ministry, and a grace given him by the exclusive choice of God himself.[73] Even more strikingly, Luke selects a whole range of expressions which he uses either independently or in combination. He speaks of the 'place' and 'lot' of this 'ministry', and of the apostles' 'ministry of the word', which he calls an 'overseership' or even an 'apostolate', a mission and authority which—on his view of the matter—is granted only to the Twelve.[74] John avoids the concept of 'apostle' altogether, very possibly because in his time it was already too heavily loaded with official and 'authoritarian' ideas, and seemed to threaten that awareness that Christ was directly present to all Christians which to him was the thing that mattered. The once-for-all character of the apostolic calling is completely incompatible with the idea of an organised office, the essence of which is that it remains constant even when the holders change. The apostles, who had been called by name, found, as we saw, no successors. The decisive fact about their position is that their calling is related to the person of the Lord to whom they bear witness, and not to any kind of system or organisation. The concept of an office is essentially linked with a community and with a particular 'constitution', however embryonic, within which the holders of the office have their entitlements and their legal status. The apostles, however, are not in this sense an ecclesiastical 'supreme court'; they may create an organisation'[75] but they themselves are prior to any organisation, and neither they nor their 'office' are part of it. We must not in this context draw anachronistic modern distinctions between 'purely spiritual' functions and those of ecclesiastical administration. Undoubtedly the first apostolic men of the primitive community also governed that community, possessed special honour within it, and took decisions concerning it. The vital meaning of Christian witness, embracing as it does the whole of life, would certainly lead us to assume this, and Paul and Luke confirm it. It is for this very reason that the

[73] Rom. 11:13; 12:3; 15:15; I Cor. 3:10; 9:17; II Cor. 1:11; 3:6; 4:1; 6:3f.; 8:19; Gal. 1:15f.; Col. 1:25.
[74] Acts 1:17, 20, 25; 6:4; 20:24.   [75] On this point cf. pp. 76ff. below.

apostles have to be warned against self-aggrandisement and desire for power: 'Whoever would be first among you must be slave of all.'[76] 'You are not to be called rabbi, for you have one teacher, and you are all brethren. . . . Neither be called masters, for you have one master, the Christ'.[77] But such formulations reveal how all pretensions were thought of in personal terms, and have nothing to do with a struggle for a particular office or for a position in a hierarchy.[78] Where this fact is not appreciated, the concept of the apostolate is bound to be misconstrued from the start.

The most impressive evidence against a simple organisational interpretation in terms of constitutional law is the fact that it is quite impossible to arrange the leading figures of primitive Christianity in any definite patterns, vertical or horizontal, which would allow us to delimit their mutual official rights and duties. This is relevant in particular to the many and various Catholic attempts to attribute to Peter a special 'primacy' over the Twelve, and to reconcile his rights with the claims of Paul and with the supposed status of James.[79] The only result of all such efforts is a tangle of overlapping and mutually destructive jurisdictions, not made any more comprehensible by superimposing as an afterthought attempts to blunt the edge of the legal approach by crediting the early Christians with a first love which for the moment made it unnecessary to work out the institutional system of the Church with greater precision. There is no evading the fact that it is the underlying legalist conception itself which is inappropriate. The Protestant critical approach, however, is at bottom not much better; for while indeed acknowledging the apparent contradictions that exist, it then interprets them as nothing more than the crudities and obscurities of the original patriarchal situation—in other words, once more tacitly relating everything to the notion of a definite, even though at first only 'embryonic', constitution. The result of thinking along these lines is the well-known presentation of the primitive community in terms of various mutually competitive tendencies in ecclesiastical politics. The attempt is then made to associate these tendencies with particular apostles such as Peter or James, on the assumption that the different points of view must still be expressed in the extant texts. We must re-

[76] Mk. 10:44 par.

[77] Matt. 23:8–10.

[78] Cf. E. Schweizer, Das Leben des Herrn in der Gemeinde und ihren Diensten, 1946, pp. 19ff.

[79] A crude example of this method is to be found in the essay by P. Gaechter, 'Jerusalem und Antiochia. Ein Beitrag zur urkirchlichen Rechtsentwicklung', ZKT 70, 1948, pp. 1ff. For the difficulties which from the very first were raised by the particular problem of incorporating Paul into the apostolic circle cf. J. Wagenmann, Die Stellung des Apostels Paulus neben den Zwölf in den ersten zwei Jahrhunderten, 1926.

ject absolutely any view of the apostles either as model, peaceable members of the hierarchy, or as jealous, quarrelling consistory councillors. The whole way of thinking in terms of ecclesiastical law and ecclesiastical politics implied in such a picture is completely foreign to primitive Christianity.

This, of course, is not meant to imply that the affairs of the primitive community were easy to superintend or free from tension. There is no need to idealise away the personal and practical conflicts that undoubtedly existed. We know from the Pauline Epistles how serious were the differences of opinion on particular questions, and how hard the men in authority found it to get along with one another. Even Luke in his glossy presentation has not been able wholly to suppress these unhappy features. The decisive factor, however, was not one of the importance of particular offices or of the competence of ecclesiastical authority. That which in spite of everything held the primitive church and its 'apostles' together was not the unity of an organised Church but the unity of their witness to Christ and of their vocation. For this vocation and its authority a hierarchical or organisational basis was not of decisive importance. Here and there such things may have been associated with the image of apostolic authority; but such instances are not accessible to us now, and in any case did not at first determine the course of future developments.

This is as much as can prudently and without *a priori* argument be extracted from our sources; and this means that we must also recognise our limitations. For the earliest period we can discern no more than the rough outlines of the concept of an apostle. In particular we do not know how a Peter or a James or any one of the Twelve saw and understood his specific authority, so to speak, from the inside. On this subject there is only one apostle whose thoughts we know with any degree of precision, and he—in this respect as in every other—is to be regarded as an exception: the apostle Paul.

CHAPTER III

Apostolic Authority and the Freedom of the Congregation in the Thought of Paul

IT IS precisely on those questions which are essential to our present purpose that in the case of the apostle Paul we are particularly well informed. Individual details of his life, his call, his relations with the first apostles and with his congregations, may remain obscure; but on the fundamentals of his apostolic self-consciousness we have in the Epistles[1] an abundance of statements as definite as they are direct, made indeed with reckless candour.

Everything that Paul says, writes, or teaches is worked out not on the neutral ground of general considerations, but as an integral part of his own work and purpose, of the dramatic struggle of his own life. And an extraordinary life it was—even for an apostle. Paul quite rightly knew and acknowledged that both as a person and as a public figure he was in the most radical sense an exception,[2] not by some accident without further significance nor by human choice, but an intentional, incomprehensible exception created solely and deliberately by God's saving election. Peter, the Twelve, and many other apostles had been disciples of Jesus in his lifetime; James had at first been cool or even hostile toward his brother and Lord; but Paul was plucked in mid-career from the life of a raging enemy and persecutor to be an apostle.[3] For this monstrous begetting he paid the price all his life long. It was because of this that he referred to himself as 'the least of all the apostles, who am not worthy to be called an apostle'.[4] The grace and the burden of such an election was for Paul all the more palpable in that it was precisely to him, the unworthiest of the apostles, the one called, so to speak, as an afterthought, that a unique task was committed. Christ had entrusted to him the entire pagan world; Paul is *the* apostle of the Gentiles. It was his duty to put aside the old law of God, which for the rest still counted as a holy thing, and to take the Gospel to all nations. From the day

---

[1] In what follows Ephesians and the Pastorals, as being non-Pauline, are not taken into account; Colossians and II Thessalonians have been made use of as probably genuine. Omitting their evidence, however, would make no essential difference to the general picture.

[2] I Cor. 15:8; cf. p.35 below, n. 26.   [3] Gal. 1:13ff.   [4] I Cor. 15:9.

when the Risen Lord confronted him directly and with blinding sudden-ness in the way this was the whole content of his life. Without a moment's pause he began on his work; without losing his way, or allowing him-self to become bogged down in details, he carried it on year after year systematically and resolutely, building only on ground of his own breaking, hurrying from city to city, from province to province, in order to cover the whole world as far as Spain before the return of Christ. And everywhere he went he planted the standard of 'his own' law-free Gospel, by which all men were to be brought into subjection to Christ.

This claim, which Paul put forward as his own to the exclusion of all other apostles, was so tremendous that making it good inevitably meant trouble. Wherever he appeared, controversy arose over his preaching and his person. Nor was it only the gentile authorities and populace with whom he came into conflict, or the Jews who pursued him, the renegade, with their inextinguishable hatred: within the Church, too, Paul had throughout his life to fight for his message and his standing. It is true that the first apostles and the authorities in Jerusalem extended to him the hand of fellowship; but they seem nevertheless to have regarded his impetuous and radical methods with doubt and uneasiness, and the more emphatically Judaeo-Christian members strove constantly to restrict his influence, and to assert as far as possible the continuing validity of the Law for gentile Christians. Even in his own congregations opposition was constantly being stirred up, set in motion by 'deceitful workmen',[5] and growing on occasion into open rebellion. Such continual guerrilla warfare, added to the contro-versies about fundamentals and the immense loneliness attendant upon all the inward and outward cares of his mission, never succeeded, how-ever, in bringing his work to a standstill. Paul never 'lost heart';[6] 'in ill repute and good repute'[7] he pressed on unceasingly with his plans, and at the end was able to make a claim which no man dared contest— that his success was without parallel. He had achieved more 'than any of them', and God's calling and grace toward him had not been 'in vain'.[8]

In such a life the question which might otherwise have remained in the background was bound to become a central theme: whence did Paul derive his authority? What was its nature and significance? How was it made effective? What possibilities were open to him, to what rights could he appeal? So far as a developed doctrine is concerned, Paul is the true founder and discoverer of the Christian concept of authority; and in this connection he does not begin from the com-munity as a whole or from any particular individual Christian. The starting-point, both for him personally and as an objective fact, is his

[5] II Cor. 11:13.
[6] II Cor. 4:1.
[7] II Cor. 6:8.
[8] I Cor. 15:10; cf. II Cor. 11:23.

apostolate. But the ideas which he developed in this context were from the first of wider relevance. They became fundamental for the Christian conception of authority in general, and determined the Christian approach to the questions of freedom and discipline even, to some extent, in later times when the concept of spiritual office had become dominant.

We will not attempt to pursue the question, who specifically were the opponents with whom Paul had to contend?[9] They vary from time to time and from place to place. In so far as they display the character of a 'party', operating beyond the limits of any one congregation, the feature they have in common is a more or less definite Judaistic legalism; and it is for this reason more than any other that they are opposed to Paul. Hostility on these objective grounds is combined, however, with personal enmities and misgivings about the rightness of his conduct. In part, too, the 'servants of Satan' and 'false apostles'[10] who invaded Paul's congregations patently did their utmost to enlist the support of other, higher authorities against him, possibly even the apostles at the head of the primitive Jerusalem community.[11] It is, however, an important fact, and in view of our earlier remarks an especially significant one, that though these personages, spiritually outstanding as they are, superior to Paul in every respect, and distinguished moreover by their personal connections with Jesus, are ranked above Paul, yet this personal precedence is not maintained as a matter of fixed Church order or superior ecclesiastical office. Paul, therefore, is not defending himself against the authority of a sacral, 'hierarchical' ecclesiasticism, and it is quite wrong to draw parallels between him and Luther in this context. Furthermore, we have always to reckon with the fact that his own views on the nature of the Church and on the meaning in principle of apostolic authority are theologically more developed, more deeply thought out, and more advanced than those of his opponents. The latter therefore should not be taken too seriously. Paul has to deal with more or less arbitrary and obstinate convictions, products of the immensely strong traditions of Judaism, not to mention naïve presumption and partisanship bound up with suspicion of and distaste for himself personally; but he does not yet have to contend with an articulated anti-Pauline theology, not at any rate so far as his conception of apostolic and Christian authority is concerned. We should be careful to avoid the mistake of making a conjectural reconstruction of such a theology

[9] On what follows cf. esp. E. Käsemann, 'Untersuchung zum II Kor.: Die Legitimität des Apostels', ZNW 41, 1942, pp. 33ff.; also A. G. Hebert, 'St Paul's Defence of his Apostolate', Theology 51, 1948, pp. 323ff.

[10] II Cor. 11:13-15.

[11] W. G. Kümmel (in H. Lietzmann, An die Korinther I. II, 1949⁴, p. 210) disagrees with this view.

by reversing his own polemical theses. It is enough to have his own words and opinions presented with complete clarity.

Paul knows himself called to be an apostle of Jesus Christ.[12] Even though he does not stress his apostolic rank so frequently as the modern interpreters of his sense of vocation customarily do, and though the boundaries of his own authority vis-à-vis other, non-apostolic colleagues remain fluid, nevertheless this is the fact from which his self-confidence derives, the firm basis of his claims; and here, when occasion demands, he resolutely takes his stand. With this apostolate from Christ come two things: first, complete autonomy and independence as regards all other human claims and authorities, and secondly, association with and membership of the unique group of those who were 'apostles before him'.[13] Paul joins them as someone of equal status, endued with equal authority; and it is this particular consequence of his calling which is plainly for Paul the crucial matter. Communion with the first apostles and with Jerusalem is of great moment to him; he sees it as absolutely indispensable to the meaning and success of his work.[14] That is why, after three years of missionary activity, he sets out in person for Jerusalem; and again, fourteen years later, when his law-free gospel is already making headway, and is for that very reason running into stiffer resistance, decides—on the basis, as he emphasises, of a 'revelation'— on a second journey, to submit the gospel which he is preaching among the gentiles formally to 'those who are of repute' at Jerusalem. It is clear, therefore, that Paul made great efforts to obtain their agreement, and he is proud of the fact that, in his opinion, he received it without reservation.[15] It is he who goes to them, not they who come to him; in that fact there is unmistakably a certain recognition of the primacy of the mother-church and its leaders. On this occasion, too, Paul is ready to promise the regular support required of him for the 'saints' in Jerusalem, and organises a collection in all his congregations, enjoining it both by word of mouth and in writing.[16] This was done not for the reason that the Christians in Jerusalem were especially poor or needy, though there may have been some element of this;[17] primarily,

[12] This consciousness is decisively dependent upon the actual event of his call. Paul did not experience his apostolate as an endowment with any kind of 'gift', and accordingly never refers to it as a χάρισμα, as J. Wobbe, *Der Charis-Gedanke bei Paulus*, 1932, pp. 74f., rightly emphasises. Equally, however, it was not a matter of an ordinary human vocation, but of a call by Christ himself.

[13] Gal. 1:17. [14] Gal. 2:2; cf. Phil. 2:16.

[15] Gal. 2:1ff. For a correct exposition of this passage cf. H. Schlier, *Der Galaterbrief*, 1949, pp. 34ff.

[16] Gal. 2:10; Rom. 15:25ff.; I Cor. 16:1ff;. II Cor. 8:1ff.

[17] The phrase εἰς τοὺς πτωχοὺς τῶν ἁγίων τῶν ἐν Ἰερουσαλήμ in II Cor. 8:13ff., Rom. 15:26 suggests this interpretation; but there is a concealed ambi-

however, Paul is stressing the presence of a debt of gratitude to the primitive community, binding on all gentile Christian congregations: 'If the Gentiles have come to share in their spiritual blessings, they ought also to be of service to them in material blessings.'[18] It may, indeed, be that in Jerusalem this contribution was seen as implying rather more, namely a formal payment of dues which it was right should be laid upon the young churches for the benefit of the primitive community.[19] For Paul, however, it was nothing of the sort, and in time it came to take on in his own mind a more far-reaching, positive significance. It is no casual remark when he asks the Christians in Rome, who were not involved in the collection, to pray earnestly to God that his 'service for Jerusalem may be acceptable to the saints'.[20] There is no longer any question, for Christians at any rate, of suppressing Paul; and therefore acceptance of the collection can now serve as a sign that, in spite of all the tensions, the unity of the Church is unbroken, and as a renewed recognition of Paul's law-free mission.

That Paul never ceases to fight for this sense of fellowship and mutual obligation within the Church is a salient feature of his ministry, and something which partly explains his universal pre-eminence among missionary leaders.[21] His congregations are no independent guilds of initiates, absorbed in themselves and their own religious life; they are all involved one with another in their acceptance of the original witness to Jesus and his Resurrection, and in their common submission to him as Lord.[22] Above all, therefore, they are linked to the original Jewish congregation, which first proclaimed this testimony and thereby communicated it to them.[23] Or did the word of God, by any chance, originate with the Gentile Christians, and are they the only ones it has reached?[24] By the same token Paul knows that he, too, as an apostle is not simply working on his own, but is linked, as we have already said, to those who were 'apostles before him'. They are bound to acknowledge

---

guity here, inasmuch as πτωχοί like ἅγιοι is a title of the eschatological people of God, and may have been adopted as such by the primitive community: cf. H. Schlier, op. cit., p. 46.

[18] Rom. 15:27.

[19] On this question cf. W. G. Kümmel, Kirchenbegriff und Geschichtsbewusstsein in der Urgemeinde und bei Jesus, 1943, pp. 25, 53 n. 85, and the literature cited there; also M. Goguel, L'église primitive, 1947, pp. 35f., 262ff.

[20] Rom. 15:30.

[21] Cf. R. Bultmann, art. 'Paulus,' RGG² IV., 1930, p. 1025.

[22] I. Cor. 11:16; also, on the specific topic of the collection for Jerusalem, I Cor. 16:1; II Cor. 9:1ff.

[23] Cf. I Thess. 2:14, and the similar ideas concerning the relation of the Gentiles to the Jewish nation as a whole in Rom. 11:16ff. Also relevant here, as Schlier remarks, is Rom. 15:19, where Paul describes the extent of his missionary work in terms of an arc beginning at Jerusalem.

[24] I Cor. 14:36.

him, just as he for his part acknowledges their witness, and passes it on to his own congregations.[25]

For Paul, however, this 'ecclesiastical' connection implies absolutely no sort of subordination of his own authority and person to any other of supposedly higher status. In a twinkling he shifts his whole emphasis, and elaborates his arguments in quite the opposite direction, as soon as any one depreciates him on principle by comparison with the first apostles, or tries to interpret his different historical position as implying a lower rank than theirs, or his recognition of their precedence in time as an admission of dependence upon them. Paul is indeed the least of the apostles, a departure from the norm, the 'afterbirth', a monstrosity[26] in their circle; but that does not alter the fact that God separated him from the womb, and in his grace called him to be an apostle of Christ, whose 'bondman'[27] he now is. The fundamental event, which brought Paul his apostolate, his gospel, and his success, was the encounter with Christ on the Damascus road; it was because of this that even the great apostles at Jerusalem could not do otherwise than recognise his authority. It is clear, however, that for Paul it was his 'gospel' that mattered, not personal recognition for its own sake. The question at issue in Jerusalem was not 'whether one allowed that Paul had received his call through the appearing to him of the Risen Lord, but whether one was prepared to grant that what he had received in this vision of the Risen Christ was the call to the Gentile mission'.[28] But there was in fact never any chance of separating the two.[29] His law-free gospel was a right and proper thing because he had been called to act as its minister, and his apostolic ministry was to be demonstrated in the proclamation of this

[25] I Cor. 15:1ff., cf. 11:23. It may be assumed that the piece of traditional material passed on by Paul in 15: 3b–5 derives from the primitive community: cf. J. Jeremias, *The Eucharistic Words of Jesus*, 1966, pp. 101ff.; E. Lichtenstein, 'Die älteste christliche Glaubensformel,' *ZKG* 63, 1950/52, p. 5; K. G. Rengstorf, *Die Auferstehung Jesu. Form, Art und Sinn der urchristlichen Osterbotschaft*, 1952, pp. 89ff. The characteristic error of earlier exegetes in assuming that by his use of the phrase παρέλαβον ἀπὸ τοῦ κυρίου Paul meant that he was appealing to a special revelation granted directly to himself nowadays no longer needs to be refuted: cf. Kümmel, *Korintherbriefe*, p. 185.

[26] According to G. Björck, *Conject. Neot.* 3, 1938, pp. 3ff., this is the only sense of the term of abuse ἔκτρωμα, and its use in I Cor. 15:8 must not therefore be 'interpreted in terms of the way in which Paul became a Christian' (Kümmel, *op. cit.*, p. 192). This may, however, be doubted; it would be quite understandable if in a literary context the word was not confined strictly to its crude basic meaning.

[27] G. Sass, 'Zur Bedeutung von δοῦλος bei Paulus', *ZNW* 40, 1941, pp. 24ff., shows that this term implies not merely the idea of subjection, but above all that of being an emissary in whom Christ reposes especial confidence.

[28] Kümmel, *Kirchenbegriff und Geschichtsbewusstsein*, p. 9.

[29] Cf. H. Von Campenhausen, 'Der urchristliche Apostelbegriff', *Stud. theol.* 1, 1948, pp. 110f. and the literature there cited.

particular gospel. On this point Paul does not yield a single step. He lays stress on the fact that even in critical situations he never kowtowed to the Judaisers nor 'yielded submission' to them.[30] Instead, he had himself gone over to the attack, publicly denouncing and putting to shame no less a person than the Apostle Peter for his cowardly compromise.[31]

This 'equality of status' and this recognition of his teaching and person by the first apostles do no more, however, than define Paul's position in a purely external way; they tell us nothing of its inner nature. For this we must turn to Paul himself, who is easily the outstanding witness to the distinctive quality of the idea of the apostolate described in the preceding chapter. For him, to be an apostle of Christ was something that came 'not from men, nor through man',[32] but from Christ, who had called him and given him authority independent of all human control; but equally it also meant that he was bound wholly to Christ, and that Christ was at all times to be the sole content and the only norm of his preaching. 'For what we preach is not ourselves, but Jesus Christ as Lord'.[33] The apostle exists in order to communicate to the world the wonderful mysteries that have been entrusted to him. To this extent he is merely an underling, an 'agent', with nothing autonomous about him. The only virtue which it is open to him to practise is faithfulness.[34] But this does not mean that it is simply a matter of a lifeless, mechanical faithfulness, concerned only to hand on traditional formulae and data—although even these may have their value.[35] Christ, the Gospel, the preaching of the Cross—these virtually identical realities are to determine and to transform through and through the life of Christians who have been touched by them; and the apostle's own preaching must have the same character, that is to say, it must be forceful, vital, overwhelming. It is therefore precisely the 'objective content' of the work which calls for total, personal, and passionate commitment on his part; only the human involvement of the apostle without reserve is adequate to make Christ truly present in his lordship and power. This, however, makes no difference to the fact that the apostle acts and possesses authority only in another's name. He is a 'witness'[36] to someone else, and the witness's own person and merits as such are devoid of interest.

Paul takes this concept of the apostolate very seriously in practice as well as in theory. Whenever in the course of controversy he comes up against those who stress their rank or superior status he meets such

[30] Gal. 2:4f., adopting the correct reading, οἷς οὐδέ.
[31] Gal. 2:11ff.   [32] Gal. 1:1.   [33] II Cor. 4:5.
[34] I Cor. 4:1-2.   [35] Cf. I Cor. 11:23; 15:1-3; II Thess. 4:15, etc.
[36] I Cor. 15:15. For an explanation of the μάρτυς-concept cf. H. Von Campenhausen, *Die Idee des Martyriums in der alten Kirche,* 1936, pp. 28f.

pretensions with biting severity[37] or with unconcealed and lofty irony. Even the apostles in Jerusalem are not spared the rough side of his tongue. In their own circles no doubt they are honoured and revered as 'pillars'; but Paul seizes on this title for the 'men of repute'—'those who were reputed to be something,' 'who were reputed to be pillars'— with such ceremonious emphasis that he at once makes it perfectly clear how he himself despises such considerations, even before stating explicitly: 'What they were makes no difference to me; God shows no partiality.'[38] Even the supreme privilege of the original apostles, namely that they had been the companions and eye-witnesses of the earthly Jesus, a privilege on which Paul's disciple Luke was one day to lay even greater stress, makes not the least impression on Paul himself: 'From now on, therefore, we know no one after the flesh; even though we once knew Christ after the flesh, we know him thus no longer.'[39] Mere historical continuity and tradition entitle no one to be regarded as a specially privileged person or source of authoritative decisions; even the Apostles are not that. This is made plain in the moment when even an apostle is in danger of betraying the meaning of faith in Christ. Paul knows that this is a real possibility; that is why he opposes Peter 'to his face', when he 'acts insincerely'. Indeed, he abandons any and every conceivable authority, in principle even his own, the moment it runs counter to the 'gospel': 'But even if we, or an angel from heaven, should preach to you a gospel contrary to that which we preached to you, let him be accursed.'[40] Paul savagely underlines the unconditional, ineffaceable validity of this principle by immediately repeating it: 'As we have said before, so now I say again, If any one is preaching to you a gospel contrary to that which you received, let him be accursed.'[41] The possibility of error is always present; and apostolic authority contrary to the truth of Christ and of his gospel there cannot be: 'For we cannot do anything against the truth, but only for the truth.'[42] Just as in the case of Jesus himself the authority of the apostolic man is wholly bound

---

[37] II Cor. 11:14; Gal. 4:17.

[38] Gal. 2:6; cf. W. Förster, 'Die δοκοῦντες in Gal. 2', ZNW 36, 1937, p. 288.

[39] II Cor. 5:16: cf. Kümmel, Korintherbriefe, p. 205.

[40] Gal. 1:8; cf. II Cor. 11:4.

[41] Gal. 1:9. Most exegetes take the word προειρήκαμεν as referring to instructions given orally on an earlier visit to Galatia: cf. H. Schlier, Galaterbrief, pp. 14f. But the emphatic combination of 'before' with 'now' (ἄρτι πάλιν) is not meant to indicate a lapse of time but to intensify the force of the repetition. Arguments to the contrary based on I Cor. 7:3 and Heb. 4:7 are mistaken. In neither case are we concerned with the repetition of an immediately preceding statement, nor indeed with an incident that occurred some time in the past, but with a second citation of a passage of Scripture already quoted some sentences earlier. In so far, therefore, as these instances provide a relevant parallel, they agree rather with the interpretation given here than with the opposite exegesis.

[42] II Cor. 13:8; cf. I Thess. 2:13.

up with the scandalising truth of the message through which it exercises its effect, and from which by its very nature it cannot be separated.

This abandonment of personal, human self-assertion applies, however, not only where matters of seniority or election are concerned. Paul's view is exactly the same when instead his opponents enlist personal qualities or religious abilities against him, or conversely deplore their absence in himself. In this connection the controversies in II Corinthians are instructive. Here Paul is standing up less for his gospel than for himself as a man against the slanderous assertions that he is unspiritual, physically infirm, and unreliable. He dare not even—so they say—make any real use of the rights which he himself claims; all he can do is talk, and even then he never gets away from his own ego. He is not a real apostle, nor a genuine man of the Spirit.[43] Faced with such accusations Paul is in a difficult position. He knows that they are false, and that he must rebut them if both his position in the community and his entire work are not to be undermined, and the victory to go to the 'false apostles'.[44] But he can do this only by justifying himself, even though he is in fact accountable to no human tribunal but only to his Lord.[45] For him what is at stake is his commission and call and thus the very cause itself; but it looks as though he were 'commending' simply his own person. It is vital that he destroy this impression, and so we arrive at the strange zigzag course of his reply; he makes his apologia, but almost as if his heart were not in it. He champions his rights and his status with great asperity; but every time he has finally made his point, he turns aside and strikes out everything he has just said, explaining that all this is utterly futile and of no account, indeed, strictly speaking, it is childish and senseless, mere 'foolishness':[46] 'You forced me to it.'[47] Paul knows that he has no grounds for anxiety; he can stand any comparison with the Judaistic 'super-apostles'[48] with whom his opponents confront him: 'Whatever anyone dares to boast of—I am speaking as a fool—I also dare to boast of that.'[49] If they glory in the flesh, and if you are willing to have it so, then I can too: 'Are they Hebrews? So am I. Are they Israelites? So am I. Are they descendants of Abraham? So am I. Are they servants of Christ? I am a better one—I am talking like a madman—with far greater labours, far more imprisonments, with countless beatings, and often near death.'[50] Paul knows himself far superior to his opponents in precisely those miraculous

[43] For the evidence in detail cf. Käsemann, art. cit., ZNW 41, 1942, pp. 34–36.
[44] II Cor. 11:13. On the question who are the opponents Paul has in mind here, cf. the recent study by J. Dupont, Gnosis. La connaissance dans les épîtres de S. Paul, 1949, pp. 249ff.
[45] I Cor. 4:3f.; cf. Rom. 14:4, 12.
[46] II Cor. 11:1, 16f.; 12:1.
[47] II Cor. 12:11; cf. 11:21.
[48] II Cor. 11:5; 12:11.
[49] II Cor. 11:21.
[50] II Cor. 11:22f.

spiritual experiences, 'visions and revelations', in which they take such pride.[51] He is one who speaks with tongues,[52] and an ecstatic;[53] he has experienced translation, and been given knowledge of heavenly mysteries, of which he may not speak, since they were really meant only for himself and could well be allowed to remain a matter of indifference to those around him.[54] From the human point of view Paul would be perfectly right to 'boast' about such things if he wished.[55] Of his own motion, however, he refuses to do so; and if by their lack of confidence in him his congregation force him to talk of such things, then he speaks of his experiences with pointed detachment, as though they were those of some remote, third person—'on behalf of this man I will boast.'[56] The same applies to the 'signs of a true apostle', the miracles which his opponents profess to miss in Paul, but which nevertheless he has shown in abundance among his people in Corinth.[57] How much better it would have been, had they themselves taken up the cudgels on behalf of their spiritual father, and spared him the dangerous business of setting out his own claims to glory![58]

The defence of his right to respect, however, is not in fact quite so simple a matter for Paul as this might make it appear. The mortifying and dangerous thing about the hostile criticism is that distaste and incomprehension have not found expression in sheer lies, but that in the insinuations against Paul truth is apparently mixed with the falsehoods. Paul has, for example, to allow the accusation that he 'lacks skill in speaking', and admits that he has not mastered the art of free, enthusiastic utterance (which must be what this referred to) with the virtuosity of which his rivals, as men of miraculous spiritual power, can boast.[59] Above all, his personal manner, which his critics are now contrasting with the proud tone of his letters, was plainly not always engaging nor at first encounter convincing,[60] for Paul was a sick man. He himself gives the Galatians great credit for the fact that at their first meeting, which indeed took place only because of an attack of his affliction,[61] they did not allow themselves to be discouraged, but 'received him as an angel of God', and instead of 'spitting in his presence' (a prophylactic gesture designed to ward off evil) were ready to be won over despite his illness.[62] Any success of which Paul can 'boast' is not,

---

[51] II Cor. 12:1.   [52] I Cor. 14:18.   [53] II Cor. 5:13.
[54] II Cor. 12:2ff.; cf. Käsemann, art. cit., pp. 67ff.
[55] II Cor. 12:6.   [56] II Cor. 12:5.
[57] II Cor. 12:12; cf. Kümmel, Korintherbriefe, p. 213: 'Nowhere else does Paul speak of σημεῖα τοῦ ἀποστόλου; he may therefore be seizing on a catch-word which his opponents applied to themselves.'
[58] II Cor. 12:11.   [59] II Cor. 10:10; 11:6; cf. Käsemann, art. cit., p. 35.
[60] II Cor. 10:1, 10f.
[61] The words δι' ἀσθένειαν in Gal. 4:13 are to be taken in this sense: cf. Schlier, Galaterbrief, p. 148.   [62] Gal. 4:14.

therefore, the effortless achievement of someone with great and un-impaired natural endowments, but is wrung with toil and pain from a tortured body.

There can be no doubt that Paul suffered grievously under these bitter burdens that so restricted his work and his reputation. He confesses that three times he begged his Lord to free him from this 'thorn in the flesh', 'this messenger of Satan to buffet me'; but his request was not granted. Paul saw his affliction first of all as a cross which had been given him to bear in order to counterbalance to some extent his unusual spiritual gifts, and to ensure that the 'abundance of revelations' granted to him should not lead him astray into overweening arrogance. But this purely personal interpretation plainly did not satisfy him. Before all else Paul is an apostle; and so, just as he tries to understand everything that befalls him in terms of this calling, in the end he interprets his illness too on this basis, and in this way wrests from it a positive meaning. The Lord, in the answer which taught him to overcome his temptation, had told him: 'My grace is sufficient for you, for my power is made perfect in weakness.'[63] This meant that in withholding human abilities from him Christ as 'Lord of the Spirit'[64] was precisely not leaving Paul in the lurch, but rather for the first time making him fully an apostle, one who could do nothing of himself but everything by grace alone. The old conception of the apostolate hitherto had been forced to distinguish between human and divine elements in the one endowed with authority. In the election of Paul, the depraved persecutor of the Church, it had already undergone a unique development; now that development is carried to its logical conclusion 'to show that the transcendent power belongs to God and not to us'.[65] The reason why the life of the apostle testifies so clearly to the glory of the grace of Christ is precisely that it has to do so in a wretched specimen of humanity, broken by suffering. Indeed, the witness is to two things at once; the life of God is shown forth in the dying of the man, and the dying of the man in the life of the apostle. In the work of the apostolate his outward and inward miseries find their common purpose.[66] Paul is 'afflicted in every way, but not crushed; perplexed, but not driven to despair; persecuted, but not forsaken; struck down, but not destroyed'. His life is a daily dying, a continuing participation in a doom of death which condemns him to suffer, and which is the very same that Christ himself endured in the days of his flesh. For that very reason, however, the life of Jesus is also present in him here and now, and will at the last day be revealed 'in his body' as total life and glory.[67] What room is there

---

[63] II Cor. 12:7-9.   [64] II Cor. 3:18.
[65] II Cor. 4:7.   [66] II Cor. 7:5.
[67] II Cor. 4:8-10; cf. I Cor. 15:29-32; II Cor. 1:3-11; 4:16f.; 6:4-10; 11:23-33; cf. Kümmel, *Korintherbriefe*, p. 213: 'In the concrete fact of the

here for human boasting? Everything that might once have distinguished him Paul counts as 'dung', and casts behind him, simply in order to gain Christ.[68] Paradoxically enough, however, he can now boast of his suffering and infirmity: 'By the grace of God I am what I am.'[69] It is when Paul is weak that he is strong.[70]

It should by now be clear that when Paul speaks in this way he is not merely making a virtue out of the necessity of his bodily and spiritual sufferings, nor is he simply attempting an *ad hoc* defence against the attacks aimed at his person. What he says is to be understood in terms of the very heart of his faith in Christ, which is faith in the Crucified; and it is on this basis that his words define the fundamental meaning of his existence both as Christian and apostle. Life in Christ is life in hope, and can be comprehended only as the very antithesis of all earthly satisfaction, just as the Cross is the sign of divine life only in antithesis to all the glamour and glory of the world. Christ's glory and the glory of this age, the wisdom of God and the widsom of men, boasting of one's natural powers and boasting of one's weakness, are things that can never co-exist nor be made, so to speak, compatible with one another. Paul consciously holds fast to this truth not only as a man but also in his role as an apostle; it characterises his mode of operation. 'If I were still pleasing men, I should not be a servant of Christ.'[71] Paul carries out his work 'in weakness and in much fear and trembling',[72] and explicitly refuses to commend his testimony by means of the glamour of bewitching rhetoric or of supposedly higher wisdom.[73] It is by *suffering* for his congregations that he brings about their salvation.[74] Only so can he remain truly the apostle of his Lord, the crucified Christ, who is to the Jews a scandal and to the Greeks foolishness, but who in this human nothingness at the same time reveals to both of them the power of God and the wisdom of God.[75]

By contrast the false apostles who 'boast' and 'commend themselves'[76] are dishonest workmen, who have disguised themselves in angels' garb.[77] But even in cases where Paul's judgment on other teachers, those who are working alongside himself, is thoroughly friendly and appreciative in tone, he still condemns the attitude of their adherents, who attach themselves to these men simply because the latter display

---

apostle's activity we see the working out of man's eschatological participation in the glory of Christ, the reality in the present of the eschatological future.'

[68] Phil. 3:8.   [69] I Cor. 15:10.
[70] II Cor. 12:10; cf. also 11:30; 12:9f.; Rom. 5:3.   [71] Gal. 1:10.
[72] I Cor. 2:3; cf. I Thess. 2:2.   [73] I. Cor. 2:1, 4, 13.
[74] II Cor. 1:6.
[75] I Cor. 1:22–24; cf. H. Von Campenhausen, 'Glaube und Bildung im Neuen Testament', *Stud. Gen.* 2, 1949, pp. 184f.
[76] II Cor. 11:13f.   [77] II Cor. 5:12; 10:12, 18.

special abilities or dazzling gifts. They fancy that in acquiring superior knowledge they have outgrown their first apostle, and become out-standingly 'spiritual'; but Paul tells them that in thinking like this they merely display their 'fleshly' nature, and prove themselves childish and incapable of grasping what the Gospel is really about.[78] And with searing irony he contrasts his own way of life, which wears itself out in service, with the spiritual self-indulgence of the supposedly perfect. God has set the apostle in the lowest place of all, like the gladiators condemned to death in the arena. 'We are fools for Christ's sake, but you are wise in Christ. We are weak, but you are strong. You are held in honour, but we are in disrepute. To the present hour we hunger and thirst, we are ill-clad and buffeted and homeless, and we labour working with our own hands.' The servants of Christ are treated as scapegoats in every land; day after day they are given over to death. But while their outward man is perishing, their inner man is clothed with Christ's future and his invisible glory; it is not destroyed, but 'renewed every day'.[79] Paul is here speaking of his life as an apostle;[80] but in so doing he shows his erring congregation as if in a mirror the true pattern of all Christian living.[81]

Paul's understanding of the apostolic and Christian life is thus thoroughly dialectic. In the context of the concept of authority, how-ever, it is essential that the emphasis should not be laid solely on the negative aspect of its human failures and frustrations. If it is true that the apostle 'dies' daily,[82] it is also true that the power of Christ is genuinely present in his mortal body. In every passage in which Paul speaks of his weakness, his sufferings, and his failure[83] he also speaks in the same breath of the mighty operation of Christ through him, of Christ's victory and triumph. Christ constantly snatches him back from death to life again. 'For though we live in the world, we are not carrying on a worldly war, for the weapons of our warfare are not worldly but have divine power to destroy strongholds. We destroy arguments and every proud obstacle to the knowledge of God, and take every thought captive to obey Christ, being ready to punish every disobedience, when your obedience is complete.'[84] Paul knows of no activity on God's

[78] I Cor. 3:1ff. The preceding section, 2:6ff., shows that Paul is not here intending to condemn 'wisdom' as such. The passage must be understood dialectically, as in the similar treatment of 'boasting' in II Cor. 11f.

[79] I Cor. 4:9–12; II Cor. 4:11, 16.

[80] But not simply of his own—I Cor. 4:9 refers to the lot of the apostles in general. The community has a share in the work of the apostles only by inter-cession (Rom. 15:30; II Cor. 1:11; Phil. 1:19f.; II Thess. 3:1f.; Phmn 22) and —though Paul's case is the exception—by material support (II Cor. 11:7ff.; Phil. 4:10ff.; cf. Rom. 16:2).

[81] Cf. on this point L. Cerfaux, 'L'antinomie paulinienne de la vie aposto-lique', RSR 39, 1951–2, pp. 221ff.

[82] I Cor. 15:31.   [83] Cf. p 40. n. 67 above.   [84] II Cor. 10:3–6.

business which is not accompanied by the living demonstration of God's presence in power.[85] 'I can do all things in him who strengthens me.'[86] This confidence is of crucial importance for his relationship with his congregations. In his dealings with them he has no use for a prudent reserve which considers the possibility of miscarriage or failure, and so prefers not to promise too much either to himself or to others,[87] but to leave the outcome in suspense. With bold determination he seeks out his opponents, and confronts them with his vizor up: 'I warned those who sinned before and all the others, and I warn them now while absent . . . that if I come again I will not spare them—since you desire proof that Christ is speaking in me.'[88] If in the eyes of his flock Paul has hitherto seemed weak, just as Christ himself was crucified in weakness, in future he will demonstrate God's power in his dealings with them, just as Christ lives by the power of God,[89] that is to say, in direct confrontation[90] he will provide evidence of that very authority which some would like to deny him. Then there will be proof on which side there have been nothing but inflated claims and high-sounding words and on which side the real power of the Spirit is to be found[91]—and for many of those involved this will be a far from pleasant experience.[92]

Paul is plainly counting on the collapse of the opposition which has been formed behind his back, once it is confronted with the moral— and perhaps not merely moral[93]—force of his personal presence; for like every apostle he is most certainly armed with miraculous spiritual powers.[94] That is why he dares to use this power which is entrusted to him.[95] It is precisely because Paul does not desire to be anything on his own account, and dares to champion only that which Christ does in him, that Christ does in fact both work and speak through him un-equivocally and irresistibly—for salvation, where men will hear, and for destruction, where they forbear. 'For we are the aroma of Christ to God among those who are being saved and among those who are perishing, to one a fragrance from death to death, to the other a fragrance from life to life.'[96] But who, he goes on, is sufficient for these things?—and answers his own question crisply, without wasting time talking about himself: unlike some other apostles Paul devotes himself single-mindedly and unreservedly to his ministry, and what he speaks

---

[85] Cf. II Cor. 2:14: πάντοτε, ἐν παντὶ τόπῳ.   [86] Phil. 4:13.

[87] Cf. Rom. 15:29; οἶδα δὲ ὅτι ἐρχόμενος πρὸς ὑμᾶς ἐν πληρώματι εὐλογίας Χριστοῦ ἐλεύσομαι; cf. I Thess. 2:1.

[88] II Cor. 13:2-3.   [89] II Cor. 13:4; cf. 10:1ff.   [90] Cf. Gal. 4:20.

[91] I Cor. 4:18-21.   [92] II Cor. 12:20f.   [93] Cf. I Cor. 5:5.

[94] Rom. 15:18f., 29; II Cor. 12:12; Gal. 3:5. He himself, however, 'is interested in them only as integral parts of his apostolic ministry, whereas his opponents regard them in isolation as revelations of the irruption of the other world into history:' Käsemann, art. cit., p. 63.

[95] II Cor. 13:10.   [96] II Cor. 2:15-16.

'in Christ' comes indeed from God, and is uttered in God's sight.[97] That on the words of the messenger hangs the fate of those who listen to him, as with the words of Christ himself, is the common conviction of the primitive Church;[98] but no one, so far as we know, dared as Paul did, by surrendering his whole existence to death, to make his own person the medium of this authority, so that at every level of the self he is as it were permeated with Christ: 'It is no longer I who live, but Christ who lives in me.'[99] In the whole Pauline corpus there is not one sentence which seeks either to qualify or to retract this all-embracing confession.[100] In his own person a cipher,[101] but endued with the supreme authority, that of God himself—that is how Paul presents himself to his congregations. We must now enquire what in fact such a claim must have meant and did mean to them.

Our answer must start from Paul's concrete responsibility toward his congregations. He is their missionary, their founder, and their leader. These young Christians are his 'children', and he is their spiritual father.[102] He is the one who 'conceived them in Christ Jesus through the gospel',[103] or, in another image, 'bore' them, in order that Christ 'might be formed' in them.[104] He is continuously providing them with the food appropriate for them,[105] cherishing them 'like a nurse',[106] and watchfully accompanying them through every step of their development. And as with any natural parent-child relationship, so too this spiritual parenthood knows all the most intense feelings of care and love, pain and disappointment, jealousy and impatience, and exultation at that ultimate bond of free affection in 'righteousness and peace and joy in the Holy Spirit' which is to hold sway in the kingdom of God.[107] In all the literature of the world there are no documents more personal than the letters of Paul to his congregations.[108] In the context of many different occasions we see reflected in them the ups and downs of mood, the striving after the real meaning of life, the safeguarding of fellowship 'in the Lord', or its recovery when threatened. Paul knows that his congregations need him, and cannot as yet do without him,[109] and his disquiet increases when alien, destructive influences seek to intrude

[97] II Cor. 2:16–17.

[98] Matt. 10:15 par.; 10:40 par.; Joh. 16:8ff.   [99] Gal. 2:20.

[100] Even Phil. 3:12–14 is not a qualification of this union with Christ; it simply stresses that its meaning is dynamic and points to the future consummation.

[101] Gal. 6:3; II Cor. 12:11. There is no need, with Käsemann (art. cit., p. 51 n. 107) and others, to understand such remarks of Paul's as ironic.

[102] I Cor. 4:14; II Cor. 12:14; Phil. 2:22; I Thess. 2:11.

[103] I Cor. 4:15.

[104] Gal. 4:19.   [105] I Cor. 3:1f.   [106] I Thess. 2:7.   [107] Rom. 14:17.

[108] Not to mention those to individual members! Cf. Philemon and such passages as Phil. 4:3.

[109] Phil. 1:24ff.

between him and his people. Moreover, the nature of his relationship with them seems to be such that there is no reason why it need ever come to an end. For the more mature the congregation becomes, with the result that Paul is able to repose more confidence in it, and needs the less to exercise reticence in what he writes, the more inward and indissoluble becomes the bond that unites them—and will continue to unite them until the 'day of Jesus',[110] the returning Lord, to whom Paul has betrothed those who are his, 'as a pure bride'.[111] The relationship is thus a permanent and reciprocal one, which will reach its term only at the last day.[112] Thus the congregation's boast is that the apostle has always behaved toward them with sincerity, 'not by earthly wisdom, but by the grace of God', while the apostle's boast is that his congregation flourishes; and this boast has nothing worldly about it, because it is simply the proof and confirmation of the authority which God has permanently committed to him,[113] the 'seal' attached to the whole meaning of his life's work.[114] The congregations are his joy and crown,[115] his letter of recommendation, 'to be known and read by all men',[116] proving, should anyone be in doubt on the matter, whether or not he has truly been called by Christ and has fulfilled his divine commission.[117] Paul 'lives' by the faithfulness of his children,[118] whom he holds in his heart.[119]

It is implicit in the nature of such a 'paternal' relationship that primarily it is simply Paul himself who is *the* authority; and one should not be in too much of a hurry to build a massive superstructure of legal theory or theological reflection on top of something which is simply the inevitable concomitant of his situation as a missionary in an alien, heathen environment. It is in I Corinthians that we see most clearly how indispensable for the young churches in those early days were firm regulations and clear decisions on all questions of belief and in every department of the moral life and of the ordering of the community. Paul feels it incumbent upon him to answer every question put to him, and he discusses, decides, and regulates all those matters that call for clarification,[120] in accordance with the 'authority' which has been given him for the building up of his congregations.[121] Paul also reproves with merciless frankness, when he has ocasion to do so. He can even demand that the names of those brethren who do not conform to the rules should be made public, in order that the rest may avoid their company until

---

[110] II Cor. 1:14; Phil. 2:16. [111] II Cor. 11:2.
[112] II Cor. 4:14; I Thess. 3:13; cf. E. Lohmeyer, *Grundlagen paulinischer Theologie*, 1929, pp. 193ff., 220ff., 229f.
[113] II Cor. 1:12–14; I Thess. 2:20. [114] I Cor. 9:2.
[115] Phil. 4:1; I Thess. 2:19. [116] II Cor. 3:2; cf. 4:2.
[117] II Cor. 3:3; 4:12; cf. 8:24; 9:3; cf. also I Thess. 1:7ff.
[118] I Thess. 3:8; cf. II Cor. 7:4, 7. [119] Phil. 1:7f.
[120] I Cor. 11:34. [121] II Cor. 10:8; 13:10.

they reform.[122] On occasion Paul, who is constantly subjected to claims from every quarter,[123] declines to be burdened further with troubles and disappointments;[124] or again, he may threaten his refractory children with the spiritual 'rod'.[125] He knows too what of love and respect is owed to his position as such,[126] and what, both inwardly and outwardly, he is entitled to by reason of his labours. Thus he lays great stress, for example, on the fact that he has just as good a right as any other missionary to be supported economically by his congregations, and that if he forgoes this right it is solely because he himself freely chooses to do so.[127] The churches founded by him belong to him. Paul refuses to tolerate it, when rivals force their way into his field of work uninvited, and stir up trouble against him,[128] however glad he may be at all times of helpers of goodwill.[129]

All this, as already pointed out, is really a matter of course, and in itself presents no particular problem. For the truly astounding feature of the situation we must look in quite the opposite direction, and consider the fact that Paul, who both as one called to be an apostle of Christ and as a teacher of his churches is a man of the very highest authority, nevertheless does not develop this authority of his in the obvious and straightforward way by building up a sacral relationship of spiritual control and subordination. Quite the contrary; whenever there seems to be a possiblity of this, it is balked by Paul himself, who rejects in set terms either his right or his desire to construct such an authority: 'Not that we lord it over your faith; we work with you for your joy, for you stand firm in your faith.'[130] Again: 'You were called to freedom, brethren',[131] and: 'Do not become slaves of men.'[132] Such expressions are not, of course, based on an appeal to freedom as an automatic human right which Christians too possess within the Church; Paul is referring to the freedom in the Spirit, which belongs to the baptised children of God who have been liberated by Christ. This freedom is not only in conflict with any attempt to reimpose the old Jewish law; it is just as essential to maintain it whenever new, personal authorities arise within the congregation itself and seek to domineer over men's faith, or when Christians attach themselves to particular teachers

---

[122] II Thess. 3:14 (possibly not genuine); cf. II Cor. 2:1.

[123] II Cor. 11:28.   [124] Gal, 6:17.   [125] I Cor. 4:21.

[126] II Cor. 2:3; 7:7; Phil. 2:30.

[127] I Cor. 9:6ff.; II Cor. 11:7ff.; Phil. 4:14; I Thess. 2:5ff.; II Thess. 3:3ff.; cf. Gal. 6:6. In addition to the motives emphasised in these passages Paul was no doubt also influenced by the desire to keep his independence, and to avoid from the start giving any sort of occasion for false suspicions. It was thus all the more galling for Paul that his opponents should maliciously misrepresent this circumspection of his as lack of confidence in himself and his position.

[128] I Cor. 4:15; II Cor. 10:14f.   [129] I Cor. 3:5f.

[130] II Cor. 1:24.   [131] Gal. 5:13.   [132] I Cor. 7:23.

and apostles, and quarrel over their individual qualities as if these were the things that mattered. 'What then is Apollos? What is Paul? Servants through whom you believed, as the Lord assigned to each.'[133] When the congregation came to the faith, they became subject not to their apostles and teachers of the moment, but directly to Christ himself. They are his property, and all God's human 'fellow-workers'[134] can for their part do no more than help men toward this decisive direct relationship. Hence it is these workers who belong to the congregation, and not the other way round.[135] To this rule even the apostolic 'founding father', Paul himself, is no exception. He is, it is true, the one who 'like a skilled master builder' laid the foundation, Christ, on which everything has to be built thereafter.[136] But this makes no difference to the freedom of the congregation: 'Was Paul crucified for you? Or were you baptized in the name of Paul?'[137] The Apostle takes his place in the community *for* Christ, not *before* him.

This means that the power of command which he exercises is from the outset fundamentally limited. Paul has to guide his congregations; he sees the mistakes they are making, he is constantly aware how much they are still lacking in the spiritual maturity and 'perfectness' which ought to be theirs.[138] But his position is not that of the prudent pedagogue, who will train his pupils up to freedom only a little at a time; Christian freedom is already a fact at all times, and must be recognised as such. It is bestowed on all Christians when they believe on Christ and are baptised; it is the necessary fruit of the Holy Spirit: 'Anyone who does not have the Spirit of Christ does not belong to him.'[139] However imperiously Paul the apostle may demand a hearing for Christ, however ingenuously he may put himself forward as a pattern for imitation,[140] yet he cannot simply give orders. He does not himself create the norm, which is then to be obeyed without further ado, but instead the congregation of those who possess the Spirit must follow him in freedom; and it is this freedom which he has in mind when he addresses them. They must themselves recognise in his instructions the 'standard of teaching' to which they are committed,[141] and to which Paul in a sense merely 'recalls' them,[142] in order that they may affirm it for themselves, and freely and joyfully make it their own once more.[143]

---

[133] I Cor. 3:5.   [134] I Cor. 3:9.   [135] I Cor. 3:21ff.; II Cor. 4:5.
[136] I Cor. 3:10ff.; cf. Col. 2:6f.   [137] I Cor. 1:13.
[138] I Cor. 3:1ff.; 14:20; Phil. 3:15.   [139] Rom. 8:9.
[140] I Cor. 4:16f.; 10:33; Phil. 3:17; I Thess. 4:1.
[141] Rom. 6:17. According to R. Bultmann, *TLZ* 72, 1947, p. 202, this verse is a secondary gloss.
[142] Rom. 15:15; I Cor. 4:17; 15:1.
[143] Cf. also the emphasis on προθυμία (II Cor. 8:12), which comes from the heart, μὴ ἐκ λύπης ἢ ἐξ ἀνάγκης (II Cor. 9:7), at the very moment when Paul is pressing them to make a serious effort to raise their contribution to the collection for Jerusalem.

'Be imitators of me, as I am of Christ!'[144] Those Christians who follow his example become, as Paul has it in a characteristic phrase, 'fellow-imitators' with him.[145] It is this direct relationship of all the baptised with Christ which constitutes the determinative background to all actual controversies, and gives them at once their pressing seriousness, their spiritual tension, and their forward thrust. No more for his children than for Paul himself is the bond uniting the believer to Christ an occasion for relaxing in a feeling of tranquillity, as if no real mishap could ever occur again.[146] On the contrary, the danger to those who have been made partakers of Christ's freedom becomes greater than before,[147] the moment they cease to hold on to him. 'We must not put Christ to the test.'[148] 'God is not mocked'; and only he who truly 'sows' to the Spirit, and no longer to the flesh, 'will from the Spirit reap eternal life'.[149]

Paul, the apostle, knows what is at stake, and he knows in whose Name he admonishes 'by the grace given to him',[150] and has to speak. It is implicit for him in the fundamental confession of Jesus Christ that the ancient basic moral commandments are not open to discussion; within the Church they must be observed. The real difficulties begin only when instructions have to be given which go beyond these elementary principles into matters of detail, at the point where the sphere of relative decisions, of distinguishing between what is humanly good and better, begins. The paradigm of such a discussion is his treatment of the Corinthians' questions on the problem of marriage.[151] The commandment of the Lord forbidding divorce is taken for granted;[152] and Paul therefore needs to apply the old Law only analogically.[153] But on the wider questions relating to the possibility of marriage or celibacy he can, as he emphatically states, do no more than give advice, and put forward his own conviction as one who 'by the Lord's mercy is trustworthy'.[154] He believes, nevertheless, that he too 'has the Spirit of

[144] I Cor. 11:1.
[145] Phil. 3:17. Linguistically, it is true, this could be an instance of a 'tautological formation', in which case συμμιμητής would simply be equivalent to μιμητής; so W. Michaelis, TWNT 4, 1942, p. 669 n. 13.
[146] I Cor. 4:4, 9ff; 9:16; II Cor. 7:11; Phil. 2:12; 3:12ff.; I Thess. 3:5.
[147] Rom. 13:11.   [148] I Cor. 10:9.
[149] Gal. 6:7f.   [150] Rom. 12:3; 15:15.
[151] I Cor. 6:12–7:40. Cf. H. von Campenhausen, Die Askese im Urchristentum, 1949, pp. 30ff.
[152] I Cor. 7:10.   [153] I Cor. 7:39.
[154] I Cor. 7:25. In my opinion Käsemann (art. cit., p. 59) has read too much into Paul's words, when he insists that 'even the δοκιμή of the apostle is not something which anyone is free to criticise'. It is true that the dialectic of the mutual relationship, based on faith, could be developed in this direction, and that such a development would in fact be in keeping with Paul's own ideas; but Paul himself did not press his thinking on the subject to this extreme.

God',[155] and if at any time he declines to give an authoritative decision,[156] this is definitely not the result of perplexity or uncertainty as to the right course. In giving advice Paul also bears in mind what is best for his people; but even so he may not 'lay any restraint upon them',[157] and must allow them their liberty in any matter that does not concern Christ and his word. Paul therefore deliberately refuses to interpret his authority in such a way that it could be extended beyond its proper sphere of upholding the truth of the Gospel to become a source of legal norms of any kind for the life of the Church.

But even when it is a question of the essential knowledge and preservation of the truth of the faith he avoids putting himself in a position of unqualified supremacy over his congregation. His 'children' are at the same time also and always his 'brethren'; and therefore he as an apostle is not their 'master' but their 'servant for Jesus's sake'.[158] 'I myself am satisfied about you, my brethren, that you yourselves are full of goodness, filled with all knowledge, and able to instruct one another.'[159] Paul is always producing new compound word-formations with συν- ('co-') in order to bring out his fellowship with his congregations in their labours, their struggles,[160] their prayers[161] and consolations,[162] their sufferings, rejoicings, and triumphs.[163] Where he must needs admonish, he frequently includes himself in the admonition by the use of a plural which is more than a mere author's 'we': 'We who are strong ought to bear with the failings of the weak.'[164] Moreover, he likes to introduce his pieces of instruction with the phrase 'You know', or 'We know',[165] or even with the minatory variant, 'Do you not know . . .?'[166] Even when, revolted to the very depths of his soul by the horror of the alleged case of incest at Corinth and by the slackness of the congregation responsible for dealing with the situation, he has already delivered his judgment in advance and from a distance, he

---

[155] I Cor. 7:40.

[156] As he does explicitly in the matter of the collection: II Cor. 8:8.

[157] I Cor. 7:35; cf. II Cor. 8:10, again on the subject of the collection.

[158] II Cor. 4:5. The love which is to abound within the community is the same as that which the apostle has for them: I Thess. 3:12.

[159] Rom. 15:14; cf. II Cor. 8:7. The modesty with which Paul in Rom. 15:15 practically apologises for his letter of instruction is also connected with the fact that here he is writing to a church which has not been founded by him, and with which he is as yet personally unacquainted.

[160] II Cor. 6:1; 8:18; Phil. 3:17; 4:3.

[161] Rom. 15:30; II Cor. 1:11.   [162] Rom. 1:12; 15:32; II Cor. 1:21.

[163] Rom. 16:7; I Cor. 4:8; 12:26; II Cor. 2:5; 4:14; 7:3; Phil. 1:29f.; 2:17f.; Col. 4:10; Phmn 23. The same motive lies behind the prominence which he deliberately gives to the συνεργοί: Rom. 16:3, 9; I Cor. 16:10; II Cor. 8:23; Phil. 2:19ff.; Col. 1:7; 4:11.

[164] Rom. 15:1.   [165] I Cor. 8:1; 12:2.

[166] Rom. 6:3, 16; I Cor. 3:16; 5:6; 6:9, 15, 19; 9:13, 24.

avoids presenting this decision, which seems to him the obvious one, as a unilateral measure taken solely by himself.[167] The congregation is to assemble, and, united with him 'in spirit' though separated in body, to carry out on the evildoer 'with the power of our Lord Jesus' what is in some sense the common judgment of them both.[168] Again and again Paul assures his readers that, although he has most certainly been given the power to take radical action, nevertheless he does not wish—or not yet—to bring it to bear; he wants only to encourage them in the good course, and not to put them to shame.[169] If a man is truly spiritual, then he ought to see for himself that he and Paul belong to the same Lord, and that what Paul writes is genuinely the Lord's bidding.[170] By thus appealing to the congregation's own judgment and sense of responsibility he takes their freedom seriously, possibly indeed more seriously than they themselves had expected. Those who put the questions would probably have preferred to receive in reply a strict and binding decree. But it is precisely at this point that the distinctively Christian aspect of Paul's methods becomes clear; and this aspect can be misunderstood only by someone who has failed to grasp the very heart of Paul's purpose.[171]

With this deference to the congregation, which is the vessel of the Spirit, goes a lively sense of what the distinctive character of his message requires in practice. It would be an altogether over-simplified and 'human' interpretation to see in the strangely permissive manner of his admonitions, threats, and appeals to his mature and yet childish congregations nothing more than a style or a technique, a more agreeable or more prudent method of giving orders or exercising jurisdiction, which sufficed for a group of believers who were ready to follow him, and was appropriate for a corporate relationship cemented by love. In that case it would amount to nothing more than a certain restraint or mitigation of authoritarian power in the ordinary sense, the thing which Paul himself either did not know or would not tolerate for a moment. In fact his authority is of such a kind that he continually brings it to bear only with reserve, reluctantly, and, as it were, merely requesting or soliciting

---

[167] It is possible that Paul is adopting this attitude all the more deliberately in this instance, because the Corinthians may have been boasting of their behaviour in the case as a supposed proof of their 'freedom': cf. I Cor. 5:2.

[168] I Cor. 5:1-5; cf. E. Schweizer, Das Leben des Herrn in der Gemeinde und ihren Diensten, 1946, p. 93 n. 16; on the actual procedure cf. pp. 134f. below.

[169] I Cor. 4:14; II Cor. 13:10; I Thess. 2:7 (on this passage cf. M. Dibelius, An die Thessaloniker, an die Philipper³, 1937, pp. 8f.); II Thess. 3:9; Phmn 8f.; cf. I Cor. 9:12, 18; also 14:37.

[170] I Cor. 10:12, 15; 14:37. The phrase προφήτης ἢ πνευματικός is a reference to the pneumatics who were setting themselves up as rivals to Paul.

[171] On this whole subject cf. H. Von Campenhausen, 'Recht und Gehorsam in der ältesten Kirche,' Theol. Blätter 20, 1941, pp. 279ff.

compliance, and confines its full and unambiguous exercise, in accordance with its essential nature, to such occasions as the true authority of Jesus himself determines. Precisely for this reason it is recognizable as the direct opposite of the false zeal of the judaising apostles,[172] and of that dead, legalistic preaching, which has nothing more to offer than all too human requirements, commands, and prescriptions.[173]

The dispensation of the Spirit and of the new righteousness, of which Paul is the minister, possesses in its gentleness and moderation a different, more powerful and more resplendent glory than that of the old Mosaic law, with its letter that killed,[174] because this dispensation is effected through candour,[175] love, [176] and patience,[177] and the winning and reconciling power of forgiveness, and no longer through punishment and destruction, imposed by an external authority. Through Christ God has reconciled the world with himself, and in the light of this fact has established within the world the ministry and word of reconciliation, that is, the Gospel preaching and the apostolate.[178] Hence Paul, too, has received authority without restriction of any kind—not, however, to use it to destroy, but to build up;[179] and it is of the very essence of this commission that he, the freeborn citizen, should like a slave be subject in unending accommodation to every man.[180] 'But we have the mind of Christ'.[181] 'Love bears all things, believes all things, hopes all things, endures all things.'[182] This love of Christ's is alive in Christ's apostle when he confronts his people as an 'ambassador for Christ', speaking, as it were, God's language, not in punishment but in pleading: 'We beseech you on behalf of Christ, be reconciled to God.'[183]

There are, however, limits to this attitude, precisely because it is Christian in character. These limits are reached where Christ and his Gospel are themselves once more abandoned and betrayed, where genuine apostasy has begun. At this point Christ's apostle no more than Christ himself can pronounce anything but anathema and condemnation.[184] We know, however, of no example of Paul's ever taking such a step with respect to an entire congregation, though he may now and then have come near to so doing.[185] So long as a church in general is still in some sense a Church of Christ, he may rebuke its members and censure them, convict, warn, and threaten them, he may conjure them

[172] Gal. 4:17.
[173] This point of view is stressed especially in Colossians: cf., for example, 2:20ff.
[174] II Cor. 3:7ff.   [175] II Cor. 3:12.   [176] II Cor. 5:14.
[177] Gal. 6:1.   [178] II Cor. 5:18f.   [179] II Cor. 10:8; 13:10.
[180] I Cor. 9:19; 10:33.   [181] I Cor. 2:16.   [182] I Cor. 13:7.
[183] II Cor. 5:20.   [184] I Cor. 16:22; Gal. 1:8f.; 5:10; Phil. 3:18f.
[185] I Cor. 5:5 records the taking of such action against an individual; cf. also Rom. 16:17f.; II Cor. 11:15.

to consider the imminent danger they are in, and pull out every stop of his anger; but for all this his approach remains one of appeal and exhortation which seeks to compel them, so to speak, without compulsion to change for the better of their own free will. The hortative and not the imperative is really the mood of the verbs in Pauline paraenesis. For the mark of every admonition is 'remembrance',[186] recollection of the basic indicative of that divine election of which the congregation have in Christ been made partakers. In the event of conflict all that is necessary, so to speak, is for the apostle to lead them back to the ground which is their common starting-point in order that they and he together may in fellowship make from there the step which should and must be taken. Thus it is that they follow him of their own free will but yet 'with fear and trembling';[187] for it is Christ who speaks to them through the apostle's mouth, and it is Christ and his word to whom they must become subject by following the apostle 'in obedience'.[188]

Paul's own conception of his authority, therefore, for all the intense emotion, and the directness which characterises it, and the many levels at which it operates, is yet of monumental simplicity in that it is at all times organised entirely round one focal point, in relation to which everything else acquires its meaning: Paul is the apostle of Jesus Christ —he is this wholly and completely and nothing but this. Because it is God's will that he should bear witness, and go on bearing witness, to the gospel of Christ in its significance as the basis of a new being, the foundation of a new life, his apostolic authority is by virtue of its very source unlimited, and death and life for men depend on his preaching. But Christ is not Lord of Paul alone; he is also the Lord of Paul's church, which is tied not to Paul but always and only to Christ through Paul. It is in Christ, who out of sheer grace calls them to his grace, that the congregation become free and are to remain free. It is this which gives Paul's approach to his congregations its distinctive character. Unequivocal though it is, its dynamic is nevertheless at the same time genuinely dialectical, a combination of powerful thrust and gentle retreat, at once threatening and inviting. The resultant stress on the

[186] The fundamental importance of this concept for the whole of primitive Christian thought has been well brought out by N. A. Dahl, 'Anamnesis', *Stud. Theol.* I, 1947, pp. 69ff.

[187] II Cor. 7:15.

[188] It is therefore hardly in accordance with Paul's own thinking, to count the concept of ὑπακοή given to the apostle (Phmn 21) as a unique exception to the general N.T. rule, on the grounds that elsewhere 'the word is always used in conjunction with religious decision' (G. Kittel, art. ὑπακοή, *TWNT* I, 1935, p. 225). The two things cannot be separated in this way. In II Cor. 2:9; 7:15, for example, it is precisely in the encounter with the apostle that religious decision takes place; and in Phmn 21 more is implied than mere human subordination.

self-limitation of the apostolic authority may have been a personal trait of Paul himself; certainly, in so far as it is consciously elaborated, it goes beyond the general concept in primitive Christianity of the apostle's role and character. It is understandable too that a later generation, even when it appealed specifically to Paul, should have failed to preserve his discovery. The later Church venerated its saints and 'good'[189] apostles in retrospect without reserve, and saw them as the possessors of an all-embracing, sacral authority, which could not be limited in any way. For them, therefore, the apostles became once more quite simply the 'foundation' of the Church.[190] Rightly understood, this image is certainly not necessarily false. It is, however, significant that Paul himself never used it, and indeed, in the context of his own 'apostolic' generation, hardly could have done so. Furthermore, he had experienced forcibly and at close quarters the dangers of a cult of personality and of human aggrandisement and error, from none of which were even apostles in any way immune. It was impossible for him, therefore, to exalt the apostles without question or reservation to a position which on his view the apostolic testimony, and therefore not the apostles themselves but only the one of whom that testimony spoke, namely the person of Jesus Christ, was entitled to occupy.

Paul also differs from the later historians and dogmatic theologians of his Church in the fact that he attaches little importance to a neat definition of specifically apostolic authority in relation to the authorities of other 'evangelists' and spiritual teachers. He constantly brackets himself with Barnabas,[191] Apollos,[192] and various other members of his congregation[193] in a way which is highly significant. Such an attitude fits in with his conception of the apostolate as entirely a matter of proclamation, not of organisation. The Church lives by her awareness of the Christ-message, the Gospel; it is on this, and not on the privileged position of certain individuals whom God has called to his service for this purpose, that all depends. The emphasis on the special character and unique importance of the original apostolic office and testimony for its own sake is completely post-Pauline; and it is only in the next generation—for example, in the Lucan and Johannine writings—that answers, and very varying ones, are first given to these questions.

The development of the idea of authority, however, does not depend simply on the concept of the apostolate, the reality of which slowly

---

[189] I Clem. 5:3.
[190] Cf. Eph. 2:20, a reshaping of Col. 2:7, where Christ himself, as in I Cor. 3:10 (cf. Rom. 15:20), is the foundation-stone. Cf. also Rev. 21:14; Matt. 16:18; Hermas, Sim. IX, 15, 4.
[191] I Cor. 9:6.   [192] I Cor. 4:6.
[193] I Cor. 12:29; cf. also p. 49 n. 163 above.

becomes a matter of past history. In the individual congregations, only some of which were of apostolic foundation, the question of the government of the community presently arises in a new form. It is in this context that we find emerging in the course of time the development of a permanent 'office', in the strict sense of that word. Once again, however, it was Paul, with his concept of the Christian community and his understanding of the idea of authority in non-official terms, who created the essential preconditions for this development; and to him therefore we must turn our attention once more.

CHAPTER IV

Spirit and Authority in the Pauline Congregation

IN THE case of Paul we know a good deal about the relationship between the 'apostle' and the churches founded by him. Elsewhere, however, things may have been quite different. Not all churches were of apostolic foundation, or had a single founder responsible for them.[1] Traffic and commerce within the Roman Empire were so intense that many must have come into existence, so to speak, spontaneously as a result of the work of itinerant missionaries or of ones whose visits were only sporadic, and then have been left, so far as their development was concerned, more or less to their own devices. The first missionaries were not seeking to 'found churches' but to proclaim Christ;[2] and if even the preaching and teaching which were their main concern present at the beginning a highly diversified picture,[3] this was naturally all the more true of the early attempts at Church order and 'constitution-making'. We know, for example, nothing of how the great Roman congregation came into being, nor what form it originally took.[4] In general, where we have neither Paul nor even Luke to guide us, imagination is accorded free but fruitless scope. Even on the subject of the original Jerusalem community we have in this respect only dubious and largely obscure indications; and how great the differences not only from province to province but even within one and the selfsame town may have been can be illustrated from the story of the faction-torn Corinthian church.

The Pauline congregations, too, undoubtedly exhibited local variations. Nevertheless, the general outlines of their life and organisation were determined by Paul himself, and the basic ideas to which he gives expression, and on which we are dependent, are the same in every case. It is these which we have now to consider. This will mean to a certain extent retreading ground already covered in the preceding chapter, since the same fundamental views are just as applicable to the internal life of the congregation as to its relationship with its own apostle or to the relations of the various apostles with one another. Above all,

---

[1] Cf. A. Von Harnack, *The Mission of Christianity I*, 1908, p. 321 n. 4.

[2] Cf. M. Goguel, *L'église primitive*, 1947, p. 156.

[3] On this subject cf. W. Bauer, *Rechtgläubigkeit und Ketzerei*, 1934.

[4] Cf., however, p. 84 nn. 43 and 44, below.

Paul communicated to the children of his mission his idea of what it meant to live the life of a spirit-filled community in Christ; and it is from this that all the other details of its internal and external life followed automatically, or at any rate ought to have done so.

For Paul, as for other early Christians, the 'Church' or 'congregation' is primarily the eschatological People of God, the new Israel, the community of God's holy and elect, who have submitted to the risen Christ as Lord, and who await his ultimate, imminent return.[5] This people now no longer consists of Jews alone, but essentially of both Jews and Gentiles; it embraces the whole world. The Old Testament concept of the people of God, however, is not the only determinative one; it now shares that role with another idea of quite a different kind, namely that of the congregation as the 'body' of Christ. They live not merely as those who wait for their Lord and believe in his presence with them, but, so to say, as this very presence itself, its incarnation in many 'members', all controlled by the one Christ-'Spirit.' United with Christ their master by the process of baptism, Christians now belong in an almost spatial sense to the heavenly world. They are only outwardly 'in the flesh', the final 'transformation' of which is still to come; in reality they are 'in Christ', who has laid hold on their whole being, and therefore both should and must determine their every action. The mythological background of this view, discernible in the later gnosis, need not occupy us here.[6] Its distinctively Christian meaning shines out in the way in which membership of Christ is thought of in Paul's writings, and given effect in real life. For the realm of Christ and of the Holy Spirit, despite their miraculous quality, are at the same time understood as the sphere of personal decision. Only by faith in the crucified and risen Christ can a man win a share in them; only by renouncing sin and the world can he maintain himself within them; and only by the mutual service of all the members of the body can the life of the Spirit develop among them and reach its fulfilment. The content of this life and of this spirit is clearly defined in Paul: it implies the rejection of a God–Man relationship determined by the demands and exertions of the 'Law', and the affirmation of the 'Gospel' of forgiveness. In this 'evangelical' sense faith in Christ effects the sonship, freedom, and sanctification before God which find expression as selflessness, purity of heart, friendship, and love toward men. In both these respects God's congregation is different from the world around it; it possesses a life that is genuinely 'new'. Everything that is contrary to this is contrary to the spiritual nature which is the community's possession in Christ; and if it is prepared to persist in this contradiction, then it is in danger of betraying and destroying its own very

[5] Cf. N. A. Dahl, *Das Volk Gottes*, 1941, pp. 209ff.
[6] Cf. E. Käsemann, *Leib und Leib Christi*, 1933.

existence. At the same time, however, the new life is not a new requirement in the sense in which the Law had set the Good before men as a
task required of them; it is a reality already bestowed 'in Christ', and
actualised as a gift of grace by the Spirit. It is the soil in which the
congregation is planted, and in which they have to grow; and all that
is required of them is that they should never leave it again.

This applies to the congregation as a whole and to each member
individually. All Christians have received the Spirit, and thus become
'spiritual' men and women.[7] For Paul, without the Spirit there is no
being a Christian, and no spiritual life. On the other hand, he definitely
does not regard unity in the Spirit as implying 'equality'. For him it is
of the essence that the underlying unity of the Spirit which has been
given to all is made concretely effective in the multiplicity of different
gifts bestowed on different people. Paul knows of no operation of the
Spirit that is formless, universal, and indiscriminately interchangeable.
One man has received this gift, another that; and the life of the Church
is to be found only in the continual interplay of a variety of spiritual
capacities, which complement one another, and which precisely in this
way reveal the fullness and harmony of the Spirit of Christ.[8] Paul
derives neither the complexity nor the omnipresence of the Spirit's
endowments from theoretical considerations; behind the language
which he uses stands the vivid experience of his missionary work. It
is clear that his preaching, when it was effective, released among the
converted a violent enthusiasm (in the technical sense of that word),
which then found expression in the most varied and surprising 'gifts'.
We hear of prophesyings and revelations, of healings and exorcisms
and 'mighty works', of miracles and parapsychological phenomena, such
as are met with at other times and places in history under the impact
of a new religion or of religious 'revival'.[9] Paul's attitude toward them
is neither sceptical nor mistrustful; he accepts them joyfully as gifts of
the Spirit of Christ. But, so far as he is concerned, the unusual and
astounding character of the phenomena is not enough in itself. The
Spirit of Christ shows itself pre-eminently as the power of sanctification
and love within the community; these alone are the infallible signs of its
presence. The new life is decidedly not a matter of mere exaltation in the
enjoyment of individual religious experiences, but of bringing all
together in the unity, love, and fellowship of the indivisible 'Body of
Christ'.[10]

[7] Cf. pp. 46f. above. [8] Cf. Rom. 12:3ff.; I Cor. 12:4ff.
[9] For a detailed examination of this point cf. H. Weinel, *Die Wirkungen des
Geistes und der Geister im nachapostolischen Zeitalter bis auf Irenäus*, 1899; and
I. Salomies, *Henkilahjat kirkossa sen alkuvuosisatoina* (= *Charismatic gifts in the
Church of the first centuries*), 1937. The latter work is unfortunately written in
Finnish.
[10] I Cor. 12–14.

On this basis Paul develops the idea of the Spirit as the organising principle of the Christian congregation. There is no need for any fixed system with its rules and regulations and prohibitions. Paul's writings do as little to provide such things for the individual congregation as for the Church at large. The community is not viewed or understood as a sociological entity, and the Spirit which governs it does not act within the framework of a particular church order or constitution.[11] 'If you are led by the Spirit, you are not under the Law.'[12] In the Church 'freedom' is a basic controlling principle;[13] for the Spirit of Christ, which is the giver of freedom, urges men on not to independence and self-assertion but to loving service. It is love which is the true organising and unifying force within the Church, and which creates in her a paradoxical form of order diametrically opposed to all natural systems of organisation. For it is not the 'strong', the capable, and the great who enjoy the 'honour' of precedence; instead, the weaker and more needy a member is, the more are all the rest to support him with their love and to 'honour' him.[14] Moreover, no one is completely useless; everyone has a possibility of making some contribution with his own gift in proportion to the faith which has been given him:[15] 'If the whole body were an eye, where would be the hearing? If the whole body were an ear, where would be the sense of smell?'[16] Paul knows how to apply this concept in such a way that by it the individual in his individuality is protected against the criticism and intolerance of his fellow-Christians: 'Who are you to pass judgment on the servant of another? It is before his own master that he stands or falls.'[17] It was just as much for the weak brother that Christ died,[18] and the immediate reality of Christ, which brings Christians together, at the same time upholds each one in his particular capacity for living. More important, however, than this restraining, almost defensive meaning of the new 'freedom' is its positive, construc-

[11] In this connection the Pastoral Epistles and Ephesians are of course not counted as Pauline: cf. p. 30 n. 1 above.

[12] Gal. 5:18. Here, as in all other passages where Paul speaks of the 'Law', it is primarily only the particular Jewish Law which is meant. But the way in which he contrasts this with the Spirit and with the 'law of Christ' (Gal. 6:2) shows that he is speaking not of the replacement of the old law with some new kind of legal regulation of life but of the end of all law, of 'legalism' in general.

[13] II Cor. 3:17.   [14] I Cor. 12:22ff.; Rom. 12:11; 14:1.

[15] An explicit statement to the effect that every member of the congregation receives his own χάρις (= χάρισμα) is not found until the post-Pauline Ephesians (4:7; cf. 4:16). Genuine Pauline utterances on this subject are not quite so clear-cut, though their general tendency is undoubtedly in the same direction: Rom. 12:3; I Cor. 3:5; 12:7, 11, 18; 14:1, 26; similarly I Pet. 4:10. For a discussion of this question cf. E. Schweizer, *Das Leben des Herrn in der Gemeinde und ihren Diensten,* 1946, p. 86 n. 3.

[16] I Cor. 12:17.   [17] Rom. 14:4; cf. I Cor. 10:29; Gal. 6:4f.

[18] Rom. 14:15; I Cor. 8:11.

tive sense. Christians do not please themselves,[19] they do not strive after 'high things',[20] they do not consider themselves and their own advantage, but that which benefits their neighbour and the whole community.[21] Sharing joys and sorrows,[22] one bears another's burden,[23] and the result is 'peace' and 'edification' and the growth of the whole congregation.

It is clear that in Paul's case such teachings are motivated by a strong practical interest. Small-minded bickerings and jealousies there had always been in the Christian congregations with their predominantly petit bourgeois composition. Paul's ideas, however, should not be interpreted merely in terms of 'church politics' or as 'good tactics'. They are of a piece with the very heart of Pauline theology, and must be taken seriously in their theological sense. Christians have in very fact died to the old 'human' nature, and thus also to the old ideas of status and social order. Among them there can be neither respect nor distinction of 'persons',[24] since there was none in Christ's acceptance of them.[25] 'He died for all, that those who live might live no longer for themselves but for him who for their sake died and was raised. . . . Therefore, if any one is in Christ, there is a new creation; the old has passed away, behold, the new has come.'[26] Only beyond death, the complete dissolution of the old man, is spiritual life to be found. The expression of this life is love; but this love is no special 'virtue', and it is equally remote from human self-effacement or respect. It is a matter of continuing in the basic attitude of the new, redeemed being. Whoever thinks otherwise is prey to an illusion, and 'deceives himself'.[27]

There is no need to point out that this radical definition of Christian existence in Paul is not to be attributed to ignorance on his part of the real difficulties and of the far from 'ideal' conditions within his congregations, nor to his having simply skated over them as a result of overenthusiastic expectations. The hard facts—namely that Christians 'bite and devour one another',[28] are overbearing and at constant feud,[29] are lacking in humility and knowledge[30]— are for him simply occasions to 'recall' them to their real, spiritual mode of being,[31] and thus to summon them back to the true path of Christian existence. And this applies twice as strongly to those who consider themselves already 'perfect'. Christians are not to stand still, nor at any stage of their life to fancy that they have reached the goal; they have to 'grow' and 'increase', and to strive in the spirit for an ever richer actualisation of the blessing which

[19] Rom. 15:1.
[20] Rom. 12:16.
[21] Rom. 15:1; cf. 12:17; I Cor. 10:24, 33.
[22] Rom. 12:15; I Cor. 12:26; 13:6.
[23] Gal. 6:2.
[24] Rom. 2:11; I Cor. 12:13; Gal. 2:6; 3:28; Col. 3:11, 25.
[25] Rom. 15:7.
[26] II Cor. 5:15, 17; cf. I Cor. 8:12.
[27] Gal. 6:3; cf. I Cor. 3:18.
[28] Gal. 5:15.
[29] I Cor. 1-4.
[30] I Cor. 8:1-7; 15:34.
[31] Rom. 15:15; I Cor. 4:17

has come among them.[32] In the realm of the Holy Spirit it simply is not true that 'You've either made it or you haven't'. Hence there is also a need in the congregation for spiritual authority, for constant admonition, encouragement, and reminder. So far we have come across these things only as the task of the apostle, the man who on the basis of his own unique commission has called the congregation to life and now leads it. Authority, however, is not restricted to him and to his direct intervention. It is precisely for this very same purpose that the Spirit bestows upon the Church his many different gifts and graces. But how can these be given concrete effect in a community which knows of no fixed 'offices' or 'constitution', no superiority or inferiority of rank, and which quite definitely does not ascribe to those with spiritual gifts, as distinct from the apostle, any sort of personal authority? The answer to this question is decisive for the meaning of the Pauline concept of authority as the principle of the life of the redeemed congregation.

For a proper understanding of the state of affairs envisaged by Paul it is not necessary that we should form a complete picture of the various spirit-endowed persons within the congregation as regards the distinctive character of their particular gifts, which in some cases can be identified only with difficulty.[33] It will be sufficient to concentrate on the two noblest gifts, which Paul himself singles out as such and links with the apostolate,[34] namely, prophecy and teaching. It is these which primarily build up and sustain the spiritual life of the congregation, whereas other capabilities, which attract attention and excite the especial wonder of the immature, such as speaking with tongues, are of little value to the community as a whole, and must therefore step into the background.[35] 'And God has appointed in the church first apostles, second prophets, third teachers, then workers of miracles, then healers, helpers, administrators, speakers in various kinds of tongues'[36]—the last-named including also the 'interpreters' of these ecstatic utterances.[37] 'But earnestly desire the higher gifts!'[38]

It is clear that this enumeration falls into two parts:[39] the random and somewhat imprecisely formulated mention of individual 'gifts' is

[32] Cf. esp. Phil. 3:12ff.
[33] They may also, as the example of Paul himself shows, be found in combination in a single person.
[34] This 'triad' later became stereotyped, and may already in Paul's time have been a traditional enumeration: cf. Harnack, *op. cit.*, pp. 348ff.; J. Dupont, *Gnosis*, 1949, pp. 203f.
[35] I Cor. 14:3, 12, 26.   [36] I Cor. 12:28.
[37] I Cor. 12:8ff.   [38] I Cor. 12:30f.
[39] On what follows cf. H. Greeven, 'Propheten, Lehrer, Vorsteher bei Paulus. Zur Frage der "Ämter" im Urchristentum', *ZNW* 44, 1952, pp. 1ff., which the author most kindly made available to me at the proof stage.

preceded by a list of three groups of people, clearly marked off as such, and arranged in sequence with an emphatic 'first', 'second', and 'third'. Concerning the 'apostles' there is no need to enlarge on what has already been said. In their case the word 'first' undoubtedly carries the additional sense of an objective precedence; the apostle possesses a unique vocation, and occupies a position of pre-eminent authority over the whole congregation—indeed, a whole group of congregations is linked to him as their missionary founder and spiritual father. It is often assumed that the prophets and teachers likewise operated outside the framework of the single congregation, and moved on as 'itinerant preachers' from place to place, but this is certainly not a conclusion that can be drawn from the Pauline epistles.[40] On the contrary, it looks as though it was their particular task to continue within the individual congregation the work which the apostle had first begun on a wider scale. The work of prophecy is to bring to men the untrammelled utterance of proclamation and revelation in which Christ is preached; teaching, however, is concerned with handing on and expounding the Christ-tradition, with impressing on men the precepts and propositions of the faith, and above all with the exegesis of the Old Testament as understood by the young Church. Probably the activities of the Christian teacher have something in common with the practice of the hellenistic synagogue and its rabbinate. In that case the teachers will have formed a rather tightly closed group, something which followed from the nature of their work, the systematic learning and teaching, 'receiving' and 'transmitting', of a tradition which was partly already formed and partly still in process of formation. The limits of prophetism, on the other hand, are less sharply drawn. In some sense the spirit of prophecy is indeed alive in the whole congregation, and may therefore make itself heard in unexpected places.[41] But this does not at all imply that all Christians are in the narrower sense 'prophets';[42] this term refers primarily only to particular, distinguished individuals, appointed by God and known to men as such. They occupy the highest place within the local congregation; and 'prophecy' is, according to Paul, that spiritual gift for which one should strive above all others.[43] Probably, therefore, its exponents are accorded higher respect than the teachers, who come third in the list, just as they themselves are surpassed by the apostles. It is the Spirit of Christ which speaks directly to men through the prophets. The work of the teacher is, of course, likewise made possible by a special spiritual endowment; but whether

---

[40] If this were so, one would certainly expect them to be mentioned in such a passage as I Cor. 9:5; cf. Greeven, art. cit., p. 9.

[41] This is suggested by I Cor. 11:5, understood against the background of I Cor. 14:33–36; cf. Greeven, art. cit., p. 7.

[42] I Cor. 12:29.   [43] I Cor. 12:31; 14:39; I Thess. 5:19f.

because it was the custom in teaching to stick more closely to tradition, and to a certain extent to be tied to a 'text',[44] or for some other reason, it is clear that in Paul the teacher's place is of less importance than that of the prophet. By contrast, the activities of the prophets are constantly compared with the way in which he himself works and preaches in his congregations. Nevertheless, the distinction which exists between the prophetic and the apostolic authority should not be overlooked.

However great the stress which Paul lays at all times on his self-effacement, his role of servant, and his rejection of the desire for power in any form, the fact remains that, as already described, his position as apostle sets him permanently over the congregation. He is not incorporated into it as a 'member', but in virtue of his direct calling by Christ has, as it were, an independent origin. The prophets, however—and this applies equally to the teachers and all others imbued with the Spirit—stand always within the community, and therefore in subjection to the testimony which they have received from the apostle. If anyone has received the gift of prophecy, says Paul, let him use it 'in proportion to', that is, in agreement with the faith.[45] In the case of the prophet this means that he is forbidden to suppress or add anything on his own authority! He stands on a 'ground' of faith which the apostle has laid, which did not begin with himself, and which therefore binds him in a different way from that in which it binds the apostle, who comes from Christ himself. This becomes clear when we consider his position within the congregation. Here the prophet, as Paul sees it, never stands on his own, but always in association with other prophets who possess equal authority with himself; and by his spirit he is united with them and with the whole community. If a revelation forces itself on one prophet, then the others must give way to him; for in all of them there is one single Spirit of God, who inspires the prophecies, and 'God is not a God of confusion but of peace'.[46] This remark, which refers in the first place to outward behaviour, of course applies all the more to the inward disposition; the prophets are not to contradict one another, but to complement and co-operate with one another. The ultimate decision, however, is always left to the congregation itself and not to any one person in authority. This does not imply a 'democratic' church organisation; the 'discerning' or testing of the spirits is itself in turn a special gift, which is practised by particular individuals equipped to do so,[47] and these may well themselves be prophets. But this does not mean that

[44] For further discussion of the role of the teacher cf. pp. 192ff. below.
[45] Rom. 12:6; cf. I Pet. 4:11.
[46] I Cor. 14:33. As Greeven, art. cit., pp. 12ff., has shown, this is not a question of subjecting the prophetic spirit to the will of the prophet as a human person.
[47] I Cor. 12:10.

the congregation is thereby relieved of responsibility for what happens. The confession of faith in Christ common to all Christians, a confession which itself can only be made 'in the Spirit', is a criterion which every member has at his disposal.[48] It is significant that Paul, both where he is specifically summoning Christians to vigilance in testing the spirits,[49] and everywhere else in his letters, never addresses one single class or group of people as though they were responsible for the spiritual well-being of the others.[50] Instead, one member exhorts and edifies another. As a matter of principle there is no 'ruling class' in the congregation, and even the 'spiritual men' are not thought of, by Paul at any rate, as a 'pneumatic aristocracy'. The function which the prophets perform is certainly of outstanding importance for the congregation; but for all that, they themselves are still incorporated into the totality of the body of Christ, and the power or 'authority' which they exercise is consequently no 'absolute' authority. This applies not only, as in the case of the apostle, to their personal status, but also to their testimony, to the extent that this is not something given once for all, but is to be judged in each specific instance and tested for genuineness.[52] Every genuine gift, whether high or lowly, is indeed an operation of the Spirit. It is therefore not human but divine, and must be affirmed and acknowledged as authoritative. But this means that its exponents, precisely because they are spiritual men, are involved in the corporate whole in which and through which the Spirit of Christ shows its power; and this Spirit alone is sovereign.

In Paul's thought, therefore, the congregation is not just another

[48] I Cor. 12:3, with the formula 'Jesus is Lord', is not, however, as yet directly intended to provide such a criterion. To judge from the context, Paul is simply trying to show that 'glossolalia is only *one* among many spiritual gifts. Even the elementary (? cultic) form of confession, "Jesus is Lord", is an example of the operation of the Holy Spirit' (Greeven, *art. cit.*, p. 3 n. 6). But it would obviously be in line with Paul's meaning here to come to a decision in keeping with this confession when testing the spirits as well: cf. Rom. 10:9.

[49] I Thess. 5:11.

[50] Farrer, 'The Ministry in the New Testament', *The Apostolic Ministry* (ed. Kirk), 1946, has maintained the opposite view: 'A great part of any Pauline epistle is addressed to an inner circle: this leaps to the eye.' Both the passages, however, which he adduces, if they suggest anything, indicate rather the opposite. The πνευματικοί of Gal. 6:1 are no more characterised as an 'inner circle' of leading members of the congregation than are the δυνατοί of Rom. 15:1, and what is said to them applies, to judge from the context, to everyone (cf. 6:2, ἀλλήλων 6:3, εἰ γὰρ δοκεῖ τις 6:4, ἕκαστος). I Thess. 5:12f., if we adopt the better reading, explicitly addresses both the προϊστάμενοι and the rest of the congregation together (εἰρηνεύετε ἐν ἑαυτοῖς); but even apart from this, the idea that there is a change in the persons addressed between 5:13 and 5:14 (ἀδελφοί!) is a purely arbitrary assumption.

[51] I Thess. 5:20f.

[52] I Cor. 14:29 shows that this was a regular occurrence, and not just a step taken when misgivings began to arise.

constitutional organisation with grades and classes, but a unitary, living cosmos of free, spiritual gifts, which serve and complement one another. Those who mediate these gifts may never lord it over one another, or refuse to have anything to do with one another. To the extent that any element of compulsion, any permanent seat of command is expressly excluded, the resultant picture of the community, understood in terms of human social order, is utopian. But, for Paul, the Church is not a human,[53] natural entity, but a sheerly miraculous, transcendent phenomenon. The preaching of the Gospel is the only thing which calls to life the Spirit through which the congregation can become what it is. Christians have the Spirit of Christ. Because of this, spontaneity, obedience and love are in fact presupposed and required of the Church as, so to speak, the 'normal' thing. When the Church ceases to be spiritual, that is to say, when within her that which is normal for the world is exalted into a law, then in Paul's eyes she is dead.

Yet the utopian character of the Pauline conception of the Church should not be exaggerated. That for Christians there can be no command by one section only, no governing class or 'spiritual executive', does not mean that Paul wanted organisational chaos, or that in his congregations everything was to be at sixes and sevens. In the Corinthian congregation it does sometimes look very much as if this was so; here there seems to have been almost no trace of fixed arrangements or conventions for regulating meetings. On the other hand, however, Paul mentions helpers, controllers and administrators, whose activity he includes among the 'spiritual gifts'; and he is plainly concerned that these people should not be despised, and that nothing should be done to make their work more difficult. 'But we beseech you, brethren, to respect those who labour among you and are over you in the Lord and admonish you, and to esteem them very highly in love because of their work. Be at peace with them.'[54] Nevertheless, the imprecise terminology which Paul uses can hardly be taken to imply a fixed 'office'. Paul

[53] Cf. I Cor. 3:4: ὅταν λέγῃ τις, ἐγὼ μὲν εἰμι Παύλου. ἕτερος δὲ, ἐγὼ 'Απολλῶ, οὐκ ἄνθρωποι ἐστε; (the reading σαρκικοί instead of ἄνθρωποι is a latter correction). Obviously the sentence does not imply that 'the spirituals have ceased to be human'; it means that they are not to live as men do, but by the Spirit: W. G. Kümmel in Lietzmann, *An der Korinther*[4], 1949, p. 171.

[54] I Thess. 5:12f. In fact it would make hardly any difference, if one were to adopt a different reading in the final short sentence, and render it 'Be at peace among yourselves' (as does, for example, RSV). In that case the supervisors would be included in the request. Moreover, the exhortation to a quiet and hard-working life which follows (5:14) is not unconnected with Paul's intervention on behalf of those who are 'over' the congregation. This passage may be compared with the corresponding exhortation in Rom. 13:1ff., which has the secular officials in mind; there is almost a parallel here in the treatment of the ecclesiastical and secular 'authorities': cf. H. Von Campenhausen, 'Zur Auslegung von Röm. 13,' *Festschrift Alfred Bertholet*, 1950, pp. 111f.

has in mind anyone who comes forward in one way or another within the congregation to take on its problems and to provide material or spiritual help. The fact that spiritual exhortation, either to comfort or to admonish, is particularly mentioned certainly does not exclude the prophets or teachers, since they were the ones to whom this ministry primarily belonged. The expression κοπιᾶν, 'to toil', which originally denoted heavy, physical labour, is a favourite with Paul in other passages where he is either speaking of his own undertakings[55] or wishes especially to commend particular colleagues.[56] Its use may have been suggested to him in the first place by the manual trade which he himself pursued to ensure his independence;[57] but on his lips it has already to a certain extent become a 'technical term'. The same seems to the word σπουδή, 'zeal', with which he describes the joyful 'commitment' which certain 'presiding' members of the congregation display in its work.[58] The meaning of the word προίστασθαι, which has been rendered here on the one hand as 'to be over', 'to preside', and on the other as to 'take on', 'take over', in practice falls roughly between these two ideas. Outside the New Testament the word is used of the activity of taking care for someone's welfare, as indeed those in high positions do for their dependants and subordinates. But when Paul uses the word he is not thinking of any definite 'governing' office within the congregation, but quite generally of any work of advising or assisting which takes place there.[59]

Nevertheless, it is true that among the gifts of the Spirit which Paul enumerates in Corinthians—though not first in the list—the gift of 'government', the art of the pilot or 'helmsman'[60] as it was called in the political imagery of the ancient world[61], is also mentioned. But even this does not imply 'government' in the strict sense of the word, but much more the gift of 'providing assistance'.[62] For an office of governor on the lines of the presbyterate or of the later monarchical episcopate there was no room at Corinth either in practice or in principle,[63] and to try to describe any particular set of duties which might be allocated to

[55] I Cor. 15:10; II Cor. 6:5; 11: 23, 27; Gal. 4:11; Phil. 2:16; Col. 1:29.

[56] Rom 16:6, 12; I Cor. 3: 8; 16:16; I Thess. 5:12.

[57] I Cor. 4:12; cf. A. Von Harnack, 'Κόπος (κοπιᾶν, οἱ κοπιῶντες) im urchristlichen Sprachgebrauch', ZNW 27, 1928, p. 5.

[58] Rom. 12:8; otherwise 12:11 would be 'pure tautology' (Greeven).

[59] Cf. G. Friedrich, 'Geist und Amt,' Wort und Dienst (Jahrb. Theol. Schule Bethel, 1952) p. 80 n. 65; Greeven, op. cit., p. 32 n. 74.

[60] I Cor. 12:28: κυβερνήσεις.   [61] Cf. H. W. Beyer, TWNT 3, 1938, p. 1035.

[62] In I Cor. 12:28 ἀντιλήψεις are listed next to κυβερνήσεις.

[63] If anyone does not see this, it is naturally difficult to provide him with sufficiently convincing proof that offices in the true sense of the word are not to be found in Paul; hence it is hardly likely that attempts to interpret him in a more or less clerical and ecclesiastical sense will cease altogether. Quite the most astonishing example of such an attempt in recent years is that of

these governors is to run immediately into great difficulties. The task of representing the congregation in its dealings with the outside world is quite out of the question. But it is obvious that even worship is still completely unorganised, and subject to no special control. Paul himself has to intervene with his admonitions in this department—to check, for example, the practice of beginning the communal meal in disorder. The solitary piece of advice which he is able to give on this point is, 'Wait for one another'.[64] Responsible presidents to see to this matter cannot therefore have been available.[65] Neither can the leaders have been regularly employed in looking after the economic affairs of the congregation, taking in hand those matters which fell outside the scôpe of a spiritual cure.[66] The instructions which Paul gives for preparing the 'collection' show that such an organisation did not exist in even the most modest and rudimentary form; otherwise he would not have had to urge each individual member of the congregation to put aside himself the odd pence which he had saved, so that they might all be pooled when Paul arrived.[67] Furthermore, both in Corinth and in Philippi it is necessary for appropriate men to be chosen for the express purpose of delivering the alms.[68] We must be content, therefore, to leave this particular gift of government undefined. The man who had proved or commended himself in these or similar matters was one who had received this gift from the Spirit, and could in this way make himself useful to the congregation. The same probably applies to teachers and prophets, who in primitive Christianity are most certainly not to be thought of as unrestrained enthusiasts.[69]

B. Hennen, 'Ordines sacri. Ein Deutungsversuch zu I Cor. 12, 1–31 und Rm. 12, 2–8,' *Theol. Quartalschrift* 119, 1938, pp. 427ff. Hennen neatly distributes the Pauline charismata among all the various clerical offices to be found in developed Catholicism—right down through acolytes, exorcists, lectors, and doorkeepers. Thus, for example, the γλώσσαις λαλοῦντες are the lectors, who supposedly had to recite Hebrew texts in public worship, and so on. How far, by contrast, even Catholic scholars are prepared to go in recognising a 'charismatic hierarchy', independent of ordination and ecclesiastical institution, may be seen, for example, in O. Casel, 'Prophetie und Eucharistie', *Jahrbuch für Liturgiewissenschaft* 9, 1929, pp. 1ff. It is still true, however, that the static legal concept of 'hierarchy' is quite unsuited to express the distinctive character of the idea of charisma.

[64] I Cor. 11:33.

[65] Cf. Schweizer, *Das Leben des Herrn*, p. 96 n. 3; Greeven, *art. cit.*, p. 39.

[66] So H. Lietzmann, 'Zur altchristlichen Verfassungsgeschichte', *ZWT* 55, 1914, pp. 98ff., and *History of the Early Church* I, pp. 145f.; II, pp. 58f., in agreement with the ideas of Hatch and Harnack; cf. p. 82 below.

[67] I Cor. 16:2; II Cor. 9:3f.

[68] I Cor. 16:3; II Cor. 8:19, 23; Phil. 2:25, cf. 4:18. The term ἀπόστολος in this context does not imply an apostolate like that of Paul himself, but simply designates the authorised representative of the congregation: cf. H. Von Campenhausen, 'Der urchristliche Apostelbegriff', *Stud. Theol.* 1, 1948, p. 102.

[69] Cf. also p. 73 n. 128 below.

It is possible to inject a little more colour into this rather general idea of beneficent rule or administration by taking into account an even wider category of persons, though still without exhausting the whole range of those who might be considered in this connection. There are those whom Paul speaks of as 'firstfruits' of their congregations. Thus for example, in the last chapter of Romans he greets 'my beloved Epaenetus, who is the firstfruits of Asia for Christ'.[70] The present tense indicates that by 'firstfruits'—the word which Paul uses is precisely the impersonal, originally cultic term[71]—a permanent distinguishing quality is implied. And indeed nothing is more natural than that those who were the first converts at the foundation of a missionary congregation should be held in special respect by those who joined at a later stage, and should occupy a position of trust in the community.[72] They may have made their houses available for the missionary and for the meetings of the congregation, and have carried a large share of the burdens connected with these aspects of church life.[73] A passage in I Corinthians makes this even clearer: 'Now, brethren, you know that the household of Stephanas were the first converts in Achaia, and they have devoted themselves to the service of the saints.'[74] Here, then, it is a matter of a whole family,[75] which took on the work involved in the early days, and made sacrifices for the young Church. Special house-churches are also found in Colossae,[76] and in Rome at the home of Aquila and Prisca, Paul's 'fellow workers'.[77] With regard to Stephanas Paul urges in addition that Church members should voluntarily 'be subject' to him and to anyone who 'co-operates and labours with him' in the general interest.[78]

With an eye on later developments in the doctrine of ecclesiastical office the question is much debated how such administrators and leading figures attained their 'position'—were they chosen by the congregation, or appointed by the apostle, or subsequently confirmed in their position by him? In view of the actual circumstances and of the nature of these positions of authority it should be obvious that such a question is completely futile, and ought not even to be asked. Stephanas, as Paul stresses, himself 'volunteered' for his service; in the case of Archippus at Colossae, who has 'received' a particular 'ministry in the Lord', and is to take care to fulfil it, a call by the congregation may have been involved;[79] and others, such as Philemon, demonstrate their faith and

---

[70] Rom. 16:5. In Rome itself Epaenetus apparently has no special role to fulfil.

[71] Cf. G. Delling, *TWNT* I, 1935, p. 484.

[72] For this reason I Clem. 42:4, and, later, Origen, *Hom. Num.* XI, 4, see in these persons the first office-holders.

[73] Cf. Rom. 16:23; Acts 18:7.

[74] I Cor. 16:15. [75] Cf. also I Tim. 1:15ff. [76] Col. 4:15.

[77] Rom. 16:4f. [78] I Cor. 16:16: ὑποτάσσησθε. [79] Col. 4:17.

love 'toward all the saints' in completely unspecified ways.[80] Such arrangements and relationships arise spontaneously, and do not allow of legal definition. For Paul each such ministry rests in principle not on some human organisational plan nor on an arbitrary decision; it is the employment of a gift which the Spirit bestows. The one who exercises it has received it for the greatest possible advantage of all, whether or not, like Phoebe at Cenchreae, he is explicitly designated a 'servant' of the Church.[81] In the nature of the case no sharp dividing line can be drawn between particular tasks, which of course there may also have been,[82] or between spiritual and practical service.

That there was a rapid turnover of those who exercised these various ministries is nowhere stated, nor is it intrinsically probable. Normally, therefore, those whose gifts had put them in a position of trust will have received their ministry on a permanent basis, or at any rate for a fairly long time. Consequently, it is entirely possible that they would be described not only in terms of their gift, as Paul himself commonly describes them, but also by the activities which they pursue and the position within the congregation which they acquire as a result. Thus, Philippians is addressed not only to 'all the saints' but also, for the first time, to the 'overseers and servants' of the congregation, their 'bishops and deacons'.[83] In view of the universal usage of later times one can hardly regard this specific collocation of terms as no more than an indefinite 'description of office'.[84] We are dealing with established terms for offices, one might say with titles, even though these are of a very general and neutral, and entirely non-sacral, origin and nature.[85] Moreover, Paul makes no bones about recognising this arrangement, and indeed by the very fact of singling them out for mention gives especial prominence to the persons so described.[86] In all probability Philippians is one of the latest of the Pauline Epistles. If then the stereo-

[80] Phmn 5.

[81] Rom. 16:1. It is generally assumed that the term διάκονος here is already to be understood, as in Phil. 1:1, as a title of office. This is not impossible, but it seems to me unlikely.

[82] As suggested, for example, by Col. 4:17, and as in the case of the representatives chosen to deal with the collection: cf. p. 66 n. 68 above.

[83] Phil. 1:1.

[84] So F. Loofs, 'Die urchristliche Gemeindeverfassung mit spezieller Beziehung auf Loening und Harnack', Theol. Stud. und Krit. 63, 1890, pp. 682f.

[85] In the main this is shown by the non-Christian usage of the words: cf. H. W. Beyer, TWNT 2, 1935, pp. 614ff.; and H. Karpp. RAC 2, 1952, pp. 394ff.

[86] Why he does so cannot be determined. The widespread view that Paul specifies these men because they were the ones who brought the gift of money mentioned in the epistle is just as impossible to prove as the bold hypothesis of E. Lohmeyer that special reference was made to them because at the time of the letter they had been thrown into prison (Philipper, Kolosser, Philemon, 1930, pp. 12f.)

typed terminology in this passage is more than merely the reflection of a local idiosyncrasy, we may perhaps say that there a later stage of church development is already emerging. It would be quite wrong, however, to suggest that in Paul's mind a congregation without a fixed form of 'office' was as yet immature, with a purely provisional organisation, and that until it had acquired a fully developed constitution it would not have fulfilled its essential nature. Any sort of basis for such an interpretation is completely lacking; and in fact the exact reverse is the truth. The congregation lives by the Spirit, and it is as a result of the manifold gifts of the Spirit that it develops its various members. Where the Spirit and love are sovereign it is already 'perfect' in Christ, and in need of absolutely no further organisation. Particular concrete arrangements and ministries may arise within the life of the congregation, but they do not as such establish any new system, any sacred law. They are incorporated without further ado into the prevailing outlook; and their validity rests on the fact that they are the product of gifts which the Spirit has given. And this they remain, even when they become a continuing feature of community life, and thus in some sense 'official'. There is, however, no question of offices in the strict sense, and absolutely none of sacral offices on the lines of the later 'hierarchy'.

This may be seen from the way in which, in Paul's writings, the authority of such ministries is conceived and implemented. The gift of the Spirit which is the basis of each ministry within the congregation cannot be 'handed on', but in every instance is directly bestowed by the Spirit himself. The tension fundamental to any office, namely that between personal capacity and the duties imposed, is therefore lacking. In this context, to pursue a certain 'calling' is simply to exercise, to confirm, to prove a particular gift that has been received; and it is the presence of this gift which demonstrates a true 'call', and makes its implementation possible. Paul knows of no 'obedience' in the strict sense of the word toward those in authority within the congregation, such as he demands toward Christ and therefore also in principle toward Christ's apostle.[87] His characteristic admonition is rather to the effect that the congregation should 'acknowledge' the work of their helpers and administrators, and so far from despising it should gratefully support it as a recognised activity of the Spirit. We see here a continuation of the distinctive conflict which characterised Paul's own relationship with his congregations, in that he as an apostle could 'properly' command them, and yet for the sake of their freedom and the nature of his commission did not wish to do so.[88] For the person in authority within the congregation there is still only the life of humility, of the mutual subordination of every member, and of a spontaneity as great in serving as in obeying. The ultimate either-or of a divinely authoritative decision,

[87] Cf. p. 52 n. 188 above. [88] Cf. pp. 49ff. above.

which the apostle knows has been entrusted at any rate to him personally, has not been put at their disposal.[89]

The ideas which Paul elaborates to direct the ministry of these persons in authority are not, in so far as they are pieces of general edification, peculiar to Paul. The rejection of force and compulsion, the
requirement of freedom and voluntary co-operation, the demand for
cohesion and unity, and the insistence on the spiritual nature of all
leadership, are found elsewhere in primitive Christianity.[90] Pauline,
however, is the radical theological approach by which this attitude is
given a christological basis, and related totally to the concept of the
Christian's having died to the world; though Paul may here be thinking
less of the life of the Church and its ministers than of the special character of his own apostolic activity and of the personal destiny of
suffering which that lays upon him.[91]

The most striking feature of Paul's view of the Christian community
is the complete lack of any legal system, and the exclusion on principle
of all formal authority within the individual congregation.[92] This is no
accident; it accords too well with Paul's emphasis on the new being
of the Church, which has put off the old human nature, with his rejection of external prescriptions and commands, and with his unconditional
allegiance to love, humility, and freedom. What makes it all the more
remarkable, however, is that at this time, as we shall see, in all probability there already existed, at any rate in Judaeo-Christian congregations, a definite patriarchal 'office', that of the presbyters.[93] Nevertheless, it is not necessary to interpret this difference polemically as
the result of a deliberate contrary decision on the part of Paul. The
Pauline mission on a large scale did not start from Galilee or Jerusalem,
but from Antioch; and it should be noted that we hear nothing of a
presbyterate at Antioch in the early period. Teachers and prophets are
the ones at the head of affairs there.[94] Paul may, therefore, simply have
followed this existing pattern when he founded his congregations.

Furthermore, his vision of the structure of the community as one of
free fellowship, developing through the living interplay of spiritual
gifts and ministries, without benefit of official authority or responsible

[89] This question will be considered in more detail in Chapter VI.

[90] Cf. H. Von Campenhausen, 'Recht und Gehorsam in der ältesten Kirche',
Theol. Blätt. 20, 1941, pp. 282ff.

[91] Cf. p. 41f. above.

[92] It is the fact that this is done on principle which constitutes the new element
as compared with the mere absence of constitutional thinking, which is a
general characteristic of the Church's beginnings: cf. pp. 28f. above.

[93] Cf. pp. 76ff. below.

[94] In the light of Acts 11:27; 13:1ff. (cf. 11:20; 15:32); 21:10ff., this can
hardly be seriously questioned, even if the statements which Luke makes on
the subject may be doubtful in certain details.

'elders', did not at once disappear after his death. Hebrews, Barnabas, and even the Didache, still adhere basically to this picture of Church 'organisation', despite the fact that the internal and external difficulties involved in maintaining it are already discernible. Paul is writing to young, enthusiastic, 'convert' congregations, practically without tradition of any kind, and seemingly knowing no limits to their spiritual zeal and impetus. Here 'anyone' may have a psalm, a piece of teaching, or a revelation to offer, with which he can edify the whole company of the brethren,[95] and if he does, he can take the floor.[96] Paul has both to exhort his converts to order and decorum in their assemblies, and on the other hand to warn them against 'quenching' the Spirit.[97] In time, however, the number of persons actively participating becomes smaller, and the group of 'leading' helpers and ministers consequently stands out more clearly from the crowd. Furthermore, the conceit of the 'spiritual' men, and the tendency to pay them excessive respect, both features which had given Paul a great deal of trouble, are once again becoming noticeable. In the long run it was impossible that the overall concept of Church life, and the evaluation of the 'gifts' at work within it, should remain unaffected by these changes.

The documents mentioned show at first only faint traces of the altered situation. A basically new conception of the 'Church' is not discernible. They are still addressed to the congregation as a whole, to the 'holy brethren',[98] the 'saints',[99] the 'children of love and peace'.[100] The Church, now as earlier, is regarded as the people chosen out of all the nations,[101] to whom God has spoken in these last days by his son,[102] a people formed and gathered around his word. 'For the Lord is there wherever the doctrine of the Lord is preached.'[103] Certain signs of fatigue, however, cannot be overlooked. There are instances of apostasy and withdrawal from the congregation; and in Hebrews these are dealt with as a matter of fundamental importance.[104] It is becoming necessary to urge upon Christians the duty of regular attendance at public worship,[105] for which fixed liturgical forms are beginning to be drawn up.[106] Above all, false doctrine has now become a serious danger;

[95] I Cor. 14:26; cf. p. 61 above, the portion of the text relating to n. 41.

[96] I Cor. 14:30.   [97] I Cor. 14:40; I Thess. 5:19f.   [98] Heb .3:1.

[99] Heb. 6:10; Barn. 6:16; 19:10; Did. 4:2; 10:6.

[100] Barn. 21:9; cf. 1:1; 4:6; 7:1; 9:7; and the simple forms of address, τέκνα and τέκνον, Did. 3; 4:1; 5:2.

[101] Barn. 3:6; 5:7; 7:5; 13; 14; Did. Inscr.; 9:2 (for a different interpretation of this last passage cf. M. Dibelius, 'Die Mahlgebete der Didache', ZNW 37, 1938, p. 34.)

[102] Heb. 1:2.   [103] Did. 4:1.

[104] Heb. 6:1ff.; cf. also pp. 222ff. n. 41 below.

[105] Heb. 10:25; Barn. 19:10; Did. 4:2; 16:2.

[106] This is clearly true at any rate for Did. 7ff.; for Hebrews cf. the excursus 'Kultus und Gottesdienst' in H. Windisch, Der Hebräerbrief², 1931, pp. 94ff.

the congregation is warned against it, and against allowing itself to be diverted from the traditional way of salvation by new teachings.[107] In such circumstances the example of 'leading members' takes on increased importance, that not only of those still active but also of those now fallen asleep who preached the word of God in earlier days.[108] In the closing section of Hebrews we find in addition to the general salutation to 'all the saints' a special greeting to those who set the standards for the congregation.[109] This passage emphasises their responsibility for the souls entrusted to them, over whom they must 'watch' and for whom they will one day have to give account, and, even more urgently than Paul, commends to the congregation the duty of following the lead of such men and of respecting their wishes.[110] In principle, indeed, the nature of their authority has not changed. The congregation is to hearken to the warnings and encouragements of its leaders and to 'bear with' them,[111] but it is not simply placed under their control. Christians are to 'consider' and 'remember' the spiritual work these men have done for the whole body,[112] in order that the latter may perform their ministry with joy 'and not sadly', for that would be of no benefit to the congregation itself.[113]

In certain respects the Didache lays even greater stress on this free and spiritual character of community life. The congregation possesses the 'capacity to discern right from left',[114] and can test the spirits. Hence it also tests the prophets, the ranks of whom now include a number of charlatans who travel from place to place simply exploiting for their own benefit the material advantages of the profession. In such circumstances an accord between the man's life and his teaching, the absence of personal covetousness and indulgence, is seen as the safest criterion for recognising a true prophet.[115] No longer, as in Paul's day, is it a question of confessing the Lord but of imitating his 'way of life'.[116] This does not imply, however, that the high respect paid to prophets is in any way lessened. On the contrary, once a man of the Spirit has been tested and found genuine, he is immune from further criticism, and must be accepted 'as the Lord' himself.[117] If he speaks in the Spirit— which in this context means in ecstasy—one may no longer seek to tempt or test him.[118] No rules of any kind may be laid down either for

---

[107] Heb. 12:3; Did. 6:1; 11:1f.   [108] Heb. 13:7.
[109] Heb. 13:24.   [110] Heb. 13:17.
[111] Heb. 13:22.   [112] Heb. 13:7.
[113] Heb. 13:17.
[114] Did. 12:1. 'Right' and 'left' here have the sense of 'good' and 'evil', 'beneficent' and 'destructive': cf. F. J. Dölger, *Die Sonne der Gerechtigkeit und der Schwarze*, 1918, pp. 37ff.
[115] Did. 11:3ff.; cf. Hermas, Mand. XI.   [116] Did. 11:8.
[117] Did. 11:8.   [118] Did. 11:7.

his private life[119] or for his behaviour in public worship.[120] In this way a certain attitude of superstitious awe, quite unknown in Paul's writings, springs up toward the men of extraordinary spiritual powers. The new problems that arise are dealt with more from a practical and moral standpoint than in a fundamental and theological way. There is a search for binding norms, which are derived particularly from the dominical utterances of the Gospel tradition.[121] The 'doctrine' which determines membership of the Church[122] consists primarily of ethical and cultic prescriptions. Confession of Christ has lost its central, Pauline position as 'the Gospel', and the congregation is at least in danger of delivering itself up to a law—certainly new, and allegedly Christian, but a law none the less—and to particular leaders who are men of 'spiritual power'.

Nowhere, however, had any of this, as we have already stated, become a matter of clear and conscious policy. In particular there is no inclination of any kind to make a transfer in principle of the freedom and responsibility of the congregation to specific human tribunals or authorities. The prophets command attention only as the voice of the Spirit and of the Lord, which rings out in their utterance.[123] 'For he who desires to be saved looks not at the man, but at Him who dwells and speaks in him, and is amazed at him',[124] and respects him 'as the Lord'.[125] In that event, however, the prophet does not merely, like the apostle in Paul's letters,[126] have a claim to love and material support, but also to 'honour' and to be kept 'in memory day and night'.[127] Furthermore, the congregation can itself appoint tested and worthy men to be bishops and deacons, who then attend to the work of prophets and teachers, that is to say, they take over the direction of public worship. Such men are not to be despised, but given recognition, 'for they are the honoured men among you along with the prophets and teachers'.[128] It is true that these honoured men take over the initiative

---

[119] Did. 11:11. The reference in this passage is to the case of a prophet living with a maiden in 'spiritual marriage'; cf. R. Knopf, *Die Lehre der zwölf Apostel*, 1920, p. 32.

[120] Did. 10:7. [121] Did. 4:13; 15:4. [122] Did. 6:1; 11:1.

[123] Barn. 16:9. [124] Barn. 16:10. [125] Did. 11:8.

[126] I Cor. 9:14; Gal. 6:6. [127] Did. 4:1f.; cf. I Cor. 11:2.

[128] Did. 15:1-2. In this passage, therefore, there is an explicit statement that the bishops exercise in principle the same function as the charismatic leaders of the congregation. That the bishops had only lately risen to this spiritual function from a subordinate position in which their concerns were economic and practical is a conclusion which cannot be derived from the text, and which the Pauline evidence makes entirely improbable. That it is necessary to lay particular stress on their equal status with the prophets calls for no explanation other than the fact that they are not, or not yet, masters of free prophetic utterance (Did. 10:7), and are no wandering miracle-workers—which is what the prophets in the Didache have become—but simply leaders of public wor-

and control in other aspects of congregational life as well; but in principle responsibility for the state of the Church is still vested in the congregation as a whole. To the whole body apply, as always, the exhortations to peace and harmony, to just judgment,[129] and to mutual instruction in penitence.[130] The distance from Paul is discernible more in the interior matters of spiritual attitude and values than in the details of organisation or in the overall character of the Church's self-awareness.

The converse is true in the so-called First Epistle of Peter. This document is directed to the 'chosen exiles', the Christian 'Diaspora' of Asia Minor,[131] and seeks to rally churches threatened by an approaching persecution in deep and serious commitment to Christ, the 'Shepherd and Guardian' of their souls.[132] Here we find the classic description of the new Christian self-consciousness as this had been fashioned pre-eminently by Paul: the Church forms the 'chosen race, the royal priesthood, the holy nation', which the Lord has called out of darkness into his own marvellous light.[133] Once again the Church is seen as a 'brotherhood',[134] filled with many different 'gifts', which in 'a gentle and quiet spirit'[135] of humble subjection[136] make harmonious music that God may be glorified in her through Jesus Christ. 'If anyone fulfils a ministry, let him do so by the strength which God supplies.'[137] 'As each has received a gift, employ it for one another, as good stewards of God's varied grace.'[138] Closer inspection, however, reveals that the one-time abundance of gifts has become very much restricted. Strictly speaking, we hear only of the work of preaching and of practical services, among which the duty of hospitality is to be especially inculcated.[139] Most important of all, however, is the fact that the congregation as a whole is now thought of in terms of a new model. It is no longer a unified cosmos of differing, 'organically' cohering gifts, but is organised, or rather, stratified in such a way that the relationship of the 'young' to the governing 'elders' is like that of children to their parents. Lest the resultant relationship should conceivably seem somewhat

---

ship elected by the congregation. It is noteworthy that, when there are no prophets in a given place, it is not they but the poor of the congregation who receive the contributions due to the prophets (Did. 13:4); but this feature may merely be the result of lack of agreement between the literary sources underlying the work: cf. Goguel, *L'église primitive*, pp. 113 n. 3; 264f.

[129] Did. 4:3.   [130] Barn 19:12; Did. 5:3.   [131] I Pet. 1:1.

[132] I Pet. 2:25. The word ἐπίσκοπος cannot here have its technical sense, for I Peter apparently knows only of elders within the congregation, not bishops.

[133] I Pet. 2:9.

[134] I Pet. 2:17; 5:9. The word ἀδελφότης occurs in this sense only in these passages, and takes the place of ἐκκλησία, which is not used: cf. H. Von Soden, *TWNT* I, 1933, p. 146.

[135] I Pet. 3:4; cf. 3:8ff.; 4:7ff.

[136] I Pet. 2:13; on this subject cf. p. 82 n. 29 below.   [137] I Pet. 4:11.

[138] I Pet. 4:10.   [139] I Pet. 4:9; cf. Heb. 6:10f.; 13:2; also Did. 11.

restrictive, the author of the Epistle emphasises as strongly as he can that it must never be a matter of unilateral control and subordination on the lines of human government.[140] The 'shepherds' are to display neither arrogance nor coercion—nor, of course, avarice—and the congregation 'likewise' are to follow them willingly and joyfully. For all that, however, there is no mistaking the fact that we are now moving into the sphere of a community-structure built on lines fundamentally different from those of Paul's, and of a different understanding and rationale of spiritual power or authority. It is no mere coincidence that this pseudonymous document addressed to the congregations of the early Pauline mission field is issued under the name not of Paul but of Peter, that is, of the one who in the eyes of Jewish and Gentile Christian alike was the premier authority for the mission which originated from Jerusalem and was independent of Paul.[141] On the deeper meaning of the concept of community here espoused, the one which later was to emerge triumphant, the Epistle has, however, as yet nothing to say.

[140] I Pet. 5:1ff. For more detailed discussion cf. pp. 82ff. below.

[141] This also reflects the widespread settlement of Palestinian Christians in Asia Minor, which must have taken place toward the end of the first century: cf. E. Hirsch, *Studien zum vierten Evangelium*, 1936, pp. 149ff.; H. Lietzmann, *History of the Early Church* I, 1949, p. 213f.

CHAPTER V

The System of Elders and the Beginnings of Official Authority

THE ONLY authority known to Paul as instituted by God in advance, and therefore to some extent independent of the congregation, is that of the apostle. Everything else is a matter of 'gifts', and has validity only as a function of the life of the Spirit which has been awakened in the congregation. The community cannot generate this life from within herself, it is given to her; but there is no need for her to accept its manifestations uncritically. She incorporates them, and recognises them as genuine operations of her spirit as occasion requires. Such recognition may lead to the taking over of permanent ministries or functions by those who possess the gifts; but it establishes no automatic personal authority superior to that of ordinary members nor any subordination of one Christian to another. It is true that in Paul we find a grading of various gifts, and also certain modest beginnings of an organisation within the community; but there is no direct line of development from his conception to the idea of functionaries controlling all the members and responsible for them, called to this particular work and qualified by their appointment. But the elders, as we have already encountered them in I Peter, are all these things. In detail their authority appears still to be fluid, and susceptible of varying interpretations. It may be understood as concerned more with practical or more with spiritual affairs. The position of these 'fathers'[1] within the system may be explained either as more official and authoritarian or as more patriarchal and moral in kind. But however the matter is viewed it remains true that these are the 'honoured' men, the outstanding and normative figures within the congregation. With the system of elders we move into the sphere of a fundamentally different way of thinking about the Church, which can only with difficulty be combined with the Pauline picture of the congregation, and certainly cannot be derived from it.

The system of elders spread swiftly, and put down roots even in Pauline churches. It had important advantages to commend it, and the transition may in many cases have been barely perceptible. Neverthe-

---

[1] This word best conveys the emotional overtones of the concept of the 'elder'; cf. p. 162 n. 73 below.

less, when compared with Paul's approach, it presents not merely a new phase but a new line of development, the first and decisive prerequisite for the elaboration of a narrowly 'official' and 'ecclesiastical' way of thinking. This is not to be taken to mean that the system of elders was historically later than the Pauline type of congregation. The opposite may well be true, and in any event the gap between them is not large. Luke knows of the existence of a group of elders in the later stages of the original Jerusalem community. The apostles first appoint the Seven for the hellenistic section of the congregation,[2] and these are scattered with their flock.[3] Then, at the Apostolic Council, quite abruptly the elders make their appearance. They seem here to be a kind of congregational representation,[4] and later form a special group with James, the Lord's brother, at their head as a first bishop.[5] Luke plainly regards a board of elders as part of the normal equipment of a Christian congregation. He wastes no words on their emergence in Jerusalem, even represents Paul and Barnabas as appointing elders wherever they go.[6] But however unhistorical the latter picture may be, there is absolutely nothing improbable in itself in the statement that there were elders at Jerusalem, and it may be entirely in accordance with the facts.[7] There had for a long time been elders at the head of every Jewish congregation, especially in Palestine,[8] and the idea of organising themselves in a similar way must have suggested itself to the Jewish Christian community. The system of elders is therefore probably of Judaeo-Christian origin (using that term without any particular theological emphasis), just as bishops and deacons were at first at home only in Gentile Christian congregations.[9] The designations and the types of

[2] Acts 6:2ff. According to A. M. Farrer ('The ministry in the N.T.', *The Apostolic Ministry* (ed. Kirk), 1946, pp. 138ff., 143) the Seven were in essence elders, and K. H. Rengstorf, art. *TWNT* 2, 1935, p. 630, also thinks that the model for them may have been the governing body of a Jewish congregation. Dom G. Dix ('The ministry in the early Church, c. A.D. 90–410', *The Apostolic Ministry* (ed. Kirk), pp. 232f.) suggests a link with the seven *parnashim* who were responsible for the care of the poor in Jewish congregations. There is still, however, no satisfactory explanation of this isolated incident. The parallel which Farrer draws between the Seven and the Seventy (Lk. 10:1ff.) is quite imaginary.

[3] Acts 8:4ff.; 11:19.

[4] Acts 15:2, 4, 6. A single previous mention occurs at 11:30.

[5] Acts 21:18.   [6] Acts 14:23f.

[7] In detail, peculiarities and deviations from the standard situation are, of course, perfectly conceivable, and it may be that in time the Qumran scrolls will throw more light on these.

[8] It is worth noting that, as in the case of the Christian elders at a later date, the 'official' character of the Jewish elder was not at first very marked; the presbyterate was a 'dignity'. Cf. W. Nauck, Excursus: 'Zum Problem der πρεσβύτεροι in den Pastoralbriefen', *Die Herkunft der Pastoralbriefe* (Diss. Theol., Göttingen) 1950.

[9] Out of the abundance of earlier literature on this subject (to which O. Lin-

organisation, it is true, quickly mingled and interpenetrated; but in the early days their separate existences were equally clearly marked. Just as Paul and the sources dependent upon him know nothing of elders, so conversely Acts, I Peter, James, and Revelation mention only elders but neither bishops nor deacons. In these latter documents we may attempt to grasp the distinctive character of the concept of authority in the setting of the new 'patriarchal' overall vision of the Church.

Despite their Jewish or Judaeo-Christian origins there can never have been a time when the Christian elders were simply identical with their contemporary Jewish counterparts. The Jewish elders, as civic and religious representatives of their community, are entirely bound by the Law and the Tradition; these are the legally obligatory norms. In every problem of life the Jewish congregation is referred to its ancient heritage, 'expounded and represented in each generation by the eldest members of the community. Its whole piety centres on the Law revealed to the people of Israel in earliest times, on the transmission, appropriation, and exposition of which the utmost care and love is expended.'[10]

The elders are professional guardians of the Law, and for that reason also leaders of their communities. Compared with them eschatological expectations play in normal circumstances no decisive part, and prophets none at all. In the Christian Church the situation was from the start entirely different. She was most decidedly not living any longer by the Law and by the past, but by her experience in the present of a new sovereignty of God, and by her hope for a final manifestation of that sovereignty in the future and for the return of her Lord. In her midst prophecy awakes to new life, and therefore the guardians of the old inheritance, the men of experience and those skilled in the Law in the Judaistic sense can no longer, as they once had done, provide the exclusive norm. But that did not imply that there was nothing for them but to disappear. The old divine covenant and its revelations are not

---

ton, *Das Problem der Urkirche in der neueren Forschung*, 1932, provides an excellent guide) I would like to draw special attention to the great essay by H. Lietzmann, 'Zur altchristlichen Verfassungsgeschichte', *ZWT* 55, 1914, pp. 97ff. (cf. *History of the Early Church*, 2 1938, pp. 56ff.). In more recent writing cf. M. Goguel, *L'église primitive*, 1947, pp. 110ff.; E. J. Palmer, 'A new approach to an old problem: the development of the Christian ministry', *The Ministry and the Sacraments* (ed. A. C. Headlam and R. Dunkerley), 1937, pp. 768 ff.; K. L. Schmidt, 'Le ministère et les ministères dans l'église du N.T.,' *RHPR* 1937, pp. 314ff.; *TZ* 1, 1945, pp. 309ff. For a Judaeo-Christian origin of the monarchical episcopate J. Jeremias, *Jerusalem zur Zeit Jesu* II B, 1929, pp. 132ff., has argued especially strongly; on the other side of the question cf. K. G. Goetz, 'Ist der מבקר der Genizafragmente wirklich das Vorbild des christlichen Episkopats?' *ZNW* 30, 1931, pp. 89ff. The Dead Sea Scrolls have given new impetus to this discussion.

[10] H. Greeven, 'Propheten, Lehrer, Vorsteher bei Paulus', *ZNW* 44, 1952, p. 40.

simply dead in the new present, but fulfilled; that is to say, they have still to be known, but now they must be taught in a new way in accordance with their preparatory and predictive meaning. To this extent a link with the old tradition remains. The decisive factor, however, is that the Church, too, possesses its own, new tradition, and has to safeguard that. The Lord whom she now serves with an obedience no longer legalistic but free is himself a reality not only of the future and also, by means of his Spirit, in some sense of the present; he is at the same time an objective fact of the past, and his words and deeds and above all his resurrection must be attested and handed down as such.[11]

On this basis, as we have seen, rested the special and unique respect accorded to the apostles within the Church. But it could equally well provide the basis for the idea of a permanent and universal office. Within Judaeo-Christian congregations an explicit rationale of this kind was probably not at first required. Here the tradition of Jesus was cherished with meticulous care; here authority was valued, as is shown by the honour paid to the apostles and the Lord's relatives. Hence the order of elders also was adopted as something customary, something natural, and by no means alien to the new community. The elders represented tradition, and were at the same time the natural leaders and the exponents of the idea of order in general. The two things go together. Wherever a tradition is cherished, it is no good relying merely on enthusiasm; there must also be the natural pre-conditions to ensure and make possible the reliability of the transmission from one generation to the next, from the old to the young. And wherever, conversely, age is at the head of affairs it is protected by 'tradition', and for its part also takes care that that tradition is preserved. Both motives had already played their part in Judaism; they now passed over into Judaeo-Christianity, and could also reckon on a sympathetic reception in the hellenistic world. Only Paul is out of step. Paul knows of no leading figures to whom is entrusted the safe keeping of the Gospel on behalf of everyone else, and *a fortiori* it never occurs to him to call upon facts of the natural order to supply the framework for the community. Paul bases everything on the Spirit. But however significant this may be for him and for his particular 'style', the distinctive approach which he exhibits at this point should not be pressed too far in interpreting his theological thinking. For Paul, too, knows and affirms the special Christian tradition which is no less a primary constituent of the Church than is the Spirit. It is simply that he drew no conclusions from it for the life and organisation of the community. The next generation were unable to maintain this position. The increasing remoteness of the Church's beginnings,

[11] On these points cf. further H. Von Campenhausen, 'Tradition und Geist im Urchristentum', *Stud. Gen.* 4, 1951, pp. 351ff.

the emergence of heretical deviations, the growth in numbers, and to some extent also the flagging zeal in the congregations made it essential in time to develop everywhere a responsible cadre of leaders, and ultimately to arrange for the formal appointment of authorised officials. There is, however, no need to assume that office as such, even if it is of natural origin and thus by definition cannot be termed 'spiritual' in the sense of being a direct divine endowment, must therefore be set in diametric opposition to the Spirit. Even the new authority of the 'elders', acquired by human appointment, should not be thought of as in essence 'human', nor as such is it bound without question to prove 'legalistic'. The only relevant consideration is the way in which it is thought of in practice and explained in principle. It is not unspiritual just so long as it remains obedient to the Spirit of Christ, and performs that service of the Gospel of Christ for which it was appointed. Only where this original evangelical relation is inverted, and the authority of the official as such is made absolute, is the primitive Christian concept of the Church abandoned; and at first this question nowhere arises.

The internal contingencies which lead to the establishment of office are already becoming plain in the writings of Luke, who tries to comprehend the message of Christ throughout in a Pauline sense as 'Gospel', but at the same time champions the un-Pauline system of elders. It is significant that he supports this with the idea that in degenerate times the genuine apostolic tradition cannot do without specially qualified guardians. The twentieth chapter of Acts tells how Paul on his last journey to Jerusalem, not having time to visit his old congregation in Ephesus, arranges for their elders to meet him at Miletus, in order that he may take his leave of them there. The speech which Luke puts into his mouth on this occasion has the character of a last will and testament.[12] Paul looks back over his life as an apostle, and for the last time swears to the purity of his conduct and of his sentiments. His 'course' is coming to an end, and the ministry which he 'received from the Lord Jesus, to testify to the gospel of the grace of God' has been fulfilled.[13] At this solemn moment what matters is to prepare the elders for the crises that lie ahead, and to strengthen them for their task within the Church: 'Take heed to yourselves and to all the flock, in which the Holy Spirit has made you guardians, to feed the church of the Lord which he obtained with his own blood.'[14] Paul 'knows' that fierce wolves will break in, and will win adherents with their perverted teachings.[15] It is vital, therefore, that they should be 'alert' and on their guard against such people, lest the long labours of the apostle should

[12] Cf. M. Dibelius, 'Die Reden der Apostelgeschichte und die antike Geschichtsschreibung', *Aufsätze zur Apostelgeschichte*, 1951, pp. 133ff.

[13] Acts 20:24.   [14] Acts 20:28.   [15] Acts 20:29f.

go for nothing.[16] The elders are to follow his example in their work, and to suppress all tendency to cupidity and avarice.[17] With this in mind Paul commits them to 'God and to the word of his grace', which is able to build up his own and bring them eternal redemption.[18]

Obviously, what underlies this speech attributed to Paul is the danger, which later became acute, of false teaching; and it is on this basis that its meaning must be understood. It is the genuine, ancient, well-known apostolic testimony which is at stake, and which has to be maintained in face of the false mysteries of gnosticism.[19] The judicial body which more than any other is entrusted with this task is that of the elders of the congregation. They have been appointed by the Holy Spirit, and on them falls the whole weight of responsibility for protecting the sheep from being led astray. The immemorial image of the shepherd,[20] which Paul himself had never used in this way,[21] now makes its appearance, and serves to describe the work and status of the elders in a suitably emphatic manner. It is noteworthy that in connection with this function they are also described as 'guardians', ἐπίσκοποι. The conjecture seems plausible that Luke has here deliberately introduced this older term, which was current in the Pauline mission field, but which he himself nowhere else employs,[22] in order to equate those thus described with the 'elders' in his sense, and thus to fuse the two traditions.[23] The warning against misusing one's official position for material gain is also typical and instructive. Along with the warning against discord and quarrelling this is a constantly recurring feature of early Christian writing.[24] There is, however, no justification for de-

---

[16] Acts 20:31.   [17] Acts 20:33ff.   [18] Acts 20:32.

[19] It is against this that Paul's assurance that he has concealed nothing from his people, but has declared to them 'the whole counsel of God', is particularly directed: Acts 20:20, 27; cf. Irenaeus, *Adv. haer.* III, 4, 2. The rendering adopted by Dibelius (*op. cit.*, p. 134), 'I omitted nothing which is beneficial to you', conceals the specific reference of this 'apologetic utterance'.

[20] Cf. W. Jost, ΠΟΙΜΗΝ. *Das Bild vom Hirten in der biblischen Überlieferung und seine christologische Bedeutung,* 1939.

[21] I Cor. 9:7 is not concerned with establishing any authority, but simply illustrates by analogy the right of a worker in the congregation. By contrast, the inclusion of the shepherd in the non-Pauline Ephesians (4:11), when this verse is compared with the parallel passage in I Cor. 12:28, is very significant. In line with this is the heightened evaluation of the apostles as the foundation of the Church, cf. p. 53 n. 190 above.

[22] The ἐπισκοπή, 'apostolate', of Judas in Acts 1:20 does not have a technical sense.

[23] In the same way Acts 6:2 portrays the Seven, who are entrusted with the διακονεῖν τραπέζαις, as the model for the later deacons, without actually using the word.

[24] In later times this danger was to some extent overcome by choosing as bishops for preference men of substantial means; for examples cf. H. Achelis, *Das Christentum in den ersten drei Jahrhunderten* II, 1912, pp. 6ff.

ducing from this that the special function of bishops was originally purely 'economic' or financial.[25]

In James too, as mentioned earlier, there are references only to elders or presbyters, not to bishops and deacons. With its traditional, eminently practical, and ethically oriented exhortations it is especially close to Judaism and at the farthest extreme from Paul and Pauline theology. Of the structure and shape of the congregation presupposed by the letter little can be determined. Toward the close of his remarks, however, appears the direction to call 'the elders of the church' in cases of sickness, so that they may restore the sufferer to health with prayer and anointing with oil 'in the name of the Lord'.[26] It would seem, therefore, that the elders regularly exercise a function[27] which in Paul's writings belongs to particular spiritual men who have received the gift of healing. There may also be a suggestion that the elders act as confessors and intercessors, whose duty it is to care not only for the bodily but also for the spiritual welfare of the 'sick';[28] but this is not absolutely certain.

I Peter has already been mentioned briefly in the preceding chapter. Here there is an attempt to preserve to a certain degree the multiplicity of Pauline 'gifts', and at the same time an emphasis on the Spirit-controlled freedom of the Church's life which rules out from the start any one-sided, authoritarian conception of church government. The structure of the congregation as a whole, however, is already very much altered. In accordance with natural categories, not spiritual gifts, it is divided into 'classes',[29] among which are included the representatives of an office conceived on patriarchal lines: slaves form a pair with masters, wives with husbands, and the younger with the elder. From a purely linguistic standpoint it would be possible to understand the words 'old' and 'elder' simply of seniority in age, and thus of those members

[25] Cf. also p. 68 n. 86 above, and p. 85 n. 54 below.

[26] James 5:14f.

[27] M. Dibelius, *Der Brief des Jakobus*, 1921, p. 233: 'This must refer to men holding the official position of elder within the congregation, and it is precisely with this official character of theirs that the power to heal is connected.'

[28] This might be concluded from the juxtaposition of James 5:15 and 5:16; cf. the thorough discussion in B. Poschmann, *Paenitentia secunda*, 1940, pp. 54ff.

[29] The significance of classes as part of the order of creation is not limited to the congregation; Christian obedience applies also πάσῃ ἀνθρωπίνῃ κτίσει. On the interpretation of this phrase cf. M. Dibelius, *Rom und die Christen im ersten Jahrhundert*, 1942, p. 17 n. 2; and H. Teichert, 'I Petr. 2, 13—eine crux interpretum?' *TLZ* 74, 1949, pp. 303f. It certainly includes the heathen civil authorities, and in the case of slaves is precisely their subjection to heathen masters which 2:18ff. has in mind. What is involved, therefore, is an all-pervading principle of right subordination and association to which the casual use of ὁμοίως as a connecting word in 3:1, 7; 5:5 gives involuntary but eloquent expression.

of the community who are full of years and experience.[30] But the fact that they are also addressed and appealed to as 'shepherds' decisively excludes any such limited interpretation. 'Tend the flock of God that is your charge, not by constraint but willingly, not for shameful gain but eagerly, not as domineering over those in your charge but being examples to the flock. And when the chief Shepherd is manifested you will obtain the unfading crown of glory.'[31] This reference to Christ as the 'Arch-shepherd' is significant.[32] The author, 'Peter', who modestly describes himself simply as 'a fellow elder[33] and a witness of the sufferings of Christ', may have wished to avoid in his exhortations any appearance of arrogating to himself a superior status, and therefore recalls his hearers to the returning Lord as the ultimate and proper authority; he is the true 'shepherd and bishop'[34] of souls.[35] That persons of human distinction should thus yield precedence to the 'Lord' is again thoroughly Pauline in feeling; but on the other hand the elders, precisely by virtue of the fact that they are shepherds under the command of the Chief Shepherd, acquire a share in his pastoral office and work, and as eminent 'examples' to their flock are authorised to present Christ's supreme example.[36] This new and, so to speak, 'hierarchical' feeling finds its most grandiose expression in the Revelation of John. Here twenty-four elders surround the eternal throne of God, dressed in white robes, and wearing golden crowns which they cast down before the throne whenever they raise their voices in praise to God and to the Lamb.[37] It is true that this picture is not concerned with earthly beings and types, but with the heavenly council of spirits gathered around God

[30] So T. Spörri, Der Gemeindegedanke im ersten Petrusbrief. Ein Beitrag zur Struktur des urchristlichen Kirchenbegriffs, 1925, p. 117.

[31] I Pet. 5:2-4.

[32] Similarly Heb. 13:20 refers to Christ as τὸν ποιμένα τῶν προβάτων τὸν μέγαν, and alludes, just as does I Pet. 2:24f., to the redemptive significance of his sufferings.

[33] I Pet. 5:1; on the subject of this word cf. p. 119 n. 304 below.

[34] I Pet. 2:25. In a similar way Ignatius, Pol. Inscr.; 8:3; Rom. 9:1; and Polycarp, Phil. 5:2, refer to Christ as διάκονος πάντων when holding him up as a model for the deacons.

[35] The term ἐπίσκοπος in this context is not of course meant in any 'official' sense, but may nevertheless, as in Acts 20:28, contain an allusion to the title of bishop: cf. Farrer, art. cit., pp. 161ff.

[36] Christ's moral example is also emphasised in I Pet. 2:21ff. That the heavenly shepherd will one day examine and pass judgment on the earthly shepherds is an idea found also in Hermas, Sim. IX, 31, 4ff.; and later, for example, in Clem. Alex., Paed. I, 37, 3. The Epistle of Polycarp also uses the shepherd image in an official sense (6:1): cf. W. Bauer in Die apostolische Väter, 1923, suppl. vol. to the Handbuch zum N.T., ed. Lietzmann, p. 289. The Martyrdom of Polycarp (19:2) calls Christ ποιμένα τῆς κατὰ τὴν οἰκουμένην καθολικῆς ἐκκλησίας.

[37] Rev. 4: 4, 10; 5: 11,14; 7: 11; 11: 16; 19:4.

himself;[38] but their activity is undoubtedly meant to reflect that of the earthly presbyterate of the Church, or is at any rate, for all its glowing colours, depicted as the same in outline.[39]

With the early Roman sources we arrive at a new stage of organisational development. In I Clement[40] and in Hermas the 'leading'[41] men of the congregation are termed both bishops and presbyters.[42] The fusion of the two titles, of which we have so far seen strong hints, is in Rome therefore already an accomplished fact; and the presbyteral constitution has completely intermingled with elements of an episcopal system,[43] which in Rome probably preceded it.[44] Nevertheless, the terms 'presbyter' and 'bishop', 'elder' and 'overseer' are not equivalent in meaning. In these documents as in all other instances 'bishop' is an official designation. It refers to a particular position and function, in fact that 'episcopal office'[45] which is permanently undertaken by specific members of the congregation. On the other hand, the borderline between the official and the patriarchal authority of the 'elders' is fluid. The same term may indicate that they are regarded either as 'presbyters' or simply as reverend 'old men', and one merges into the other. Age as such in itself bestows a dignity and a certain right to respect,[46] especially when at the same time it testifies to a long life of proven worth in the Christian community.[47] Consequently the presbyterate contains not merely the presiding members in the strict sense, but alongside them and of equal status with them 'reverend' men of every kind; prophets, teachers, old and proven pastors and counsellors, and later also confessors and ascetics, by custom—like the elders in the

---

[38] Ignatius, Trall. 3: 1, apparently ventures on the direct comparison: πρεσβυτέρους ὡς συνέδριον θεοῦ. Later on, the descriptions in Revelation are referred to the presbyters standing 'to the right' and 'to the left': cf. E. Hennecke, 'Zur apostolichen Kirchenordnung'. *ZNW* 20, 1921, pp. 242f.

[39] The number twenty-four may be an allusion to the twenty-four sections of the Jewish priesthood, each headed by a 'chief': I Chron. 24:5ff.; also 25:1ff.

[40] I take it for granted that I Clement, although it speaks directly only of conditions at Corinth, is nevertheless to be regarded as also supplying evidence of the first importance on the state of affairs at Rome. The assumption of R. Sohm, *Kirchenrecht* I, 1892, pp. 165 ff., that I Clement provoked a change of constitution in Rome itself, and in fact established the monarchical episcopate there, is pure conjecture.

[41] I Clem. 1:3; 21:6; Hermas, Vis. II, 2, 6; III, 9, 7; cf. Acts 15:22; Heb. 13:1.

[42] Bishops: I Clem. 42:4f.; Hermas, Vis. III, 5, 1; Sim. IX. Presbyters: I Clem. 1:3; (3:3); 21:6; 44:5; 47:6; 54:2; (55:4); 57:1; Hermas, Vis. II, 4, 3; III, 1, 8.

[43] Deacons are coupled with bishops in the characteristic manner in I Clem. 42:4f.; Hermas, Vis. III, 5, 1; Sim. IX, 26, 6.

[44] In Romans Paul assumes that the situation at Rome is the same as that at Corinth. The operation of charismatic gifts is described in Rom. 12 in precisely the same way as in I Cor. 12.

[45] I Clem. 44:1, 4: ἐπισκοπή.   [46] Cf. esp. I Clem. 3:3.

[47] I Clem. 63:3; Mart. Pol. 9:3.

Jewish synagogue—occupy the front seats in the congregation.[48] For this reason Hermas, perhaps with an undertone of censure,[49] calls them πρωτοκαθεδρῖται, 'occupants of the first seats'.[50] If we wish to single out from these 'front-row men' those members who in the narrower sense are active in positions of responsibility, then we must either refer to them, as Clement does, as 'appointed',[51] or, with Hermas, as 'leading elders'[52]— or even, from the start, by the explicitly official title ἐπίσκοπος, 'overseer' or 'bishop'.[53] In what the essential work of the bishops consists is made clear in I Clement: like the priests of the old covenant they 'present the gifts', that is to say, they are the leaders of worship, and at the celebration of the Eucharist they offer prayer on behalf of the congregation—as indeed the Didache already testifies.[54]

The tradition of the Pauline type of community has therefore been combined, as in I Peter, with the presbyteral system,[55] and, again as in that Epistle, the patriarchal element has taken precedence over the pneumatic. This development is all the more sharply emphasised by the fact that on the one hand I Clement exhibits an impoverishment of

[48] Cf. K. Müller, *Beiträge zur Geschichte der Verfassung der alten Kirche*, 1922, pp. 3f.

[49] Cf. Matt. 23:6.

[50] Vis. III, 9, 7; cf. Mand. XI, 12; Sim. VIII, 7, 4; and James 2:2f.

[51] I Clem. 54:2; cf. Titus 1:5.

[52] Vis. II, 4, 3; cf. I Tim. 5:17. The phrase used here, καλῶς προεστῶτες, should not be taken (as it is by E. Schweizer, *Das Leben des Herrn*, p. 99 n. 17) to refer to a special gift distinct from the gifts of the other presbyters.

[53] On this subject cf. R. Knopf, *Das nachapostolische Zeitalter*, 1905, pp. 161ff.; K. Müller, 'Die älteste Bischofswahl und -weihe in Rom und Alexandrien,' *ZNW* 18, 1929, pp. 274ff.; and the survey of the relevant material in F. Gerke, *Die Stellung des I. Klemensbriefes innerhalb der Entwicklung der altchristlichen Gemeindeverfassung und im Kirchenrecht*, 1931, pp. 107ff. In I Clem. 21:6 we find a similar mention of the προηγούμενοι alongside the πρεσβύτεροι. The former term must denote either the πρωτοκαθεδρῖται as distinct from other worthy members of the congregation, or again perhaps the 'overseers' as distinct from the rest of the 'honoured' men. Usage is still fluid.

[54] Cf. Gerke, *op. cit.*, pp. 112ff. It should not be concluded from this, however, that the bishops were originally appointed purely for liturgical purposes, any more than as 'business officers' (cf. p. 81f. above). From the beginning, their activity must have been of a comprehensive kind, and not restricted to any particular 'department': cf. pp. 64ff. above. In principle the same will have been true of the deacons who were put under them. Naturally, however, in view of their subordinate position the latter will have been concerned to a greater extent with practical matters; indeed, the use of the very word διάκονος calls to mind waiters and butlers, and may perhaps derive from their serving at the congregational meals. By contrast, ἐπίσκοπος is completely denotative and 'devoid of specific content' (Linton, *op. cit.*, p. 107). On this whole subject cf. also H. W. Beyer, artt. διάκονος and ἐπίσκοπος, *TWNT* 2, 1935, pp. 90ff., 614ff.

[55] The literary problem of the Pauline and the hellenistic philosophical traditions is discussed by L. Sanders, *L'hellénisme de Saint Clément de Rome et le paulinisme*, 1943.

spiritual content, and that on the other its concern is precisely to justify and to protect the rights of the appointed elders against a rebellious congregation. For the first time the presbyteral system is explicitly accounted for as a datum of tradition; and from this account quite definite legal consequences are then deduced. To this extent it is understandable that Sohm saw I Clement as the beginning of canon law in the Church.

The occasion of the document is well known. At Corinth tension between a section of the congregation and their leaders had reached the point of open conflict, in the course of which a group of the latter had been driven from their position of control and stripped of their liturgical functions. In Clement's words it was a case of 'abominable and unholy rebellion', started by 'a handful of impetuous and self-opinionated persons',[56] which had led to strife and dissension;[57] 'the "unhonoured" rose up against those "in honour", those without reputation against those with a good name, the foolish against the wise, "the young against their elders" '.[58] The youth of these foolish persons is no doubt primarily a product of the rhetoric which contrasts them with the 'old', that is, with the elders of the congregation. They are also described as 'arrogant' men,[59] gifted in argument,[60] and can hardly have been totally unimportant, seeing that at any rate they succeeded in bringing the majority of the congregation over to their side.[61] They may also have felt themselves to be endowed with the Spirit.[62] This would fit in with the state of the Corinthian congregation as we know it from Paul. In contrast to the ideal picture which Clement for obvious reasons paints of their past,[63] it looks as though the old turbulence and disruption, the religious arrogance and the chaotic craving for freedom, had still not died out. It is easy to understand how such a congregation would be all the more likely to come into conflict with the representatives of the presbyteral system in proportion as the latter had perhaps as yet not occupied their position for long, and may have been seeking to extend and reinforce their all too recent authority.[64] On the other hand, it may have been no more than an 'outbreak of faction fighting,' with no significant principle at stake.[65] Dogmatic issues are nowhere

---

[56] I Clem. 1:1; cf. 21:5. In 47:6 stress is laid on the small number of the troublemakers.

[57] I Clem. 14:2.   [58] I Clem 3:3.   [59] I Clem. 14:1; 57:1f.
[60] I Clem. 21:1, 5.   [61] I Clem. 44:6.
[62] So P. Meinhold, 'Geschehen und Deutung im I. Clemensbrief', *ZKG* 58, 1939, pp. 82ff.
[63] I Clem. 1:2ff.; cf. 57.
[64] Cf. M. Goguel, *La naissance du christianisme*, 1946, p. 418 note.
[65] So A. Von Harnack, *Einleitung in die alte Kirchengeschichte: Das Schreiben der römischen Kirche an die korinthische aus der Zeit Domitians*, 1929, p. 73.

mentioned.[66] We can no longer discern the background and the real point of the quarrel, and must be content to see it as Clement portrays it, in order that we may deduce at least his own view of office within the Church. That much at any rate is possible.

When Clement, in the name of the Roman congregation, demands that recognition be once more accorded to the ejected presbyters, this in his eyes is an appeal for that peace and concord without which no Christian congregation can exist. The maintenance of this good is to him a spiritual concern, and supplies the basic theme of the Epistle, to which he constantly returns. The most important outcome of more profound, 'divine' knowledge is consequently this: that a congregation is bound to act at all times within the lawful order commanded by God.[67] In his relationship with the Corinthians Clement feels himself for this reason to be a successor of their own apostle, Paul. He draws repeatedly on I Corinthians,[68] making extensive use of its exhortations to humility, of the imagery of the body and its members,[69] and of the hymn in praise of love.[70] In fact, however, the meaning of all these passages has been shifted to make them support a particular moral and social demand. The miracle of the new life is now understood as the fulfilment of order and law: 'The man who with humility of mind and constant gentleness, without altering in his resolve, fulfils the decrees and commandments given by God, is enrolled and numbered among those who are saved by Jesus Christ.'[71] That everything should be done 'decently and in order' is, indeed, an idea which Paul himself could express at the appropriate moment. In Paul, however, it occurs only as a peripheral comment, an obvious truth which ought not to be forgotten. For Clement it has turned into a piece of sacred knowledge which touches the essence of the Church, a fundamental, exalted truth, which he makes the content of his whole sermon. It is no longer faith in Christ which directs and defines what concrete application is to be made of the idea of order; this idea is now extolled as, so to speak, an autonomous principle of an abstract and formal kind, the power controlling both the world and the Church, and the true norm of the spiritual life. In practice this means that Christians ought not to disturb the existing situation in the Church; their task is to fit into its beautifully articulated

---

[66] W. Bauer, *Rechtgläubigkeit und Ketzerei im ältesten Christentum*, 1934, pp. 99ff., thinks that in this respect Clement has kept silence on the crucial issue; but this is highly improbable in itself, and contrary to all analogy.

[67] I Clem. 40:1.

[68] Cf. esp. I Clem. 47. Next to I Corinthians, which is understood entirely as concerned to uphold peace and good order, Romans is Clement's major Pauline source. But this too is ransacked only to supply moral teaching: cf. W. Bauer, *op. cit.*, pp. 222f.

[69] I Clem. 37:5-38:4.   [70] I Clem. 49.

[71] I Clem. 58:2 (Harnack's translation).

and organised community, and by patience and docility to maintain harmony, peace, and universal order—mere abstract ideas which, when combined, all come to mean more or less the same thing. The concepts of humility and love are in their turn defined to accord with the same notion.

Nevertheless, the fact that the Church is seen as a totality organised in accordance with definite basic rules does not mean that it ceases to be an organism, a living complex of various parts, which are united in one Spirit and have an obligation of mutual love and respect. 'The great cannot exist without the small, nor the small without the great.' It is precisely in the reciprocal complementarity, in the 'mixture', that the advantage lies.[72] One member must consider another; no one is to praise himself—he must wait for someone else to praise him[!].[73] Such exhortations, however, do nothing to alter the fact that order within the community can now be realised only by an analysis of rights and duties, and therefore also by allotting to individuals superior and subordinate positions, which they must maintain at all times. Hence even in the Church women are subject to men, the young to the old, and the general body—the 'multitude' as Clement likes to call them[74]— to the presbyters,[75] or alternatively to the bishops and deacons appointed for the purpose; and the latter are in turn to carry out their appropriate ministry with humility.[76]

The innovators in Corinth have sinned against this fundamental order of Christian and of all right living; they have dispossessed the elders, and exalted themselves[77] in their place over the flock of Christ.[78] Such conduct is intolerable. 'The Most High is the protector and defender of those who minister with a pure conscience to his all holy Name,'[79] and the elders who perform the sacred service for the congregation[80] have a right to deference from them.[81] For Clement the

---

[72] I Clem. 37:5.   [73] I Clem. 38:1f.

[74] πλῆθος is a technical term for the Christian congregation: cf. Gerke, op. cit., pp. 129ff.

[75] I Clem. 21:6.   [76] I Clem. 44:3.   [77] I Clem. 16:1.

[78] The term ποίμνιον is frequently used: I Clem. 16:1; 44:3; 54:2; 57:2. Clement does not describe the presbyters themselves as ποιμένες, nor does he use the verb ποιμαίνειν of their activities. The ποίμνιον-concept, however, does not primarily connote for Clement the fact that the flock belongs to Christ, nor is he thinking of the living process of pastoral care, but rather of the objective organisation and subordination which seem to go with the image: μόνον τὸ ποίμνιον τοῦ Χριστοῦ εἰρηνευέτω μετὰ τῶν καθεσταμένων πρεσβυτέρων (54:2). Cf. Gerke, op. cit., pp. 125f.

[79] I Clem. 45:7.

[80] I Clem. 44:3; cf. Gerke, op. cit., pp. 116ff. In Clement the concept of λειτουργία is strongly coloured by LXX usage, and undoubtedly has a sacral sense.

[81] I Clem. 57:1.

truth of this proposition should be obvious at once to every judicious and pious mind. Not only is it to be deduced from the Old Testament, it also follows directly from the origin of the existing office itself. Clement refers to the ordered nature of the cosmos,[82] and to the disciplined organisation of the Roman army,[83] and then dwells in detail on the regulation of the cult by Moses, whose actions in giving a special place to the priests and in binding the laity[84] by their own separate rules constitute a type of the Christian dispensation. With wise foresight Moses in this way made confusion and controversy over the priestly office impossible from the start;[85] and the apostles proceeded in exactly the same way in the Christian Church.[86] The higher the knowledge of which Christians have been considered worthy, compared with the devout of the Old Testament, the more serious is the responsibility which they bear for the maintenance of order,[87] and the greater is the danger, if they wantonly violate it.[88] This brings Clement to the decisive point. There now follows the famous passage in which he lays down the legal status of the episcopate as an order and institution of the Church created by the apostles and valid for all time: 'Our apostles also knew, through our Lord Jesus Christ, that there would be contention over the name of bishop. For this reason, being possessed of complete foreknowledge, they appointed the above-mentioned men, and then made a decree that, when these died, other reliable men should take over their office. Now, that men who were appointed by them, or later by other respected persons with the agreement of the whole church, who have ministered to the flock of Christ blamelessly and in all humility, peaceably and nobly, and who for a long time have received the highest testimony from all—that such men should be deposed from their ministry we do not consider just. It will be no small sin on our part if

---

[82] I Clem. 20.   [83] I Clem. 37.

[84] Jewish and Christian examples of this concept (of which this is the first occurrence in Christian literature) are collated by R. Knopf, *op. cit.*, p. 114. The word does not occur in the LXX, but appears to have been already common at this time in pagan cultic terminology: cf. O. Kern, 'ΛΑΟΙ – Laien,' *ARW* 30, 1933, pp. 205ff. It acquires its sharply derogatory sense of 'unsanctified, profane' only as a result of the clericalism of the fourth century; at first the 'layman' was simply a member of the '*laos*' of God: cf. Dix, *op. cit.*, p. 285.

[85] I Clem. 40f.; 43.   [86] I Clem. 44:1.

[87] Herein lies the *tertium comparationis*. Clement finds in both the Old and New Covenants the working out of a definite τάξις which separates the cultic ministers from the laity, and this seems to him significant. 'He does not, however, treat the Old Testament legislation without more ado as laying down laws for the Christian office, nor does he interpret the Christian office as a continuation of that of the Old Testament': W. Wrede, *Untersuchungen zum Ersten Klemensbrief*, 1891, p. 91.

[88] I Clem. 41:4. On the correct arrangement of this section cf. J. Klevinghaus, *Die theologische Stellung der apostolischen Väter zur alttestamentlichen Offenbarung*, 1948, p. 61 n. 1.

we depose from the episcopal office those who blamelessly and in holiness have made the sacrificial offerings. Blessed are the presbyters who have already completed their course, and have been allowed to reach a happy and undisturbed end! They need no longer fear that someone will drive them from the place which has been appointed for them!'[89]

The conclusion is obvious. The congregation is instructed in everything pertaining to salvation by the documents written by the Holy Spirit,[90] and so it must now restore the officials it has injured; but the 'leaders of rebellion and schism'[91] are to 'bow their necks' and 'adopt an attitude of obedience'.[92] Clement wishes them to quit Corinth voluntarily, in order that the flock may once again be able to live at peace with its presbyters.[93] If they make this heroic decision,[94] any other congregation will be only too glad to make them welcome (54:3). It is along these lines that this written directive from Rome proposes to put an end to the 'very disgraceful' situation,[95] and to ensure that the presbyteral system in Corinth, which has been so badly shaken, is firmly established once more. It is true that we do not know how matters did work out in detail; but that the decision went in accordance with the advice from Rome is confirmed by the testimony of Dionysius, Bishop of Corinth, written some time later.[96]

Wherein then lies the importance of I Clement for the development

---

[89] I Clem. 44:1-5. Dix, *op. cit.*, pp. 257ff., attempts to prove that the arrangement for continuing the episcopate refers not to the filling of the local office but to the retention of the special apostolic authority to make the appointment, the theory being that, before this could be vested in the local, supposedly monarchical, official, it was first handed on to individual outstanding figures (cf. p. 108 n. 229 below). He accordingly offers an alternative translation (*op. cit.*, p. 262) of the relevant passage from I Clem. 44:2f., which yields the required meaning. The Greek in question, and his rendering, are as follows: . . . καὶ μεταξὺ ἐπινομήν, δεδώκασιν ὅπως ἐὰν κοιμηθῶσιν, διαδέξωνται ἕτεροι δεδοκιμασμένοι ἄνδρες τὴν λειτουργίαν αὐτῶν. τοὺς οὖν κατασταθέντας ὑπ'ἐκείνων ἢ μεταξὺ ὑφ' ἑτέρων ἐλλογίμων ἀνδρῶν συνευδοκησάσης τῆς ἐκκλησίας πάσης κτλ. . . . 'And later on they made a second enactment that if they (themselves) should die, other tested men should succeed to their own liturgy (of appointing local episkopoi and deacons). Those Corinthian episkopoi, therefore, who were appointed by them or afterwards by other men accounted (as apostles, ἐλλογίμων) with the agreement of the whole Church . . .' From a purely linguistic point of view, this is certainly a possible translation. It is, however, hardly surprising that no one had ever before hit upon this fantastic suggestion, which indeed sorts well enough with a theory of episcopacy, but which has absolutely no connection with what Clement actually says, and what the whole tenor of his letter is concerned to emphasise.

[90] I Clem. 45:1.   [91] I Clem. 51:1.
[92] I Clem. 63:1.   [93] I Clem. 54:2.

[94] To encourage them to do so Clement points to the examples of pagan rulers who offered themselves in sacrifice or went into exile: I Clem. 55:1. Parallels in philosophical writings will be found in L. Sanders, *op. cit.*, pp. 41ff.

[95] I Clem. 47:6.   [96] Cf. Eusebius, *HE* IV, 23, 11.

of the doctrine of ecclesiastical office? It is obvious that Clement does not feel himself to be innovating, but rather championing the old, immemorially valid order against wanton and totally unjustified revolution. In accordance with this he develops his theory of the apostolic origin of the presbyteral system, and of the consequent lifelong tenure of the office, once it has been bestowed. It is quite impossible to maintain that in saying this he is putting forward something completely unheard of. In his concern with the concrete situation of conflict Clement only works out more precisely and systematically something which must have been taken more or less for granted in every church where the system of elders had gained control. It may be that in Corinth this had not yet completely come about; but in Rome it must already have done so, and in Syria and Asia Minor too the system must by this time virtually have taken over.[97] Where it does exist, it is accepted without question as apostolic. This is assumed even by Acts, James, and I Peter. Clement has only underlined this assumption, and elaborated it as a general principle. According to his account of the matter the apostles tested those in every congregation who were their firstfruits 'in the Spirit,' and then made them into bishops and deacons. An Old Testament text, adapted to fit the situation, reinforces the correctness of this assumption by showing that it was prophesied long ago.[98] In accordance with the purpose of his letter Clement strongly emphasises that the apostles already had future difficulties in mind when they set up their system of church order;[99] but Luke makes the same assumption,[100] and other writers of the later period press the point even more.[101] It is, so to speak, self-evident that the apostles did such a thing, since they were wise and filled with the spirit of prophecy. Clement's particular contribution is simply this: the apostolic ordinances under consideration are not directed against heresy nor do they have as their content religious and moral instructions, in the narrower sense, which the elders are to uphold. Instead, it is the system of elders as such which is created simply for the sake of order, and which is therefore placed permanently under the protection of an express apostolic injunction. It thus acquires a weight and significance which it has not hitherto possessed, and though in itself a purely formal, insti-

---

[97] As Ignatius, Polycarp, and the Pastoral Epistles indicate.
[98] I Clem. 42:4f. In such cases it is quite inappropriate to speak of 'deliberate falsification'.
[99] I Clem. 44:1. The same is assumed to be true of Moses: 43:6.
[100] Acts 20:29; cf. p. 80 above.
[101] Cf., for example, II Tim. 3:1ff., and above all II Pet. 3:3 (cf. Jude 17f.). On this subject cf. J. Munck, 'Discours d'adieu dans le Nouveau Testament et dans la littérature biblique', in *Aux sources de la tradition chrétienne* (Mélanges M. Goguel), 1950, pp. 155ff.

tutional thing it now becomes an essential and binding part of the apostolic tradition. To this extent it may be said that here for the first time the structures of canon law are included in the category of doctrines and dogma, and given the same sacral and immutable character.[102]

This is also to say that the system of elders takes on, more than it has done hitherto, the quality of a definite, fixed 'constitution', and that the senior patriarchal figures within the community are themselves now regarded as invested with a clearly defined office. They are the officers of the congregation, and by virtue of their office can expect obedience from it, and exercise authority over it. It is no longer a question of individuals, chosen on a particular occasion, and entrusted by the apostles with a function or task within the Church, but of an institution, which has to be preserved as such, and which must be respected in the persons of its representatives. The point at issue is that of 'order' within the congregation. One result is to increase the formalisation of the idea of 'office', so that the responsibilities of the elders as 'shepherds' and leaders of their community are no longer left completely open, but that their position now corresponds to a quite definite ministry, which they and they alone have to fulfil in accordance with fixed rules. They are the Christian cultic officials, and the cult now requires that a clear distinction be drawn between 'priests' and 'laymen'. For Paul and those in the Pauline tradition, especially the author of Hebrews, the cult was obsolete and of no significance. Clement accepts it once more as an obviously essential datum, and to that extent also affirms the concept of priesthood as an indubitable requirement of the sacral system.[103] It would, however, be perverse on the strength of this to ascribe to his bishops and deacons fully developed priestly attributes in the sense of the later concept of 'character'. Clement has nothing of that sort in mind. Even the Old Testament cultus serves him as a pattern only in a quite general sense, by virtue of the fact that it is well ordered; and there is no suggestion that it should be taken over as a whole by the Church, or that anything corresponding to it should be developed.[104] Nevertheless, the line of demarcation between the 'multitude' and the elders is in this way made

[102] On the concept of apostolic tradition in general cf. pp. 149ff. below.

[103] In the case of Clement's cultic ordinances, however, we are not dealing with a distinctive, sacral idea of law, which might be defended as something parallel and equivalent to the universal 'concept of order'. Clement reverences order in all its manifestations as a sacred principle, but considers that it is supremely in the sphere of the Church that especial importance attaches to it: so Klevinghaus, *op. cit.*, pp. 57ff. A dissenting view is expressed by G. Holstein, *Die Grundlagen des evangelischen Kirchenrechts*, 1928, p. 63.

[104] Cf. Wrede, *op. cit.*, p. 91; Knopf, *op. cit.*, p. 113; Klevinghaus, *op. cit.*, pp. 66ff.

a very positive and 'official' one. The latter now stand in a special 'place,' and henceforward may never be driven from it.[105]

Even this principle, however, can hardly be regarded as a sudden innovation. The assumption that the spiritual leaders and those in charge of public worship were originally changed at will is a purely arbitrary one with, as we have seen, little probability even for the Pauline churches;[106] and where a group of 'elders' was already in existence the exact opposite may almost be taken for granted. It is contrary to the very idea of an elder and of a shepherd and guardian appointed by the Spirit that the 'young' should be able to renounce their obedience to him as they see fit, with the result that he must then simply step aside. All that Clement does is to find a special way of emphasising this truism by relating it to the cultic task which the elders have been commissioned to perform, and to the fact that the sacred character of worship calls for regularity and order. But this does not mean that the congregation is, as it were, put under the control of its elders, or subjugated to an authoritarian form of church government. However decidedly Clement intends to safefuard the rights of the office-holders, the assumption from which he always starts as a matter of course is that they for their part are not at fault in any respect, but on the contrary have fulfilled their ministry 'blamelessly'.[107] The decision whether they have in fact done so plainly belongs to the congregation. The bishops, therefore, are not flatly declared to be 'irremovable'; but a baseless dismissal, one where no offence has been proved, is a gross injustice, something wholly contrary to the nature of the office and of its solemn institution within the congregation. It may be that full justice is not done to the true significance of the events at Corinth by presenting them in this light; but, if we simply take the decision as Clement formulates it, it is 'no more than an ethical platitude'.[108] To raise any further questions—concerning, for instance, the divine or human, the alterable or unalterable character of this legal axiom—would be to introduce into the text problems which lie wholly outside its purview. The characteristic mark of Clement and his religious thinking is precisely that for him the all-embracing principle of right organisation and order is just as much a natural as a divine, a secular as an ecclesiastical principle, and must hold good everywhere and at all times. That is why he supports it, as the fancy takes him, with arguments and examples both sacred and profane, Old Testament and Christian, from popular philosophy and politics. He is convinced that a rightly

---

[105] I Clem. 40:5; 41:2; cf. 63:1. On this concept of τόπος cf. J. Munck, *Petrus und Paulus in der Offenbarung Johannis,* 1950, pp. 75f.

[106] Cf. p. 67f. above.

[107] I Clem. 44:3f.; cf. p. 89 above.

[108] A. Ritschl, *Die Entstehung der altkatholischen Kirche*², 1857, p. 362.

instructed[109] congregation is bound to agree with him on this point in all circumstances, and he avoids anything[110] which might look like unilateral constraint or coercion of what is their own decision.[111] God's congregation at Corinth are to give ear of their own freewill neither to Clement nor to the Roman church, but to the Holy Spirit who has spoken to them through Clement's letter.[112] Only in this way can they win God's good pleasure; for 'insolence, arrogance, and presumption are proper to those who are cursed by God. Meekness, humility, and gentleness are marks of those who are blessed by him.'[113]

The primitive Christian concept of the independent responsibility of the congregation as a whole is therefore in no way abandoned. This much, however, is clear, that a concept of order and subordination understood in such formal and static terms is bound from the start to favour the tendency to assume that in cases of disagreement the 'reverend' officeholders, as the group in authority, must be in the right, and that their opponents are to be treated as malicious disturbers of the peace, who are lacking in proper humility. It is significant that our Epistle, for all the unctuous prolixity and seriousness of its edifying discourses, nevertheless leaves us completely in the dark concerning the real situation and the crucial points of conflict in the Corinthian troubles. The abstract concept of order has become completely detached from any specifically Christian meaning—that is to say, one connected with Christ and the Gospel—and thus threatens to lose altogether its concrete and historical actuality. The empty generalities and the lack of any really penetrating human and religious insights, which characterise I Clement, are however by no means devoid of practical implications; for the decision has already been reached in favour of a particular side. The political and social self-awareness, in the widest sense, of the official Church with its natural morality spon-

[109] I Clem. 40:1; 45:1f.; 46:6f.; 53:1; 62:2f. Where Paul would have appealed to the Spirit-given capacity of the congregation to form a right judgment, Clement recalls them to the biblical norm which they have learned.

[110] Even the example of the Roman army (I Clem. 37:1ff.) is not intended to commend blind 'military obedience', but only brings out, as in the imagery of the flock (cf. p. 88 n. 78 above), the idea of a well-articulated system, which produces a σύγκρασις throughout the army, provided that everyone fits into his appointed place. In this respect the analogy agrees with the image of the body and its members which immediately follows it (I Clem. 37:5).

[111] This point is stressed by S. Lösch, 'Der Brief des Clemens Romanus,' *Studi dedicati alla memoria Paolo Ubaldi*, 1937, p. 187, although he does in fact regard the Epistle as evidence for a supra-ordinate Roman authority, in opposition to R. Van Cauvelaert, 'L'intervention de l'église de Rome à Corinthe vers l'an 96,' *RHE* 31, 1935, pp. 267ff.

[112] I Clem. 56:1; 59:1; 63:2. There are no grounds for supposing that the Roman envoys, as Bauer, *op. cit.*, pp. 115f., conjectures, also resorted to less spiritual and more material methods to attain their ends.

[113] I Clem. 30:8.

taneously thrusts itself forward, and in the place which the Gospel has left vacant sets its own ready-made system. As a result the diffuse, respectable sentiments of the sermon acquire a positive platform, and ecclesiastical organisation the needed safeguard and reinforcement of an edifying presentation.

In this way the elders and church officials win the victory over the slackening energies of the Christian proclamation; and wherever there is a struggle over the rights of ecclesiastical office, again and again it is I Clement which the adherents of officialdom like to adduce in support of their position.

On the other hand, the extent to which I Clement proved influential should not be overestimated. A warning against doing so is provided by yet another Roman document, which likewise quickly won universal regard, namely the *Shepherd of Hermas*. Here, taking the work as a whole, the church officials are hardly mentioned, despite the fact that the voluminous work, in the manner of penitential sermons, discusses every possible concrete instance of morality and immorality in the life of the congregation. It may perhaps date from a generation later than the letter to Corinth; but this time the author does not belong to the group of elders. He is a prophet who by virtue of his visions and spiritual illuminations has received authority to speak to the 'saints',[114] that is, to his own church and to the churches throughout the world. It is stated that he had already wished at an earlier stage to give his book to 'the presbyters'; now Clement, on whom such duties fell, is to send it to the cities abroad, while Grapte, probably a respected Roman deaconess, is to instruct the widows and orphans out of it.[115] The 'Clement' referred to here, who conducts the correspondence of the congregation with other churches, is certainly the celebrated author of the Epistle to the Corinthians.[116] It appears, therefore, that the most harmonious relations exist between the men of the Spirit and the officials. Hermas mentions the apostles of the early days, the bishops, the teachers, and the deacons, all in the same breath.[117] The fact that he also addresses an edifying exhortation and call to repentance to the 'leaders of the church', as he does to all Christians, is no evidence to the contrary.[118]

---

[114] Vis. III, 8, 9–11.   [115] Vis. II, 4, 2f.

[116] This is chronologically possible, because the relevant portions of the *Shepherd* are said to have been already written at an earlier date. On the whole controversy cf. M. Dibelius in *Die apostolischen Väter* (suppl. vol. to Lietzmann's *Handbuch zum NT*), 1923, pp. 422 f.; and Goguel, *op. cit.*, p. 417 n. 2.

[117] Vis. III, 5, 1. In Sim. VIII, 7, 4; IX, 25, the apostles and teachers appear as ideal figures of the past, who preached to the whole world. What particular ministry the spiritual men or the officials performed, it is hard to say: cf. Dibelius, *op. cit., ad loc.*, and in the Excursus, pp. 634f.; Goguel, *op. cit.*, pp. 152ff.

[118] The same applies to the oft-discussed passage, Vis. III, 1, 8f. Hermas, who would like to defer modestly to the presbyters, is ordered to take his seat

The leaders appear once more as 'shepherds' of the congregation, and, as in I Peter, the image is used to convey that theirs is the supreme responsibility for the flock, and that they will one day have to make their account. 'Woe to the shepherds' if their sheep go astray! Will they argue that they were misled by the sheep?[119] It will be noted that Hermas, too, takes the superior status of the church leaders for granted. Nevertheless, we do not come to know the officials in his writings exactly from their most impressive angle. Hermas sees things with the eyes of the poor, to whom he belonged, and he shows the leaders amid all the narrowness and triviality of everyday church life. Remarkably there is now no mention at all of the liturgical functions which are so prominent in Clement.[120] In their place the proper use of possessions plays a correspondingly greater part.[121] The deacons in particular are denounced for making themselves rich from the property of widows and orphans,[122] and the first apostles are praised for the express reason that they embezzled absolutely nothing.[123] Even the prophets on occasion demand money for prophesying, and thereby prove themselves false prophets.[124]

Squabbling and petty jealousies seem to be even more prevalent within the congregation. Even those Christians who have shown themselves 'always faithful and good . . . strive among themselves for precedence and honour',[125] and for the first seats in the assembly,[126] and cannot keep the peace.[127] This complaint applies especially to the group of 'leading' figures.[128] The bishops, teachers, and deacons ought to get on well together, to listen to one another, and to fit together like well-hewn stones in the structure of the Church.[129] 'How do you expect to instruct the elect, if you yourselves have no training?'[130] Thus it is that for the first time we hear of the inner contradiction between the worth of the official and the spirit and authority of his office.[131] It is a problem which in the history of the concept of office constantly increases in importance, and is never resolved.

---

before they do. The fact that in the whole book there is not a trace of rivalry between the prophetic and official authorities indicates that Hermas richly deserved the honour paid him here as 'the type of the Christian who has done true penance': cf. Dibelius, *op. cit.*, pp. 454, 457, 635.

[119] Sim. IX, 31, 5f.

[120] Nevertheless they did, of course, continue to exercise them, as Justin, I Apol., 67, 6, testifies.

[121] Sim. IX, 27, 2.   [122] Sim. IX, 26, 2.   [123] Sim. IX, 25, 2.

[124] Mand. XI, 12.   [125] Sim. VIII, 7, 4.

[126] *Ibid.*; cf. pp. 84f. above.

[127] Hence the constantly recurring exhortations to εἰρηνεύειν: Vis. III, 6, 3; 12, 3; Mand. II, 3; Sim. VIII, 7, 2; 7, 5; IX, 31, 4; 32, 2.

[128] Vis. III, 9, 7.   [129] Vis. III, 5, 1.   [130] Vis. III, 9, 10.

[131] This problem also exercises Hermas in connection with his own prophetic commission: Vis. III, 1, 6; 3, 4; 4, 3; 10, 6ff.; V, 4f.

In the period between Clement and Hermas a fundamentally new picture is presented by the letters of Ignatius, Bishop of Antioch, written on his last journey, which took him to Rome as a martyr. They reveal an advanced stage of developed hierarchical order,[132] which is connected with the fact that they are of Syrian provenance, and possible also with the particular circumstances of life in the metropolis of Antioch. In Ignatius a system of monarchical episcopacy has already been implemented, so that all important functions are in principle in the hands of the one bishop. The clergy itself no longer constitutes a single group of 'reverend' and 'leading' men over against the rest of the congregation, but is sharply divided into grades. The 'spiritual garland' of the presbyterate[133]— this impersonal term is now the normal usage in place of the older form, 'presbyters'—surrounds the one bishop as his 'council';[134] and below them both stand the 'servants of the church of God',[135] the deacons. This class of 'godly men'[136] causes Ignatius some anxiety;[137] for while on the one hand he assures them of his warmest love,[138] he finds himself on the other obliged to urge that these fellow-workers 'so especially dear to him',[139] who are 'entrusted with the ministry of Jesus Christ',[140] should be a great deal more conscious of their spiritual responsibilities. They ought not to be merely 'ministers of food and drink', and they must guard themselves against reproach as they would against fire.[141] Behind these remarks there is patently the anxiety which we have already encountered elsewhere concerning abuse of a position which brings with it the control of wealth.

The overall picture of a three-level clergy which emerges is in accordance with what was to be the main line of ecclesiastical development, and later on prevailed even in the West; but the spiritual interpretation which Ignatius gives to it is quite distinctive. His concept of the Church is not legal and constitutional, like that of I Clement;[142] nowhere does

---

[132] On what follows cf. the excursus by W. Bauer in *Die apostolischen Väter* (suppl. vol. to Lietzmann's *Handbuch zum NT*), 1923, pp. 201ff.

[133] Magn. 13:1. [134] Magn. 6:1.

[135] Trall. 2:3. [136] Magn. 13:1.

[137] Cf. H. W. Bartsch, *Gnostisches Gut und Gemeindetradition bei Ignatios von Antiochien*, 1940, p. 160 n. 1.

[138] According to Bauer, *op. cit.*, p. 202, the reason for this is to be found in Ignatius's personal experiences with the deacons in the course of his journey: cf. Eph. 2:1; Philad. 11:1; Smyrn. 10:1; 13:1. This angle alone, however, does not provide an adequate explanation.

[139] Eph. 2:1; Magn. 2:1; Philad. 4:1; Smyrn. 12:2.

[140] Magn. 6:1. [141] Trall. 2:3.

[142] This point was made as long ago as 1894 by E. v. d. Goltz, *Ignatius von Antiochien als Christ und Theologe*, pp. 161f. A. Von Harnack, *Die Briefsammlung des Paulus und die anderen vorkonstantinischen Briefsammlungen*, 1926, p. 34, also gave it as his opinion that 'the Catholic system for undergirding both doctrine and the Church by the dogma of the apostolic office of the bishops, and

he attach any weight to the apostolic origin of the structure of the Church. Ignatius experiences the contemporary Church, as it is, as a living mystery. In its totality it is united to Christ, who was God's incarnate 'Word' to this world,[143] and has thereby itself become 'in both flesh and spirit'[144] a mysterious divine reality belonging to the eternal order. These are mythological thought-forms, similar to those which are found in Colossians and, above all, in Ephesians.[145] What is new is that these ideas are now combined with a clear conception of the official structure of the congregation. The Church as a spiritual reality

---

their apostolic succession, was far from his mind'. The concept of an apostolic παράδοσις does not occur in Ignatius: cf. B. Reynders, 'Paradosis. Le problème de l'idée de tradition jusqu'à Saint Irénée,' *RTAM* 5, 1933, pp. 160f. Nevertheless, the contrary is continually asserted, starting with Eusebius, *HE* III, 36, 4. But the fact that Clement, the Roman, puts forward the idea of succession *in nuce* is absolutely no justification for 'interpreting' Ignatius to the same effect, when he nowhere does so; for the opposite view cf. R. Seeberg, *Lehrbuch der Dogmengeschichte* I², 1920, p. 243. The frequent allusions to the apostles (Eph. 11:2; Rom. 4:3) and comparisons with them (Magn. 6:1; 13:1; Trall. 2:2; 3:1; Philad. 5:1; Smyrn. 8:1) have, in Ignatius, a different motive and purpose. To him the apostles are the sacred figures of the past (Trall. 13:2; Philad. 9:1), through whom Christ acted (Magn. 7:1), and with whom he was intimately associated (Trall. 12:2). In the same way the presbyters today gather round the one bishop (cf. pp. 100f. below), and are subject to him as the apostles intended (Trall. 7:1; at a later period the number of presbyters in any one congregation was for preference fixed at twelve: cf. Achelis, *op. cit.,* p. 15 n. 12). Such comparisons, however, are analogically or typologically intended, and are not concerned with a legal succession. If this were not so, one would be forced to the absurd conclusion that the bishop was of more importance than the apostles, whereas Ignatius expressly emphasises his own inferiority to them (Trall. 3:3; Rom. 4:3). The only scholar who has correctly perceived the import of these facts is, so far as I know, M. Werner, *Die Entstehung des christlichen Dogmas,* 1941, pp. 655ff.; but the explanation which he offers is completely fantastic: the new dignity and authority of the bishop are to rest on the fact that he 'as president of the congregation must constantly be prepared for martyrdom', and that consequently the right of the martyr to judge and to reign with Christ has been applied to him in advance in the present. And yet this right of the martyr, of which Ignatius knows nothing, has already been extended by Paul (I Cor. 5:5) to all Christians.

[143] Magn. 8:2.

[144] This phrase (Philad. 7:1; Pol. 1:2; 2:2), which recurs continually, is bound up with the anti-docetic confession of the genuine sufferings of Christ and of the redemption effected in and through the body. On the problems connected with this, which have not yet been completely clarified, cf. H. Schlier, *Religionsgeschichtliche Untersuchungen zu den Ignatiosbriefen,* pp. 102ff.; Bartsch, *op. cit.,* pp. 102ff.

[145] On this subject cf. esp., H. Schlier, *op. cit.,* also *Christus und die Kirche im Epheserbrief,* 1930; *Die Kirche im Epheserbrief,* 1949; E. Käsemann, *Leib und Leib Christi,* 1933; also H. Von Campenhausen, *Die Auffassung der Kirche im Altertum von den apostolischen Vätern bis zum Anfang des 4. Jahrhunderts.*

is manifested only in the particular form of an episcopal church system with presbyterate and deacons. This form is again and again affirmed and emphasised by Ignatius in the most solemn way; but it is not a subject which is open to discussion. 'Without these there is nothing which can be called a church.'[146] This articulation and organisation of the community is a given reality, and therefore the episcopal office and the whole clergy system share intrinsically in the holiness of the whole, which is the body of Christ. The unity of the Church is an ultimate value, for it is the hallmark of its divine nature and of its union with Christ and with the Father himself.[147]

If Ignatius never tires of lauding the unity, the concord, the harmony and peace, the sympathy and the close, indivisible affection which prevail within the Church,[148] this is because he is locked in battle with heresy. He harries the fissiparous false teaching of gnosticism with passionate persistence: 'Shun schisms as the source of all evil!'[149] This is meant quite literally. Ignatius will not tolerate any separatist worship or separatist groups within the congregation. It would, however, be wrong to see his demand for unity solely from this angle, and to judge it as in essence no more than a polemical conception or a piece of church politics. On the contrary, it is here that we come up against the fundamental concerns of his whole theology and soteriology.[150] Unity is for Ignatius the all-embracing cosmic and ecclesiastical principle, within which everything comes to its divine fulfilment: 'One prayer, one petition, one mind, one hope in love in the spotless joy which is Jesus Christ'—who is himself the one who came forth from the one Father, in whom he is and to whom he has returned.[151] There is, therefore, nothing better than this unity.[152] It is typical of Ignatius that he does not conceive of unity as something monolithic, as unity, so to speak, in a mathematical sense, but as harmony and fundamental agreement, as union in sympathy, and as the sequence and concord of an abundance of parts. In this context he likes to use musical imagery;[153] and later

---

[146] Trall. 3:1; cf. Pol. 6:1.

[147] Cf. Schlier, *Ignatiosbriefe*, pp. 97ff.; Bartsch, *op. cit.*, pp. 10ff.; L. Stählin, *Christus praesens*, 1940, pp. 60ff. The concept of ἕνωσις (ἑνότης, ἑνοῦσθαι) is lacking in all the other Apostolic Fathers, and indeed—with the exception of *Ephesians*—from the New Testament itself.

[148] The expressions which Ignatius uses in this context are: ἕνωσις, ἑνότης, ἑνοῦσθαι· εἰρήνη, εἰρηνεύειν· ἀγαπᾶν· ὁμοιότης, ὁμονοία, ὁμοήθεια· συμφωνος· συναρμόζεσθαι· ἀμέριστος· ἐπὶ τὸ αὐτὸ εἶναι φεύγειν· μερισμόν: for the relevant passages cf. E. J. Goodspeed, *Index patristicus*, 1907.

[149] Smyrn. 7:2; cf. Philad. 2:1; 9:1, 3; 7:2; 8:1.

[150] Bartsch is right to see the theology as Ignatius's starting-point, but he lays a rather one-sided stress on this idea; for a criticism of his view cf. Stählin, *op. cit.*, pp. 75ff.; Klevinghaus, *op. cit.*, p. 82 n. 2 and p. 106 n. 1.

[151] Magn. 7. [152] Pol. 1:2.

[153] Eph. 4; Philad. 1:2; Rom. Inscr. (cf. Bartsch, *op. cit.*, p. 107); 2:2.

tradition has in fact made him into a hymn-writer and the inventor of antiphonal singing.[154] But this symphonic ecstasy never causes him to lose sight of the real Church and its hierarchy. Outside the true sanctuary the bread of life is not to be found.[155] The Church is a supra-terrestrial, cosmic entity, and the unifying power of peace that is in her is known in eternity;[156] but it is made visible only in the perfected harmony of the congregation, its orders and individual members, 'in order that the unity may exist in flesh as well as in spirit'. Just as Christ was united to his Father, so must Christians be subject to their presbyters and deacons, and all of them to the bishop,[157] must avoid the poisonous food of heresy,[158] and must join harmoniously in one spiritual chorus, as those who are gathered in one temple, around one altar, before the one Christ.[159]

This union is union around Christ and his genuine passion, endured 'in the flesh'. This passion is celebrated in the sacramental reality of the Church, constituted by the assembly of the whole congregation around its clergy and bishop. The sacred, divine meaning of this requirement is illustrated over and over again in reiterated and yet constantly shifting images. Thus, the congregation, it is asserted, follow their bishop as Christ followed the Father, and the presbyters as they would the apostles, and reverence their deacons as they would the command of God.[160] Or, it is joined to the bishop as the Church is joined to Christ and Christ to the Father;[161] or again, as the apostles were joined to the Father, the Son, and the Holy Spirit.[162] These comparisons between the Church and the divine order come so naturally to Ignatius that on occasion they may even be inverted: Ignatius takes refuge in the Gospel as in the flesh of Christ, and in the apostles—as in the presbyterate of the Church.[163] He also concerns himself with the mutual cohesion of the orthodox churches;[164] but the word 'church' in such passages always signifies the concrete, individual congregation organised around the bishop, and gathered 'in one place' in the 'physical and spiritual'

---

[154] Cf. Villier–Rahner, *Aszese und Mystik*, 1927, p. 27. Ignatius does indeed incorporate passages from hymns into his letters: cf. C. F. Burney, *The Aramaic Origin of the Fourth Gospel*, 1922, pp. 161ff.

[155] Eph. 5:2; cf. Philad. 3:2.

[156] Eph. Inscr. (cf. Stählin, *op. cit.*, pp. 61f.); also Bartsch, *op. cit.*, p. 32.

[157] Magn. 13:2.

[158] Trall. 6. In using this imagery Ignatius has in mind the Eucharist and the separatist worship of the gnostics: cf. Bartsch, *op. cit.*, pp. 103f.

[159] Magn. 7:2.

[160] Smyrn. 8:1; cf. Magn. 6:1; 7:1; also Trall. 2, where, however, the text appears to have been somewhat dislocated: cf. Bartsch, *op. cit.*, p. 160 n. 1.

[161] Eph. 5:1; Magn. 7:1; 13:1; Smyrn. 8:1.

[162] Magn. 13:2.   [163] Philad. 5:1.

[164] Philad. 10; Smyrn. 11:2f.; Pol. 8:1; cf. Bauer, *op. cit.*, pp. 68f.

56537

unity of Christ.[165] It is true that the concept of the 'catholic Church' is also already emerging[166]—indeed, Ignatius is the first writer in whom it appears; but it may be asked whether this attribute of catholicity is not simply once again the quality of being one and at one, and not yet the 'oecumenical' Church found 'in every place'.[167]

This whole outlook naturally endows the person of the bishop with supreme significance. Whereas the presbyters are for preference compared to the apostles,[168] he presides like the Lord,[169] nay rather, like God himself over the congregation.[170] He is in very truth the one around whom the unification of the Church is accomplished: 'All who belong to God and Jesus Christ are with the bishop.'[171] The bishop keeps in touch with each individual member of the congregation personally;[172] he tackles everyone in the most appropriate way;[173] he bears the infirmity of all, and should therefore also be 'refreshed' by all.[174] He is the centre of his congregation. Ignatius in fact attempts to vest all important functions in the bishop. The bishop alone is entitled to lead public worship and to dispense the sacraments;[175] if anyone else wishes to do so, this is only permissible by his commission, by delegation, so to speak, of the episcopal rights.[176] Marriages are to be contracted only with the bishop's consent, and even the most secret vows of the pious should be made known to him, though to him alone.[177] Naturally it is also part of this man's duty to instruct his congregation, and thus to save them from false doctrine,[178] but taking the Epistles as a whole it is astonishing how little weight is put upon this side of his work. This is significant. A bishop who is no orator may even keep silence altogether[179]— for it was out of God's silence that Christ came

<hr>

[165] Eph. 13; cf. Stählin, op. cit., p. 62. [166] Smyrn. 8:2.
[167] Cf. F. Kattenbusch, Das apostolische Symbol II, 1800, p. 922: 'καθολική here means virtually μία μόνη.'
[168] Magn. 6:1; 7:1; Trall. 2:2; 3:1; Philad. 5:1; Smyrn. 8:1.
[169] Eph. 6:1.   [170] Magn. 3:1; Smyrn. 9:1; Pol. 6:1.
[171] Philad. 3:2.   [172] Pol. 4:2.   [173] Pol. 1:3; 2:1f.
[174] Trall. 12:2.   [175] Magn. 3:1; Trall. 12:2.   [176] Smyrn. 8.
[177] Pol. 5:2. The difficult sentence concerning ascetics, ἐὰν γνωσθῇ πλέον τοῦ ἐπισκόπου, ἔφθαρται, is translated by Bauer, op. cit., p. 278, as follows: 'If more respect is paid to him than to the bishop, he is lost.' To exalt the bishop by thus suppressing and depreciating others is not, however, Ignatius's way. It is more probable that the words should be understood as forbidding public boasting by the ascetics; so (following Lightfoot) A. D'Alès, RSR 25, 1935, pp. 489ff.: 'If he makes himself known to anyone other than the bishop, he is lost.'   [178] Pol. 1:2; 5:1.
[179] Eph. 6:1. With reference to Eph. 15 and Philad. 1, H. Chadwick, 'The silence of bishops in Ignatius', HTR 43, 1950, pp. 169ff., has very pertinently emphasised, in oppositon to Bauer, op. cit., p. 206, that this is not simply a case of avoiding embarrassment with regard to an ungifted colleague. The idea is rooted in the total conception of the bishop as τύπος θεοῦ (Magn. 6:1); in God there is an abyss of silence (Eph. 19:1), cf. Schlier, op. cit., pp. 37f.

forth as the Word;[180] he may also be young, and yet retain the respect of the congregation and the presbyterate.[181] Everyone whom the Lord of the house sends to look after the affairs of the household must be received as if he were the one who sent him.[182] The crucial point for Ignatius is the sheer fact that the bishop is there, in his appointed place. He is the 'hub'[183] of the congregation, with reference to which it can orient itself, or a firm, immovable rock,[184] or again, like an anvil on which the blows of God's enemies fall.[185] Even the image of the shepherd, which Ignatius uses but rarely, takes on this distinctively representative and ritual character: where the shepherd is, there the sheep must follow; wolves indeed lie in wait for them, but on the 'unity' of the flock their power is broken, and they can accomplish nothing.[186]

If we go on to ask about the concrete authority or legal powers belonging to the bishop, then we shift the view of the matter in a way which makes it no longer true to Ignatius. Ignatius is not concerned with legal axioms, but with the essence of a holy fellowship embodied in the bishop, the clergy, and the congregation in conjunction. The bishop is, as it were, only the apex or the focal point of the whole. No special arguments are marshalled in support of his authority. It is true that the congregation is subject to him and to 'those who are over it';[187] that it is in harmony with the bishop[188] 'in a single obedience';[189] that it follows him'[190] and is constant and sincere in obeying him;[191] and that the man who resists the bishop cannot be submissive to God.[192] Ignatius, however, throughout avoids treating the powers, the authority, and the 'rights' of the bishop in isolation, and setting them off against other authorities. 'Wherever the bishop appears, there let the people be';[193] whatever brings honour to the one also brings honour to the other.[194] His authority, therefore, is apparently limitless; but it has, so to speak, no proper legal ground on which to take its stand. This not only points to the *de facto* limits of the governing power, which in this period were still narrow even for the monarchical bishop, but also accords with the inner logic of a concept of the Church in terms of musical or cosmic harmony. Despite the new general approach the old Pauline idea of the reciprocal subordination and mutual love of all

[180] Magn. 8:2. That silence surpasses speech is a typically gnostic idea: cf. Bartsch, *op. cit.*, pp. 53ff.

[181] Magn. 3:1.   [182] Eph. 6:1.   [183] Cf. Stählin, *op. cit.*, p. 64.

[184] Pol. 1:1.   [185] Pol. 3:1.

[186] Philad. 2:2; the bishop is also referred to as a shepherd in Rom. 9:1.

[187] Magn. 6:2.   [188] Eph. 4:1; Magn. 2; 3:1; 13:2; Pol. 6:1.

[189] Eph. 2:2.   [190] Smyrn. 7:1.   [191] Eph. 20:2; Magn. 3.

[192] Eph. 5:2.

[193] Smyrn. 8:2; cf. Magn. 4; 7:1; Trall. 2:2; Philad. 2:1; 3:2; Smyrn. 9:1; Pol. 4:1.

[194] Eph. 2:1; cf. Pol. 8:1. In a similar way Trall. 12:2 links the honour paid to God, to Christ, and to the apostles.

the members is here still very much alive.[195] The bishop is under an obligation to exercise tireless yet patient care for all;[196] but at the same time all Christians are still his brothers and sisters.[197] 'Let no one's position make him arrogant; for faith and charity form "the whole", and nothing is to be preferred to them.'[198] In his view of official position Ignatius is peculiarly 'ecclesiastical', but he is never 'clerical'.

It is therefore not easy to define the nature of the authority of the Ignatian bishop. The congregation is to pay heed to the bishop, in order that God may pay heed to them;[199] but to what—or to whom—is the bishop in his official capacity to pay heed? In Ignatius's thought it is not a dogmatic tradition which confronts the bishop with the norms binding upon him; but equally it is neither a specific commission which he has received nor a clearly defined official ministry. Ignatius refuses to be tied to the 'archives' of the traditional Scriptures,[200] and he never backs up what he is saying by appealing to his episcopal authority;

---

[195] Magn. 6:2; 13:2; Trall. 13:2; Pol. 6; 7:2. This idea is still to be found in Polycarp, Phil. 10:2, in the form of a quotation from the N.T. Eph. 5:21; but in the Pastoral Epistles it has completely disappeared.

[196] These admonitions occur in the letter to Polycarp, which from 6:1 onwards is, however, at the same time clearly a letter to the whole congregation in Smyrna: cf. Bauer, op. cit., pp. 278f.

[197] Pol. 5:1.

[198] Smyrn. 6:1; cf. Eph. 14:1. The word τόπος, here translated 'position', is taken by Schlier, Ignatiosbriefe, p. 128, as referring to 'a somewhat higher level of gnostic being'. Against this interpretation, however, we have the evidence of Pol. 1:2 and Polycarp, Phil. 11:1, where, exactly as in I Clement, τόπος denotes position within the Church, and that a gnostic term should have been adopted to express this is neither demonstrable nor probable. It would be more plausible to think, as Bauer, Rechtgläubigkeit, p. 73, does, in terms of 'something like a gnostic anti-bishop in Smyrna'; but this too remains pure hypothesis. The concept of 'love' in Ignatius's letters seems on the one hand to be coloured by gnostic ideas of a 'Love'-aeon, and on the other to owe a good deal to the experience of the agapē or 'love-feast' within the congregation: cf. Käsemann, op. cit., pp. 154f.

[199] Pol. 6:1.

[200] Philad. 8:2. It is difficult to determine precisely the meaning of this much-discussed passage: cf. Bauer, Handbuch (supp. vol.), pp. 260f.; Schlier, Ignatiosbriefe, p. 109 n. 2; Bartsch, op. cit., pp. 40ff.; and Klevinghaus, op. cit., pp. 98ff., who sees in it a reference to the 'Jewish-Gnostic apocryphal Gospels'. Be that as it may, what is clear both here and elsewhere is the magisterial character which Ignatius gives to the preaching of the Christian gospel; this has not yet become for him, as it does in the later period, 'tradition'. Not once does he mention the institution of the Eucharist, even though the Eucharist itself is of such importance to him: cf. Bartsch, op. cit., pp. 125ff. Revealed truth and its exposition are still indissolubly linked in his mind; no more than Paul does he give thought to the question of possible 'false' interpretations. Ἑρμηνεύειν, in the sense of scriptural exegesis, therefore means authentic exegesis': Klevinghaus, op. cit., p. 98. As in Paul, ἑρμηνεία is therefore a gift of the Spirit and inerrant.

in fact, not once does he explicitly refer to himself as bishop.[201] Ignatius feels himself to be a man of the Spirit; and it would appear that it was as such that he bestowed on himself the epithet 'Theophoros', 'God-bearer'.[202] He knows 'the natures of the heavenly beings, the hierarchies of angels and the musterings of the powers, the visible and the invisible worlds', and is aware that this gives him a superiority over others.[203] The Spirit of God, which lives in his fleshly being, cannot be deceived,[204] and bursts forth miraculously in inspired, prophetic speech.[205] It may be that this element of enthusiasm has been intensified by his martyr's destiny, just as on the other hand that same destiny imposes on him, the individual Christian torn from his congregation and pressing forward toward his ordeal, all the more the duty of humility, making any kind of 'boasting' impossible.[206] This gift of prophecy, however, is not in principle linked with martyrdom; nor is it, as in Paul, thought of as a 'gift' in the strict sense. Instead, it is simply a case of an exceptional heightening of the general 'spiritual' nature, as this is made known to and bestowed upon Christians as a corporate body, even though the 'children' among them are not as yet able to comprehend it.[207] For Ignatius all Christians are, like himself, 'God-bearers', Christ-bearers, and bearers of holiness;[208] and they no longer live 'in a human way', if only they meet in the unity of the congregation, submitting to the bishop as to Christ himself.[209]

We are, therefore, dealing here with a distinctive combination of pneumatic and official or ecclesiastical thinking. The Church is the locus of the process which makes Christians into spiritual men and women, and the bishop who stands at their head is therefore called above all else to embody this spiritual ideal and to fulfil it ever more and more perfectly. Only so can he hope to be equal to his position.

On this point there is no need to confine our attention to the statement

[201] The only exception is Rom. 2:2, and here the reference to himself is in the third person. Similarly, Polycarp nowhere calls himself bishop in his letter to the Philippians.

[202] Ἰγνάτιος ὁ καὶ Θεοφόρος is the regular form in which he describes himself in the introductions to his letters. That this description, as Bauer, op. cit., pp. 189ff., has suggested, may be linked with Ignatius's imminent martyrdom, is contradicted by the decisive way in which he speaks of the martyr's crown as a future dignity which he has yet to win, and by the reference in Eph. 9:2 to all the Ephesian Christians as χριστοφόροι.

[203] Trall. 5.   [204] Magn. 3:2.

[205] Philad. 7; cf. Bauer, op. cit., pp. 259 f.; F. J. Dölger, 'ΘΕΟΥ ΦΩΝΗ,' Antike und Christentum 6, 1936, pp. 218ff., 290f.

[206] Cf. H. Von Campenhausen, Die Idee des Martyriums, 1936, pp. 69f.

[207] Trall. 5:1.

[208] Eph. 9:2; cf. F. J. Dölger, 'Christophoros als Ehrentitel für Martyrer und Heilige im christlichen Altertum,' Antike und Christentum 4, 1934, pp. 73ff.; 5, 1935, pp. 79f.

[209] Trall. 2:1.

which Ignatius makes about himself, and which as such may perhaps call for special evaluation;[210] the same lessons are inculcated in a highly suggestive way by the exhortations which Ignatius sends to his episcopal colleague, Polycarp of Smyrna. The conviction that the bishop must be a man who is continually growing, that he must become more than he already is,[211] here finds forceful expression. Nor is this a matter of general admonitions to strict moral self-discipline and vigilance, but of an explicitly 'spiritual' demand that he should 'lack nothing, but abound in every gift of grace'. Polycarp, like Ignatius, is to open himself to invisible, supra-terrestrial things.[212] He is to make time for unceasing prayer, to increase in insight, and to 'keep his spirit awake and on the watch'.[213] He stands under the 'episcopal' governance of God the Father and of Christ himself,[214] the bishop of all and the High Priest of priests, whom he is to actualise to his congregation.[215] He is borne up by God, as he for his part bears all his people;[216] and if he does 'nothing without God',[217] and fills his position diligently, then men will discern that he possesses genuine, divine legitimation, and did not acquire his office 'by his own efforts or those of others'.[218] Ignatius knows of no special grace associated with a particular office, nor does he remind the bishop, as the Pastoral Epistles do, of his ordination. As a spiritual man, however, he is to fulfil the unending spiritual tasks which his office imposes upon him, for all and in co-operation with all.[219] For 'no Christian has a right to his own life; but he rests in God'.[220]

The ideal of church office here displayed might be called not just a spiritual but also a cultic ideal. To say this is not to think merely of the

[210] In my own view the striking restlessness which Ignatius displays in his letters is not to be understood *solely* as a product of his situation as a martyr-to-be; it is also a concomitant of the unremitting demands of his spiritual ideal.

[211] Pol. 3:2.

[212] Pol. 2:2. In view of the context this passage might equally refer to the knowledge of what is hidden within men; but knowledge of terrestrial and supra-terrestrial spirits makes a good combination.

[213] 1:3.   [214] Pol. Inscr.

[215] Philad. 9:1: καλοί οἱ ἱερεῖς, κρεῖσσον δὲ ὁ ἀρχιερεὺς ὁ πεπιστευμένος τὰ ἅγια τῶν ἁγίων, ὃς μόνος πεπίστευται τὰ κρυπτὰ τοῦ θεοῦ, αὐτὸς ὢν θύρα τοῦ πατρὸς κτλ. This passage is a figurative application of the concept of priesthood, but one where specifically sacrificial ideas play no part: cf. Klevinghaus, *op. cit.*, p. 105. As against Klevinghaus, *op. cit.*, pp. 109f., however, I find no trace elsewhere in Ignatius, any more than in Clement of Rome, of an appeal to the O.T. cult legislation as normative.

[216] Pol. 1:1.   [217] Pol. 4:1.   [218] Philad. 1:1.

[219] Such requirements are not to be interpreted, as they are by Werner, *op. cit.*, p. 653 n. 46, as mere maxims of ecclesiastical politics, implying 'that Polycarp, in Ignatius's opinion, makes his episcopal authority felt much too little'.

[220] Pol. 7:3.

special liturgical function which the bishop exercises.[221] Ignatius's total conception of the Church and of Christianity possesses a cultic character in this respect, namely that salvation becomes a reality only in unison with the activity of the visible congregation, performed both in the spirit and in the flesh; in this way the church exhibits the divine world, and actualises it through its own way of life. Its 'unity', and to a less extent the Gospel or the 'Word',[222] shape and maintain that life. This unity, however, cannot exist without the bishop. He is the central point of the divine mystery of the Church; hence he must and shall also be more than the rest a 'spiritual' man.

On his home ground the 'bishop of Syria'[223] will not have been the only one to uphold this distinctive concept of the Church and church office as a spiritual mystery. Its origins are still matter for conjecture. On the one hand, it is plainly connected with the enthusiasm of the teachers and prophets, which marks the very beginnings of the history of the Antiochene church;[224] and on the other, it points to the gnosis, which won its strongest support in Syria.[225] Ignatius, however, is neither a prophet in the Pauline sense nor a gnostic in the heretical. He is no prophet, because he perceives and acknowledges the presence of Christ only in the Church officially governed by and united around the bishop; and for the same reason he is also no gnostic, because the mystery of unity, which is the point at issue, can only be achieved here, in the actual, visible community which 'in flesh and spirit is, so to say, nailed to the Cross' of the Lord.[226] It is one and the same passionate conviction which rejects gnostic docetism and affirms the visible Church, which seeks the spiritual life and demands the organised structure of office. The episcopal office in Ignatius has absolutely nothing in common with Roman ideas on the subject; but in liturgy and cultic theory, especially that of the Greek Orthodox Church, his thought was to have a long and significant influence.

The third document bearing on the concept of office and official authority which has come down to us from this early period is the so-called Pastoral Epistles,[227] which claim to have been written by the

---

[221] This aspect is far too strongly emphasised in the fantastic over-valuation of the cultic element in G. P. Wetter, *Altchristliche Liturgien I: Das christliche Mysterium*, 1921, and also, in my opinion, by Schlier; on the whole question cf. Bartsch, *op. cit.*, pp. 99ff. The dissertation by G. Cloin, *De spiritualiteit van de Ignatiaansche Bisschops-Idee*, Nijmegen, 1938, is completely worthless.

[222] Ignatius no longer separates the Gospel from the Law: cf. Klevinghaus, *op. cit.*, p. 83.

[223] Rom. 2:2.   [224] Cf. p. 70 above.

[225] In Ignatius's day it may even have predominated; cf. Bauer, *Rechtgläubigkeit*, pp. 65ff.

[226] Smyrn. 1:1.

[227] On what follows cf. M. Dibelius, *Die Pastoralbriefe,*[2] 1931. My own somewhat divergent standpoint is presented in *Polycarp von Smyrna und die*

apostle Paul toward the end of his life, but which cannot in fact derive from him. They must have been composed in Asia Minor in the first half of the second century, and their author was in all probability himself a presbyter or bishop, since the problems and duties of these officials are among his principal concerns. The Pastoral Epistles are neither occasional pieces, as is to a certain extent the Shepherd of Hermas, nor genuine letters, such as I Clement or the Epistles of Ignatius. They are a systematic work, incorporating older traditions and possibly even written sources, which may be classed as 'writings on church order'. They are cast in epistolary form, and contain a number of messages couched in highly personal terms, in which 'Paul' expresses himself on the subject of his situation, his person, his apostolic calling, and his anxieties and hopes for the future. In this way the theological warnings against false teaching, and the practical instructions for the running of the congregation, which are the major topics, are given an air of verisimilitude and a warm and urgent tone. The rules for the congregation, and the instructions to its leaders, in many respects follow the widespread pattern of the so-called *Haustafeln*, which enumerate the duties and virtues appropriate to the old and the young, masters and slaves, husbands and wives, and so also for the bishops, presbyters, and deacons in office. These three offices are, however, for the most part not mentioned in the same breath. Where bishops and deacons occur, the presbyters are commonly missing, and where the presbyters are under discussion, there is no reference to bishops and deacons.[228] This argues for the hypothesis that the Pastoral Epistles are interweaving different traditions, which up to this point have followed separate courses. They thus provide further evidence for the gradual fusion of the Pauline-episcopal tradition with the traditions of the system of elders as this, according to the indications in Acts, came into existence in Asia Minor, though it is, of course, also attested elsewhere by the Roman sources.

In the Pastoral Epistles the 'bishop' is always spoken of in the singular. The simplest explanation of this fact is that monarchical episcopacy is by now the prevailing system, and that the one bishop has already become the head of the presbyterate, even if his supreme position is not nearly so strongly emphasised as it is in the Epistles of Ignatius. It is in keeping with this that the Pastoral Epistles no longer take the form of letters to congregations, but are directed to individual men, Timothy

---

Pastoralbriefe (Proceedings of the Heidelberg Academy), 1951, where further literature is cited.

[228] Cf. Dibelius, *op. cit.*, p. 36. In Tit. 1:5ff. we have a clumsy attempt to combine the two groups. There is no reason to suspect an interpolation; this is simply an instance where the author of the Epistles is himself acting as 're-dactor'.

or Titus. These are portrayed not simply as personal disciples and intimate confidants of the apostle; they are also nothing less than his official representatives, who are to give effect in Asia Minor and Crete to the teachings and instructions set out in the letters. It may be asked whether this does not perhaps reflect a particular quasi-metropolitan position which may have been granted to outstanding figures of the post-apostolic generation.[229] Too little is known, however, about the precise situation obtaining at this time to allow of any conclusion on this point. The status of the apostle's disciples, who are to appoint presbyters and to proclaim the apostolic teaching, is most simply understood in the light of the purpose which the whole fiction is intended to serve. They exist merely to ensure that as universal and unquestioned a validity as possible is ascribed to the instructions given in the letters. In this respect the Epistles, despite the fact that they are addressed to individuals, are essentially 'catholic'. Timothy and Titus figure in them as models of faithful and conscientious church officers. The tasks which they have to handle fall entirely within the sphere of the individual congregation; we learn nothing, for instance, concerning the relationship of congregations to one another, the exchange of news, acts of mutual aid, and suchlike. In part, those addressed are persons within the individual congregation who are, however, entrusted with functions which can be exercised only by a governing bishop, and who are already beginning to rise above the level of their 'fellow-elders'.[230] Nevertheless, the borderline between that authority and function of the bishop and those common to all the elders is in some other respects not sharply drawn.[231] This corresponds to the actual situation at the beginnings of the monarchical episcopate.

The relevant passages should be expounded in accordance with this general picture.[232] In those sections of the Pastorals which are signifi-

---

[229] From a consideration of the Pastoral Epistles, III John, Revelation, and I Clement (cf. p. 90 n. 89 above), and of men such as Polycarp, Dix, op. cit., pp. 263ff., attempts to deduce that before the rise of the local monarchical episcopate there were apostolic plenipotentiaries, especially authorised to perform ordinations, whose sphere of activity was not limited to a single congregation. In the last analysis this is pure historical fiction, designed to uphold the dogma of the 'apostolic ministry'; for a critique cf. T. W. Manson, The Church's Ministry, 1948, pp. 61ff.

[230] On the term 'fellow-elder' cf. p. 119 n. 304 below. Chief among the functions which mark out the recipients of the letters is their judicial authority over the presbyters: I. Tim. 5:19; cf. p. 147 below.

[231] The list of virtues appropriate to the bishop is markedly unspecific, and in this respect closely akin to the ideal pictures, e.g., of the good army commander, compiled by pagan writers: cf. Dibelius, Pastoralbriefe, pp. 84, 100; A. Vögtle, Die Tugend- und Lasterkataloge des Neuen Testaments, exegetisch, religions- und formgeschichtlich untersucht, 1936, pp. 51ff., 73ff., 237ff.

[232] For this reason the sharp juristic dividing-lines which Schlier, 'Die

cant for the question of church government we are dealing with admonitions and instructions which a cleric from Asia Minor, possibly himself a bishop, wrote for the benefit of his colleagues in order to teach them in Paul's name the right conduct and form of their ministry. Clad in this supreme authority he can speak with the utmost freedom, combining at will words of his own with traditional elements, statements of principle with illustrative material, legal with religious dicta, and including also a great many contemporary allusions. He himself must have been an outstanding personality, much more fully and deeply educated in the things of the spirit than, say, Clement of Rome, even if at the same time he was not so original and fertile in expression as Ignatius. The exceptional value which his Epistles have for precisely the subject we are discussing is obvious.

If we ask what particular tasks fall to the cleric, the first point to strike one is that the cult in general is never mentioned. In the Pastorals, in Clement, and even to a certain extent in Ignatius, interest in things cultic has markedly receded. In its place a different subject, though one which does indeed play its part in assemblies for public worship, engages the attention of our Paulinist: the apostolic teaching now figures as the sustaining power and the backbone both of church life and of the official activity of its leaders. For the first time the office is treated as essentially and comprehensively a teaching-office.[233] The apostolic teaching is that with which the holders of the office have been 'entrusted',[234] and which they must above all proclaim and uphold. This does not mean, however, that their position has ceased to be one in which they are concerned with every aspect of church life, or that the whole 'care of the church' has not been committed to them.[235] The Church's preacher is also to be her example,[236] her judge,[237] and the 'corrector of the recalcitrant'.[238] Practical and economic affairs also come into the picture,[239] and the customary warning has to be given against covetous malpractices.[240] At the heart of everything, however,

---

Ordnung der Kirche nach den Pastoralbriefen', *Festschrift Friedrich Gogarten*, 1948, pp. 38ff., draws between the functions of the apostle's disciple and of the local church officers seem to me completely contrary to the intention of the Pastorals themselves. Such an attempt is only possible if the letters are accepted without question as Pauline, or if, as Schlier does, one simply ignores the question of authenticity altogether.

[233] A full account of the words used in connection with this teaching function will be found in Schlier, *op. cit.*, p. 47.

[234] In I Tim. 1:11; Tit. 1:3, this is true even of the apostle himself.

[235] I Tim. 3:5; cf. Tit. 1:7.   [236] I Tim. 4:12; Tit. 2:7.

[237] I Tim. 5:19ff.; Tit. 3:10f. For a more detailed discussion of this aspect cf. pp. 143ff. below.

[238] II Tim. 2:25.   [239] I Tim. 3:2, 8; 5:16ff.; Tit. 1:8.

[240] I Tim. 6:5–10, 17; Tit. 1:11.

stands the 'sound doctrine',[241] a phrase which covers a great deal more than just dogmatic truths. Elders who 'labour in preaching and teaching' are to be prized above the rest,[242] and even Timothy, 'the man of God, equipped for every good work', is above all else an 'evangelist' and 'a workman who has no need to be ashamed, rightly handling the word of truth'.[243] To this extent it may be said that the Pastoral Epistles once more give effect to the prophetic function which Paul had formerly set at the very centre of the congregation's life.[244] Preaching, convicting, and exhorting, however, hardly appear any longer as the direct fruit of the Spirit; the official preacher holds fast to the undistorted tradition and to the sacred, inspired Scriptures which the apostles have left behind them. Moreover, responsibility for the trusteeship of this inheritance is no longer vested in the congregation as a whole, but in the bishop and the elders as the professional holders of an established office, committed to them for this purpose.

The background to this altered situation is the fight against gnostic false teaching, which has flared up on a wide front. Traces, explicit or implicit, of polemic against the heretics, their poisonous quarrelsomeness, their supposedly completely childish myths and fantastic speculations,[245] their ascetic extravagances, and their moral depravity, are everywhere to be found. To counter them, what matters is to set the genuine 'gospel of the glory of the blessed God'[246] once more upon the lampstand by holding fast to the original apostolic preaching.[247] Perhaps one ought in fact to say: what matters especially is to protect the memory and the teaching of the apostle Paul against the heretics' misuse of his name. For there can be no doubt that our author is striving to preserve genuine Pauline traditions, into the meaning of which he has penetrated much more profoundly, and to which he pays much more careful attention, than do either Clement or Ignatius of Antioch. The emphasis on grace as opposed to works, on the binding importance of salvation as a present reality, on the unity of faith and action, corresponds to a legitimately Pauline concern, even though it is not applied as radically or energetically as Paul would have done.[248] On the

---

[241] I Tim. 1:10; 6:3; II Tim. 1:13; 4:3; Tit. 1:9, 13; 2:1. The phrase derives from the vocabulary of popular philosophy.

[242] I Tim. 5:17.   [243] II Tim. 3:17—4:5—2:15.

[244] A first step toward the position taken in the Pastorals can be seen in Ephesians, where charismatic gifts are predominantly associated with preaching: cf. Käsemann, op. cit., p. 146. But here preaching itself is still the effect of a gift, or rather of various different gifts.

[245] The derisive tone of spiritual superiority toward the heretics, something quite unknown to Paul or Ignatius, here appears for the first time: cf. H. Von Campenhausen, 'Glaube und Bildung im Urchristentum', Stud. Gen. 2, 1949, p. 191.   [246] I Tim. 1:11.   [247] On this subject cf. pp. 161f. below.

[248] Cf. R. Bultmann, art. 'Paulus', RGG 4², 1930, 996; E. Aleith, Das Paulusverständnis in der alten Kirche, 1937, pp. 15f.

other hand, it is also possible to detect a new concern, namely to give
prominence to the biblical idea of creation, to the universal requirements of a morality as much natural as Christian, and to the rights of
reason and of a rational Christian training, in a way which is quite
definitely no longer Pauline, but which nevertheless makes its bow
under Paul's aegis. If gnostics and Marcionites as, so to speak, ultra-
Paulinists, threaten to snap the bond between spiritual and natural
human life altogether, then a Paul will oppose them who by contrast
stresses precisely the self-evident and the given in the created order,
and in resolute opposition to all 'unwholesome' and extraordinary
opinions falls back on the great simple basic facts of the Christian
doctrine of salvation and morals. With these a pious Christian congregation ought to be content, and not let itself become involved in controversy about new notions which confuse the original teaching:[249] 'O
Timothy, guard what has been entrusted to you. Avoid the godless
chatter and "antitheses" of what is falsely called " knowledge"!'[250]

It is the intention of 'Paul' that the holder of church office—and by
that is meant office invested with authority, as in the system of government by elders—should now make himself known publicly as a sup-
porter of this attitude. The gnostic heretics seem as yet not to possess
such an office, or at least not to perceive its full significance. Their
leaders are merely 'teachers', who heed 'deceitful spirits',[252] and their
followers attach themselves to them in accordance with 'their own
likings'[253]—a phrase which means that the leaders base themselves
entirely on their own spiritual gifts,[254] and thus obtain, as others had
formerly done in Corinth, the free recognition of their adherents. They
may even have appealed to Paul to justify their position, though the
possible reference in this passage does not come out very clearly. What
is clear is the overall conception which the Pastorals set up in opposition
to them. The picture which emerges of the congregation has a great
deal in common with the demands put into the mouth of Paul in Acts
on the occasion of his farewell to his elders at Miletus.[255] The 'Pauline'
Epistles at present under consideration likewise derive their instructions
for church life from the prophetic foresight of the departing apostle,
who in the Spirit plainly saw the coming evils;[256] and by doing so they
set these instructions in the same, humanly affecting light.[257] The only
difference is that here the development has been carried further. On the

---

[249] II Tim. 2:14, 24; cf. I Tim. 6:4.
[250] I Tim. 6:20f. There may be an allusion here to Marcion's *Antitheses*:
cf. W. Bauer, *Rechtgläubigkeit*, p. 229; Campenhausen, *Polycarp*, p. 12.
[251] I Tim. 1:3, 7; Tit. 1:11.   [252] I Tim. 4:1.   [253] II Tim. 4:3.
[254] This is suggested by II Tim. 2:18, and possibly also by the 'arrogance'
with which they are reproached: I Tim. 6:4; II Tim. 3:4.
[255] Cf. pp. 8off. above.   [256] I Tim. 4:1ff.; II Tim. 3:1ff.; 4:3.
[257] Cf. especially II Tim. 3:6ff.

one hand, the efforts of the false teachers are becoming more clearly recognisable; and on the other, church office has itself reached a higher degree of perfection, in that it now has a less 'patriarchal' character, is more precisely defined as 'office', and is already articulated into various grades. In accord too with the situation of a later time is the more than literary audacity with which the Pastorals make themselves out to be genuine Pauline letters. Their author is concerned to ensure the appearance of authenticity against any doubts that may be raised; and he ingeniously corroborates this with numerous details quite peripheral to his real purpose.[258] A similarly deliberate procedure is to be found elsewhere only in II Peter, which also probably comes from Asia Minor, and here too it is the product of the same anti-heretical concern. The latter work, however, is satisfied simply with combating the gnostics at the theological level, whereas in the Pastorals the polemic against their doctrines is combined with remarks on morals and church order to form a unified whole, and it is as a unified whole that it is designed to make its effect.

This, of course, does not mean that we are required to expound every sentence and every detail in terms of this confrontation with heresy. This is impossible in the first place because in the church regulations which the Pastorals collate there is undoubtedly considerable purely traditional material. Moreover, our author obviously has a direct interest in the problems of right ecclesiastical order and constitution. Alongside the traditional description of the elders and the virtues which they ought to possess he considers the personal question of the spiritual relationship between the office-holder and his office. This is a new approach. In Clement the spiritual office was described, so to speak, from the outside, namely in terms of the way in which it ought to appear to the eyes of the other members of the congregation; and in Ignatius the subjective and objective elements are still not treated separately, but are found side by side and in combination. In the Pastoral Epistles a fundamental question of all 'pastoral theology' is posed as such for the first time; and it is precisely this which proves them to be letters by a genuine 'shepherd of souls', written to help other shepherds of the Church who were exercised by new problems and responsibilities.

'The saying is sure: If any one aspires to the office of a bishop, he desires a noble task.'[259] The spiritual office is no longer regarded as a status or mere dignity, befitting those of advanced years, for which a man gradually matures, and to which with age and merit he must automatically attain. It is an office, something which can be aspired to and achieved, something therefore which can perhaps even be applied for, when a 'post' falls vacant. This situation is considered quite normal, and is confirmed by an old saying as having obtained for a long time.

[258] Cf. Campenhausen, *Polycarp*, p. 8.   [259] I Tim. 3:1.

In principle the case of the presbyterate will have been no different.[260] The elders are installed in their office, and are clearly entitled, if they prove satisfactory, to material reimbursement.[261] The youth of an office-holder is no reason to deny him the respect which is his due.[262] In this way spiritual office now becomes one of the professions. Once again it more closely resembles the Jewish office of elder, which in itself called for no special 'spiritual' qualifications in the sense of a miraculous endowment of divine grace, but was a position entrusted to worthy members of the congregation. It is very significant that now purely natural abilities and qualifications are listed among the conditions for elevation to the spiritual office. The virtues of moderation, good sense and peaceableness stand side by side with the particular requirements of hospitality, a capacity for teaching, a well-run household, and a good reputation—the last-named, bearing in mind the pagan environment, being obviously indispensable.[263] Recent converts to Christianity are not eligible.[264] Appointments must always be made with the greatest caution; before the ordination of deacons there must be a testing period.[265] Faith is regarded as especially well established where the family has been known to be pious, and the Holy Scriptures have been read among them, for generations.[266] All the virtues which a Christian requires in civil and family life he also needs for the governance of the congregation: 'If a man does not know how to manage his own household, how can he care for God's church?'[267] If a man has been given office, then others naturally expect him to prove himself worthy of it, and a minister who passes this test is rightly highly regarded.[268] Men ought not to despise their spiritual monitor.[269] Elders, as officials of the

---

[260] As U. Holzmeister, ' "Si quis episcopatum desiderat, bonum opus desiderat" ,' *Biblica* 12, 1931, p. 41, rightly emphasises, a certain difficulty is implicit precisely in the fact that it is the episcopal office and not the presbyterate which is mentioned in this passage. For by the unanimous principle of the later Christian Church the office of a bishop is the very thing a man should not 'aspire to'. For this reason Holzmeister would like to take *episcopatus* in this verse in the wider sense of *sacerdotium*, and to apply it as in I Clement to office-holders in general. This would mean that references to the bishop in the Pastorals should be treated as 'generic'. A similar position is taken by C. Spicq, *Les épîtres pastorales*, 1947, pp. 91ff. In fact, however, the λόγος cited may well derive from a period when the episcopate had not yet become monarchical, and when therefore an official differentiation between bishops and presbyters was not yet general. In my view, however, this does not exclude the possibility that at one time it might have been applied to the monarchical bishop as well, after the period of transition was over.

[261] I Tim. 3:15; 5:17; in the light of 5:18 the phrase διπλῆ τιμή must mean, so to speak, 'double rations': cf. Dibelius, *Pastoralbriefe*, pp. 47f.

[262] I Tim. 4:12; cf. Ignatius, Magn. 3:1.   [263] I Tim. 3:2ff.; Tit. 1:6ff.

[264] I Tim. 3:6.   [265] I Tim. 3:10.

[266] II Tim. 1:5; cf. 1:3–II Tim. 3:15f.   [267] I Tim. 3:5; cf. 5:8.

[268] I Tim. 3:13.   [269] Tit. 2:15.

congregation whose lives are for this reason more public than other men's, also have the right to special protection: charges against them are not to be admitted except on the evidence of at least two or three witnesses.[270]

Of course, office is still essentially a 'ministry'.[271] But the respect due to it and to its standing has been greatly accentuated in every possible way. No longer is there any mention of the active co-operation or responsibility of the congregation. The most we find is the admonition that Timothy must always be respectful when correcting the elderly,[272] or that he is to honour those Christian widows who are active as deaconesses.[273] There is no longer any effort to achieve a living mutuality in the relationship between the official and the community, such as was still being commended in I Peter.[274] For this very reason, however, the new individual dialectic between the office-holder and his office, between his own abilities and that which his spiritual calling requires of him, now develops seriously for the first time.

That the nature and work of the office is 'spiritual' is firmly established, despite all the naturalistic assumptions, as self-evident. Primitive Christianity and the early Church know of no concept of office which is content with secular, legal, or practical considerations. This is doubly clear where the office is so decidedly understood as a teaching one. On the work of the man who holds it depends, in the view of the Pastorals, not only his own salvation but also that of those who listen to him, his congregation.[275] In their interest he must be present at every turn, invited or uninvited, to teach and admonish, to rebut and contest false and corrupting ideas,[276] and to supply in his own person the living example of his teaching.[277] He must also be ready, in the service of the gospel, to suffer for the sake of the elect, as the apostle himself does;[278] for 'all who desire to live a godly life in Christ Jesus will be persecuted'.[279] A man from whom so much is required must be aware of what is spiritually necessary to enable him to carry out his work. He must 'take heed' to himself.[280] It would be a serious matter were he to fall into

---

[270] I Tim. 5:19; on this point cf. p. 147 below.

[271] And its holder a minister of Christ: I Tim. 1:12; 4:6.   [272] I Tim. 5:1f.

[273] I Tim. 5:3. There is a significant difference here not only from Paul but even from Ignatius, who similarly commands bishop Polycarp not to look down on slaves in dealing with his people: Pol. 4:3. In this latter passage it is still the weak members who are to be protected; in the Pastorals it is those who would be worthy of respect in any case who are to be honoured by the spiritual officer.

[274] The attempt of Schweizer, op. cit., p. 88, to weaken this impression is abortive. There is in fact no suggestion that the governing clergy were tested by the congregation (Schweizer himself admits, p. 91, that this is 'not brought out very strongly'). I Tim. 3:10 (as Schweizer agrees, against Lock, A Critical and Exegetical Commentary on the Pastoral Epistles, 1924) is not relevant here.

[275] I Tim. 4:16.   [276] II Tim. 4:2.   [277] I Tim. 4:12; Tit. 2:7.

[278] II Tim. 4:5–II Tim. 3:11.   [279] II Tim. 3:12.   [280] I Tim. 4:16.

frivolous self-conceit.[281] It is God alone who can give him the strength which he needs in his work,[282] and he must therefore strive to prove himself worthy in the presence of God,[283] 'to be strong in the grace that is in Christ Jesus'.[284] It was to this effect that Timothy, the true model of every preacher of the gospel, was encouraged and exhorted by Paul.

If anyone should wonder whence the holder of this office is to derive the personal courage and strength for his task, all that can be done is to remind him of the fact of his call, or in concrete terms, of the act by which he was consecrated or ordained through the laying-on of hands of the presbyters.[285] On that occasion the cleric was entrusted with the apostolic tradition which is his guide, and thereby he was once for all armed and empowered for the good fight which he has to fight in the service of Christ.[286] The personal responsibility which he undertook at his call is a heavy one; and not all have remained faithful to it.[287] But 'God did not give us a spirit of timidity but a spirit of power and love and self-control'.[288] If he loyally fulfils his ministry, if he never tires of rekindling the grace communicated to him,[289] he can go his way with a good conscience, and hope some day, like Paul himself, to finish his course in peace, and to receive the crown of righteousness.[290] Both the responsibilities and the promised rewards of the office have increased; but the real spiritual mainstay of the one who holds it is shown to be the thought of his duty as a teacher and of the call which he received at his ordination. The 'man of God'[291] is supported in the task of governing the Church not by any gift directly bestowed on himself, nor by his natural capacities, however useful these may be, but by the apostolic tradition and his own apostolic commission, that is to say, by the office itself and by the authority which accrues to him from it. The conferring of the office is just as much a concrete, ecclesiastical act as a spiritual and 'sacramental' one. It is all one whether a group of presbyters or, in Timothy's case, the apostle himself carried this out;[292] none of them act in this context merely as the commissioned representatives of men, but as the authoritative agents of God.[293] The decisive action in per-

[281] I Tim. 3:6.

[282] I Tim. 1:12; even the apostle is helpless in his own strength.

[283] II Tim. 2:15.   [284] II Tim. 2:1.   [285] I Tim. 4:14.

[286] I Tim. 1:18; 4:14; II Tim. 2:2.

[287] I Tim. 1:19.   [288] II Tim. 1:7.

[289] II Tim. 1:6. That the word ἀναζωπυρεῖν in this passage has a sacramental connotation is suggested by Ignatius, Eph. 1:1.

[290] II Tim. 4:7f. This passage explicitly states that the promise is not limited to the apostle: οὐ μόνον δὲ ἐμοί, ἀλλὰ πᾶσι τοῖς ἠγαπηκόσι τὴν ἐπιφάνειαν αὐτοῦ.

[291] I Tim. 6:11; II Tim. 3:17.

[292] II Tim. 1:6; cf. p. 000 n. 35 below.

[293] In Timothy's case this aspect of the matter is especially emphasised by the fact that the prophets also played a part in his ordination: I. Tim. 1:18; 4:14.

forming the ordination is plainly the laying-on of hands, which is regularly employed also in baptism and in other rites for communicating power and the gift of the Spirit.[294] It is therefore undoubtedly correct to define this ordination as a sacramental act which imparts to the recipient effectual grace appropriate to his office.[295] This is the basis of the self-awareness of the office-holder, though in the last analysis this cannot be termed self-awareness but only an awareness of a spiritual call; and it is also the basis of the public status and recognition which he, as a duly appointed officer within his congregation, is allowed to claim—always bearing in mind that he in his turn has to do everything in his power to match this claim by his spiritual stature and to justify it by his actions.

Our presentation so far has shown that in its essential nature office in the Pastorals is not a product of Pauline tradition. It springs up in the soil of the system of elders, an originally Jewish institution which was taken over at first in a 'patriarchal' form. Renewed emphasis on the idea of tradition now intensifies its authoritarian quality, and at the same time gives it more markedly the character of an office.[296] It hereby

---

Here, therefore, as in Acts 13:2, it is a case of an 'inspired choice', such as is frequently mentioned in later Church history (cf., for example, Clem. Alex., *Quis dives* 42, 2), but which naturally could never become the regular practice. Further examples will be found in Achelis, *op. cit.*, vol. 2, pp. 8f. There are no grounds for following Behm, *Die Handauflegung im Urchristentum*, 1911, p. 50, in interpreting this prophetic attestation to mean that it was only in this way that Timothy 'received the inner assurance that he was charismatically equipped for his work', and that the ordination which followed was a mere formal acknowledgment of this fact. This exegesis has been put forward a number of times, most recently by Schweizer, *op. cit.*, p. 114; it implies that Timothy's ordination was, in the words of J. W. Falconer, *From Apostle to Priest*, 1900, p. 27, nothing more than 'the simple and impressive recognition of his fitness for such a work'. There is, however, no justification for thus assimilating the Pastoral Epistles, which no longer think in charismatic terms, to the Pauline conception: cf. J. Wobbe, *Der Charis-Gedanke bei Paulus*, 1932, p. 68.

[294] Cf. the material in Behm, *op. cit.*, and J. Coppens, *L'imposition des mains et les rites connexes dans le Nouveau Testament et dans l'Église ancienne*, 1925; E. Lohse, *Die Ordination im Spätjudentum und im Neuen Testament*, 1951.

[295] Because E. Schweizer 'really cannot accept this', he is obliged (p. 113 n. 26; 115 n. 35) to resort to the desperate expedient of asking whether I Tim. 4:14 and II Tim. 1:6 might not possibly refer to baptism. He makes the same suggestion in 'Die neutestamentliche Gemeindeordnung,' *Ev. Theol.* 1947, p. 355; and a similar comment, this time on I Tim. 5:22, is already to be found in H. Weinel, *Die Wirkungen des Geistes und der Geister im nachapostolischen Zeitalter*, 1899, p. 216. Cf. N. Adler, *Taufe und Handauflegung. Eine exegetische Untersuchung von Apg. 8, 14-17*, 1951, pp. 67ff.

[296] A remnant of the old patriarchal conception of the elder may perhaps be detected still in I Tim. 5:17.

becomes even further removed from the men of the Spirit within the Pauline congregation. In a different respect, however it is moving back toward Pauline ideas, for the authority of the new office possesses a spiritual affinity with that of the apostle himself. For, like Paul's apostolate which derives from Christ, it too is based on an objective divine call and act of institution, the rightness of which, because of this divine nature, cannot be doubted. Moreover, by virtue of its preaching commission the responsibility attaching to it is once more all-embracing and of the same decisive importance for salvation; and the church official, if he faithfully fulfils his ministry, can like Paul be certain of God's continual assistance. What has changed, however, is the interior attitude to vocation. In Paul's case the monstrous tension between his vocation and his natural self was overcome by surrendering his merely human existence and, in a daily dying, receiving new life from the Spirit alone. The disciple of Paul's whom we meet in the Pastoral Epistles, in his less dramatic ministry,[297] also sets store by the natural gifts of God's created order, and the sanctifying power with which even he cannot dispense he receives through loyal adherence to the apostolic tradition. This means that for him too it is not his own person which is decisive but the truth of his testimony. This explains how the Pastorals can go beyond the apostle's disciples, Timothy and Titus, and approximate the Church's new office to the authority of the apostle himself; but the effect of so doing is, of course, to make the authoritarian element loom much larger than it does in the case of Paul. Hardly any attention is now paid to Paul's own characteristic concern to refract and relativise all authority in order to ensure the freedom of the congregation and their direct contact with Christ. It is clear that in face of the confusion of gnostic notions and the menace of disorder and defection in the churches no further interest is taken in this aspect of the matter. It is regarded as far too dangerous. Even so, office in the Pastorals cannot be labelled as one-sidedly sacral or authoritarian. Two factors of fundamental importance stand in the way of such a development. First, the one endued with the grace appropriate to his office is not thereby automatically in some magical way made immune from sin and error. He is admonished to safeguard the 'gift' bestowed upon him, and to give proof of it, just as much after he has received it as before; and it is perfectly conceivable that he should prove unfaithful, and 'make shipwreck of the faith'.[298] In this respect the grace of office corresponds exactly to the concept, found in primitive Christianity in general and in Paul in particular, of the communication of grace

---

[297] As Schweizer, *op. cit.*, p. 30, pertinently remarks, it is 'no longer a matter of a special call to the ministry of an apostle, but of consecration in a quite general sense'.

[298] I Tim. 1:18f.; II Tim. 4:10.

in baptism.[299] This too is an 'objective' sacramental act, an effective means of grace, but not for that reason an automatic insurance against corruption; instead it simply heightens the seriousness of men's responsibility. Secondly, and this is supremely important, the organisation of the spiritual leadership is never put forward in the Pastorals as a self-contained sacred law which corresponds as such to the will of God, and must be preserved as irrefragable. Such ideas, characteristic of I Clement, nowhere occur.[300] Instead, the true substantial reality behind the spiritual office, the ultimate reason for its existence, its activity, and its demand for obedience from the congregation, is seen as the 'sound teaching', the genuine apostolic tradition with its very definite and religiously essential content. It is this which gives the office its meaning and the specific character of its authority. By this normative tradition, therefore, it must itself be measured, and to this, if need arise, it must take second place.

This, however, is an inference which the Pastorals, as distinct from Paul, no longer explicitly draw.[301] Office is seen as a piece of right ecclesiastical organisation, and at the same time and supremely as the instrument by which the apostolic teaching is to be preserved within the Church. But as for the question how the givenness of the office is related to preaching as the proper spiritual task of those who hold it, this basic theological problem of church order is no longer posed. All that can be stated beyond a peradventure, in view of the numerous fixed regulations on the subject of office and of church life which are recorded in the Pastorals, is this: canon law has arrived and, what is more, is regarded as entirely legitimate. The Pastoral Epistles do not bear witness to a canon law which is only just beginning, but to one which is already fairly well developed; and they see that law as an integral part of the spiritual nature of the Church and its offices. The bishop is responsible for the whole sphere of the faith and moral life of the congregation, and as their teacher and guide is bound to regard it as important that certain organising rules and regulations should exist and be observed. One difference from the genuine Paul is that these rules are now given a certain emphasis. Another is that they also take

[299] Occasionally, as in II Tim. 1:6 or 2:2, there is some doubt whether baptism or ordination is in question: cf. p. 116 n. 295 above.

[300] This also constitutes a difference in fundamental principle between the Pastorals and Ignatius: cf. Goltz, *op. cit.*, p. 116.

[301] Schweizer, *op. cit.*, p. 78, unquestionably goes too far, therefore, when he states categorically that the authority of a Timothy or a Titus is nothing more than the authority of the 'word' itself which has been entrusted to them: 'In the moment when they go aside from this word to speak their own words they are no longer what they are. To be exact, it is not they who are able to rule the churches, but only the word which they preach.' What is significant about the Pastorals, however, is that they nowhere formulate pointed Pauline alternatives of this sort or even contemplate them.

on the validity of apostolic tradition to the same degree as propositions and confessions of faith; and from the fact that their relative theological importance is not expressly discussed the danger undoubtedly arises that in the course of time they may petrify into something equally sacred and unassailable. To set against this, however, there is the prominence given to the 'good confession' as the thing of central and decisive importance for the Church, and absolutely binding upon her officers as well. The precise question how law and order within the congregation are to be related to this ultimate authority, and how the spiritual teaching authority of the church officer and his powers as a governor relate to each other, is, as we have said, not raised; and we must therefore be content to leave it open until a later stage of the Church's history.

Very close to the Pastorals both in time and place is the Epistle to the Philippians of Polycarp, bishop of Smyrna.[302] This letter may, indeed, be somewhat earlier than they,[303] but it reflects very much the same stage in the development of spiritual office,[304] just as it is also

---

[302] So much seems to me pretty well certain. In my *Polykarp von Smyrna und die Pastoralbriefe*, 1951, however, I believe that I have shown that they are intimately connected with him personally, and at the very least must have been written under his influence.

[303] According to the prevailing view the Epistle dates from some time in the second century. If, however, the not improbable hypothesis of P. N. Harrison, *Polycarp's Two Epistles to the Philippians*, 1936, is correct, and the letter should be divided, then the major portion may perhaps be dated more precisely in the fourth decade of that century: cf. Campenhausen, *Polykarp*, pp. 39f.

[304] It is striking that in Phil. 5:1; 6:1; presbyters and deacons are mentioned, but not bishops. That in Polycarp's day there should have been no episcopal office in Philippi is more than improbable, for it is precisely in this city that bishops occur as early as Paul's time (N.T. Phil. 1:1), and the combination of bishops and deacons is also constantly found elsewhere. That the bishop in Philippi, as Bauer, *Rechtgläubigkeit*, pp. 77f., suggests, may have been a heretic, is a makeshift solution supported by nothing in the Epistle itself. Instead, the most probable answer is that in Philippi the episcopal office was exercised by a number of men, and that Polycarp, for whom this title already had a monarchical significance, for this reason simply included them among the presbyters in the earlier manner, as I Clement also does. Despite his personal connections with Ignatius, Polycarp did not take up the other's determined fight for monarchical episcopacy, but in the preamble to his letter puts himself on a level with his own presbyters: Πολύκαρπος καὶ οἱ σὺν αὐτῷ πρεσβύτεροι means 'Polycarp and those who are presbyters with him' (*contra* Bauer, *Handbuch*, supp. vol., p. 285; *Rechtgläubigkeit*, p. 74). He therefore sees himself as their συμπρεσβύτερος—a term which we have already encountered in I Pet. 5:1, and which is also attested as current in this sense in Asia Minor by Irenaeus, *Ep. ad. Vict.*, cited in Eusebius, *HE* V, 24, 14, and by the anti-Montanist writer, *ibid.* V, 16, 5. Later συμπρεσβύτερος, συλλειτουργός, συμμύστης, and the corresponding Latin equivalents were to become the standard forms of address from bishops to their presbyters: cf. Achelis, *op. cit.*, II, p. 16. In Polycarp, however, the original close association of bishop and presbyters, of episcopate and presbyterate, is still reflected, so that in this respect too the affinity with the Pastorals

fighting on the same anti-gnostic theological front. The epistle supplies us with the first concrete example of a cleric, the presbyter Valens of Philippi, who failed to 'understand' the responsibilities of his position, and who had to be deposed from his office in consequence of an act of embezzlement.[305] He is not, however, to be completely cut off from the Church for this, and given up for lost, but both he and his wife, who was his accomplice, are to do penance.[306] Apart from this episode, the epistle throws little new light on our problem.

The documents of the sub-apostolic age which we have discussed thus fall naturally into three definite groups, from three different provinces of the Empire; and each of the three groups displays a different concept of ecclesiastical office and of the powers pertaining to it. The three might almost be classified as embryonic forms of the Roman Catholic, the Greek Orthodox, and the Lutheran thinking on this subject. In Rome the bishop is primarily the supreme cultic official of his congregation, in Syria he is its spiritual example and sacral focus, in Asia Minor he is above all the ordained preacher of the apostolic teaching. These are the three main possible evaluations of church office; and in later Church history we hardly ever again find them in isolation and in such pure form as we do here in Clement, in Ignatius, and in the Pastoral Epistles. This is not due simply to an accident of transmission, by which all the documents from one particular area happen to represent the same attitude. There is, of course, no reason to say that different viewpoints on this matter could not have co-existed in the same community from the very first; but in fact the approaches to a theology of church office were highly complex from the start, and varied from one geographical area to another. This variation in basic principles is all the more striking in view of the palpable fact that in practice the development of office followed more or less the same course everywhere. In all three areas this began from the patriarchal system of elders, which formed the load-bearing framework of the 'catholic' church organisation. Pauline traditions acted at the most as a certain spiritual corrective, as I Peter already makes clear; but no longer, even in Corinth, were they able to determine the main lines of the congregational structure. The replacement of the original patriarchal concept by one based on the idea of 'office' in the strict sense was also a process which began everywhere at an early stage;

---

is very strong (cf. p. 108 above). On the whole subject cf. Campenhausen, *Polycarp*, pp. 34ff.

[305] Polycarp, Phil. 11:1. The deposition is not explicitly mentioned, but would seem to be implied in the tone of the passage, and possibly also by the phrase, 'qui presbyter factus est aliquando apud vos'; cf. Bauer, *Handbuch*, suppl. vol., p. 294.

[306] Polycarp, Phil. 11:4.

and with it went the division of the single office into different grades, each with a clear technical definition. In I Clement this process is still only beginning, and in Ignatius of Antioch it is manifestly already complete, while in this respect the Pastorals fall somewhere between the two. The various degrees of development correspond to some extent to absolute chronology; but they are more closely related to the general drop in the developmental graph as we follow the Church from east to west.

Furthermore, when dealing with the beginning of the second century, we must guard against the assumption that the system of elders was everywhere an automatic feature of church life. That this was not so is shown by the Didache, which was discussed in the preceding chapter, and the caution applies all the more in the case of gnostic groups.[307] We can only regret that the later polemical writers, in their confused accounts of gnostic doctrines, have left us so little information about the organisational practice of their opponents.[308] It could happen, however, that the orthodox, even while engaged in a struggle against certain gnostic teachings, still retained their free and flexible form of association. This is the lesson of the epistles known as II and III John,[309] which we have still to consider before concluding this chapter.

Their author describes himself as 'the elder'.[310] By so doing, however, he is not representing himself as a member of a local 'presbytery'.[311] Instead, all his thoughts and actions prove him to be still unaffected by any form of ecclesiastical constitution. Not once does the Elder feel himself to be restricted to a particular individual congregation, but exerts his influence over a wide area by means of letters and emissaries. He should not therefore be thought of as a kind of 'super-

[307] Even as late as the gnosticising Acts of John there is still no sign of a fixed pattern of congregational life; on this subject cf. the unpublished Heidelberg theological dissertation by C. L. Sturhahn, *Die Christologie der ältesten apokryphen Apostelakten*, 1951.

[308] Cf. another unpublished Heidelberg dissertation: H. Kraft, *Gnostisches Gemeinschaftsleben*, 1950.

[309] These documents are undoubtedly closely related to I John and to the Fourth Gospel: cf. pp. 136f. below.

[310] II Joh. 1; III Joh. 1. E. Hirsch, *Studien zum vierten Evangelium*, 1936, pp. 177f., regards this term as a deliberately mysterious allusion, intended to be interpreted as referring to the apostle and evangelist John, who is the author's hero. The whole letter is thus a fiction, and as such contains at best faded recollections, and possibly nothing more than pure 'inventions of a novelistic kind.'

[311] E. Käsemann, 'Ketzer und Zeuge. Zum johanneischen Verfasserproblem', *ZTK* 48, 1951, pp. 292ff., is the only recent writer to revive this interpretation. But his assertion that it would be impossible to 'excommunicate' an 'elder' in the sense of an authoritative exponent of tradition understands this title much too systematically as implying a rank or a definite 'dignity'.

intendent';[312] he figures rather as a prophet or teacher of the earlier type, one of those 'elders' and fathers to whose testimony Papias and Irenaeus later appealed.[313] His followers are known to one another, and enjoy mutual fellowship.[314] Whole congregations look to him as their spiritual father,[315] or have members who enjoy his especial confidence,[316] and who give hospitality to travelling brethren and evangelists.[317] Their mutual commendation and 'testimony'[318] apparently take the place of more formal organisation, and are sufficient to preserve the teaching of Jesus and the 'truth' in which those who are genuinely 'children' of the elect churches[319] walk,[320] by which they test their teachers,[321] and in which they abide.[322]

Now, however, the Elder, with his principles of freedom and of trusting wholly to the power of the truth, has encountered abrupt resistance in one particular congregation, unfortunately unnamed. Diotrephes, 'who loves the pre-eminence,' has refused the letters which the Elder has sent, and has forbidden anyone to receive his messengers.[323] To what extent doctrinal as well as personal differences may have played a part in this we cannot say;[324] but in any case we are here concerned with a conflict on a matter, so to speak, of canon law, which is of fundamental importance.[325] The man of the Spirit, subject to no organisation and to no local authoritative body, clashes with the leader of the organised single congregation, who, it would seem, is already claiming monarchical rights for himself.[326] He may, therefore, be described with confidence as a bishop, and as one who is fighting, just as Ignatius has required, for the solidarity of his congregation around himself. In

[312] As suggested by A. von Harnack, *Entstehung und Entwicklung der Kirchenverfassung und des Kirchenrechts in den ersten zwei Jahrhunderten*, 1910, p. 48, in accordance with his hypothesis of a 'pneumatic universal and missionary organisation'; similarly, E. Gaugler, 'Die Bedeutung der Kirche in den johanneischen Schriften,' *IKZ* 15, 1925, pp. 37f.; *contra* Schweizer, *op. cit.*, pp. 53ff.

[313] Cf. pp. 162f. below.   [314] II Joh. 12; III Joh. 12.

[315] II Joh. 1:13, though, as 1:4 shows, some of their members may not.

[316] III Joh. 1.   [317] II Joh. 10; III Joh. 5ff.

[318] III Joh. 3, 6, 12. Schweizer, *op. cit.*, p. 50, also stresses that the Johannine writings as a whole are 'very poor' in details of any specific tasks which might be connected with particular church offices.

[319] II Joh. 1.   [320] II Joh. 4.   [321] I Joh. 4:1.

[322] II Joh. 9, cf. 2.   [323] III Joh. 9f.

[324] The letter itself nowhere reproaches Diotrephes with doctrinal error, and, as the succeeding verses show, hardly regards him as 'an enemy of Christ, worthy of condemnation', as Schweizer, *op. cit.*, p. 92, asserts, and as Bauer, *Rechtgläubigkeit*, p. 97, would like to assume.

[325] H. Windisch, *Die katholischen Briefe*[2], 1930, p. 141; *contra* W. Lockton, *Divers Orders of Ministers*, 1930, p. 142.

[326] Cf. T. Zahn, *Einleitung in das Neue Testament* II[4], 1924, p. 581; R. Seeberg, *Lehrbuch der Dogmengeschichte* I[3], 1920, p. 244, n. 2; T. Craig, *The Beginning of Christianity*, n.d., p. 276: 'It is clear that this Diotrephes not only *loved* the pre-eminence but he *had* it.'

one respect, indeed, he goes even further than Ignatius, inasmuch as he 'puts out of the church' all those members of the congregation who are not prepared to give way to him.[327] Here then we come across an example of the exercise of that particular kind of episcopal authority which was to be of decisive importance in the wider development of spiritual office. For the moment, however, we must be content to point out the distinctive way in which the Elder reacts to Diotrephes's behaviour. He is deeply angered, but he does not put forward his own rights in opposition to those of the other man, nor does he waste time discussing his opponent's claims. He falls back on the living authority with which he is endowed by the 'truth'; and thus armed he proposes to confront Diotrephes face to face, to convict him and overcome him[328] —in just the same way as Paul did with his opponents in Corinth.[329] Theologically, there is no sort of link with Paul; but both spiritually and in his concept of the Church this witness of a later day is still living in a totally different world from that of the duly appointed representatives of the congregation and the holders of what was soon to be a strictly monarchical office.

[327] III Joh. 10. To suggest, as Käsemann, *op. cit.*, p. 298, tries to do, that such 'excommunication', except in the case of serious moral delinquencies, could only be pronounced against a notorious heretic, is to define the situation much more sharply than the evidence warrants.

[328] III Joh. 10.

[329] Cf. pp. 43f. above.

CHAPTER VI

The Power of the Keys in the Primitive Church

IT MIGHT be thought that the present chapter must be either a post-script or an interpolation. From the very beginning the Church had rightly estimated, or at least sensed, the importance of the question of the authority to forgive sins, and how this was to be put into practice; for this authority is bound up with the essence of her faith, which is simply inconceivable without it. And yet in the practical development of church order and of spiritual office the forgiveness of sins plays at first a very minor role, and soon none at all. This is astonishing, when we consider the crucial importance for the rationale of official authority which the power to bind and to loose was later to acquire; but it is comprehensible, when we bear in mind the spiritual presuppositions and the special historical circumstances of early Christian life. In this chapter we shall collate all that can be discovered in the primitive Christian period so far discussed on the question of the power of the keys, evidence which was to be re-examined from a very much altered standpoint in the course of ecclesiastical development a century later.

For the believer, the Resurrection of Jesus meant that not only death but also the sin of the world had lost its power. Separation from sin, therefore, is just as primary and fundamental as confession of the Risen Lord for those who belong to him. The new people of the eschatological era, who are to enter into the kingdom of heaven, are a holy nation in contrast to the godless and adulterous generation around them. Baptism sunders two worlds. It is administered for repentance, 'for the remission of sins', and at that moment establishes once for all a new being. Christians are no longer 'sinners'. Here again something which before had been merely longing and labour has now become reality and ful-filment. Christians are standing within the blessed fact of moral redemption.

The positive experience of salvation is thus at all times the most prominent feature. The genuineness of this new experience, and of the new vitality that goes with it, is shown precisely by the fact that it does not pretend that the reality of sin is magically eliminated or argued away by some dogmatic theory. Men are well aware that temptations to sin remain and are effective; daily in the Paternoster they pray to be preserved from them and forgiven. They experience the power of sin in their fellow-Christians, and Jesus's admonitions to be merciful and forgiving remain very much alive not just for pagans and the unconverted but for his own congregation. By forgiving one another Christians take their place within the fellowship of forgiveness which unites them to God and to their Lord who came to seek sinners; and for this very reason they remain free, and do not relapse into the old tyranny of sin. In prayer for forgiveness, in mutual forgiving, and in the assurance that God forgives, sin's power is, so to speak, constantly brought to nought even before it has had time to raise its head afresh. This dialectical movement, from which Christian holiness proceeds, is a matter of experience for the primitive Church; but she is not yet aware of it as a problem.

'Temptations to sin are sure to come. . . . Take heed to yourselves! If your brother sins, rebuke him, and if he repents, forgive him; and if he sins against you seven times in the day, and turns to you seven times, and says, "I repent", you must forgive him'.[1] For the primitive Christian sense of holiness it is self-evident that to pardon sin, and to know no limits to such pardoning, does not imply tolerating, condoning, or overlooking sin. The will to forgive can only pass over into full forgiveness where it is met by the readiness to be forgiven; and this means in effect the readiness to confess one's sin and genuinely to give it up. In this sense the words 'Go, and do not sin again' are already included, explicitly or implicitly, in the forgiving of Jesus himself. The readiness to get rid of the sin is perhaps not a 'condition' of forgiveness, to be laid down and fulfilled as such, but it is the only attitude for which forgiveness can become a reality, and is the result to which it leads. Hence the duty of warning, convicting, and challenging the sinner is part of the duty of mercy and forgiveness, and is relevant most particularly to dealings between Christian 'brethren'. Where there is no contrition and no 'repentance', neither is there any forgiveness.

At first, however, it is less this aspect of the matter which attracts attention than the fact that forgiveness really is available, that within the Church there are no limits to the extent to which one either must or may forgive. This is more than a merely human decision; it is God's decision and God's power, confirmed by the living experience of holy fellowship in the life of the Church. This right to forgive in God's name is claimed as the new possibility open to Christianity as distinct from Judaism.[2] It is in this sense that an old saying, going back to the primitive community, is to be understood, in which Jesus expressly bestows on his disciples the power to bind and to loose: 'Truly, I say to you, whatever you bind on earth shall be bound in heaven, and whatever you

---

[1] Lk. 17:1, 3f.; cf. Matt. 18:7, 15, 21f.
[2] Cf. p. 8f. above (the Healing of the Paralytic) and Matt. 9:8.

loose on earth shall be loosed in heaven.'[3] The total identity between the judgement of the Church and the judgment of God could not be stated more emphatically. The saying does not, for example, start from the premiss that a heavenly decision has already been made, and that it is for the Church to give its judgment in accordance with this, but conversely insists that authority is really and truly vested in the sentence and decision of the Church itself, and that at the Last Day God will concur in this, recognise it as valid, and 'ratify' it.[4] It is therefore a spiritual judgment, made in the Holy Spirit of God,[5] and as such approved by God himself. God's judgment is not merely 'proclaimed' in the Church; it is exercised. Her acts are the present acts of God.[6]

In contemporary Judaism 'binding' and 'loosing' are technical terms,[7] signifying roughly 'forbidding' and 'declaring to be permitted'. This would suggest that the saying derives from the context of the early Palestinian church and its debates about the Law. The expressions are also found, however, as terms for imposing or lifting sentence of

[3] Matt. 18:18; cf. 16:19b; Joh. 20:23. This can hardly be an instance of a genuine saying of Jesus, since it presupposes in any case an already existent community with a defined membership. On the other hand, it must be very early, since it occurs twice in quite different versions within Matthew itself. It may be that neither of the two is original, just as Matt. 18: 15–17 also is not (cf. n. 7 below), since it is given in Lk. 17:3 in an even older form (and without the attached saying about authority). On Matt. 16 cf. p. 129 n. 19 below. Sufficient attention is not always paid to the need to expound the Matt. 18:18 saying first and foremost by itself, without reference to any particular setting.

[4] Cf. J. Jeremias, art. κλείς, TWNT 3, 1938, p. 750.

[5] This is indeed only hinted at by Matthew (16:17; 18:20), and not brought out explicitly until John; cf. p. 139 below.

[6] There is no justification for watering down the verse to make it accord with modern dogmatic viewpoints by drawing fine distinctions, as for example that the disciples 'directly grant only the pardon of the Church, but this has God's pardon as its consequence' (so B. Poschmann, Paenitentia secunda, 1940, pp. 11f., citing a Roman dissertation not accessible to me, F. B. Xiberta, Clavis ecclesiae, 1922. Poschmann himself allows the possibility of the exegesis given in the text).

[7] On what follows cf. (Strack-) Billerbeck, Kommentar zum Neuen Testament aus Talmud und Midrasch I, 1922, pp. 738ff.; R. Bultmann, Die Geschichte der synoptischen Tradition², 1931, p. 147 n. 1; F. Büchsel, art. δέω (λύω), TWNT 2, 1935, pp. 59f.; also R. Hermann, 'Das christliche "Selbstverständnis" und der Glaube an Gott in Christo—unter besonderer Berücksichtigung der "Schlüssel des Himmelreichs"', ZST 14, 1937, p. 697 n. 2. Hermann's attempt to interpret ἐκκλησία in this passage in terms of the Jewish congregation, and thus to salvage the pericope as a saying of Jesus, is not, however, feasible. Instead, as O. Michel, Das Zeugnis des Neuen Testaments von der Gemeinde, 1941, p. 10 n., remarks: 'Both Matt. 16:18 and 18:17 point to the complete separation of the Christian community from Israel; in Matt. 16:18 this is predicted, in Matt. 18:17 it is presupposed.' Two writers who see some influence from Jewish excommunication practice are: R. Bohren, Das Problem der Kirchenzucht im Neuen Testament, 1952, p. 27; E. Kohlmeyer, 'Charisma oder Rechts? Vom Wesen des ältesten Kirchenrechts,' ZRG 69, Kan. Abt. 38, 1952, pp. 2ff.

excommunication, and it is this meaning which comes to be of importance in the Church. Nevertheless, the two references go together. The 'teaching' of the Church is never a one-sidedly dogmatic thing, it also includes moral instruction; and the power to teach, when exercised 'with authority', always covers the power to discipline as well. The one meaning derives directly from the other.

How the application of this spiritual authority is to be thought of in concrete terms is perhaps shown by the incorporation of the old saying into a piece of instruction in church law which is handed down in the eighteenth chapter of Matthew as an address of Jesus to his disciples. In style the passage is like an ecclesiastical ordinance, and lays down the general rule for dealing with a brother who has sinned. On the nature of the sins in question nothing is said; no difference is made whether the transgression is light or serious, unconscious and involuntary or deliberate and with full knowledge, or whether it has been committed only against men or 'against God'.[8] These distinctions, which were already important in Judaism and were later to become so in the Church, as yet play no part. Anyone who detects his brother in sin is obliged, without further ado, to challenge him with it and to convict him.[9] If he is successful, then he has 'gained' the brother who was in danger, that is, the sinner has broken with his sin, it has been forgiven him, and brotherly fellowship exists as it did before. If not, however, then one or two more persons are to be brought in, so that in accordance with the Old Testament rule the matter may be established 'by two or three witnesses'. This is not, of course, a case of witnesses in the proper sense; the enlargement of the group is simply to intensify the urgency of the exhortation. If this attempt too fails, then the case comes before the judgment of the whole congregation; and if the sinner is not prepared to listen even to this, then he must be abandoned. So far as the Church is concerned, he is then nothing more than a 'heathen and a publican', that is, fellowship with him can no longer be restored, and what happens to him is none of the Church's business.[10] All possibilities have been exhausted, and as regards the Church and his own salvation he is lost.[11] The section closes with the saying about

[8] The reading ἁμαρτήσῃ εἰς σέ in Matt. 18:15 has been inserted from Lk. 17:4, and is not original.

[9] 'This word ἐλέγχειν is not just to "reprove" or "reprimand", nor merely to "convict" in the sense of demonstrating that the offence has been committed, nor again simply to "make known" or "public", but "to show someone the right path", that is, "to turn them from sin to repentance" ': F. Büchsel, art. ἐλέγχω, TWNT 2, 1935, p. 471.

[10] ὁ ἐθνικὸς καὶ ὁ τελώνης is here used in the traditional Jewish sense to denote a notorious sinner. Jesus's own intimacy with publicans and sinners is irrelevant in this context.

[11] As against Michel, op. cit., p. 67, I find not a shred of evidence to suggest the idea of an eventual return of the sinner.

binding and loosing both on earth and in heaven; the sentence that has been passed is valid and binding with God as well as with men.

Plainly the assembly of the congregation here plays the part of a final and definitive court of appeal. How it is organised, graded, or directed in such a case, or indeed whether it is at all, we have no means of knowing.[12] That the direction may have been in the hands of elders or of an 'apostle' cannot be ruled out, but there is not a single word to suggest it, and it cannot therefore have played any very decisive role. It is the Church as a whole in which this great power is vested. Her essentially spiritual character, grounded in the presence of Christ, is taken as axiomatic: 'Where two or three are gathered in my name, there am I in the midst of them.'[13] Moreover, there seem to be no juristic problems; the possibility of judgments being at fault is not considered, instead it is assumed automatically that the brethren will be unanimous and clear as to their verdict. The full assembly of the congregation can hardly be thought of as an appellate court, or as machinery to control and supervise the earlier, private 'courts'; rather it serves once more to intensify the efforts to warn and convict the sinner, before final sentence is passed. The text envisages this primarily in terms of a negative result, since it mentions only the ultimate penalty of excommunication as the extreme possibility. Of a corresponding form of 'loosing' there is no word, and it therefore cannot simply be assumed to have existed as a formal act. Nevertheless, forgiveness and not punishment is the real aim of the proceedings. That the congregation cannot tolerate any sin in their midst is indeed taken for granted, and admits of no exceptions; but nowhere is there any suggestion of interest in a typically 'ecclesiastical' concern to safeguard order, purity, or general discipline. The point of it all, the only point in fact mentioned in the text, is the winning back of the erring brother. As soon as it is seen that this has been achieved, all has come right, and the proceedings are at an end. Nor is there any question of punishment or expiation.[14] The explicit concern of the whole process with salvation and forgiveness is especially emphasised by the fact that in Matthew the pericope is incorporated into a complex dealing precisely with the duty and joy of forgiveness; it is preceded by the sayings on the rescue of the lost,[15] and followed by

[12] I would like to stress this even more emphatically than has been done by Bultmann, *Tradition*, pp. 150f., Jeremias, κλείς, p. 751, and Poschmann, *op. cit.*, p. 7, in their respective somewhat different interpretations.

[13] Matt. 18:20. The connection with the preceding passage is not original.

[14] Hence the 'binding' which cuts off the offender is not to be regarded as a means for bringing ecclesiastical pressure or coercion to bear: cf. Campenhausen, 'Recht und Gehorsam in der ältesten Kirche', *ThBl* 20, 1941, p. 293, in criticism of the position of W. Schönfeld, 'Die juristische Methode im Kirchenrecht', *ARW* 18, 1924–5, p. 81.

[15] Matt. 18:10–14.

the admonition to be ever ready to forgive and by the parable of the Unmerciful Servant.[16]

Closely connected with this passage are the famous words, preserved only by Matthew, bestowing the keys of the kingdom on Peter, where the saying conferring authority to bind and to loose is used yet again.[17] It is hardly possible to decide which of the two settings is the earlier. That the founding of the Church on Peter is unthinkable in the mouth of Jesus it is impossible to doubt,[18] despite recent attempts to prove the contrary.[19] The only real question is whether the saying derives from the primitive community or arose later. In contrast to the form of the saying already discussed the words conferring authority are here directed to Peter in person and are linked with a promise to him. Peter receives the keys, and is thus, in accordance with a widespread oriental image, declared to be the powerful steward of the house, which represents the Church. The latter is already understood as the beginning, or the earthly preparatory stage, of the kingdom of God, which the demonic keepers of hell's gates[20] cannot overcome. Jesus himself bestows this dignity on Peter, in response to the latter's confession of him as the Son of God, a confession which he was the first and only one to make, and that—as is expressly remarked—not by any natural capacities but by virtue of an illumination from Jesus's Father in heaven. Consequently, the concept of 'binding' and 'loosing' may now contain a stronger emphasis on the apostolic 'teaching authority'; but this does not mean that the disciplinary significance of the words is

[16] Matt. 18:21f., 23ff. If the parable of the tares among the wheat (Matt. 13:24) may be interpreted of the Church, then it contains a warning against violently separating the righteous from the wicked, a task which can only be performed at the Last Day: cf. J. Jeremias, *The Parables of Jesus*, 1955, pp. 53ff.

[17] For the following exegesis cf. esp. Bultmann, *Tradition*, pp. 147ff., and Jeremias, κλείς, pp. 744ff.

[18] Cf. R. Bultmann, 'Die Frage der Echtheit von Matth. 16, 17–19,' *ThBl* 20, 1941, pp. 265ff.; W. G. Kümmel, *Kirchenbegriff und Geschichtsbewusstsein in der Urgemeinde und bei Jesus*, 1943, pp. 37ff.; H. Strathmann, 'Die Stellung des Petrus in der Urkirche: zur Frühgeschichte des Wortes an Petrus Matth. 16, 17–19,' *ZST* 20, 1943, pp. 223ff.

[19] Cf. especially the comprehensive study by A. Oepke, 'Der Herrnspruch über der Kirche Matth. 16, 17–19 in der neuesten Forschung,' *Stud. Theol.* 2, 1950, pp. 110ff. In support of his argument Oepke reconstructs the messianic self-consciousness of Jesus, and makes great use not only of metrical considerations, but also of the suspicion of psychological and dogmatic prejudice on the part of his opponents. R. N. Flew, *Jesus and his Church*[2], 1945, pp. 89ff., also is inclined to accept the 'keys' saying as genuine. Most recently on this side cf. O. Cullmann, *Peter*, 1956, pp. 164ff. (A full-scale discussion is unfortunately impossible within the limits of the present work.)

[20] The original reading may have been שֹׁעֲרֵי = πυλωροί, not שְׁעֲרֵי = πύλαι, according to the attractive conjecture of R. Eppel, 'L'interprétation de Matthieu 16, 18b,' in *Aux sources de la tradition chrétienne* (Festschrift M. Goguel), 1950.

ruled out.[21] It is precisely in this context that the concept of authority must be made as comprehensive as possible. Peter has become the teacher and governor of the Church, which is founded upon him and his testimony. As such he has not one nor even two keys but, so to speak, the whole bunch in his hand.

If the provenance of these words is sought, as it usually is, in the primitive community at Jerusalem, one runs into serious difficulties. Even though Peter may from the very beginning have played a prominent and directing role, nevertheless the idea that the government of the whole Church was solemnly and exclusively conferred on him accords neither with the statements of Paul[22] nor with the picture which Acts draws of his activities in Jerusalem. However strongly the latter emphasises his importance, yet Peter at all times remains simply the leader and spokesman of the apostolic band.[23] In the later stages of the history of the Jerusalem church there is absolutely no room for such a saying. Peter has taken himself off 'to another place',[24] the Twelve have vanished altogether, and James, the Lord's brother, stands alone at the head of the congregation.[25] If one wishes to maintain a Jerusalem provenance for the promise to Peter, then it can be regarded at the most as the tendentious creation of a Petrine party, which was unable to implement its programme. This is not a very enlightening conclusion, and the text itself in any case provides no basis for a polemical exegesis of this sort.

It is more likely, therefore, that we should abandon Jerusalem altogether as the home of our pericope. It is an established fact that before his probably quite brief sojourn in Rome Peter must have worked for a longer period outside Palestine, and that later there were even Gentile congregations which honoured him, and not Paul, as their normative missionary. It is easy to conceive that the Petrine tradition was particularly cultivated and expanded in such circles. This may have been the case, for example, in Antioch or elsewhere on Syrian soil, where Judaeo-Christianity was also strong.[26] The promise to Peter is

[21] The same double connotation attaches to the concept in the Syrian *Didascalia*. It is true that primarily the Syrians always think of the authority to excommunicate and to absolve: 'They are, however, well aware of the image of "binding" by laws and regulations, and occasionally apply this to the field of ecclesiastical jurisdiction' (V. Brandner, ' "Binden und Lösen" in der altsyrischen Kirche,' *Katholik* 96, 1916, p. 302). Bohren, *op. cit.*, pp. 55ff., 83f., considers the possibility of a demonological meaning.

[22] Cf. pp. 17f. above.   [23] Cf. Strathmann, *op. cit.*, p. 253.   [24] Acts 12:17.

[25] In the Judaeo-Christian *Epistle of Peter* in the Pseudo-Clementines Peter is simply a teacher and missionary who has to account to James in Jerusalem as the head of the whole Church: cf. C. Schmidt, *Studien zu den Pseudo-Clementinen*, 1929, pp. 322ff., and p. 179f. below.

[26] Cf. B. H. Streeter, *The Four Gospels*, 1924, pp. 500ff., Strathmann, *op. cit.*, pp. 254ff.; *contra* Oepke, 'Herrnspruch', pp. 131ff.

best understood as a piece of retrospective veneration on the part of a congregation devoted to him. This is supported by the non-Pauline outlook, which no longer distinguishes between the word and the person of the apostle. Peter, the first witness of the Resurrection, the founder of their own churches, is now seen as the normative founder-figure of the Church as a whole. The latter stands on the foundation laid by him, and has received from him, together with the confession of Christ, also the comprehensive authority to bind and to loose. There is no need to look for a conscious opposition to James, or Paul, or any other apostle.[27] This also explains the 'monarchical' form of the present passage only two chapters before the 'democratic' version in terms of the congregation as a whole.[28] The two forms may quite happily be left in peaceful co-existence; for it is one and the same authority which in the one instance is exercised by Peter and the apostles, and now in the other by the whole Church.[29]

Concerning the manner in which this authority was exercised in practice unfortunately nothing can be deduced from the saying to Peter. All we have are legendary descriptions which tell us how a latter generation liked to imagine the power of the keys being used in the hands of a Peter. The story of Ananias and Sapphira, which Luke gives as his first example of Christian failure, concerns a typical case of dishonesty in matters of property, which disturbs the peace of the congregation.[30] But fault is found less with the 'covetousness' than with the stealth and deception involved. The guilty parties sought to

[27] The situation here is different from that in Joh. 21:15ff., where the command to Peter to feed Christ's sheep, while indeed equally the product of retrospective interpretation, patently clashes with other traditions: cf. E. Hirsch, *Studien zum vierten Evangelium*, 1936, pp. 179ff.

[28] A similar collocation occurs in the *Epistle of the Apostles*: in ch. 42 (Coptic version 53) the commission is explicitly given to the apostles as a group, and in 48 (59) this is followed by a passage modelled simply on Matth. 18. There is no hint of 'successors' to the apostles; this is not, however, to be explained, as J. Hoh, *Die kirchliche Busse im 2. Jahrhundert*, 1932, pp. 71f., thinks, in terms of the fictional character of the document—it is precisely in a case like this that one would expect a 'prophetic' forecast (cf. pp. 80f., 91 above)—but simply shows how far this question, of such decisive importance for the modern obsession with 'office', was from the minds of writers even at this date.

[29] The theory that Matt. 16:17f. is a Roman interpolation no longer needs to be refuted. Equally arbitrary is the view put forward by E. Buonaiuti, 'Marcione e Egesippo,' *Religio* 12, 1936, pp. 401ff., that the passage is an anti-Marcionite fabrication from the hand of Hegesippus.

[30] Acts 5:1-11. The theory of P. H. Menoud, 'La mort d'Ananias et de Sapphira, Actes 5, 1-11,' *Aux sources de la tradition chrétienne* (Festschrift M. Goguel), 1950, that Ananias and Sapphira were the first members of the Church to die, and that, because it was thought that Christians would no longer have to die, therefore a special reason for their deaths had to be found, is completely fantastic.

deceive the apostles and the congregation over what had happened, and thus 'tempted the Spirit of the Lord'.[31] Peter, however, enlightened by this same Spirit, at once sees through their machinations, and takes them to task before the assembled church. The narrative is not really interested in the question of 'penance' or church discipline, but chiefly with bringing out the holiness of the Church and the miraculous power of the apostles. At Peter's words Ananias falls dead to the ground, and his wife, who persists in the same lie, meets with the same punishment. 'And great fear came upon the whole church, and upon all who heard of these things.'[32] Nothing quite so sensational occurs in one further instance preserved in Acts.[33] Simon Magus, who has been baptised, attempts to buy from the apostles the gift of bestowing the Spirit, and for this reason Peter proclaims his doom: 'You have neither part nor lot in this matter.'[34] At the same time, however, he demands that Simon should repent and pray to Christ, and the account ends with the sinner, now thoroughly subdued, requesting the apostles themselves to intercede for him in order to prevent the execution of the sentence which has been passed.

These, as we have said, are legendary accounts, concerned to demonstrate the miraculous powers of the apostles;[35] their statements should not be pressed to yield juristic information. It is indeed quite conceivable that in the primitive period many a prophet or elder attempted to act in much the same way as is here narrated of Peter.[36] It is clear, however, that an organised public discipline of penance was in general unknown to the congregations of the first and of the early second century. The passage from Matt. 18 discussed above in this respect stands on its own. Here certainly a definite, regulated practice is envisaged, or at any rate the ideal of such a thing is sketched out; but the area in which this applied cannot have been great. The use of this completely unproblematic procedure is only conceivable under the very simplest conditions. The decisive point, however, is the silence of every other source.[37] There is no lack of references to repentance as such; but it is seen as exclusively a matter between the sinner on the

[31] Acts 5:9.   [32] Acts 5:11.
[33] Acts 8:9–13, 18–24.
[34] Acts 8:21.
[35] Acts 5:12.
[36] Cf. Rev. 2:22f. Such details cannot, however, be used as evidence for an established general principle. In particular, the theory of A. Bugge, *Das Problem der ältesten Kirchenverfassung*, 1924, pp. 43f., that absolution, as an 'application of the infallible word of God to the individual case', was regarded as a privilege of the pneumatic, is impossible to accept. Bohren, *op. cit.*, pp. 114ff., expounds the passage strictly in terms of 'canon law', and thus reads far too much into it.
[37] The vague assertion of Kohlmeyer, *op. cit.*, p. 21, that 'the development of penitential discipline in the second century on the whole follows the lines laid down in Matt. 18', leaves out of account all the vital historical differences.

one hand and God, or the fellow-man with whom he needs to be reconciled, on the other. We hear constantly of the general requirement to repent, to avoid sin,[38] to admonish the erring brother,[39] and to make use of intercession by appropriate persons.[40] Occasionally, as in Judaism, there is also the command that sin should be 'confessed'.[41] None of this, however, implies any set form of ecclesiastical act, unless one wishes to count 'liturgical' prayer in general as such.[42] The congregation as a corporate body has no official penitential procedure; and nothing of this sort can be inferred from the *Anathema* in the eucharistic liturgy.[43] Hence, so far as we can see, the leaders of the congregation nowhere exercise an individual pastoral ministry, and the power formally to bind and to loose individual members is not put into practice by them in any regular or organised way.

Quite different from this 'power of the keys' in the narrow sense are the beginnings of a general 'church discipline', which is concerned not with the salvation of the individual but with the sanctity of the congregation as a whole, which has to be kept free of gross sinners, and pruned, so to say, of its dead wood. In this context the model of Jewish excommunication may be relevant.[44] At first, however, this church disci-

---

[38] All the relevant texts are discussed *in extenso* by H. Windisch, *Taufe und Sünde im ältesten Christentum bis auf Origenes,* 1908, and B. Poschmann, *op. cit.,* and some of them by J. Hoh, *op. cit.* Windisch's exegesis is encumbered by the theory that in principle early Christianity knew of no forgiveness for serious post-baptismal sin; on this point, cf. pp. 217ff. below. But Hoh and Poschmann (the latter being the more cautious) also consider that in the early period there was as yet no official institution of penance, and detect, at the most, embryonic forms which point in this direction for the future.

[39] James 5:19f.; Barn. 19:4; Did. 4:3; 15:3; I Clem. 56:2; II Clem. 17:2; 19:2; Ep. apost. 47f. (copt. 58f.).

[40] James 5:15; I Clem. 56:1; II Clem. 15:1; 17:2f.

[41] James 5:16; I Clem. 52:1; I. Joh. 1:9; Barn. 19:12; Did. 14:1.

[42] No more than this is implied by the reference to confession of sin in Did. 4:14, 'somewhat in the sense of the later *Confiteor*' (Poschmann, p. 90). As Matt. 5:23f., 6:14f., *par.,* had already demanded, one should not come to receive the sacrament before being reconciled with one's brother: cf. Did. 14:2; Barn. 19:12; Polycarp, Phil. 6:2.

[43] The formula 'Anathema—Maranatha' (I Cor. 16:22), like the parallel formula in Did. 10:6, does not convey any 'disciplinary instructions for any kind of human court (be it the congregation as a whole or a bench of judges), entitling them to use the power of the keys against this or that unworthy member, to excommunicate this or that particular person, but it states the decision laid down by God for this specific situation. By leaving the offender to God's judgment, it thus places the responsibility entirely on the person concerned, and makes the *anathema* a summons to self-examination': G. Bornkamn, *Das Ende des Gesetzes. Paulusstudien,* 1952, p. 125.

[44] Cf. the material in (Strack-) Billerbeck I, p. 739; IV., pp. 239 ff. The importance of this institution, even in Judaism, should not be over-estimated. The studies by E. Dietrich, *Die Umkehr (Bekehrung und Busse) im Alten Testament und im Judentum,* 1936, and E. Sjöberg, *Gott und die Sünder im palästinen-*

pline is concerned only with extreme cases and exceptions; and settled, universally applicable regulations are not worked out until a much later period. Of course the Christian community at no time tolerated blatant flouting of its fundamental way of life; and if we wish to form a picture of the situation in the early days, the Pauline Epistles are much the richest source of information.[45] Nowhere is there any mention of a definite procedure such as that found in Matthew; but throughout there are traces of the wearisome struggle against the reversion to type and the degeneration which were fostered not simply by the powerful pressures of the heathen environment but also by the irresponsibility of an over-spiritual enthusiasm. It is cause for astonished admiration that despite this Paul never allowed himself to be driven along the road of a convenient, legalist casuistry, but held fast to the nature and re-sponsibility of the new being, the living obligation of every Christian, undertaken at baptism, as both the goal and the starting-point in terms of which every decision 'in freedom' must be thought out and taken. But the line has to be drawn somewhere, and the gulf between what the 'saints' once were and what they now are must never again be bridged.[46] Otherwise God himself intervenes to punish, and sends sickness or death to recall the erring.[47] Lack of moral discipline may reign in the world—Christians can do nothing to alter that; but when a brother (or, in this case, merely a 'so-called brother') wants to live the life of a lecher, a thief, a rogue, an idolator, a slanderer, or a drunkard, then the congregation should not maintain their association with such a person—'not even to eat with such a one'.[48] 'A little leaven leavens the whole lump',[49] that is to say, failure on the part of one member means the danger of infection for all. Paul is shocked that a Christian who dared to marry his own stepmother has not been instantly ejected from the congregation. He makes up for their deficiencies by passing judgment himself; and he apparently expects that the man who has been expelled will, as in the case of Ananias, be at once destroyed by Satan, in other words, that he will die.[50] In less serious cases the advice is given

sischen Judentum, 1938, find it hardly necessary to mention it. Further literature cited in Bohren, op. cit., pp. 23ff. It appears to play a larger part in the Damascus Document and in the Dead Sea Scrolls (? Essene).

[45] Cf. pp. 44ff. above.   [46] I Cor. 6:11.   [47] I Cor. 11:30.
[48] I Cor. 5:9–11; cf. 6:9f.   [49] I Cor. 5:6; Gal. 5:9.
[50] I Cor. 5:1–5. The concluding words in particular are crucial, and difficult: ἵνα τὸ πνεῦμα σωθῇ ἐν τῇ ἡμέρᾳ κυρίου Lietzmann, An die Korinther[4], 1949, p. 23, takes them to refer to 'the soul united with the spirit of Christ'; R. Bultmann, Theology of the New Testament I, 1952, p. 208f.—despite the fact that in the previous verse, within the very same sentence, πνεῦμα is unmistakably the divine spirit bestowed on the Christian—interprets it as 'the person, the true ego, here contrasted with σάρξ, the physical and corporeal life'. On either of these interpretations the meaning is, as it has always been thought to be, that

to make known to the congregation the names of those persons whose way of life leaves something to be desired, so that the rest may avoid them until they mend their ways. Such people, however, still count as brethren, and are to be brought back to the right path.[51]

On the other hand, we also find in Paul the strongest exhortations to forbearance, patience, and readiness to forgive, between all members of the same congregation.[52] Such instructions do not simply repeat the old, primitive Christian rules regarding the relationship of brother to brother, but also mirror in their own way the special difficulties of the young missionary congregations. Lack of clear understanding, and the blind zeal of their first enthusiasm, constantly threaten to embroil the newly converted in quarrels and differences of opinion, and Paul has to warn them against censoriousness, factionalism, and lack of love. One member is not to criticise another, and to seek to set up new laws; instead one should mind one's own business, and allow one's neighbour his own freedom and responsibility—the ultimate judgment belongs to Christ, and will be revealed only at the Last Day.[53] In civil disputes, if the worst comes to the worst, then an arbitration court should be set up, formed of experienced members of the Church; to go to law in the pagan courts is unworthy of a Christian.[54]

---

the sinner will be redeemed in a future life, even though nothing else in Paul supports this sense. (Bohren, op. cit., p. 112, takes the same line, though with a different explanation.) One thing, however, is not in doubt, even on this exegesis, and that is the expulsion of the offender from the Church; but M. Goguel, L'église primitive, 1947, pp. 242ff. (followed by W. G. Kümmel, in the rev. edn. of Lietzmann's Commentary, p. 174) disagrees. In my own view, the verses immediately following, down as far as the closing O.T. quotation, ἐξάρατε τὸν πονηρὸν ἐξ ὑμῶν αὐτῶν (v. 13), which are an integral part of the section in question, show unequivocally that expulsion is intended. In all probability we should look for an explanation along quite different lines. Günther Bornkamm has convinced me in conversation that here as in the rest of Paul πνεῦμα must be distinguished from the human ego which it indwells. What is meant is that the divine power which has been bestowed on the congregation and on the apostle (5:4), and in which the sinner also had his share, ought no longer to be left in his possession, but must be 'rescued' by his death, in order that it may form part of the perfection and wholeness of the Body of Christ at the Last Day.

[51] II Thess. 3:6–16 (?Pauline); cf. Gal. 6:1.

[52] Paul himself here shows them the way by his own example: II Cor. 2:3–11. To equate this offender with the man expelled for 'incest' in I Cor. 5:1ff. is quite impossible, and is attempted only to serve the dogmatic purposes of the theology of penance; this view is rejected as early as Tertullian (cf. p. 222 below). Probably, as Kümmel, op. cit., p. 198, emphasises, what is at issue is not a personal injury done to Paul, but a wrong which 'made the relationship between Paul and the congregation virtually impossible'.

[53] Cf., for example, Rom. 14; I Cor. 13; Gal. 5:13–6:5; Col. 3:12ff.; and pp. 58ff. above.

[54] I Cor. 6:1–17. The principle corresponds to the practice of the congrega-

These two seemingly opposite tendencies in Paul's exhortations are in fact complementary. Both in their stringency and in their tolerance they reflect the needs of one and the same community, which has to defend its purity and solidarity against attack from without, and to preserve peace and quietness within. Paul's decisions, on the question of sin as on every other, are in accordance with this situation. Pastoral problems relating to individuals are not discussed. Of the theological problem of 'Christian sin', at any rate in its acute form, Paul knows nothing, and the later question whether post-baptismal sin could or could not be forgiven is not as such dealt with in his writings. For the same reason there is no question either of concrete, contingent absolution within the Church. Paul made no use of the beginnings from which such a thing might have grown, even if he was aware that they existed in the early Christian congregations. The simultaneous intensification of the idea of community and of essential discipline tended rather to restrict and check such a development than to advance it.

At first it may have been the lesser Christian groups, in particular those of a gnosticising tendency and other 'personal followings', which seized on this question of the cure of individual souls, and, so to speak, discovered it for the Church at large.[55] In such circles the practice of 'perfection', and the exchange of spiritual counsel, meant that sin became a daily experience and a powerful temptation, calling for means to understand and overcome it. Today, however, this development is discernible to us only in I John, which is a companion piece to the Fourth Gospel in its present form, and is at least closely connected with the other Johannine Epistles. In the preceding chapter we have already attempted to give a sketch of the free spirituality of the Johannine world, with its horror of all hierarchical organisation and its intense confidence in the power of the 'truth'.[56] I John deals, to use modern terminology, with the basic problems of theological ethics, and in doing so is especially careful to distinguish its own position from that of gnostic libertinism, which as it makes clear over and over again, is essentially bound up with the docetic gnostic christology.[57] There is no mention either of practical rules for church order or of particular

---

tions of the Jewish Diaspora, though the motives are different: 'For the Jew, the reason for handling his own legal cases lay in his desire to deal with them in accordance with the Jewish Law': A. D. Nock, *Paul*, 1930.

[55] Something of the sort may perhaps be conjectured from the polemical colour of II Tim. 3:6. Irenaeus, *Adv.haer.* I, 13, 3; I, 13, 5f., also mentions the preference of such pastors for respectable women of high station.

[56] Cf. pp. 121ff. above.

[57] Cf. T. Häring, 'Gedankengang und Grundgedanken des ersten Johannesbriefes,' *Theologische Abhandlungen, Carl von Weizsäcker gewidmet*, 1892, pp. 173ff., especially 187ff.

gross sins; but 'sin' in general, and its conquest by true faith in Christ, has become the crucial problem.[58]

The fundamental confession of Christ which forms the introduction to the Epistle begins at once with an explication of the reality of the Christian life in which two seemingly mutually exclusive lines of thought are set side by side with uncompromising clarity: on the one hand, the Christian knows no sin, and cannot sin, if his faith is not to be a lie; on the other, the Christian does know sin, and he deceives himself, and makes God a liar, if he claims that he is sinless.[59] This contradiction cannot be resolved by referring the two lines of thought to different people, degrees of sin, and suchlike, thus by theoretical adjustment blurring the distinction between them and robbing them of their radical meaning.[60] The contradiction bears witness to a genuine movement, an event, the essence of which is fully expressed from the human side in confession of sin, and from the Godward side in the fact that Jesus Christ, the one who is truly righteous, comes to meet this confession halfway.[61] Hence the believer—to use Lutheran terminology—is simultaneously *iustus et peccator*. In his union with Christ the Christian acquires real holiness, the Evil One cannot fasten on to him, and sin loses its dominion and death-dealing power over him. Sin exists; but it no longer determines his life, because he no longer clings to it. The sanctified sinner has given up his sin and been forgiven for it, as shown by the fact that he prays for forgiveness and himself extends it to others.

[58] The fact that sin is a universal human experience is, of course, frequently expressed elsewhere: cf., for example, 'the first Christian confession of sin' (Windisch, *op. cit.*, p. 218) in James 3:2, and the second, even more comprehensive one in Polycarp, Phil. 6:1 (cf. *ibid.*, p. 353). In these cases, however, the attempt is made to get over the problem simply by exhortation or encouragement without pursuing the matter any more deeply. [59] I Joh. 1:5–2:6.

[60] A good survey of the many different attempts to interpret the passage, most of them aiming at some solution of this kind, may be found in A. Kirchgässner, *Erlösung und Sünde im Neuen Testament*, 1950, pp. 268ff. His own suggestion, that the remarks concern sinning which does not 'normally' occur, and relate specifically to the teachers of false doctrine, has no basis in the text.

[61] R. Bultmann, 'Analyse des Ersten Johannesbriefes,' in *Festg. Ad. Jülicher*, 1927, p. 138, and 'Die kirchliche Redaktion des Ersten Johannesbriefes', in *In memoriam Ernst Lohmeyer*, 1951, pp. 199ff., is of the opinion that the reference to atonement through the blood of Christ was only added by the redactor, and that the meaning of the confession of sin has thereby been distorted to accord with church dogmatics. H. Braun, 'Literar-Analyse und theologische Schichtung im ersten Johannesbrief,' *ZTK* 48, 1951, pp. 272ff., takes the same view, though somewhat more cautiously. Nevertheless, even Bultmann admits that the 'conjunction of the two ideas may be a genuine Christian paradox'; on this point cf. also E. Lohmeyer, 'Uber Aufbau und Gliederung des ersten Johannesbriefs,' *ZNW* 27, 1928, pp. 231f., 259; F. Büchsel, 'Zu den Johannesbriefen,' *ZNW* 28, 1929, pp. 240f.; E. Käsemann, 'Ketzer und Zeuge,' *ZTK* 48, 1951, pp. 306ff. In what follows Gospel and Epistles—and thus the theology of the 'redactor'—are treated as a unity.

There is, however, one absolute limit to this inexhaustible sanctity of faith; there is a 'sin unto death'. Once this point has been passed, destruction begins, and in view of this, intercession for the sinner becomes impossible.[62] The context makes it clear that this mysterious sin can only mean apostasy from Christ,[63] 'in' whom Christians live; for apostasy entails abandoning the necessary precondition for the emergence of the new being, and the foundation which alone can support it.[64] Apart, however, from this one, extremely significant exception, there is nothing which can separate the Christian from salvation. A casuistic discrimination between sins is, it would appear, deliberately rejected, since it diverts the Christian in the wrong direction away from the seriousness of guilt. It is the Christian above all who must see sin as it is: 'All wrongdoing is sin'.[65]

A faith which has grasped this fact is also acquainted with 'temptation'. John is, it seems, the first theologian who speaks quite explicitly of being tempted by sin,[66] since even Paul did not do so. In exactly the same way as Paul, however, when the latter speaks of the distress of alienation from God in the limitations of our humanity, and of the frustration of earthly life,[67] the writer of our epistle finds his only refuge in the Holy Spirit, which is his advocate with God,[68] and which gives him the assurance that his prayers will be heard. The Spirit overcomes temptation by enduing men with 'boldness', and by making it possible for the unquiet and accusing heart nevertheless to have somewhere to stand before God. At the same time he grants them the 'love' which shows itself in solid, practical action between brethren.[69] 'By this we know that we are of the truth, and reassure our hearts before him.'[70] 'And this is the boldness that we have toward him, that if we ask anything according to his will, he hears us.'[71]

It may be asked to what extent the confession of sin, the temptation, and the granting of prayer, spoken of in I John, have to be thought of as completely interior events. The words used nowhere compel us to infer a definite procedure of open confession followed by the pronoun-

[62] I Joh. 5:16.

[63] Cf. I Joh. 5:21, where the reference is either to the gnostic libertinism of sacrificial meals in honour of false gods or directly to paganism. Braun, op. cit., p. 282, would prefer to restrict the reference to the false teachers.

[64] Bultmann, 'Redaktion', pp. 192ff., would prefer to ascribe the section 5:14–21 to the redactor; but in my opinion he fails to do full justice to the special nature of this case when he sees it as destroying the whole character of the Johannine concept of sin. Braun, op. cit., p. 277, also uses misleading generalisations, when he speaks of 'different kinds of sins, for which intercession is or is not effective'. For more on this problem, cf. p. 222 n. 41 below.

[65] I Joh. 5:17; cf. 3:4; also Bultmann, 'Analyse', p. 147.

[66] I Joh. 3:20.   [67] Rom. 8:26f.; cf. II Cor. 12:9.   [68] I Joh. 2:1.

[69] I Joh. 2:10; 3:11, 14, 18; 4:11f., 20.

[70] I Joh. 3:19.   [71] I Joh. 5:14.

cing of absolution. On the other hand, however, if we note what importance is attached to making brotherly fellowship a reality of the most
intense and passionate kind, it is hard to imagine that these spiritual
experiences did not correspond to personal spiritual encounters, or that
there was not the kind of pastoral care which we find, for example, in
early monasticism. Be that as it may, 'John' knew something about the
power of the concrete and individual word of help and encouragement,
when this is spoken with authority. It is against this background that
we are to interpret the distinctive form which the Fourth Gospel gives
to Jesus's final appearance to his disciples. Here the old saying conferring the authority to bind and to loose occurs for the last time.[72] John,
who elsewhere has rejected so much synoptic material or found no use
for it, has not only preserved this saying, but has made a most prominent place for it in his Gospel. On the very occasion when the risen Jesus
simultaneously appears for the first time to his assembled disciples and
also takes his leave of them, he bequeaths to them this word. Till that
moment the disciples had been shut away in anxiety and loneliness;[73]
now joy reawakens within them,[74] because the risen Lord gives them
'peace'.[75] He breathes into them his own Spirit,[76] and commits to them
his own authority: 'Receive the Holy Spirit. If you forgive the sins of
any, they are forgiven; if you retain the sins of any, they are retained.'[77]
Easter and Pentecost have become one. Jesus has not left his own deso-
late, like 'orphans';[78] for the power of his Spirit remains with them to
'help' them,[79] and in that power they themselves can now bestow forgiveness and achieve dominion over sin.

The inversion which John has made in his traditional material is
significant. In both versions in Matthew the 'binding' of sin comes
before the 'loosing'. The effect of this is to emphasise the disciplinary
aspect of church authority, that which is concerned with protecting
the community against the sinner. By contrast John puts the right of
forgiveness first, and the retaining of sin remains in undiminished force
only as, so to speak, the reverse of this. It should not be supposed that
this was because John was 'liberal' in his attitude to sinners. On the
contrary, it was his wish that Christians should not even exchange

[72] That Joh. 20:23 is simply a variant form of Matt. 16:19; 18:18, follows from
the similarity of meaning and structure, and cannot be disputed. All that has
been dropped is the semitisms. Κρατεῖν in the sense which it must have here
is, in any case, quite unusual: cf. R. Bultmann, *Das Evangelium des Johannes*,
1941, p. 537 n. 4.

[73] Joh. 20:19.   [74] Joh. 20:20.   [75] Joh. 20:19, 21.

[76] This is a gesture of blessing: cf. F. Horst, 'Segen und Segenshandlung in
der Bibel', *Ev. Theol.* 7, 1947–8, p. 28.

[77] Joh. 20:22f. E. Meyer, *Ursprung und Anfänge des Christentums* I, 1921, p. 30,
renders: 'If you confirm the sins of anyone, they are confirmed.'

[78] Joh. 14:18.   [79] Joh. 14:16, 26.

greetings with one who denied the truth about Christ, 'for he who greets him shares in his wicked work'.[80] But in the power to forgive, John sees something to which the Church must attach supreme value, because she herself lives by the power of forgiveness. It is not merely particular individual sinners who need forgiveness, but all Christians; and they are continually instructed to receive it. The power of the keys is the primary authority of the Christian Church in general.

One further small alteration is perhaps worthy of attention. According to Matthew sins forgiven on earth *shall* be forgiven in heaven—the saying is here looking forwards to the coming Last Judgment. For John, however, sin, as soon as it has been forgiven here, *has* already also *been* forgiven in heaven.[81] Inasmuch as the eschatological decision is hereby transferred into the present, this corresponds to a universal characteristic of Johannine theology, and calls for no further notice; but the perfect tense is significant none the less. It underscores the contemporary relevance of the consoling word of grace for the tempted, who yearn not for assurance as to the future but for actual forgiveness, and thus 'boldness', in the present.[82] It is a matter of inward, spiritual distress, not of the fulfilment of wishes for the future.[83]

This is the reason why the gift of the Spirit is so solemnly emphasised in the present passage. This and the power to forgive sins are two parts of a single endowment. It is therefore in the Spirit that the latter is exercised, and it remains—if we may infer so much—pre-eminently the province of those who are 'spiritual' men in the narrower sense of the word. We might perhaps think in terms of a small group of spiritual elect within the congregation, such as that which is addressed as 'Lady' in II John,[84] or, better still, of the 'Elder' himself, who works among

[80] II Joh. 11.

[81] In the MS tradition the present ἀφίονται, ἀφίενται, predominates over the perfect ἀφέωνται, but the latter can hardly, as J. Jeremias, *TWNT* 3, 1938, p. 753 n. 88, argues, have arisen simply by 'assimilation' to κεκράτηνται (Joh. 20:23b). It is more likely that ἀφίενται is a *lectio facilior*. Jeremias, in agreement with P. Joüon, *L'Évangile de Notre-Seigneur Jésus-Christ*, 1930, p. 593, would then, nevertheless, like to go on to interpret this present, which he considers the original reading, as future in sense.

[82] What is emphasised is the immediacy of the decision, and the fact that it applies without question and at once; it is not implied that the human sentence is linked with a divine judgment that has already taken place: cf. H. J. Cadbury, 'The meaning of John 20,23; Matthew 16,19 and Matthew 18,18,' *JBL* 58, 1939, pp. 251ff., in reply to J. R. Mantey, 'The mistranslation of the perfect in John 20,23, Matthew 16,19 and Matthew 18,18', *ibid.*, pp. 243ff.

[83] This is also entirely in keeping with I Joh. 5:15, where requests made to God are said to be already granted. By contrast, the past tense in Mk. 11:24 (ἐλάβετε) conveys no more than the most complete certainty ('as good as received'), since the actual fulfilment lies in the future (ἔσται).

[84] II Joh. 1:5. Cf. F. J. Dölger, *Antike und Christentum* 5, 1936, pp. 211ff., 296; W. Foerster, art. κυρία, *TWNT* 3, 1938, pp. 1094f.

his 'children' as their head and pastor, or, like Peter, 'feeds' his lambs.[85] Apart from the basic religious principle involved, which could be expressed in practice in various ways, nothing can be determined with certainty. In particular it would be decidedly perverse to interpret the Twelve,[86] to whom Jesus is speaking, as the prototype of an official group of presbyters, thus designating the latter as invested *ex officio* with the power of the keys. The passage in question, however, as little reflects a definite presbyteral constitution as the Petrine version of the same saying does a monarchical episcopate. The disciples figure here as representatives of the Church, and as models of spiritual authority in general. It is certainly no accident that John is the one writer who avoids ever referring to them as 'apostles', the title that carries the solemn overtones of office.[87] Moreover, gospel and epistles alike nowhere show the least trace of any Church organisation or constitution based on office—III John indeed seems actively to resist such a development.[88] 'John' thus stands aloof from the 'ecclesiastical' development which pointed to the future form of the Church.

Such reflections on sin and repentance as occupy the attention of the average Christian in this period are not marked by a deeply spiritual theology or pastoral concern. Their primary interest is the avoidance of those grosser sins and lapses which now become ever more frequent. But even where the struggle against sin and sinners begins in this spirit there is at first no thought of having officials to control and direct the processes of penance. This is most clearly apparent in the Shepherd of Hermas. This Roman document, for all its considerable length, is a single extended penitential sermon, in the course of which individual sins, classes of sins, and methods of expiation are reviewed and dis-

[85] Joh. 21:15ff. In this supplementary chapter, however, there is also a special Petrine interest (cf. p. 131 n. 27 above), the significance of which is hard to assess. P. Gaechter, 'Das dreifache "Weide meine Lämmer".' *ZKT* 69, 1947, pp. 328ff., offers a purely juristic exegesis in terms of office congenial to Catholic thought, which fails to do justice to the text.

[86] They are not described as such in the text, and in any case, if we are to be precise, not only is Judas Iscariot missing, but also Thomas: cf. Joh. 20:24.

[87] Cf. H. von Campenhausen, 'Der urchristliche Apostelbegriff', *Stud. Theol.* I, 1947, pp. 126f.

[88] In the case of Joh. 20:23, therefore, it goes without saying that 'it is not a special apostolic authority which is here bestowed; the congregation as such is armed with this power': Bultmann, *Ev. Joh.*, p. 537. Käsemann, *op. cit.*, pp. 302ff., however, goes much too far in the opposite direction when he sets out to interpret this Johannine position in the light of the specific ecclesiastical situation of the writer, whom he conjectures to have been excommunicated. The strict Roman Catholic standpoint is represented by J. B. Umberg, 'Die richterliche Bussgewalt nach Joh. 20,23,' *ZKT* 50, 1926, pp. 348ff., who does nothing to advance the solution of the historical problems. According to O. Michel, 'Der Abschluss des Matthäusevangeliums', *Ev. Theol.* 1950–51, p. 24, the spiritual authority in this passage is linked with 'the priestly office and its authority' (?).

cussed. It is dominated by a primitive moralism combined with certain 'Christian' religious elements of a fantastic kind. Repentance itself is left, as it was before, to the individual, whose task it is to improve himself and to make contrite reparation for past sins of omission and commission, by prayer, fasting, almsgiving, and similar exertions. For soon, when the Lord comes, it will be too late.[89] Hermas's own exhortations are given with the authority of a prophet who can command the attention of the whole Church;[90] and homilies of the same kind might certainly be delivered by an elder or bishop. But this does not mean that either the man of the Spirit or the church official is concerned with a regular programme of penitential discipline.[91] There is neither confession nor absolution in this sense; nor is there any mention in Hermas of excommunication as an ecclesiastical sentence to expel or punish the sinner. It is clear that the strict principles which Paul had championed are in general no longer implemented, and have fallen into desuetude.

Even the fight against false doctrine was not at first able to do much to alter this situation. It is true that, as we have seen, it forced the Church everywhere to draw distinctions and to make decisions, and in so doing tightened the bonds uniting orthodox congregations, and intensified and developed the power of the spiritual office. As early as Acts we find the elders being charged with the struggle against false teaching,[92] and in Ignatius the emphasis on episcopal government is closely linked with the task of defence against those who would lead the Church astray. But even Ignatius has nothing to say about the readmission of penitents or about excommunication; and in view of the completeness with which he expresses himself on all the other duties of a bishop his silence on the matter of penitential discipline simply cannot be accidental.[93] As for the use of any procedure of this sort against heretics, it is not even considered. The 'loosing' of their sin is not, in Ignatius's view, within the authority of any church official, but of Christ alone,[94] who forgives 'all'.[95] The bishop, indeed, would like to coax such people, and win them back gently to obedience to

[89] That Hermas is concerned to proclaim to the Church a 'last' rather than a first repentance has in my view been convincingly demonstrated by Poschmann, op. cit., pp. 134ff., against the positions of H. Windisch, H. Koch, E. Schwartz, M. Dibelius, and other exponents of the 'no repentance after baptism' theory (cf. p. 133 n. 38 above); cf. also pp. 222ff. below.

[90] Vis. II, 4, 2; cf. pp. 000f. above.

[91] Cf. Hoh, op. cit., p. 37.

[92] Cf. p. 80 above.

[93] That the admonition to the bishop to be 'gentle' already implies his 'disciplinary authority over the sinner' (so Poschmann, op. cit., p. 99) is a hazardous assertion.

[94] Philad. 3:2; Smyrn. 4:1.   [95] Philad. 8:1.

himself in order to heal their wounds.[96] But these are precisely the ones who have broken the unity of the Church,[97] and plainly set no store by it whatsoever. Hence one can only hope for their return, and pray to God to enlighten them.[98] Experience suggests, however, that it is hardly ever possible to convert them,[99] and consequently no mention is made of the bishop's bringing them back to a right mind.[100] The primary duty of the congregation, therefore, is simply to keep away from these tempters with their incurably diseased minds,[101] and to refuse to lend an ear to their evil counsels.[102] The bishop too must be content with keeping his sheep together; any sentence he may pass on the heretics will have no significance for them, whatever it may have for his own people. It is quite misleading to use the concept of 'excommunication', which occurs only at a much later period, to describe this action.[103]

The Epistle of Polycarp and, above all, the Pastorals reflect fundamentally the same situation. The only difference is that more stress is laid on the action which a church official is obliged to take against the heretics, and the regulations go into more detail. He is called to be the guardian of sound doctrine, and to take his stand against the disobedient workers of mischief who are active everywhere in the churches. Even here, however, the reference is not to those who acknowledge his control. The men in question have gone astray in the darkness of their own wickedness, and are disobedient and insubordinate;[104] they are the first to stir up strife,[105] they offer open resistance,[106] and unfortunately also attract adherents.[107] The duty of the Christian leader is to accept their challenge, to correct them vigorously, and to try also to convert them, taking care to 'be unfailing in patience and teaching'.[108] 'The Lord's servant must not be quarrelsome but kindly to everyone, an apt teacher, forbearing, correcting his opponents with gentleness. God may perhaps grant that they will repent and come to know the truth, and they may escape from the snare of the devil, after being

[96] Pol. 2:1.
[97] Smyrn. 7:1; 9:1; cf. Magn. 4; Philad. 7:2.
[98] Philad. 3:2; 8:1.   [99] Smyrn. 4:1.
[100] Of the two passages which Poschmann, *op. cit.*, p. 98, would cite to the contrary, Eph. 10:1 is better taken to refer to the heathen (so W. Bauer, *Handbuch*, p. 209), while Eph. 3:1 is not relevant.
[101] Eph. 7:1.   [102] Eph. 9:1; Trall. 6; Philad. 2f.; Smyrn. 4:1; 7:2.
[103] So Poschmann, *op. cit.*, p. 99 n. 1. By contrast Hoh, *op. cit.*, p. 75, with whom Poschmann is in specific disagreement, is quite correct in his definition of the situation, even though the phrase which he uses to describe it—a 'Christian boycott'— is singularly unattractive: 'However severely stigmatised the heretics may be, no sentence of exclusion is passed against them, and one looks in vain for any final severance. . . . Rather it is their conversion which is looked for.'
[104] I Tim. 1:6f.; 4:1; 6:3; Tit. 1:10,16.   [105] I Tim. 6:5.
[106] II Tim. 3:8; 4:15; cf. II Tim, 4:10ff.
[107] II Tim. 3:6f.; 4:3f.   [108] II Tim. 4:2f.; Tit. 1:13.

captured by him to do his will.'[109] The prospect of their restoration, however, is plainly not thought to be very great. In most cases such seducers simply go from bad to worse.[110] The only hope is that in time men will see through their absurdity, and that like the miscreants of every age they will at least achieve no lasting success.[111] The principal emphasis falls once more on the warning not to be too intimate with the heretics, and preferably to avoid them altogether. For the ordinary church member this rule applies without qualification;[112] but even the bishop or presbyter must understand clearly that as a matter of experience long arguments with such people lead nowhere.[113] The right thing is to have nothing to do with their childish myths,[114] and the best of all is to keep out of their way.[115] If a heretic has been warned once or twice to no effect, then there is no point in running after him any longer. He is plainly obdurate, and must bear the consequences of his behaviour himself.[116]

This ruling is primarily intended to quieten or ease the moral scruples of a conscientious church leader who can bring himself only with reluctance to give up altogether his efforts to redeem an erring member.[117] In the end such a one has to be written off, just as the impenitent brother in Matthew is abandoned after three attempts at correction.[118] In the present passage there is no reference to a public act in set canonical form; and to this extent there is no question of a formal 'excommunication', which must to some degree presume prior recognition of the competence of the official concerned on the part of the person expelled. The significance in practice of such an exclusion as this passage provides for depends entirely on the personal standing of the man who enforces it. A celebrated case in point from this very period is afforded by the encounter between Polycarp of Smyrna and Marcion. Marcion hoped to win this great and influential bishop to his own side, but his request for 'recognition' met with a rough rejection: 'I recognize you, I recognize you—as the firstborn of Satan!'[119]

[109] II Tim. 2:24ff.; cf. Polycarp, Phil. 6:1, and Irenaeus, Adv. haer. III, 3, 4, on Polycarp as an effective and successful converter of heretics.

[110] II Tim. 3:13.   [111] II Tim. 3:8f.   [112] II Tim. 2:21; cf. Polycarp, Phil. 6:3.

[113] I Tim. 6:20f.; II Tim. 2:14, 23ff.

[114] I Tim. 4:7; II Tim. 2:23.   [115] II Tim. 3:5; 4:15.   [116] Tit. 3:10f.

[117] This is the sense in which Irenaeus, Adv. haer. I, 16, 3, appears to take the passage in question; cf. also III, 3, 4; IV praef. 2.

[118] J. Jeremias, Die Briefe an Timotheus und Titus, 1935, p. 56, and art. κλείς, p. 752, would prefer to expound the passage in question entirely in line with Matt. 18:15ff., and therefore assumes that the final warning and expulsion 'certainly took place at a general meeting of the congregation'. The parallel, however, cannot be pressed so far.

[119] Mart. Polycarp XXII, 2, in the expanded form found in the Moscow MS. (Lightfoot, Apostolic Fathers, p. 198); Irenaeus, cited in Eusebius, HE IV, 7; on this incident cf. Harnack, Marcion², 1924, pp. 4f.

This rebuff may have had the effect of making it impossible for Marcion to carry on his activities among the orthodox churches of Asia Minor undisturbed. A little later, however, he would seem to have found a friendly reception at Rome, at any rate until some years afterwards, when here too matters came to an open breach.[120] Furthermore, if heretics did not regard the attitude of the bishop as binding even within one single congregation, all the more was there a lack of any cohesion in the Church at large[121] which would automatically give universal effect to a measure taken in one particular place.[122] It thus becomes clear what a so-called 'excommunication' could at the most imply at this time, and what it could not.

[120] According to a story deriving from Hippolytus Marcion had already been excommunicated earlier on by his own father, the bishop of Sinope. This information, however, is both less unequivocal and more problematical than Harnack, op. cit., pp. 23–26, assumes. Harnack is certainly right to emphasise that in the time of Hadrian there was no such thing as 'excommunication in the sense of later Church practice'; nevertheless he still retains the misleading concept of 'excommunication', and places a purely external limitation on its significance (which in other respects he considers to have been even greater than it was later to become) by his comment that 'at this period excommunication from the congregation was as yet valid only for that one church'. Dix, 'The Ministry in the Early Church,' The Apostolic Ministry, 1946, pp. 202f., rightly stresses the lack of solidarity in the church at Rome.

[121] So far as I have been able to discover, the earliest intimation of notice of a formal excommunication being communicated to neighbouring churches occurs in Tertullian, De pud. 7, 22: 'Simul apparuit (sc. moechia et fornicatio),. statim homo de ecclesia expellitur nec illic manet nec gaudium confert repertrici ecclesiae, sed luctum'—Tertullian is expounding Lk. 15:8ff.—'nec congratulationem advocant vicinarum, sed contristationem proximarum fraternitatum.' The same presumably held good in the case of the decisions to exclude Montanists: cf. Adversus Praxean 1.

[122] In this context the details which Irenaeus, Adv. haer. III, 4, 2, (=Eusebius, HE IV, 11,1) relates concerning Cerdo are significant:... οὕτως διετέλεσεν ποτὲ μὲν λαθροδιδασκαλῶν, ποτὲ δὲ πάλιν ἐξομολογούμενος, ποτὲ δὲ ἐλεγχόμενος ἐφ' οἷς ἐδίδασκεν κακῶς καὶ ἀφιστάμενος τῆς τῶν ἀδελφῶν συνοδίας. As early as the Latin translation (abstentus est) and Rufinus (arcetur) this 'secession' was understood as 'excommunication'. The question whether Cerdo was repeatedly admitted to penance and received back into the Church, or whether 'he never got past the exhomologesis' (Poschmann, op. cit., p. 221, in agreement with H. Koch, 'Die Sündenvergebung bei Irenaeus,' ZNW 7, 1908, p. 37 n. 2), is posed in terms that are historically false, as Poschmann's own warnings against an anachronistic, modern understanding of penance indicate (op. cit., p. 31 n. 1, p. 38 n. 1). Cf. also the Syrian fragment of the letter from Irenaeus to Victor (Harvey, vol. II, p. 497) concerning the Valentinian Florinus, who had boasted of his status as a Roman presbyter. The only subject mentioned, however, is the rejection of his compromising and perplexing writings, though it is possible that at the time of the letter Florinus himself was no longer alive: cf. T. Zahn, Forschungen zur Geschichte des neutestamentlichen Kanons und der altkirchlichen Literatur 4, 1891, pp. 803ff. On the other hand, the beginnings of an excommunication practice in the true sense are to be found in the apocryphal Epistle

This much, however, may be said: as a result of the bitter struggle which the official leadership had to carry on against the false teachers a desire was in fact awakened to subject these disturbers of the churches' peace if possible to a firmer discipline. This is apparent from the way in which the author of the Pastoral Epistles imagines his apostle to have acted. Hymenaeus and Alexander, who have made 'shipwreck of their faith', may have been early heretics whose names were held in honour by the gnostics of his own day. These men, 'Paul' now makes plain, 'I have delivered to Satan that they may learn not to blaspheme'.[123] Underlying this is a reminiscence of I Cor. 5. Since in that instance a carnal sinner was expelled in the power of the Spirit, and delivered up to bodily death, our author also credits his apostle retrospectively with corresponding miraculous powers in other cases.[124] Now, however, it is no longer simply a question of separation and death, but of 'discipline,' which punishes with sickness those who would lead their brethren astray, or seeks to put pressure on them in some other way to compel them to give up their 'blasphemy' and rebellion.

Yet this is still a case of wishful thinking on the part of a polemical writer, or of a legend similar to that of Peter, Ananias, and Sapphira. The very fact that the apostle's intervention is presented as taking more or less miraculous form shows that there is still no standard official procedure for punishing heretics. Within the congregation itself, however, this period of conflict sees the official spiritual leadership become sufficiently mature to take into its own hands the overall control of church affairs, and with this the disciplinary 'training' of the congregation. This does, of course, have its significance for the fight against heresy as well. III John illustrates how an energetic ecclesiastic can counter undesirable outside influences simply by threatening or enforcing an 'excommunication'.[125] Nevertheless, the decisive factor is not the struggle against heresy, but the general development of the

---

to the Corinthians 21: τούτους οὖν ἀπωθεῖσθε ἀφ᾽ ὑμῶν καὶ ἀπὸ τῆς διδαχῆς αὐτῶν φεύγετε, and 39: . . . οὓς ἀπωθεῖσθε ἐν δυνάμει τοῦ κυρίου (Greek text as reconstructed by Harnack, *Sitzungsberichte der Berlin. Akademie*, 1905, pp. 25, 28). The case of the Philippian presbyter Valens, of which we learn from Polycarp, Phil. 11, and which Poschmann, *op. cit.*, p. 103, adduces, is not relevant: cf. p. 120 above. The proposition in general terms that anyone who does not overcome the sin of avarice is contaminated with idolatry, and will be reckoned (*iudicabitur* = λογισθήσεται) among the heathen, or: will be judged (*iudicabitur* = κριθήσεται) with the heathen, gives us nothing concrete. All we can be sure of is that Valens lost his position as presbyter, and that it was still possible to hope for the amendment of his wife and himself: '. . . *quibus dominus* [n.b.!] *det paenitentiam veram.*'

[123] I Tim. 1:20.

[124] Cf. M. Dibelius, *Die Pastoralbriefe*[2], 1931, p. 21; M. Goguel, *L'église primitive*, p. 243.

[125] Cf. p. 123 above.

Church's law. Naturally enough this first becomes visible in the form of spiritual discipline for the clergy as a separate professional body.[126] In the Pastorals we already find the ruler of the church required to accept complaints against a member of the presbyterate after formally hearing the witnesses, and then publicly to call the offender to account and to censure him.[127] The author here certainly has in mind the full church meeting, which to this day still participates in such proceedings.[128] Clerics who have been guilty of serious offences invariably forfeit their official position.[129] The passage in question, however, indicates that it is already quite normal to think of the bishop as a judge, or at least as the presiding member of a church court.[130] Paul had already required the Corinthians to settle their disputes before suitable members of their own congregation; now the bishop and the presbyters have plainly become the judicial body within the competence of which such matters customarily fall. The decision of such a church court, however, is in no sense to be regarded in the same light as a purely secular matter. As the sentence of a court appointed by God it automatically becomes a 'spiritual' judgment, and so the penalties which may have to be imposed forthwith acquire the character of ecclesiastical penance.[131] A phrase in I Timothy probably allows us to go a step further. Timothy is admonished to guard against bias, and not to show favouritism. For the same reason he is not to be hasty in 'the laying on of hands', in order that he may not share the guilt of other men's sins.[132] The phrase, 'the laying on of hands', immediately suggests ordination, and if this interpretation is correct, then the passage contains an exhortation to proceed with caution in the appointment of clergy. But the explicit emphasis on the 'sins' of others, bearing in mind also the context in which the remark occurs, suggests much more strongly the re-admission of contrite sinners or 'penitents'.[133] If this exegesis is correct,

---

[126] On this point cf. again the complaints of Irenaeus to Victor of Rome concerning the presbyter Florinus: p. 145 n. 122 above.

[127] I Tim. 5:19f.

[128] Cf. Hoh, op. cit., p. 79; Poschmann, op. cit., p. 103. There is no need to confine the reference of the explanatory clause: ἵνα καὶ οἱ λοιποὶ φόβον ἔχωσιν, as Dibelius, Pastoralbriefe, p. 50, does, to the rest of the presbyters only.

[129] Polycarp, Phil. 11,1; cf. p. 120 above.

[130] In Polycarp, Philippians, the presbyters too are regarded as judges, as is shown by the admonition that they are to be ἀπεχόμενοι πάσης ὀργῆς, προσωπολημψίας, κρίσεως ἀδίκου. The ruling that complaints against the clergy are to be admitted only when they are supported by two or three witnesses (I Tim. 5:19) suggests that the normal custom was to bring them before the bishop or the presbyters, but without this safeguard.

[131] How easily the one passes into the other may be seen from, for example, Didasc. apost. II, 47, 1f.; cf. K. Rahner, 'Busslehre und Busspraxis der Didascalia apostolorum', ZKT 72, 1950, p. 279.

[132] I Tim. 5:22.

[133] So Dibelius, op. cit., pp. 50f.; also P. Galtier, 'La réconciliation des

then we have here the earliest witness to a practice of formal absolution to be performed by the head of the congregation.

With this development we cross the threshold of a new era. This brief comment by 'Paul' gives no hint of the enormous importance which the regulation of the official power of the keys was to acquire in the course of the second century. It does indicate once more, however, that the Pastorals are later than the Epistles of Ignatius, and developmentally, if not in terms of absolute chronology, much later than the Shepherd of Hermas. They belong to the very end of the sub-apostolic period. For in the next generation, or at most the next but one, the great controversy flares up concerning the nature of repentance, and the part which the episcopal office ought to play in the forgiveness of sins. The fact that the episcopate was able to come off victorious in this conflict was decidedly not due to any detailed rights in the conduct of public penance which it had acquired in the preceding period, but to its moral and spiritual authority as a whole; and this, as was explained above, in embryo certainly antedates the crisis over gnosticism.[134] Because, however, gnosis compelled the Church to pay special attention to the ideas of tradition which from the start were associated with the episcopal office, and to elaborate them, when it came to the matter of establishing the authority of the office on firm foundations, it was this aspect which was the first to be developed and fully worked out, whereas the questions of repentance and discipline remained to begin with in the background. It is therefore to the problems of tradition and teaching authority in the form which they took at this time that we must next turn.

---

pécheurs dans St Paul', *RSR* 3, 1912, pp. 448ff.; *DTC* VII. 2, 1922, cols. 1306ff.; and 'La réconciliation des pécheurs dans la première épître à Timothée', *RSR* 39, 1951/2, pp. 317ff.; W. Lock, *A critical and exegetical Commentary on the Pastoral Epistles*, 1924, pp. 63f.; B. S. Easton, *The Pastoral Epistles*, 1948, p. 160. The majority of Catholic scholars, however, such as G. Wohlenberg, *Die Pastoralbriefe*, 1906, pp. 183f., opt for an interpretation in terms of ordination to the priesthood; cf. esp. J. Coppens, *L'imposition des mains et les rites connexes dans le Nouveau Testament et dans l'Église ancienne*, 1925, pp. 125ff.

[134] Cf. pp. 76ff. above.

CHAPTER VII

Tradition and Succession in the Second Century

THE SPEEDY triumph of the presbyteral system, and the accompanying beginnings of officialdom in the Church, are not to be explained simply in terms of practical and sociological advantages or of the pressure of external circumstances. It is true that the benefits of settled government and of an organisation which could ensure responsible provision for maintaining and stabilising congregational life in face of the threat to the Church from fatigue, degeneration, and fragmentation were certainly not without influence. But the elders and the governing bishops would never have been able to win that decisive recognition of their dignity and authority which they did had not something in their position corresponded from the start to the religious nature of the Church and to its spiritual needs. What this element is we have already described;[1] it is the concept of tradition, which is supremely embodied and assured in the institution of office. What is more, the affirmation and preservation of tradition are inevitable concomitatnts of faith in Christ.[2] As belief in a particular, historical manifestation and resurrection of the Lord this faith is throughout bound up with a 'testimony', and without the continuance of this testimony in what has always been thought of as a 'tradition' it cannot endure. It is probable that the first, patriarchal beginnings of office in the Church go back to its earliest days. Only in the course of the second century, however, do Christians become aware of the spiritual affinity between tradition and office, and of their close practical association from the time of the foundation of the Church, and work out the theological significance of this. The result of their ˙hinking is the concept of succession, and belief in the 'apostolic successic n' of bishops. The attempt has often been made to trace these ideas bac ˙ into the apostolic period itself; but to do so is to ignore the significan ˙e of the intermediate development, and is in any case without an adequa ˙e basis in the sources. A brief review of the earlier evidence may bring this home to us, and at the same time demonstrate once more the antiquiˑy and importance of the concept of tradition, which is basic

---

[1] Cf. pp. 79f. above.
[2] On this point cf. H. von Campenhausen, 'Tradition und Geist im Urchristentum', *Stud. Gen.* 4, 1951, pp. 351ff.; also N. Monzel, *Die Überlieferung*, 1950.

and definitive for the second century doctrine of office in the Church.

Paul already acknowledges and affirms the concept of tradition, which had indeed always been familiar to him as a Jew,[3] though he gives it a new form, deriving from Christ.[4] Although he himself has seen the Lord, in dealing with the Corinthian enthusiasts he appeals to the older, stereotyped tradition of the resurrection, which he himself 'received', and then in his turn passed on.[5] The testimony in this form, just as it is, he calls the 'Gospel', thus asserting its complete harmony with the living preaching of Christ which he himself practises. For the latter would no longer be possible, indeed, could not exist, if the historic primal testimony of the apostles, on which it is based, were disputed or denied.[6] All that is distinctive about Paul's attitude is that at the same time he neither knows of nor desiderates any official whose job it is to 'take charge of' this testimony within the Church, and to be its continuing representative.[7] The 'edifying' and formation of the Church is left entirely to the Spirit, who does indeed flow from the apostolic witness and the Gospel,[8] but who operates freely throughout the Body of Christ, and whose manifold gifts cannot be organised in any kind of official system.[9] This attitude, at first surprisingly effective, cannot be explained solely in terms of Paul's explicit and theologically argued rejection of any kind of authority based on official position. It is plain that he simply has not reckoned with the possibility that there might be a need for special measures to safeguard the fundamental apostolic witness. To his inward vision this witness is as unambiguous and compelling as the fact of which it speaks had been that day outside Damascus,

---

[3] The technical terms παραλαμβάνειν (I Cor. 11:23; 15:1,3; Gal. 1:9,12; Phil. 4:9; Col. 2:6; I Thess. 2:13; 4:1; II Thess. 3:6) and παραδιδόναι (I Cor. 11:2,23; 15:3; II Thess. 2:15; 3:6) in Paul are primarily Jewish in connotation, but their spiritual meaning has been expanded and transformed in a christological sense: cf. O. Cullmann, 'Le problème de la tradition dans le paulinisme', *RHPR* 30, 1950, pp. 12ff.; also W. G. Kümmel, 'Jesus und der jüdische Traditionsgedanke', *ZNW* 33, 1934, pp. 105ff. There is no need here to engage in the debate on the further problems which arise in this context.

[4] This applies even to the cases where Paul appeals to sayings of Jesus as a legal norm (I Cor. 7:10; 9:13); they are still words of the Lord, and no longer those of the old Mosaic law and its 'traditions' (Gal. 1:14).

[5] I Cor. 15:1ff.; cf. J. Jeremias, *The Eucharistic Words of Jesus*, 1966, pp. 101ff.; E. Lichtenstein, 'Die älteste christliche Glaubensformel', *ZKG* 63, 1950, pp. 1ff.; H. von Campenhausen, *Der Ablauf der Osterereignisse und das leere Grab*, 1952, pp. 8ff.

[6] I Cor. 15:14f.

[7] The existence of the 'teachers' might be adduced against this view. It is, however, significant that Paul never refers to the function of instructing and handing on the tradition, which in all probability was the one they exercised, as such, and that in his writings generally they play a much less prominent part than the prophets: cf. pp. 60f. above.

[8] Gal. 3:2.   [9] On this point cf. pp. 62f., 69f. above.

when he comprehended it so fully that no further instruction or interpretation was necessary. He is well aware of the dangers that his gospel
may be betrayed or denied. What he is not acquainted with, and therefore has not yet allowed for, is a gradual, almost imperceptible drying
up and disappearance of that tradition which he sees as something so
unitary and translucent that, once it has been proclaimed to all the
world and heeded, there is, so to speak, no longer any possibility of its
being forgotten. On the contrary, all that can happen is that its meaning
should be ever more fully unfolded by the Spirit, and made effective.
It is enough, therefore, to exhort the Church to be faithful, and to
recollect what it already possesses. There is, moreover, all the less need
for Paul to think about possible changes in a distant future, seeing that
he looks for the return of Christ within a very short time, and indeed
hopes to experience that event during his own earthly life.[10]

In the succeeding period the problem of tradition could no longer
be dealt with so simply. The concept itself gains in both scope and
importance. The apostolic witness and traditional teaching take in more
and more material, historical, legal, and dogmatic; and in view of the
conflicts between various doctrines and their exponents the question
which are the genuine and original teachings can no longer be set aside.
Tradition as such is now open to question. The object at once of doubt
and emphasis, it becomes a problem, and true tradition is distinguished
from false. It would be simply perverse, however, to see this development as something like a deliberate rejection of the sovereignty of the
Spirit in favour of 'mere' tradition. In the period which we are considering both these things go together; belief in the Spirit as something alien
to tradition, something encountered only in direct religious experience,
is no part of Early Christianity, but only of the later Middle Ages and
of modern times.[11] Even the gnostic false teachers do not desire anything of that kind. Indeed, it is precisely they who wish to proclaim the
faith of Christ as a new revelation; and this means safeguarding its
true tradition, for the proof and preservation of which they consequently
make considerable efforts. That in the process they increasingly abandon
the factual and historically rooted in order to pursue a fantastic and
non-historical myth is our modern verdict, and one which is entirely
justified; but it is also irrelevant, if what we are considering is the
gnostics' own intentions and their own assessment of themselves. The
truth is that on all sides sacred tradition is sought out, discovered, and
prized; and equally universal is the conviction that it can be rightly
received, understood, and propounded only in the Spirit. Tradition is

[10] I Thess. 4:15.
[11] Even Ignatius, Philad. 8:2, is not to be taken in this sense. The reference
here is to the conflict between free, oral tradition and the written documents,
not to an opposition of Spirit to tradition in general: cf. p. 103 n. 200 above.

regarded as something miraculous, transforming Man himself; and it is this which explains the fact that the teaching of tradition is combined with mysterious and sacramental acts. The man who is to receive the truth must not only—as in orthodox Judaism—be instructed and informed; he must at the same time be transformed in his very nature, be filled with the Spirit, and thus become himself a 'spiritual' man.[12] On this point too the Catholic and the heretical gnostic Christian are in essential agreement. Where, however, the Catholic Church parts company with the majority of the early heretical groups is that Catholicism does not entrust the tradition which gives this light and learning simply to any chance spiritual leaders, teachers, and prophets, but forms a group or class of responsible men who, at first by virtue of being the elder and more experienced members of the community, then increasingly 'ex officio' undertake the work of teaching and instruction.

The position of elder in the Church was, as we saw,[13] not established for the sake of the tradition or of the teaching ministry. At first it was simply a matter of following the Jewish model and general necessity. In many cases, though not in all, the liturgical function of the elders was also felt to be especially important.[14] But so soon as the danger that believers would be led astray by false teachers became acute, the natural consequence was that these men were called upon and put forward to act as guardians and witnesses of the genuine tradition. The crucial question in this situation is this: in what relationship is the authority of the office placed to that of the tradition? In the early stages, however, the question is neither posed nor answered in this form. This much alone is clear, that there is as yet no official monopoly of the task of representing and safeguarding true doctrine and the apostolic witness —any more than there is the opposite, anti-clerical emphasis on the 'priesthood of all believers'.[15] Where there are elders who are faithful to their calling, it seems to be taken for granted that they lead and instruct the congregation. But this no more excludes the activities of other, 'free' teachers than the operations of non-apostolic evangelists and missionaries of the primitive period were inhibited in practice by the fact that they were doing the same work as the apostles.[16]

It is in this light that we are to understand the earliest document

[12] Cf. P. T. Camelot, Foi et gnose . . . chez Clément d'Alexandrie, 1945, p. 90 n. 3: '. . . and it should be remarked in passing that it is this which constitutes the essential difference between Christian tradition and Rabbinic traditions.'

[13] Cf. pp. 76ff. above.

[14] Cf. on the one side Clement of Rome, pp. 91f. above, and Ignatius of Antioch, pp. 100f., 106f. above, and on the other the Pastoral Epistles, pp. 109f., and Polycarp, pp. 119f. above.

[15] This first makes its appearance in the Montanist polemic of Tertullian: cf. pp. 228f. below.

[16] On prophets and teachers in the second century cf. pp. 178ff. below.

which turns its attention to the office of elder as such, and enlists its help against the heretics, namely the Lukan Acts of the Apostles. In the first chapters, which are a reworking of older material, it seems, however, almost as though the Apostles (which for Luke means the Twelve, to whom even Paul does not belong) have been elevated into a judicial body solely responsible for all rulings and decisions, from whom all preaching has to emanate, and by whom it must be supervised. Moreover, it is they who mediate the Holy Spirit to new congregations.[17] But this view cannot be maintained. Luke adheres to it sympathetically for a time, since it corresponds to his ideal picture of the peace and order of the earliest period; but he then goes on to show how God, in guiding the Church, goes too fast for these Apostles by himself calling preachers and prophets and by bestowing his Spirit where the Apostles least expect it. Again and again there is nothing for the latter to do but to recognise what the Spirit has already done, and to confirm it with praise and thanksgiving, while the newly won Christians gratefully join the community.[18] Then Paul moves the mission into completely new areas and situations. Whatever the piety which he displays in his dealings with the primitive community, he is not subject to it.[19] The later, historically untenable conception of the central government of the whole Church by the Apostles is thus not supported by Luke. He does, however, prepare the way for it, in accordance with his usual propensity for edification, by laying the principal stress in his highly impressionistic picture on the cohesion, the harmony, the orderly behaviour, and the inner spiritual continuity of that model apostolic age.[20] In this sense he is also describing the beginnings of office in the Church.

It is obviously of great consequence to Luke to trace the various ecclesiastical offices of his day, or at least their models and prototypes, back to the origins of the Church. The 'seven men' in Jerusalem are for him the prototype of the deacons, although he knows quite well that they were in fact something different, and therefore avoids using that

---

[17] I do not propose to analyse here the much discussed texts and individual sections of material relevant to this question, viz., Acts 8:14ff., 25; 9:26ff., 32; 11:22; 12:17; 15:1ff., 22ff.; 16:4; 21:15. The study by N. Adler, *Taufe und Handlegung. Eine exegetische theologische Untersuchung von Apg. 8, 14-17,* 1951, is strictly Catholic in its conclusions, and sees the passage in question as the earliest evidence for that form of the laying-on of hands, originally practised only by the Apostles, whereby is communicated the Spirit 'which the Christian disciple receives after his baptism, the rite which we today call Confirmation' (p. 111).

[18] Acts 8:4ff., 26ff.; 9:3ff.; 10, esp. 10:34ff., 44ff.; 11:15ff., 19ff.; 15:7ff.; 16:6ff.

[19] Acts 9:26ff.; 11:30; 15:2ff.; 21:17ff.

[20] Cf. M. Dibelius, *Die Reden der Apostelgeschichte und die antike Geschichtsschreibung,* 1949, pp. 49f. (=*Gesammelte Aufsätze zur Apostelgeschichte,* 1951, p. 155).

term to describe them directly.[21] 'Elders' in his story occur not only—
though at a somewhat later stage—within the primitive community
itself,[22] they are also appointed in the mission-field by Paul and his
colleagues.[23] At the same time, Luke suggests, they have the status of
'bishops'; for the Spirit has 'set' them in the churches as 'overseers'.[24]
In this capacity it is the duty of the elders to defend the truth and
sanctity characteristic of the original Christians against false teachers;
and this, as Luke emphasizes, corresponds to the express intent and
commission of Paul himself.[25] They are to remain faithful to the teaching and example of Paul; and Luke clearly attaches the greatest importance to this historic, objective continuity. It is not, however, also urged
that an unbroken chain of consecration is of any special significance,
though simply as a historical fact Luke would certainly have considered
this entirely possible. Something which he patently does regard as important is regular, solemn installation in office. Not only the aid and
attestation of the Spirit but also a public appointment, an 'ordination',
forms an integral part of receiving a ministry in the Church.[26] Prayer
and laying-on of hands are apparently indispensable; there is also
mention of preparation by fasting.[27] The whole congregation takes part
in the action,[28] even though not in the sense of a 'democratic' poll of
all the members.[29] In Jerusalem it is the Twelve who take the leading
part in the proceedings, in Antioch the prophets and teachers, in the
mission field Paul and the other missionaries. At the time all this proceeds from historical necessity, not as yet from any definite legal requirement. To discuss the anachronistic question whether such ordinations
were sacramental or non-sacramental in character, and on what canon
law principles they were then based, is simply to manufacture artificial

[21] Acts 6:2ff.; cf. p. 77 above.

[22] Acts 11:30; 15:2ff.; 21:18; cf. p. 77 above and n. 29 below.

[23] Acts 14:23.

[24] Acts 20:28.

[25] Acts 20:31, 35; cf. pp. 8of. above.

[26] Acts 6:1ff.; 13:2f.; 14:23,26; 15:40. The choice of Matthias (Acts 1:23ff.),
which is also conducted in a highly formal manner, does nevertheless have a
different character to the extent that here the decision is by lot; an Apostle may
not be chosen simply by men, but must be appointed by God or by Christ
himself.

[27] Acts 13:2; cf. 14:23; also E. Peterson, 'La Λειτουργία des prophètes et
des didascales à Antioche,' *RSR* 36, 1949, pp. 577ff.

[28] This is explicitly mentioned only in Acts 1:15; 6:2ff., but may be taken as
automatic, in line with all other analogous stiuations in the Early Church: cf.
esp. I Clem. 44:3 (p. 156 n. 45 below) and Hippolytus, Apost; Trad. 2:1.

[29] To say that the Apostles in Acts 6:6 merely 'confirm' the choice of the
congregation by their act of appointment is certainly to understate the case,
while to maintain that the selection of the Lycaonian elders in Acts 14:23 was
made in a 'completely authoritarian' manner is perhaps to overstate it; but cf.
E. Schweizer, *Das Leben des Herrn*, 1946, pp. 90, 95f.

and insoluble difficulties. It is obvious that Luke is not interested in the preservation of a 'succession' in any formal sense. Once we give up trying to turn the historical statements which he does make into canonist's statements, which he either cannot make or has no intention of making, then what he is seeking to say and to commend to his readers is clear enough. Luke prizes an ordered form of appointment, in which the spiritual leaders of the congregation themselves act as instruments of the Spirit,[30] and mediate to those who have been chosen their commission and authority. The Christian congregation needed a permanent pastoral office,[31] and possessed one from an early stage, to ensure that the teaching and example of the first 'eye-witnesses and ministers of the Word'[32] should be set forth undistorted before the eyes of later generations. This, however, does not depend on particular valid forms, nor on a link with particular people who happen to be lawfully consecrated. The connection is inward and spiritual, and the continuity concrete and historical, not merely sacramental or juristic.

This way of thinking about the matter is continued in the Pastoral Epistles,[33] which theologically are close to Luke.[34] Here too the dominant—though even more strongly emphasised—idea is that the noblest task of this office in the Church consists in safeguarding the apostolic tradition; here too great store is set by personal recollections of Paul; and here too ordination is taken seriously, indeed it is seen as the indispensable source of strength for carrying out the spiritual duties of the office. The connection of the persons addressed, namely Timothy and Titus, with Paul is repeatedly emphasised. Nevertheless it seems questionable whether the intention is to do more than bring out the fact that the teachings and directions here given are the true and original ones.[35] In any case the Pastorals do not put forward any theory of succession as a fixed canonical and dogmatic principle. In view of the very carefully considered form in which they are composed, however, it is perhaps not quite inconceivable that something of the sort had already crossed the author's mind as a pipe-dream or as a first tentative move

[30] In Acts 20:28 it is the Spirit alone, and not the human mediators, who is mentioned.

[31] Acts 20:28: ποιμαίνειν τὴν ἐκκλησίαν τοῦ θεοῦ.

[32] Luk. 1:2.

[33] On what follows cf. pp. 106ff. above.

[34] Cf. H. von Campenhausen, Polycarp von Smyrna und die Pastoralbriefe, 1951, pp. 45f. n. 207.

[35] In II Tim. 1:6 Paul reminds Timothy explicitly of the divine gift present in him as a result of the laying on of Paul's hands. In the other reference to the subject, however, namely I Tim. 4:14, which is of equal weight, it is only the presbyterate (with the co-operation of the testimony of the prophets) which is mentioned. The combination of these two passages certainly does not give the impression that any special stress is laid on a 'sacramental' link with the apostle as the primary fount of order.

in this direction with a view to defending the authority attaching to the office.[36] The Pastorals seem no longer acquainted with any teachers or guardians of the tradition other than official ones; or rather they are familiar with them only in the camp of the false teachers who lead Christians astray, and whose wilful arrogance,[37] sordid motives,[38] and more than dubious adherents[39] are described only in tones of the utmost contempt. The author, however, does not go to the lengths of explicitly rejecting any teaching activity except that carried out by official representatives or given official approval—at this early stage such a course is very definitely not practical politics. Moreover, the other documents of the sub-apostolic period on inspection warn us against going too far in expounding the Pastorals in a 'catholic' sense; even without our doing this they are already advanced enough. In this context there is no need to consider the completely different concept of office in a church order such as the Didache,[40] or a prophecy such as that of Hermas.[41] Even Ignatius of Antioch, the foremost champion of episcopal authority, is equally unacquainted with the concept of an 'apostolic tradition'[42] and in no way calls for consideration as a proponent of any succession theory.

Even Clement of Rome does not take us very much further in this direction.[43] He is, however, the first to base the rights of the office-holder on the idea that this office derives from the apostles, and is to be respected for that reason: God sent Christ, Christ sent the apostles, and the apostles appointed the first bishops and elders. There exists, therefore, in accordance with God's will a beautifully constructed sequence and system,[44] an unbroken continuity in the institution of the office, and in this sense also a succession. It makes no difference, however, whether the apostles themselves are thought to have made their 'firstfruits' into bishops, or whether after their day other 'approved men' installed tested candidates in the office[45]—so far as their present position and their rights in the congregation are concerned it comes to

---

[36] J. Ranft, *Der Ursprung des katholischen Traditionsprinzips*, 1931, p. 265, sees I Tim. 2:5ff. and II Tim. 2:2 in particular as already giving 'an explicit line of succession' which, in his opinion, is 'analogous to the rabbinic lines' (p. 269). That it is given in indefinite terms could be the result of the proleptic (in our view, pseudonymous) form of the Epistle, and does not exclude the possibility that it was meant to be, or could have been, seized upon by a Catholic bishop or teacher from, as it were, the other end. The use which Irenaeus makes of the Pastorals in this respect is significant.

[37] I Tim. 4:1; II Tim. 4:3.   [38] I Tim. 4:2; Tit. 1:11.   [39] II Tim. 3:6f.

[40] Cf. pp. 71ff. above.   [41] Cf. pp. 95ff. above.   [42] Cf. pp. 102f. above.

[43] On what follows cf. pp. 84ff. above.   [44] I Clem. 42.

[45] By the ἐλλόγιμοι ἄνδρες, who made the appointments after the apostles' time, clearly the presbyters are meant: cf. K. Müller, 'Die älteste Bischofswahl und –weihe in Rom und Alexandrien', *ZNW* 28, 1929, pp. 275f.; H. Lietzmann, *History of the Early Church* I, 1939, p. 204. M. A. Siotis, 'Die klassische und christliche Cheirotonie in ihrem Verhältnis', Θεολογία 20–22, 1951, pp. 116f.,

the same thing. Clement is here thinking not in 'sacramental' but in soberly juristic terms. It is a striking fact that he makes absolutely no mention of consecration or of the laying on of hands, and it is therefore impermissible arbitrarily to supply such elements.[46] It is something else, however, which is the really crucial fact: Clement still has nothing to say in this context about tradition. The concept plays no part in his thought about the apostles,[47] and his use of it in any connection is far from pronounced, and lacks any theological significance.[48] The fact is that while the episcopal office as an institution does indeed derive from the apostles in Clement's writings, he does not regard the bishops as mediators of apostolic tradition. This means that at bottom his concept of office lacks the most important element, namely the connection with tradition, with the result that the question of spiritual authority, which is essentially linked with the ministry of teaching and preaching, correspondingly receives from him no attention whatever.[49]

The decisive step in the development of the concept of tradition was taken during the generation after that of the author of the Pastorals, about the middle of the second century.[50] It is about this time that the

dissents, but his distinction between office and priesthood is anachronistic. It is therefore a possibility that these presbyters were in their turn ordained by the apostles; but it is significant that Clement never even considers this, but instead emphatically keeps the two cases distinct in order to declare their equivalence in law: cf. I Clem. 44:2f: (οἱ ἀπόστολοι) ἐπινομὴν δεδώκασιν, ὅπως, ἐὰν κοιμηθῶσιν, διαδέξωνται ἕτεροι δεδοκιμασμένοι ἄνδρες τὴν λειτουργίαν αὐτῶν (i.e., their firstfruits). τοὺς οὖν κατασταθέντας ὑπ' ἐκείνων ἢ μεταξὺ ὑφ' ἑτέρων ἐλλογίμων ἀνδρῶν συνευδοκησάσης τῆς ἐκκλησίας πάσης . . . τούτους οὐ δικαίως νομίζομεν ἀποβάλλεσθαι τῆς λειτουργίας.

[46] This does not exclude the possibility that the laying on of hands may *in practice* have been carried out at Rome. The rite itself probably derives from Jewish models: cf. for its history: W. Bacher, 'Zur Geschichte der Ordination', *MGWJ* 38, 1894, pp. 122ff.; J. Behm, *Die Handauflegung im Urchristentum nach Verwendung, Herkunft und Bedeutung in religionsgeschichtlichem Zusammenhang untersucht*, 1911; J. Coppens, *L'imposition des mains et les rites connexes dans le nouveau testament et dans l'église ancienne*, 1925; Ranft, *op. cit.*, pp. 164ff, 294ff.

[47] The only occurrence of the word παράδοσις is at I Clem. 7:2, and even the apostles' preaching is mentioned only once, and that without any particular emphasis: 42:4.

[48] Cf. B. Reynders, 'Paradosis. Le progrès de l'idée de tradition jusqu'à saint Irénée', *RTAM* 5, 1933, pp. 16of.

[49] Not once does Clement describe the elders as 'shepherds', despite the fact that the idea of the ποίμνιον is completely familiar to him; they appear exclusively as cultic officials. It may be, however, that his reticence on this point has something to do with the fact that the Corinthian bishops were not spiritually of the same calibre as their 'rebels'.

[50] The ideas which follow have been developed at greater length in my essay 'Lehrerreihen und Bischofsreihen im zweiten Jahrhundert', *In memoriam Ernst Lohmeyer*, 1951, pp. 240ff.; for a dissentient view cf. E. Stauffer, 'Zum Kalifat des Jakobus,' *ZRGG* 4, 1952, p. 21 n. 33.

ideas of 'transmitting' and 'receiving' tradition acquire new theological importance and a markedly technical meaning. The origins of this phenomenon are, however, not to be sought in the circles which elaborated the ecclesiology of the Great Church; instead they take us into the world of the gnosis and its cult of the free individual teacher. At any rate, within the Christian world it is the gnostic Ptolemaeus who provides the earliest evidence known to us of this new, theologically oriented usage. In the *Letter to Flora* he speaks explicitly of the secret and apostolic tradition (παράδοσις) which supplements the canonical collection of Jesus's words, and which by being handed on through a succession (διαδοχή) of teachers and instructors has now come to 'us', that is, to him or to his community.[51] Here the concept of 'tradition' is plainly used in a technical sense, as is shown particularly by the collocation with the corresponding concept of 'succession'; for 'just as *paradosis* originally signifies a passing on from one person to another *diadoche* implies the receiving of something passed from hand to hand'.[52] These concepts are frequent within gnosticism in other connections. Special teachings, which cannot rely on meeting with general agreement, are derived from ancient traditions, not accessible to everyone, which are supposed to have been given orally or in writing by particular apostles to particular chosen persons. To name the original witnesses, and even the intermediaries, by whom such secret traditions were disseminated, presents no problem. Basilides appeals to Glaucias, Peter's interpreter, and through him to Peter himself;[53] Valentinus is

[51] Ptolemaeus in Epiphanius, Panar. 33, 7: . . . ἀξιουμένη τῆς ἀποστολικῆς παραδόσεως, ἣν ἐκ διαδοχῆς καὶ ἡμεῖς παρειλήφαμεν μετὰ καὶ τοῦ κανονίσαι πάντας τοὺς λόγους τῇ τοῦ σωτῆρος ἡμῶν διδασκαλίᾳ. Cf. G. Quispel, 'La lettre de Ptolémée à Flora,' *VC* 2, 1948, pp. 32ff. Reynders, *op. cit.*, pp. 172f., has recognised, and rightly emphasised, the full significance of this passage for the question of tradition, namely that this is the only pre-Irenaean attestation of that conception of παράδοσις which from now on is the determinative one. Reynders, however, was not able to exploit his discovery fully, and in particular failed to recognise the importance of Hegesippus in this connection (cf. pp. 163ff. below), because he confined himself to instances of the one catchword παράδοσις, and did not bear in mind the διαδοχή-concept. Following Reynders, Dix., *op. cit.*, (p. 77 n. 2 above), pp. 202ff., also stresses the gnostic origin of the διαδοχή-idea. In addition it would seem that the Marcosians also appealed to their 'apostolic' (i.e., Pauline) tradition. According to the ironic references in Irenaeus, Adv. haer. I, 21, 2, they appeal to the ἀπολύτρωσις of Jesus Christ as proclaimed by Paul, with the explanation: εἶναι ταύτην τὴν ὑπ' αὐτῶν ποικίλως καὶ ἀσυμφώνως παραδιδομένην.

[52] T. Klauser, 'Die Anfänge der römischen Bischofsliste', *BZTS* 8, 1931, p. 196.

[53] Clem. Alex., Strom. VII, 106, 4; Hippolytus, however, gives a different version (Elench. VII, 20, 1): Βασιλείδης τοίνυν καὶ Ἰσίδωρος, ὁ Βασιλείδου παῖς γνήσιος καὶ μαθητής, φησὶν εἰρηκέναι Ματθίαν αὐτοῖς λόγους ἀποκρύφους, οὓς ἤκουσε παρὰ τοῦ σωτῆρος κατ' ἰδίαν διδαχθείς.

supposed to have been instructed by Theodas, a disciple of Paul;[54] the Carpocratians appeal to Mariamne, Salome, or Martha, the Naassenians to Mariamne, to whom James, the Lord's brother, 'handed on' the teaching.[55] All these inventions exhibit the same method, and have the same end in view: they justify the unfamiliar and exceptional features, which might make a particular teaching suspect as 'innovation', by deriving them from a definite tradition, and they validate the tradition itself by identifying witnesses and chains—at first still fairly short— of witnesses by name. They thus reflect the typical difficulties into which the gnostic, and indeed any independent body of teachers was bound to fall when faced with the defenders of the faith of the average orthodox church member, and in this sense they are apologetic and defensive. There is therefore no cause for surprise that the idea of an exactly verified tradition, confirmed by definite named witnesses, did not emerge first where men thought of themselves as 'catholic', but rather in the opposing camp. Why should an orthodox congregation, filled with the Spirit, aware that it had been linked from the beginning with other, like-minded congregations, have any doubts at all that the teaching to which it was accustomed was the original truth, proclaimed by the apostles? Demonstration first becomes necessary when men feel themselves in a minority,[56] and only secondarily when it becomes necessary to engage in controversy with this minority because it is disputing some body of truth of one's own which is normally taken for granted.[57]

The concept of tradition, of 'handing on' and 'receiving' a teaching from the distant past, was not of course something new invented by the gnostics. It was not, however, Judaism which they took as their model, nor did they, at a century's distance, resume the connection with Paul, who in any case used different terminology to refer to the concept.[58] Their predecessors were closer at hand. For centuries the concepts of *paradosis* and *diadoche* had figured in the philosophical education of antiquity in order to explain the, as it were, genealogical reproduction of traditional teaching from the original master in his

[54] Origen, Contra Celsum, V, 62.

[55] Hippolytus, Elench. V, 7, 1. According to Irenaeus, Adv. haer. I, 23, 4 (=Eusebius, HE III, 26, 1) Menander too was a Σύμωνα διαδεξάμενος

[56] This is the case with every teacher who champions unusual teachings in a group of pupils. This general proposition is not intended to imply anything either way concerning the relative strength of the gnostic and catholic streams within the Church at this time.

[57] With the exception of Marcion the gnostics for the most part were cautious about making such a challenge, and confined themselves to praising their own, higher insight compared with that of the Church.

[58] Paul (like the rest of the N.T.) never speaks of διαδέχεσθαι and διαδοχ but of παραλαμβάνειν (cf. p. 150 n. 3 above).

disciples and the later heads of the school.[59] For no more than the Church did ancient philosophy know of a communication of teaching without the idea of a community within which this could take place, or at least a personal contact between the earliest figure and his successors. Exactly as in the later lists of bishops these philosophical *diadochoi*[60] are, when occasion requires, numbered by their 'generations' from the founder of the school,[61] and the term *diadoche* no longer signifies (as *paradosis* does) the content of the teaching, but instead the link created by the process of handing on and receiving, and so the philosophical school itself (αἵρεσις). There is an analogous development in the Church, when the idea of *diadoche* or *successio* (the Latin rendering) is used later to denote both the sequence and the actual lists of bishops. With these originally philosophical terms we find ourselves in the world where gnostic teachers of the type of Valentinus or Ptolemaeus would also have felt at home. They thought of themselves as 'philosophers' just as, on the Catholic side, did such men as Justin or Clement of Alexandria. Thus the terminological common factor in this case expresses also the objective historical and sociological affinity. And if, for the Christian philosophers, it is now no longer a matter of the philosophical teachings of the revered head of a school but of divine revelations, this merely provides one more reason for taking the duty of transmission seriously, and for examining and upholding its sacred and absolute reliability. In so far as Christian teaching possesses a mysterious and theosophical character, which calls not only for instruction but also for initiation and illumination, the *paradosis*-concept of the mystery religions, with their trafficking in secrets, may also have influenced the linguistic usage.[62] Finally, in the motley world of hellenistic education, as we know it especially through Clement of

---

[59] On this subject cf. the remarks, unfortunately very brief, of A. Deneffe, *Der Traditionsbegriff*, 1931, pp. 8ff., and more recently L. Koep, art. 'Bischofsliste,' *RAC* 2, 1952, pp. 407ff. As early as the end of the second century B.C. the Alexandrian Sotion had written a work with the title Διαδοχὴ τῶν φιλοσόφων. On the philosophical concept of tradition cf. Clem. Alex., Strom. I, 62, 1; 64, 5; Hippolytus, Elench. I, 4, 5.

[60] In church writers the expression occurs with a non-official connotation, e.g., in reference to Mark and Colarbasus, οἱ τῆς Οὐαλεντίνου σχολῆς διάδοχοι in Hippolytus, Elench. VI, 53, 3, and, in a somewhat different but equally typical sense, of Menander in Irenaeus, Adv. haer. I, 23, 4.

[61] Thus, e.g., col. M5 l. 77 of the *Academicorum philosophorum index Herculanensis* (ed. Mekler, 1912), as conjecturally restored, reads: Πλάτωνος ὄγδοος διάδοχος.

[62] Reynders, *op. cit.*, p. 169, conjectures that this may be true of Justin. Ranft, *op. cit.*, pp. 179ff., saw it as an explanation in every instance, because the philosophical parallels were not available to him. Cf. also the Naassenian psalm cited in Hippolytus, Elench. V, 10, 2: καὶ τά κεκρυμμένα τῆς ἁγίας ὁδοῦ γνῶσιν καλέσας παραδώσω.

Alexandria,[63] any mixture or cross-fertilisation of ideas whatever is conceivable; and so there is no need to exclude the influence of hellenistic Judaism and its traditions altogether.[64] Nevertheless, this in itself will not have provided the starting-point for the anti-Judaistic gnostics.

The emergent Catholic Church at first displays a negative attitude to this gnostic concept of tradition, and only adopts it for her own use with a good deal of hesitation. She mistrusts the ever-spreading flood of secret revelations and traditions, constantly bearing something new on its swirling waters, and attempts to confine herself to that which is primal, fixed, and laid down once for all, that which is not in any sense secret but is known to all, and can indeed be handed on and maintained only as something known and incontestable. This may be the explanation why even as early as the Pastorals their author, in his polemic against gnostic 'myths', 'genealogies', and 'old wives' tales', avoids the concept of tradition (παράδοσις), and speaks instead of that 'property which is entrusted' (παραθήκη), the deposit of the apostolic teaching.[65] This is essentially a juristic metaphor, which stresses not the idea of link or association but specifically that of inviolability; a man can in no sense do as he pleases with money or property that has been deposited with him, but only keep watch and ward over it.[66] This idea of the Church's teaching authority is tending far more in the direction of a 'scriptural' principle than toward the justification of a free, oral, dynamically shaped tradition.[67] Similarly, Polycarp summons his hearers to abandon false teachings and to turn back to the 'word passed down to us' from the beginning;[68] and the Epistle of Jude is fighting

[63] As himself a teacher Clement has the same mental picture of the oral apostolic tradition as Ptolemaeus: cf. Strom. I, 11, 3; VI, 61, 3: ἡ γνῶσις δὲ αὕτη κατὰ διαδοχὰς εἰς ὀλίγους ἐκ τῶν ἀποστόλων ἀγράφως παραδοθεῖσα κατελήλυθεν: also Camelot, op. cit., pp. 90ff. To do as some have done, and try to find in this an imitation of the idea of episcopal succession is hardly chronologically possible, and in fact stands the whole process on its head: for a statement of this view cf. D. van den Eynde, Les normes de l'enseignement chrétien dans la littérature patristique des trois premiers siècles, 1939, pp. 196, 224ff.

[64] The concept, e.g., of 'philosophy' in Col. 2:8 may point in this direction: cf. G. Bornkamn, 'Die Häresie des Kolosserbriefes,' TLZ 73, 1948, p. 13 n. 2 (=Das Ende des Gesetzes. Paulusstudien, 1952, p. 143 n. 12).

[65] I Tim. 6:20; II Tim. 1:12, 14.

[66] Cf. Ranft, op. cit., pp. 199ff., 250f., 299ff., 304. Ranft himself would like nevertheless to approximate the concept of παραθήκη more closely to that of παράδοσις. It is a striking fact, however, that, as Reynders, op. cit., pp. 166f., rightly observes, the use of παράδοσις cannot be demonstrated even in Papias, despite Eusebius, HE III, 39, 7 and 11.

[67] This is made clear less in individual passages such as II Tim. 3:15f. than in the feeling of the Epistles as a whole, with their constant exhortations to loyalty, adherence to what was originally laid down, and the curbing of unnecessary speculation. A striking feature is the little use which is made of the O.T.   [68] Polycarp, Phil. 7:2.

the same battle when it speaks of the faith which was 'once'—that is, 'once for all', and not transmitted in constantly changing form—'delivered to the saints'.[69] This mood gives rise to a delimiting of the apostolic 'canon', the contents of which are fixed and unambiguous in contrast to all later supposedly genuine traditions.[70] Even Irenaeus is much more of a scriptural theologian than is normally realised or admitted. Only as an extra—or rather, only under the pressure of controversy with the false teachers—does he himself in a small number of passages accept the concept of tradition in order to show that by this yardstick too the Catholic Church is still superior to its opponents.[71]

With this purpose in mind not only Irenaeus but also Papias, Clement of Alexandria, and here and there even Hippolytus of Rome as well, appeal to the 'Elders' who had been acquainted with the apostles or with their disciples.[72] In this context the word has no official overtones (though naturally it is not incompatible with tenure of the presbyteral office). It signifies the 'old' leaders of the Church, the spiritual 'fathers' of former times.[73] In this general form the appeal is typically 'catholic', in that the writers refrain from naming particular witnesses or individual apostles.[74] It adduces only the earliest generation of Church leaders as

[69] Jude 3. On the other hand, the latest of all the N.T. writings, II Peter, speaks in 2:21 of the παραδοθείσῃ ἁγία ἐντολῇ, and III Corinthians (cf. Harnack, op. cit., p. 145n. 122 above) explicitly of παραδιδόναι and παραλαμβάνειν —in a characteristic misapplication of I Cor. 15:3.

[70] On this point Marcion, though limiting the canon far more severely, belongs with the Great Church, fighting on the same front against the gnostic traditionalists. His exclusive attachment to one single apostle, Paul, recalls, it is true, the special traditions of the gnostics (cf. p. 158 above), but is arrived at— Irenaeus, Adv. haer. I, 27, 2 (διαδεξάμενος δέ αὐτὸν [sc. Κέρδονα] Μαρκίων) notwithstanding—by a basically different route: the canon takes the place of 'tradition'. The text of the canon is determined by a process of criticism, and the exposition which he gives of it in the 'Ἀντιθέσεις is not traditionalist but systematic in intention.

[71] Cf. pp. 170ff. below.

[72] The 'traditions of the Elders' have often been collected and discussed: cf. G. Ficker in Hennecke - N.T. Apokryph, 1924, pp. 540ff.; F. Loofs Theophilus von Antiochien, 1930, pp. 310ff. On Hippolytus cf. A. Hamel, Kirche bei Hippolyt von Rom, 1951, pp. 106f.

[73] Cf. H. Koch, 'War Klemens von Alexandrien Priester?', ZNW 20, 1921, pp. 43ff., esp. pp. 46f.; T. Zahn, Forschungen zur Geschichte des neutestamentlichen Kanons 6, 1900, p. 83: ' "Father" would best represent the meaning of the term ὁ πρεσβύτερος as used by Irenaeus, Clement, Hippolytus, and Origen.' For Origen cf. also Comm. Ser. Matt. 10 (Klostermann, p. 18).

[74] Even when it is a case of the testimony of one single πρεσβύτερος, this anonymity continues to be a characteristic feature. Even more unspecifically 'ecclesiastical' is the suggestion of the Anti-Montanist (quoted in Eusebius, HE V, 16, 7) that the Montanists prophesied παρὰ τὸ κατὰ παράδοσιν καὶ διαδοχὴν ἄνωθεν τῆς ἐκκλησίας ἔθος. The Montanists themselves are acquainted with a διαδέχεσθαι of the Spirit, which will never be allowed to cease in the Church: Eusebius, HE V, 17, 4; cf. III, 31, 4.

a broad group, in connection with the general truth which has been taught in the Church 'from of old'. In controversy with the gnostics, however, it is then also possible, if occasion demands, to mention particular witnesses and chains of witnesses by name, from which the continuity of the church tradition may then be directly inferred. In this connection Polycarp of Smyrna especially plays a paradigmatic role; for quite apart from his personal standing as a revered bishop and martyr he forms, on account of his unusually great age, a living link between the apostolic era and the third, or even the fourth, post-apostolic generation.[75] So late as the middle of the second century he is able to testify in Rome, as Irenaeus records, that he is 'the one and only survivor of his generation who received from the apostles the truth which is passed on by the Church (and not by the "sects")'.[76] Later it is calculated that Irenaeus too, who in his youth had heard Polycarp speak, can be held to go back to the Apostle John and to the first sub-apostolic generation.[77] Such an appeal in confirmation of one's own tradition corresponds exactly to the gnostic methods of proof against which it is used, and which, as similar but far better and more trust-worthy evidence, this time in favour of the true tradition, it seeks to refute.

The idea of 'succession' acquires a new, specifically catholic form only when it is linked with the succession of monarchical bishops. In this way it becomes something more solid, universally applicable, and convincing that it could ever be when adduced to provide *ad hoc* proof of the links between a particular teacher and his disciples. We can in fact indicate with some probability the precise point at which the changeover to this new pattern of succession was made, and name the man responsible. To all appearance it is Hegesippus. Hegesippus is known to us as a Christian man of letters from the East who about the year A.D. 180 wrote a great work in which, to quote Eusebius, he 'pre-sented the undistorted tradition of the apostolic preaching in the simplest possible form'.[78] It would seem that this work has only been lost in fairly recent times; but Eusebius has preserved some important fragments.[79] In one such fragment Hegesippus recounts how he went by sea to Rome in the time of Bishop Anicetus, and stayed there during

---

[75] The date of Polycarp's death is now to be placed either in the year 177, with H. Grégoire, 'La véritable date du martyre de S. Polycarpe', *Anal. Boll.* 69, 1951, pp. 1ff., or in 168, with W. Telfer, 'The date of the martyrdom of Polycarp', *JTS* NS 3, 1952, pp. 79ff.; cf. further Campenhausen, *Polycarp*, pp. 18f.

[76] Irenaeus, Adv. haer. III, 3, 4 (=Eusebius, *HE* IV, 14, 5).

[77] Eusebius, *HE* V, 20, 1.

[78] Eusebius, *HE* IV, 8, 1.

[79] On Hegesippus cf. Zahn, *op. cit.*, pp. 250ff. The fragments have been collected by H. J. Lawlor, *Eusebiana*, 1912, pp. 98ff.

the whole pontificate of Soter—an indication which takes us down to roughly the sixtieth year of the century. On the way to Rome he also stopped at Corinth. (Possibly, therefore, he came from Asia Minor.) Such journeys, which are, for instance, attested also in the case of Clement of Alexandria,[80] were nothing out of the ordinary for cultured Christians in those days. In the case of Hegesippus there is no reason to doubt that his pilgrimage for the purpose of ecclesiastical and theological study was very particularly aimed at helping in the fight against heresy. As one result of his investigations he records his conclusion that the Corinthian church had lived 'in the right word' up to the time when Primus was bishop,[81] and that the situation was just the same at Rome, where Soter 'succeeded' Anicetus, and was himself succeeded by Eleutherus, that is, each took over from his predecessor in the succession of teaching and office. Hence, 'in each succession (διαδοχή) and in each city things are as the Law and the Prophets and the Lord preach'.[82] For Hegesippus the very fact of this unanimous agreement in doctrine is a sign that the doctrine in question is the original one. In addition, however, he makes the attempt in some sort to demonstrate historically the existence of a continuous tradition. He refers to the unbroken chain of bishops, which guarantees the undistorted transmission of doctrine in all orthodox churches. In so doing he is not as yet bringing out a juristic or even a sacramental continuity, which might be capable of safeguarding the teaching office as such; he is thinking rather of the actual links between spiritual teacher and taught, by which a continuous tradition is established. That is why he lays particular emphasis as regards Rome on the fact that Eleutherus, who succeeded Soter, had already been Anicetus's deacon in the time of the latter's episcopate; for this shows that there did indeed exist here an unbroken progression in the teaching and handing on of the faith. Nevertheless, we can already discern in this passage how the word *diadoche* is beginning to change its meaning in an ecclesiastical direction.[83] The intellectual continuity of a teaching succession becomes something like succession to the highest teaching office in the Church, a succession which is maintained in each congregation, and which must be maintained in order that the existence of a living chain of tradition may be taken as proven.

What Hegesippus has to tell of his own activities in Rome takes us even further in the same direction. He relates that while there he 'made

[80] Cf. p. 197 below.

[81] Eusebius, *HE* IV, 22, 2.

[82] Eusebius, *HE* IV, 22, 3: ἐν ἑκάστῃ δὲ διαδοχῇ καὶ ἐν ἑκάστῃ πόλει οὕτως ἔχει, ὡς ὁ νόμος κηρύσσει καὶ οἱ προφῆται καὶ ὁ κύριος.

[83] In the passage from Hegesippus quoted in Eusebius, *HE* IV, 22, 3, διαδέχεσθαι is used absolutely; in the light of *HE* II, 23, 4, however, the object understood is not the tradition but the ἐκκλησία.

a *diadoche* as far as Anicetus'.[84] This sentence was regarded for a long time as hopelessly textually corrupt.[85] To speak of a 'succession' not merely existing but being 'made' seemed intolerably harsh. Nevertheless, if one rightly reconstructs the historical and dogmatic significance of the concept, then this further extension of its meaning does not seem at all difficult to understand.[86] Hegesippus wants to say not merely that he is asserting that there is a genuine continuity of teaching behind the bishops who hold office in his time, but that he has also proved it by compiling a complete list of the actual series of 'transmitting' and 'receiving' bishops. This demonstration of the succession or *diadoche* is now, therefore, itself termed a *diadoche*, and in this way the word acquires in this passage something like its later normal sense of 'list of bishops'. That while at Rome Hegesippus did in fact do something of this kind, or cause it to be done, seems probable in the light of other indications.[87] A decade earlier, on the occasion of Polycarp's visit, the then bishop, Anicetus, in justification of the Roman observance of Easter appealed only in quite general terms to the practice of his predecessors, 'the presbyters before him',[88] even though Polycarp had explicitly based his case on the authority of John. This hardly sounds as if there was an established Roman succession list going back to the apostles.[89] On the other hand, fifteen to twenty years after Hegesippus, Irenaeus was in Rome, and became acquainted with the list of bishops which he then incorporated into his anti-gnostic work.[90] There is

[84] Eusebius, *HE* IV, 22, 3: γενόμενος δὲ ἐν 'Ρώμῃ, διαδοχὴν ἐποιησάμην μέχρις 'Ανικήτου.

[85] Cf. Zahn, *op. cit.*, pp. 243ff.; E. Schwartz, *Eusebius Werke II: Die Kirchengeschichte*, pt. 3: Einleitung, etc., 1909, p. ccxxv n. 3; and above all, E. Caspar, *Die älteste römische Bischofsliste. Kritische Studien zum Formproblem des eusebianischen Kanons sowie zur Geschichte der Bischofslisten und ihrer Entstehung aus apostolischen Sukzessionsreihen*, 1926, pp. 447ff.; also H. Lietzmann, *Petrus und Paulus in Rom*, 1927, p. 28.

[86] Cf. E. Kohlmeyer, 'Zur Ideologie des ältesten Papsttums: Tradition und Sukzession,' *TSK* 103, 1931, pp. 241f.; Van den Eynde, *op. cit.*, pp. 73ff.; an account of earlier discussion may be found in O. Bardenhewer, *Geschichte der altkirchlichen Literatur* I², 1913, pp. 389ff., who himself comes down on the side of the traditional reading.

[87] The note already mentioned, namely that concerning Soter and Eleutherus, the successors of Anicetus, would then have been included in his later work as a kind of codicil to the list.

[88] Irenaeus in Eusebius, *HE* V, 24, 16. This bishop need not necessarily have been a contemporary of Hegesippus: cf. Dix, *op. cit.*, p. 209.

[89] Of course, it is also possible that Anicetus was well aware of the postapostolic origin of Roman practice in the matter of Easter, and therefore refrained from invoking Peter in support of his own side: S. Schmutz, 'Petrus war dennoch in Rom', *BM* 22, 1946, pp. 128ff.

[90] Irenaeus, Adv. haer. III, 3, 3 (=Eusebius, *HE* V, 6). That Irenaeus received this list and did not create it is shown by the changes of tense when he inserts his incidental comments.

nothing to suggest that this list of which he availed himself is not in fact the one composed by Hegesippus. The list cannot have been very much earlier than Hegesippus, because it presupposes the monarchical episcopate; and it was, it would seem, precisely in Rome that this development occurred only at a remarkably late stage.[91] The conjecture has, nevertheless, been put forward that the Roman list of bishops was originally not a list of episcopal officers but of non-official repositories of the tradition, and as such possibly very old.[92] But this must be ruled out. For if this were so, then the list would have taken on a very different appearance—above all, it would have turned out much shorter. In such cases, as the gnostic lists and above all the example of Polycarp and Irenaeus show, there was always and inevitably an effort to get back to the fountainhead of apostolic teaching with as few intermediate steps as possible, in order to inspire greater confidence; and for this purpose, even in the time of Anicetus, two or three, or at most four or five respected names would have sufficed instead of the full dozen of which Irenaeus makes use to bring the line down as far as Eleutherus. There is, therefore, no need to mistrust Hegesippus, when he asserts that he himself established the *diadoche*, that is, the sequence of Roman bishops, and in fact 'made' it in the sense of making a list of this kind.[93]

How Hegesippus went to work in detail on his task we can no longer say. There are no grounds for suggesting that the list is 'faked'.[94] The names which he compiled will have been communicated to him by the clergy of the Roman church, and will naturally not have been simply invented for the purpose. They may, for the most part, have belonged to actual people who had at one time played a part in the life of the congregation, and of whom something was still known or thought to be known. That the writer of I Clement should be among them is natural

[91] This is shown by I Clement; Ignatius, Romans; and Hermas. The attempts to extract the opposite conclusion from these texts, even if themselves constantly repeated, do not call for repeated refutation.

[92] This was the thesis which Caspar sought to maintain in *Die älteste römische Bischofsliste*, and took as the basis of his presentation in *Geschichte des Papsttums* I, 1930, pp. 8ff. It has never met with approval among Catholic scholars; but only the argument which here follows seems to me to tell decisively against it.

[93] Nevertheless, he cannot have incorporated it into his own work; otherwise Eusebius, who liked to quote excerpts from this early authority, would have given the text in definitive form. Harnack, *Die Chronologie der altchristlichen Literatur bis Eusebius*, 1893, pp. 180ff., was, in my view, undoubtedly right in making this point, despite the later arguments against it of C. H. Turner, 'The early episcopal lists IV', *JTS* 19, 1918, pp. 119f.; B. H. Streeter, *The primitive Church*, 1929, pp. 288ff.; and Kohlmeyer, *op. cit.*, pp. 241f.

[94] Cf. Dix, *op. cit.*, p. 208. Moreover, it looks as though Eusebius did not preserve the statements relating to Corinth and Rome in full, but abbreviated them: cf. Lawlor, *op. cit.*, pp. 65ff.

enough. The order of the names in the list may, however, derive purely from Hegesippus himself; and the whole compilation is no more reliable than the memory of the Roman church at the time on the subject of the preceding hundred years or more, a memory which was unchecked then and which we certainly have no means of checking now.

On the question how far Hegesippus was successful in his attempt, there is no need to add much to what has already been said. It was, as we have seen, becoming customary elsewhere in Catholic circles to confirm the reliability of one's own apostolic doctrines by using the gnostic method of naming teachers and series of teachers. From there it is but a small step to describing the sequence of monarchical bishops as this sort of series of teachers, and then to make use of it in controversy with the gnostics. That Christian congregations had always had monarchical bishops at their head seemed, in the second half of the second century, already obvious. Presumably, therefore, all that was necessary was to discover the details. Such a succession, verified by actual names, in the 'greatest, oldest, and universally known' church of Rome may have seemed especially valuable, and have served as a sufficient model for all.[95] In principle, however, things were exactly the same in the case of Corinth and of every other church of apostolic foundation. The argument was all the more convincing in that it did not require any one church to bear alone the burden of demonstrating the fact that the teaching was that originally given. Hegesippus was just as well able as Irenaeus and Tertullian at a later date to point to the mutual agreement on doctrine between the orthodox churches, to the recollection of outstanding individual witnesses, to the supposedly late emergence of false teaching, and above all to the writings of the apostles as these were in use in the Church. In addition there was the point that the existence of similar episcopal lists for the heretical congregations could not be generally asserted, or at any rate not in the same unambiguous and universal fashion as in the Catholic Church; and that, nevertheless, the Catholic methods of proof now corresponded precisely to those of their opponents, the fragmentary nature of which had till now never dawned on anyone. The part played by the gnosis, however, is that of middleman, linking a sociological pattern in ancient philosophy to the Church, which then trasformed it to meet its own special needs. About the same time chains of witnesses begin to play their part in rabbinic tradition too;[96] but in my own opinion there is no occasion in the case

[95] This point of view is particularly emphasised in Irenaeus, Adv. haer. III, 3, 1.

[96] Cf. W. Bacher, *Tradition und Tradenten in den Schulen Palästinas und Babyloniens. Studien und Materialien zur Entstehungsgeschichte des Talmuds*, 1914; Ranft, *op. cit.*, pp. 137ff.; and the references in Kohlmeyer, *op. cit.*, pp. 235ff., and E. Stauffer, *op. cit.*, pp. 15f.

of Hegesippus to reckon particularly with any additional influence from this quarter.[97]

Hegesippus's list, in the form in which we find it in Irenaeus, still clearly reveals the interests which led to its creation.[98] Its concern is certainly not to supply a list of the heads of the church hierarchy, and even less is it a purely factual aid to ecclesiastical chronology. The only thing that matters is the unbroken link, the bridge thrown back to the apostles as the sole legitimate founders of church doctrine. It is a list with a purpose—what we may call a 'dynamic' list. A simple series of names, without dates or further particulars, it merely enumerates the places distance at which the individual men, as they 'succeed', stand from the two apostles, Peter and Paul, who 'founded and built up' the Roman church. These two are the starting-point of the chain of tradition, but they themselves are no longer included in it. For it is their tradition which is what matters; the chain itself is, to change the metaphor, merely the pipe through which it flows unsullied. The list proves, to use Irenaeus's words, that 'the tradition of the apostles in the Church, and the proclamation of the truth, has come down to us in one and the same order and succession'.[99] In this comment the new element, if one compares it with the corresponding statements in Ptolemaeus, is the concept of 'order' ($\tau\acute{\alpha}\xi\iota\varsigma$), intended in an official sense. But it will still be a fairly long time before the concept of succession, stressed here to safeguard belief in the tradition, is detached from this original context and set up, as it were, on its own in order to divert the doctrine of spiritual office increasingly

[97] On what follows the remarks of Caspar are again fundamental; in addition to the works already cited cf. 'Die älteste römische Bischofsliste', in *Papsttum und Kaisertum* (Kehr-Festschrift), 1926, pp. 1ff.

[98] That Hegesippus, as Zahn believed, would have been a Jewish Christian can by no means be firmly established. Eusebius (*HE* IV, 22, 28) deduces this merely from Hegesippus's linguistic attainments without giving any more precise details. His gross ignorance of conditions in Palestine, however, points in the opposite direction: cf. Harnack I, p. 312; also A. Schlatter, *Die Kirche Jerusalems vom Jahre 70 bis 130*, 1898, p. 30 n. 1. Furthermore, it is not at all certain that the idea of succession would have been cultivated more in Judaeo-Christianity than anywhere else. So far as the problematic evidence of the Pseudo-Clementines is relevant here (cf. pp. 179f. below), they do, it is true, reveal an explicit interest in the apostolic tradition; but this is fixed in written form, and is committed to the Christian teachers or rabbis for safe keeping, not to the bishops. This is made clear by the *Epistle of Peter, Contest.* 2f., and the related description in Clem. Alex., *Hyp.* VII (=Eusebius, *HE* II, 1, 4). In those sections which can validly be regarded as of an early date there is nowhere any mention of episcopal succession. The sole exception (Clem. Rec. 4, 35) is accepted with confidence as early only by H. J. Schoeps, *Theologie und Geschichte des Judenchristentums*, 1949, pp. 292, 294, and precisely because of its unique attitude must be regarded as highly suspect.

[99] Irenaeus, Adv. haer. III, 3, 3 (=Eusebius, *HE* V, 6, 5).

on to new paths and to be the sole determinant of its meaning.
The technique of authenticating one's tradition quickly becomes a
popular feature of ecclesiastical polemic; but it does not always take
the form of a strict proof of succession, a move which was more particularly appropriate to controversy with false teachers. It is still, for
example, open to question whether the anonymous, so-called Anti-
Montanist in Asia Minor has this in mind when, in opposition to the
'new prophecy', he appeals to the 'tradition and succession' of the
Church.[100] Polycrates of Ephesus, too, in his controversy with Victor
of Rome, marshals a confused mass of witnesses from Asia Minor, and
only in conclusion rests his case on the *paradosis* of seven bishops, all
personally related to himself.[101] In Asia Minor as in Rome the claim to
possess the tomb of an apostle has its importance.[102] The classic
continuation of the Hegesippan method occurs at first only in Irenaeus
of Lyons, who himself came from Asia Minor, and then in Tertullian,
who was an African. Nevertheless, it will hardly have remained unknown at Rome, even though we can in fact not establish its presence
there with certainty until the third century.[103]

Irenaeus is fighting on the same anti-gnostic front as Hegesippus,
and may have derived the succession concept from him, either directly
or indirectly. Institutionalist and hierarchical thinking is by nature
uncongenial to him. This is best seen from his *Demonstration of the
Apostolic Preaching*, a later work than the *Adversus haereses*, and one
which unfortunately survives only in an Armenian version.[104] This is a
summary of basic Christian doctrine, in which Irenaeus appears as
much more independent and also, let it be said, far less significant than
in the larger work.[105] All official and ceremonial elements have disappeared, and the idea of succession, indeed the clerical hierarchy in
general, is no longer even mentioned.[106] Irenaeus bears testimony only

[100] Eusebius, *HE* V, 16, 7; cf. p. 162 n. 74 above.

[101] Eusebius, *HE* V, 24, 6: κατὰ παράδοσιν τῶν συγγενῶν, ἑπτὰ μὲν ἦσαν
συγγενεῖς μου ἐπίσκοποι, ἐγὼ δὲ ὄγδοος. Naturally these eight bishops do not
form a chain of tradition.

[102] Eusebius, *HE* II, 25, 7 (Caius of Rome); cf. also VII, 25, 16 (Dionysius of
Alexandria). H. Koch, 'Petrus und Paulus im zweiten Osterfeierstreit', *ZNW*
19, 1919/20, pp. 178f., argues persuasively that Asia had a lead over Rome in
this respect; cf. also W. Köhler, *Omnis ecclesia Petri propinqua*, 1938, pp. 26f.

[103] The succession concept has still not penetrated the pre-Hippolytan
ordination prayers of the church order of Hippolytus: cf. p. 175 n. 159 below.
On later developments at Rome cf. pp. 276ff. and 236f. below.

[104] In *Dem.* 99 there is a reference to the main work.

[105] Cf. Loofs, *op cit.*, pp. 434 ff.

[106] Cf. A. Harnack in Ter-Mekerttsian and Ter-Minassiantz, *Des heiligen
Irenäus Schrift "Zum Erweise der apostolischen Verkündigung"*, 1907, pp. 65f.
As the starting-point of the tradition Dem. 3 simply refers to 'the disciples of the
apostles'.

to the truth and the way of life which 'the prophets proclaimed, Christ confirmed, and the apostles made known, and which the Church discloses to her children throughout the world'.[107] The Church is for him the place where this primal truth is taught and believed with a living faith,[108] where Christ is invoked, and his will performed,[109] and where the Holy Spirit is present with his gifts.[110]

Irenaeus seeks to defend this truth from every possible angle in his voluminous *Exposure and Refutation of the gnosis falsely so called* (i.e., the *Adversus haereses*). He does this primarily with the help of Holy Scripture, that is, on the basis of the Old Testament and of the New Testament canon—still in process of formation—which goes with it.[111] It is this which is the true treasure of the Church. She is the paradise garden planted in this world, and her Scriptures are the fruits from which we ought to eat—in contrast to the forbidden trees of the pretentious gnostic 'knowledge'.[112] But now another difficulty arises, namely that the false teachers do not admit the validity of the witness of the genuine Scriptures; they appeal, on the contrary, to their special, secret oral traditions.[113] Thus we arrive at the point where even Irenaeus, in order not to let them slip through his fingers, has to call upon the ecclesiastical succession of bishops; and in particular the Roman episcopal list compiled by Hegesippus now fulfils its purpose. The line of argument which he develops against those who deny the authority of the Bible is lucid and effectively convincing. Our faith, says Irenaeus, by God's will rests on the preaching of the apostles, which was later written down, and only on this.[114] For it was they who received 'the authority of the Gospel', and it was to them that the Lord said: 'He who hears you hears me'.[115] But if we assume for the sake of argument

---

[107] Dem. 98. With the exception of a few passages to be discussed later, it is the rule that Irenaeus passes in this way directly from the apostles to the Church as a whole: cf. e.g., Adv. haer. III pref.; III, 12, 15; III, 24, 1; IV, 17, 5; V pref.

[108] Cf. e.g., Adv. haer. V, 20, 1; for the emphasis on faith, Dem. 3.

[109] Dem. 97.

[110] Adv. haer. II, 31, 2f.; 32, 4.

[111] Adv. haer. III, 2, 1. E. Molland, 'Irenaeus of Lugdunum and the Apostolic Succession', *JEH* 1, 1950, pp. 12ff., rightly emphasises, against the catholicising exposition of Van Den Eynde, that Irenaeus was a 'biblical theologian': 'It is not Irenaeus, but his gnostic opponents who think that Scripture has to be supplemented by tradition;' similarly Reynders, *op. cit.*, p. 175. For the content of the *paradosis* in Irenaeus cf. H. Holstein, 'La tradition des Apôtres chez saint Irénée', *RSR* 36, 1949, pp. 229ff., who nevertheless underestimates the importance of the NT Scriptures.

[112] Adv. haer. V, 20, 2.

[113] Adv. haer. III, 2, 1.

[114] Adv. haer. III, 1, 1. Irenaeus never sees Jesus or the prophets as the starting-point of the *paradosis*, but exclusively the apostles: cf. Reynders, pp. 179f.

[115] Adv. haer. III pref.

that the 'hidden mysteries' about which the gnostics invent such fantastic tales did exist, to whom would the apostles have entrusted them? Obviously first and foremost to the men whom they especially valued for other reasons, and to whom they therefore handed on their congregations and their own teaching office, namely the elders of the Church. With them alone can the man of goodwill rationally hope to find the true tradition;[116] and if by some chance—the situation is purely hypothetical!—the apostles had not left behind any writings, then men would have had to be satisfied simply with this normal and regular method of transmission. Even today this is the procedure among those barbarians who do not know the art of writing; and these people resolutely reject all the efforts of the heretics to seduce them.[117] And if, notwithstanding, differences of opinion should still develop on some minor question, yet men can hold fast to the ancient apostolic foundation-truths, for which there is demonstrably an unbroken link with the apostles themselves. Here the example of the pre-eminent church of Rome (whose list of bishops is inserted in full at this point) is especially valuable; for she, as a church with a double apostolic foundation, 'more than any other'[118] has kept safe the old tradition. One can, however, also point to the churches of Asia Minor and the successors of Polycarp, who had himself been a personal acquaintance of the apostles.[119] Entirely in the manner of Hegesippus, Irenaeus here lays stress on the fact that what is involved is a genuine chain of teaching, not merely a formal, if incontestable, series of bishops' names.[120] The episcopal rank of the mediators of the tradition is of no further consequence to him. In this context, as he likes to do in others,[121] he describes them simply as 'elders', and thus opens up the possibility of including them directly in the category not merely of teaching clerics but of the revered 'Elders' of the apostolic and sub-apostolic age. Hence it is crystal clear that in the search for the original truth there is no point whatever in following any of the teachers of the Valentinians or of other new sects but only 'the presbyters who are to be found in the Church which possesses the *diadoche* of the apostles', and has received 'together with the *diadoche*', that is, with the succession in the episcopal office, also 'the assured gift of the truth'[122]—by which is meant not any

---

[116] Adv. haer. III, 3, 1; cf. III, 2, 2.   [117] Adv. haer. III, 4, 1.

[118] This is the meaning of the vulgar Latin idiom, '*ab his, qui . . .*', as C. Mohrmann, 'À propos de Irenäus, Advers. haeres. 3, 3, 1', *VC* 3, 1949, pp. 57ff., following R. Jacquin, *L'année théologique 1948*, pp. 95ff., has shown. A further parallel occurs in *Didasc. Apost.* III, 8, 3; VI, 19, 5.

[119] Adv. haer. III, 3, 4.

[120] Cf. esp. his comment on Clement: Adv. haer. III, 3, 3.

[121] Cf. p. 119 n. 304 above.

[122] Adv. haer. IV, 26, 2: quapropter eis qui in ecclesia sunt presbyteris obaudire oportet his qui successionem habent ab apostolis, sicut ostendimus; qui

special official 'charisma' but the traditional doctrine itself.[123] The arrogant false teachers, dominated by evil impulses, are on the other hand to be mistrusted from the start;[124] and the man who for their sake abandons the teaching of the Church thereby accuses the holy presbyters of ignorance, those very bishops[125] to whom the apostles entrusted their church. He has ceased to understand that even an unlearned devout believer is better than a brazen sophist.[126] In this passage Irenaeus, like the author of I Clement, perhaps displays some doubt of the intellectual capacities of the orthodox clergy, who frequently are not so unequivocally superior to their opponents as one would wish.[127]

It is clear that the ideas bound up with office and succession, which by and large take up very little space in Irenaeus's writings,[128] have an apologetic and polemical intention. Except when they are important to the struggle against the heretics, they are nowhere pursued or developed. Irenaeus's purpose is only and always the defence of the Church, that is, of her teaching, against the false teachers with their supposedly higher but in fact spurious and totally unfounded separatist doctrine.[129] Irenaeus does not contemplate a special sacramental 'character' of the episcopate,[130] nor does he ever stress the authority of the bishops as opposed to that of the laity, or indeed to that of the other non-episcopal clergy of the Church.[131] The mere position in

---

cum episcopatus successione charisma veritatis certum secundum placitum patris acceperunt.

[123] This is the only interpretation which makes sense of the passage—the *veritas* is the *charisma*: cf. K. Müller, 'Das Charisma veritatis und der Episkopat des Irenäus', *ZNW* 23, 1924, pp. 216ff.

[124] Adv. haer. IV, 26, 1; 27, 1.

[125] Adv. haer. V, 20, 1.   [126] Adv. haer. V, 20, 2.

[127] The constant polemic against the gnostics' arrogance and pride in their learning points in the same direction.

[128] W. Schmidt, *Die Kirche bei Irenäus*, 1934, pp. 70ff., noted this correctly, but failed to give it sufficient emphasis.

[129] For this reason the comment of N. Bonwetsch, *Die Theologie des Irenäus*, 1925, p. 124, and Schmidt, *op. cit.*, p. 74, that in Irenaeus office is little short of 'necessary for salvation' is very wide of the mark. The passages quoted in support of this view speak only of the duty of following the presbyters because they have received and teach the original truth: Adv. haer. IV, 26, 2; 32, 1. They will not bear the weight of such a dogmatically oppressive assertion.

[130] Such a concept does not seem to be entertained by any writer of this period (cf. K. Müller, *op. cit.*), and in the case of Irenaeus the fact that in southern Gaul he had no episcopal colleagues close at hand makes it virtually impossible that he should have maintained the existence of a special episcopal charisma given at consecration: E. Molland, *op. cit.*, pp. 26ff.

[131] On this point cf. esp. the letter of exhortation to Victor of Rome, quoted in Eusebius, *HE* V, 24, 11ff., and the letter to the congregations in Vienne and Lyons, probably also written by Irenaeus. In the latter, it is true, the remark is

itself calls in his eyes for no special respect;[132] it must be combined with living faith. Irenaeus warns expressly against those clergy who indeed are taken for genuine presbyters by the generality and seem to enjoy an unassailable position, but who in fact serve their own lusts and, while proud of their high status,[133] are rejected by Christ, who sees the heart.[134] The only presbyters to whom one ought to listen are those who in addition to the office have succeeded also to the teaching of the apostles, and who keep themselves apart from all who give offence either in doctrine or in way of life.[135] Such warnings make it clear that official position is not the item that tips the scales;[136] what matters is the preaching and the life, which must be in keeping with that position. As for the Elders who were the immediate successors of the apostles in the task of caring for the Church, it is said that their life and teaching were indeed in harmony with one another, and that they expounded the Scriptures rightly.[137] Irenaeus feels, however, no compulsion to clarify the problem raised by these various conflicting statements, and nowhere pursues the further questions which they inevitably create concerning the nature of office in the Church.

---

made that blessed Pothinus had been entrusted with the 'ministry of the episcopate' (διακονία τῆς ἐπισκοπῆς; in Adv. haer. III, 3, 3 λειτουργία) in Lyons (Eusebius, HE V, 1, 29), but any further exaltation of clerical rank and importance is omitted. His martyrdom is narrated after those of his deacon and several of the laity. In the received corpus of Irenaeus's writings a deacon is mentioned only once: Adv. haer. I, 8, 4.

[132] Similarly, in the letter of the Gallic martyrs to Eleutherus, bishop of Rome (Eusebius, HE V, 4, 2), Irenaeus is commended for his Christian zeal with the added comment: εἰ γὰρ ᾔδειμεν τόπον τινὶ δικαιοσύνην περιποιεῖσθαι, ὡς πρεσβύτερον ἐκκλησίας, ὅπερ ἐστὶν ἐπ᾽ αὐτῷ, ἐν πρώτοις ἂν παρεθέμεθα.

[133] Reading principalis consessionis with Harvey rather than concessionis with Stieren, though the sense of the passage is almost the same in each case.

[134] Adv. haer. IV, 26, 3: Qui vero crediti quidem sunt a multis esse presbyteri, serviunt autem suis voluptatibus et non praeponent timorem dei in cordibus suis, sed in contumeliis agunt reliquos et principalis consessionis tumore elati sunt et in absconsis agunt mala et dicunt, 'nemo nos videt', redarguuntur a verbo, qui non secundum gloriam iudicat neque faciem attendit, sed in cor.

[135] Adv. haer. IV, 26, 4: ab omnibus igitur talibus absistere oportet, adhaerere vero his, qui et apostolorum, sicut praediximus, doctrinam custodiunt et cum presbyterii ordine sermonem sanum et conversationem sine offensa praestant ad conformationem et correptionem reliquorum.

[136] Nevertheless, these presbyters do still have their status. B. Poschmann, Paenitentia secunda, 1940, p. 227 n. 2, attempts without success to prove, as against J. Hoh, Die kirchliche Busse im zweiten Jahrhundert, 1932, p. 96, that this section must refer to presbyters who have already undergone 'de facto excommunication', since 'the bishop' would never in any circumstances have allowed such people 'to continue to exercise their ecclesiastical functions'. This is a circular argument and proves nothing. Moreover, Irenaeus does not say what on Poschmann's view he was bound to say, but insists on the fact that such men continue to enjoy their position in the Church and general respect.

[137] Adv. haer. IV, 26, 5.

The view which a little later is to be found in Tertullian is developed in a more precise, rational and convincing way, but in essence is no different from that of Irenaeus.[138] Tertullian thinks like a lawyer, and so from the start office occupies a definite, almost constitutionalist position within his concept of the Church. That it derives from the apostles is a thesis which in his time no longer needs to be proved; it is taken for granted.[139] The bishops are the original 'heirs'[140] who received the apostolic teaching and who can therefore still testify to it today not only in those churches which are of apostolic foundation but also in all the others which developed from them and agree with them.[141] By contrast the heretics have demonstrably no connection with the apostles, because they can never produce a series of bishops going back that far.[142] Neither, therefore, can they possess the genuine tradition, and one should have nothing to do with them at any time— even when they try to appeal to Holy Scripture.[143] This is an over-statement, made for tactical reasons, of the position already developed by Irenaeus, and one which Tertullian himself patently does not take wholly seriously; all he wants is to be sure that it is maintained in principle. Once more the concept of succession is being employed in a primarily polemical way in the controversy with the false teachers.[144] With Tertullian too it is not so much a question of a hierarchical theory as of a safeguarding of doctrine, with which nevertheless the right order of the Church, the *disciplina*, is indissolubly linked. At any rate it is not his intention to substitute the authority of the bishops for that of the orthodox tradition. The powers of the episcopate are of more legal than dogmatic significance.[145] Certainly they are the leaders[146] and presidents[147] set over[148] the congregation, and as such have a permanent[149] higher rank.[150] As 'shepherds'[151] they also have an obligation

---

[138] On what follows cf. E. Altendorf, *Einheit und Heiligkeit der Kirche. Untersuchungen zur Entwicklung des altchristlichen Kirchenbegriffs im Abendland von Tertullian bis zu den antidonatistischen Schriften Augustins*, 1932, pp. 24ff., and the material in K. Adam, *Der Kirchenbegriff Tertullians. Eine dogmengeschichtliche Studie*, 1907, pp. 41ff.

[139] Praescr. 32; fuga 13.

[140] Praescr. 37; scorp. 9; cf. A. Beck, *Römisches Recht bei Tertullian und Cyprian. Eine Studie zur frühen Kirchenrechtsgeschichte*, 1930, p. 57.

[141] Praescr. 20f., 32.   [142] Praescr. 32.   [143] Praescr. 19.

[144] Of outstanding importance in this connection are the ideas in the *De praescriptione haereticorum*, on which cf. J. K. Stirnimann, *Die praescriptio Tertullians im Lichte des römischen Rechts und der Theologie*, 1949; and B. Altaner, *TLZ* 75, 1950, pp. 613f.

[145] Cf. pudic. 21, 6: disciplinae solius officia sortitus es, nec imperio praesidere, sed ministerio.

[146] Fuga 11: duces.   [147] Cor. 1; fuga 11: praesides.

[148] Fuga 11; monog. 12: praepositi.

[149] Praescr. 41.   [150] Fuga 11.   [151] Cor. 1; fuga 11.

to teach. But they may also err,[152] and the teachers who hold no office, and who are equally part of the Church, are in no way subordinate to their control but act with spiritual authority of their own. The laity too are really and truly priests,[153] and both may and should take their priestly rights seriously; if no clergyman is available, then any Christian is authorised to conduct the Eucharist in his place or to baptise, and to be his own priest.[154]

It is easy to detect from such passages that Tertullian is a layman; and Montanism only intensified the unsacral, consciously laic features in his concept of office.[155] In Hippolytus of Rome we see how the succession theory is handled by a man who is himself a bishop, even though in other matters his attitude of mind is by no means hierarchic or clericalist. Consideration of Hippolytus brings us down to the third century. Theologically he is a disciple of Irenaeus, and sees in the Church above all a spiritual nation, the assembly of the saints, and the vessel of the Holy Spirit.[156] He is a scholar, and on ecclesiastical matters his thinking is very nearly reactionary. Nevertheless, as bishop of Rome he is at the same time the conscious exponent of a tradition of ecclesiastical law—a subject in which he takes a great interest[157]— and of a dignity attaching to his office, in which he has to assert himself against a resourceful rival.[158] Hippolytus too employs the concept of tradition almost exclusively in controversy with heretics,[159] whom he tackles with scientific thoroughness; but it is precisely in his capacity as bishop that he feels himself called to expose their errors: 'No one will refute them except the Holy Spirit handed down in the Church,

---

[152] This view, however, is found explicitly only in Tertullian's Montanist period.

[153] Exhort. cast. 7; monog. 12.   [154] Exhort. cast. 7; cf. bapt. 17.

[155] Cf. pp 227f. below.

[156] Cf. A. Hamel, *Kirche bei Hippolyt von Rom*, 1951. A. Oepke, *Das neue Gottesvolk*, 1950, p. 255, calls him 'the virtuoso of the concept of the people of God'.

[157] That the ἀποστολικὴ παράδοσις as a church order is indeed the work of Hippolytus can no longer be doubted: cf. B. Botte, 'L'authenticité de la "Tradition apostolique" de saint Hippolyte,' *RTAM* 14, 1948, pp. 177ff., in reply to H. Engberding, 'Das angebliche Dokument römischer Liturgie aus dem Beginn des dritten Jahrhunderts,' in *Miscellanea liturgica in honorem L. K. Mohlberg*, 1948, pp. 47ff.; and H. Elfers, 'Neue Untersuchungen über die Kirchenordnung Hippolyts von Rom', in *Abhandlungen über Theologie und Kirche (Festschrift K. Adam)*, 1952, pp. 169ff., in reply to P. Nautin, *Hippolyte contre les hérésies*, 1949.

[158] Cf. Caspar, *Papsttum* I, pp. 22ff.

[159] The precise term παράδοσις τῶν ἀποστόλων or ἀποστολικὴ παράδοσις occurs, apart from *Contra Noet.* 17, only at the close of the Church Order: cf. Hamel, *op. cit.*, p. 104 n. 1. It is also highly problematic whether Hippolytus, as Caspar, *Papsttum* I, pp. 11ff., thinks, concluded his *Chronicle* with a list of Roman bishops: cf. Hamel, *op. cit.*, pp. 142ff.

whom the apostles first received and passed on to men of orthodox belief. We are their successors, and share in the same gifts of high priesthood and teaching; we are numbered among the guardians of the Church, and for that reason we neither close our eyes nor keep silent as to the right teaching.' Untiringly, with all the powers of soul and body, and full of thankfulness toward God, 'we are not slack with regard to that which is entrusted to us, and we communicate to all ungrudgingly that which the Holy Spirit has bestowed upon us'.[160] Consciousness of the duties of his office and of his spiritual authority here chime together in proud assurance. For Hippolytus it is still the Holy Spirit with his abundant gifts who is the real creator of the life of the Church; but at the same time he lays great emphasis on the fact that it is the bishops who as successors of the apostles have received the Spirit. As such they stand together throughout the world[161] in order to bear witness to the apostolic truth. Hippolytus is not thinking only of canonical succession to the apostolic office by 'taking over' their teaching and their church, though the corpus of teaching is his primary interest;[162] he is also already thinking of the special sanctifying power present in episcopal consecration. The general notion, which we have seen emerging as early as the Pastorals, that ordination is an effective means of grace[163] appears in his writings now for the first time differentiated into a special grace for each office. According to the ordination prayers of the Roman church collected and recorded by Hippolytus the act of consecration is the means whereby the bishops, like the apostles before them,[164] are endued with the threefold authority of the high priesthood, the teaching, and the office of watchman.[165] Bishops now are to be ordained only by other bishops;[166] and further-

[160] Elench. I pref. 6: ταῦτα δὲ ἕτερος οὐκ ἐλέγξει ἢ τὸ ἐν ἐκκλησίᾳ παραδοθὲν ἅγιον πνεῦμα, οὗ τυχόντες πρότεροι οἱ ἀπόστολοι μετέδοσαν τοῖς ὀρθῶς πεπιστευκόσιν. ὧν ἡμεῖς διάδοχοι τυγχάνοντες τῆς τε αὐτῆς χάριτος μετέχοντες ἀρχιερατείας τε καὶ διδασκαλίας καὶ φρουροὶ τῆς ἐκκλησίας λελογισμένοι οὐκ ὀφθαλμῷ νυστάζομεν οὐδὲ λόγον ὀρθὸν σιωπῶμεν . . . ἐν οἷς πεπιστεύμεθα μὴ ἀτονοῦντες . . . ὅσα παρέχει τὸ ἅγιον πνεῦμα πᾶσιν ἀφθόνως κοινωνοῦντες . . .

[161] Compared with Irenaeus, who really envisaged the bishop only in terms of the individual congregation, this is a new 'catholic' element: cf. C. H. Turner, 'Apostolic Succession', in Essays on the Early History of the Church and the Ministry, ed. H. B. Swete, 1918, pp. 129ff.

[162] Cf. Dix, op. cit., pp. 210f., 213f.   [163] Cf. pp. 115ff. above.

[164] These prayers still make no use of the idea of succession, but simply juxtapose the Spirit-endowed bishops and the apostles. Hippolytus did not compose these prayers himself, but derived them from earlier tradition: cf. Dix, op. cit., pp. 213, 214f.

[165] Apost. Trad. 2–4; cf. K. Müller, Bischofswahl, pp. 275ff., and, in more detail, Dix, op. cit., pp. 196ff.; also Hamel, op. cit., pp. 163ff., and Elfers, op. cit., p. 201.

[166] This may not have been the original situation in Rome, any more than it was in Gaul (cf. p. 172 n. 130 above): K. Müller, Bischofswahl, pp. 293f.

more, they alone are explicitly described as priests, and represent the Church to God and God to the Church.[167] The ordination of priests and deacons is conducted in a substantially simpler manner, but is equally 'sacramental' in principle, and for this reason is sharply distinguished from mere 'appointment', for instance, of a widow.[168] Consecration is supposed to convey to the consecrated person a special gift of the Holy Spirit. A confessor or a man with the gift of healing, who demonstrably already possesses such a gift, is therefore not to receive further consecration on admission to the ranks of the clergy.[169] It is clear that the pneumatic-charismatic and the official-sacramental conceptions are here still co-existing without great difficulty.[170]

With the beginnings of sacral differentiation in consecration rites, and their increasing independence of one another, we enter a new area of speculation on the law and doctrine of the Church, an area dear to the hearts of future clerical liturgiologists and professional theologians, especially from the fourth century onwards,[171] but one which can be of importance for both ecclesiastical politics and questions of principle as well. From such tendencies Hippolytus is still in spirit quite remote. All he wants is that the old customs of the Church should be preserved, that the bishops should exercise their high office with resolution, and that the Spirit of truth and holiness should continue to be the living force it was in the time of the apostles. In this he is undoubtedly a typical example of his outgoing generation. One step—and what a long step it is! — beyond him, and in a single generation we find ourselves in the age of Cyprian.

[167] Cf. Dix, op. cit., p. 197.

[168] Apost. Trad. 11, 4f.; cf. Dix, op. cit., pp. 193f., 217. Consecration or ordination is called χειροτονία, a word which in secular usage signifies simply 'assignment, appointment'. Not until the fourth century is χειροτονεῖν in its sacral significance artificially replaced by χειροθετεῖν: cf. V. Fuchs, Der Ordinationstitel von seiner Entstehung bis auf Innozenz III (Diss. Würzburg 1930), p. 6; Siotis, op. cit., pp. 107ff.

[169] Apost. Trad. 10, 1; in the case of the man with the gift of healing this stipulation is found only in one strand of the MS tradition (Copt. C): cf. Hamel, op. cit., pp. 177f.

[170] It is not, however, still permitted to describe the bishop as a prophet, as Elfers, op. cit., p. 203, maintains. That he receives the 'firstfruits', which according to Did. 13:3 belong to the prophets, proves nothing.

[171] In this period the idea of various gifts of the Spirit, which still glimmers unmistakably through Hippolytus's concept of office, is abandoned in favour of the conception of a cursus honorum through the individual stages of the spiritual office; on this development cf. the illuminating remarks of Dix, op. cit., pp. 274ff.

CHAPTER VIII

Prophets and Teachers in the Second Century

IN THE struggle against the false teachers it was not only the apostolic tradition and the primal witness of the Scriptures which acquired new weight and significance. Among the inheritances 'received' from those earliest days, and requiring to be interpreted and maintained, was that of 'office'; and in the course of the second century this element became more and more prominent. Yet it is not office as such, as a legal and institutional fact, which is the focus of interest; what matters is the traditional body of truth which it is the duty of the office to serve and to preserve. This truth is the truth of God's Church, and belongs to that Church as a whole. It is, therefore, not surprising that in addition to the office-holders the old free men of the Spirit continue to play their part; and the Church is proud that this should be so.[1] The co-existence of these various kinds of authority is not felt to be a problem. To start in every case from a supposed opposition between two separate blocs, the official and the charismatic, is a typical modern misunderstanding. Not only do office-holders possess the Spirit, but the spirituals for their part, to the extent that they rightly belong to the Church, derive the power of their teaching from the traditional apostolic truth. The dividing line is drawn not on canonical or sociological principles but on objective and dogmatic ones.

The critical situation in which the Church finds herself, however, exerts immense pressure in the direction of intensifying official authority, because of the safeguards which this is above all in a position to offer. No one any longer even entertains the idea of basing the life and order of the Church exclusively on the Spirit and its gifts, as Paul had attempted to do. The fixed constitutional framework of the presbyteral–episcopal system is taken for granted in orthodox congregations. In the tradition and succession associated with this form of church order men see the guarantee of sound teaching; and on this assumption the spokesmen of the Church overwhelm with ridicule the fluid and fluctuating

---

[1] On this point cf., in addition to the passages from Irenaeus mentioned at pp. 169f., 172f. above, Justin, Dial. 82, 1, Tertullian—who became a Montanist because he felt this so strongly—and the Anti-Montanist in Eusebius, HE V, 17, 4.

structures of the heretical conventicle and of the 'schools' which form around individual teachers. But this does not mean that the orthodox had turned against the free teacher as such; there was still room for his ministry. In practice, therefore, the Church follows a middle course which more or less does justice to the various possibilites offered in the earlier period; but she has ceased to bear in mind the questions of principle which these possibilities had raised. The meaning of this 'catholic' development is understood only relatively, in contrast with other, extreme lines of advance which open up, only to be rejected, at about the same time—namely, on the one hand, a legalist Judaeo-Christianity which was slowly withering away, and on the other, the enthusiast 'prophecy' of Montanism. Of these two only Montanism stimulated a controversy which is of importance for our present concerns. The Ebionite Judaeo-Christians pass almost unnoticed; and if notwithstanding we do in fact deal briefly with them (precisely because they are uncharacteristic) this can be done only with considerable reservations, since the extant sources are for the most part late, do not allow us to draw a complete picture, and futhermore are still the object of very diverse opinions and evaluations.[2]

This much at any rate may be considered clear: the Jewish Christian congregations in Transjordan, in their resistance to hellenism and Paulinism revert more and more to a kind of sectarian Judaism, basing their whole life once again on the Law, so that in general they no longer produce vital spiritual leadership. So far as one can tell, the Spirit plays no part in the Jewish Christian understanding of the Church and its life.[3] In the course of salvation-history the Spirit had indeed been at work in many ways; but in Jesus as the perfect lawgiver and prophet

---

[2] In what follows I draw principally on the *Epistle of Peter*, and the *Contestatio* at the beginning of the pseudo-Clementine *Homilies*, both of which are unquestionably Judaeo-Christian. In the assessment of the pseudo-Clementines H. Waitz in his numerous studies (*ZNW* 1904, 1913, 1914, 1929; *ZKG* 1932, 1933, 1936, 1937, 1940), C. Schmidt, *Studien zu den Pseudoklementinen*, 1929, and H. J. Schoeps, *Theologie und Geschichte des Judenchristentums*, 1949, and *Aus frühchristlicher Zeit. Religionsgeschichtliche Untersuchungen*, 1950, seem to me to take on the whole a better line than E. Schwartz, 'Unzeitgemässes zu den Pseudoklementinen', *ZNW* 31, 1932, pp. 151ff., and B. Rehm, 'Zur Entstehung der pseudoklementinischen Schriften', *ZNW* 37, 1938, pp. 77ff. Since 1948 important light has been thrown on some aspects of these documents by the texts from Qumran: cf. O. Cullmann, 'Die neuentdeckten Qumrantexte und das Judenchristentum der Pseudo-Klementinen', *Neutestamentliche Studien für R. Bultmann (BZNW* 21), 1954, pp. 35–51.

[3] Cf. E. Lohmeyer, *Galiläa und Jerusalem*, 1936, p. 76; Schoeps, *Judenchristentum*, pp. 293f. The lack of endowment with the Spirit was not, however, compensated for, as some have suggested, by adopting a substitute principle of physical kinship: cf. H. Von Campenhausen, 'Die Nachfolge des Jakobus. Zur Frage eines urchristlichen "Khalifats" ', *ZKG* 63, 1950/51, pp. 133ff.

it appeared in its fullness, and so finally attained to 'rest'.[4] In other words, the teaching of Jesus is the ultimate revelation of truth and righteousness, and all that now remains is to follow it. Jesus is explicitly hailed as the 'new Moses',[5] and for this reason the Jewish Christian church, just like rabbinic Judaism, can declare that henceforward no prophet is justified in saying anything new.[6] In her life she no longer has any need of direct spiritual assistance; in her 'synagogues'[7] the concern is simply with precise exegesis and casuistic application of the numerous legal prescriptions.[8] All this means that office has lost a vital part of its personal and Christian significance.[9]

This becomes clear as soon as we examine the Ebionite conception of the apostolate. Here the apostles are the authorised founders of the Church's tradition and legislation, and absolutely nothing more. Any sort of direct 'authority' bestowed upon them, and especially on their own ideas and insights, is explicitly rejected; all that matters is what they 'learned' during their intimacy with Jesus. Their concern for the future ends with the creation of official ordinances and arrangements. They themselves form a rigidly organised college with James, the Lord's brother, at their head; and to him even Peter is obliged to render a report of his journeys. It is in keeping with this that the elders and the bishop in Ebionite congregations possess no special spiritual authority, and are but little regarded.[10] All the interest centres on the position of the class of teachers, who form a tightly organised Christian rabbinate.[11] On the model of the seventy men who 'received the chair of a teacher' from Moses[12] they are assumed to have been appointed by the apostles. For six whole years they are to be trained with the greatest care before proceeding by stages to give independent instruction. The content of their teaching is the exegesis of the received doctrine, the valid

[4] This is the view taken by the Baptism narrative in the *Gospel of the Nazarenes* quoted by Jerome, *Comm. in Is.* IV, when expounding Is. 11:2.

[5] Cf. Schoeps, *Judenchristentum*, pp. 87ff.

[6] *Sifre Lev.* 27, 34, cited in W. G. Kümmel, *ZNW* 33, 1934, p. 112 n. 27; P. Billerbeck, *Komm. z. NT aus Talmud und Midrasch* I, 1922, p. 601.

[7] Epiphanius, *Panarion XXX*, 18, 2. The term 'synagogue' for a Christian gathering, however, also occurs elsewhere, namely in the case of the Marcionites.

[8] On the intricacies of Ebionite exegesis of the Law cf. esp. Schoeps, *Judenchristentum*, pp. 188 ff.

[9] On what follows cf. esp. Schmidt, *op. cit.,* pp. 314ff. ('Die Gemeindeverfassung nach den Pseudo-Clementinen'), and Schoeps, *Judenchristentum*, pp. 289ff. ('Organisation und inneres Leben der ebionitischen Gemeinden').

[10] *Ep. Petri* Inscr.; Epiphanius, *Pan.* XXIX, 3, 8f.; *Contest.* 2f.

[11] Nevertheless, the indications in the *Contestatio* and in *Hom. Clem.* II, 38, point much more strongly to utopian schemes than to laws actually in force in the Jewish Christian scribal academy, as Schmidt, *op. cit.,* pp. 318f., and Schoeps, *Judenchristentum*, pp. 97 n. 2; 290f., believe them to be.

[12] *Ep. Petri* I.

commandments of the Law. The traditional writings from which they draw all their wisdom are kept strictly secret, and protected from falsification by minute regulations concerning their safe keeping and return. Many details recall Jewish rules on the same subject, but the precautions are carried to even more fantastic lengths; the oaths required can be closely paralleled from pagan books of magic.[13] To what extent individual regulations are still Old Testament or primitive Christian in significance, or how far they have already been gnosticised or paganised, makes little difference for our present purpose. It is obvious that either way this could never provide the basis for a vital development of spiritual authority, either in a 'free' or in an official form, since the second crucial requirement for such a development, and the one on which—especially in Christianity where there is no longer a purely legal tradition—all depends, is lacking, namely belief in the Spirit and in the special authority and responsibility which he demands and bestows.[14]

Montanism emerges as a volcanic revival movement in the second half of the second century in the gentile Christian environment of Phrygia.[15] Hence it in no way disowns any connection with earlier Christian development;[16] on the contrary, in a sense it might be seen as a reactionary phenomenon. The expectation of an imminent end of the world, and, associated with this, prophetic enthusiasm and the demand for unqualified holiness of life, here burst forth anew, and seek to make headway against the creeping inertia and worldliness of other congregations. In opposition to the tradition-bound conventionality of Church life Montanism believes in a new, revolutionary descent of the divine Spirit in person, who will now finally perfect and fulfil what hitherto had been only begun and hoped for. It is in this sense that the Montanist movement describes itself as 'the Prophecy' or the 'new Prophecy',[17] to which, as the presence of the Holy Spirit in

[13] Cf. F. Boll, 'Das Eingangsstück der Pseudo-Klementinen', ZNW 17, 1916, p. 145 n. 3.

[14] On the general principles involved cf. H. Von Campenhausen, 'Tradition und Geist im Urchristentum,' Stud. Gen. 4, 1951, pp. 351ff.

[15] On what follows cf. esp. P. de Labriolle, La crise montaniste, 1913, and Les sources de l'histoire du montanisme, 1913; W. Schepelern, Der Montanismus und die phrygischen Kulte, 1929. With the majority of present-day scholars I am of the opinion that the rise of Montanism is to be dated in the year 172 or 173, and not in 156/7.

[16] Schepelern, in his 'religio-historical study,' op. cit., pp. 159ff., shows that the main distinctive features of Montanism derive not from Phrygian paganism but from the world of the Revelation of John.

[17] Cf. the Anti-Montanist in Eusebius, HE V, 16, 4 and 16; the letter of Serapion, ibid. V, 19, 2; Clem. Alex., Strom. IV, 93, 1; Tertullian, Adv. Marc. III, 24; IV, 22; res. carn. 63; monog. 14; ieiun. 1; Adv. Prax. 1; 30; cf. also Labriolle, Sources, pp. 275f. ('Note sur l'onomastique montaniste').

person, pertains the right to unconditional and radical obedience. This claim to possess a new source of revelation,[18] and thus to surpass ordinary Christianity by putting the faith into practice for the first time, is the really novel and original element in Montanism, and places it at the head of a long line of similar heresies which have sought either like those of Mani and Muhammad to proclaim a third emissary from God or like the Joachimites with their *ecclesia spiritualis* a 'third kingdom'. The significance of this idea was not, however, at first appreciated.[19] The Prophecy caused a widespread sensation by the energy of its activities and its preaching, the seriousness of its demands, and the passionate conviction of its eschatological expectations; and it was these things which first aroused opposition. The abstruse character of its revelations, its fanatical rigorism, and above all the raving frenzy of its ecstasies made men mistrustful of the genuineness of its spirit. The result was disputations and investigations, ecclesiastical assemblies and pronouncements, in which of course the bishops and clergy take a leading part. The Church's origins meant that there could be no question of a simple rejection of prophecy *in toto*, for even if the miraculous gifts of the Spirit had become less common in the second century, nevertheless they did continue to occur here and there. What was required, therefore, was effective criteria by which genuine prophecy could be distinguished from demonic possession, and it is obvious that the Church of those days did not find it easy to arrive at them. For although the question itself was not completely new, yet it was now posed in a new form, and in the case of the Montanists the earlier rules could no longer be applied just as they stood. It will be necessary, therefore, to give a brief account of the way in which development on this point had gone so far.[20]

Paul does not yet have to deal with 'false prophets'. He is aware indeed of the ambiguity of miraculous superhuman guidance, and takes

[18] The 'Spirit' of the Montanists is effectively this from the outset, even if there is no evidence before Tertullian for his specific differentiation as 'Paraclete' from the Spirit given at Pentecost. The statement that Montanus passed himself off as the Paraclete is a distortion by later polemists: cf. Schepelern, *op. cit.,* pp. 14ff.

[19] It may nevertheless be asked whether the rough tone in which the Anti-Montanist (Eusebius, *HE* V, 16, 3) condemns any writing or instruction which goes beyond the canon should not be understood as already rebutting Montanist claims in the opposite direction: cf. W. C. Van Unnik, 'De la règle Μήτε προσθεῖναι μήτε ἀφελεῖν dans l'histoire du canon', *VC* 3, 1949, pp. 1ff. The fixation of the scheme of salvation-history in tripartite form is in any case not earlier than Tertullian.

[20] Cf. H. Bacht, 'Die prophetische Inspiration in der kirchlichen Reflexion der vormontanistischen Zeit,' *Scholastik* 19, 1944, pp. 1ff. Bacht is inclined to place the beginnings of the argument used against the Montanists back in the pre-Montanist period.

it for granted that all prophecy in his churches will be tested. This carries with it the implication that for him the ability to assess spiritual manifestations aright, and to discern their divine or demonic character, is itself a 'gift' of the Spirit, one which remains incomprehensible to the 'psychical', natural man, and is of course given to particular people.[21] But Paul hardly ever seems to have found real 'enemies' of the Gospel among those endowed with the Spirit, however much their maturity and Christian attitudes may have left to be desired. The true opponents of Christ and of the Cross are for him in the camp of the Judaistic legalists.[22] Linked with this, and with that distaste for any fixed, authoritarian organisation of the Church which in him is partly conditioned by this, is the fact that he always regards prophecy as the noblest of all gifts, in comparison with which the 'teachers', that is, the exponents of the shaping and controlling tradition in the Church, are notably less important.[23] 'Do not quench the Spirit!'[24] For detailed instructions in the matter of distinguishing true from false prophets, however, we shall search the Pauline Epistles in vain. The famous observation that no one speaking in the Spirit of God can call Jesus accursed, and that anyone who terms him 'Lord' is in the Spirit, is not made with this in mind at all.[25] All that we can extract from Paul is the fundamental, systematic principles which must be decisive in any 'testing of the spirits'; detailed rules and regulations are not given. 'Dogmatically' speaking, what would no doubt be crucial in his mind is how far any particular spirits and teachers hold to and attest the basic truth of the Gospel; or 'ethically', how far also they are prepared to submit themselves to the judgment of the congregation and of the spiritual men within the congregation, and to remain united to them in love. For the foundation on which all rests is the message of Christ and his resurrection, which puts an end to life under the Law; and the 'bond of perfectness' which embraces all spiritual life in the congregation and makes it fruitful is that Love which joys to serve and to be members of and subject to one another. To the extent that a congregation remains true to these things it is 'free' in the Spirit, and at the same time called to the fullness of all 'knowledge', and therefore needs no further, objective criteria with which to unmask its opponents. 'The Spirit searches all things',[26] and those who are truly endowed with

---

[21] I Cor. 12: 10; 14:29; I Thess. 5:20f.; cf. I Cor. 2:11f.
[22] Gal. 5:12ff.
[23] Cf. pp. 60ff. above.
[24] I Thess. 5:19.
[25] I Cor. 12:3. Paul is concerned to emphasise that even the bare confession of Jesus as Lord is sufficient indication that the person is fully possessed of the Spirit.
[26] I Cor. 2:10.

the Spirit discern at once what kind of character is evinced by the man who pushes himself forward in their assembly.[27]

In the course of time, however, the question of possible fraud or misuse of spiritual gifts begins to loom larger, and the problem of dealing with this proves not at all simple. Compulsive self-assertion and concern for his own material advantage characterise the type of the spiritual 'charlatan', the religious magus and humbug, familiar also to the heathen world.[28] The Jewish 'false prophet', Barjesus-Elymas, according to the account in Acts obstructs Paul's work;[29] the Jews in Ephesus attempt to drive out demons in Jesus's name;[30] and the baptised 'magus' Simon would like to buy the power of bestowing the Spirit from the apostles for money.[31] In opposition to such it becomes important to establish that, although the testimony of Jesus does give the Spirit of prophecy,[32] nevertheless his name is no magic incantation to be used for any purpose one pleases without at the same time submitting to him in total obedience. Any attempt to do otherwise might, as Luke shows,[33] involve mortal danger.

Even enthusiasm as such is no certain indication of true prophecy,[34] and miracles may even be conjured up by demons.[35] Frequently, however, there is still reluctance to 'test' a prophet who is speaking 'in the Spirit'; 'for every sin shall be forgiven, but this sin shall not be forgiven'.[36] Normally the Christian congregation is satisfied with scrutinising the moral qualities of dubious prophets; and when doing so it is especially important to note whether they are free from mixed motives of a materialistic kind.[37] It may even be that the instruction, preserved in the Gospel tradition, that prophets are to be known by their 'fruits'[38] is primarily concerned with moral conduct; at any rate it is frequently taken in this sense.[39] In addition it is a characteristic of false prophets that they flatter people,[40] that they tell them what they want

[27] I Cor. 14:24f.; cf. Ignatius, Philad. 7; also Schepelern, op. cit., pp. 150f. That the elect cannot be led astray by false prophets is also asserted in Mk. 13:22f.

[28] Cf. the Excursus by M. Dibelius in the Supplementary Vol. to the Handbuch zum Neuen Testament: Die apostolischen Väter 4, 1923, pp. 538ff.

[29] Acts 13:6ff.   [30] Acts 19:13.   [31] Acts 8:18f.

[32] Rev. 19:10.   [33] Acts 19:16ff.; cf. 8:21ff.   [34] Did. 11:8.

[35] Justin, Dial. VII, 3.   [36] Did. 11:7.

[37] Acts 8:20, cf. 20:33ff.; Did. 11:6,9,12; Hermas, Mand. XI, 12; II Pet. 2:3.

[38] Matt. 7:15ff. par. The conflation of the warning against false prophets with the saying about fruits is not original.

[39] Justin, Dial. XXXV, 3. Did. 11:8 suggests the τρόποι κυρίου as a criterion, and Hermas, Mand. XI lays stress on gentle, modest behaviour (8), and on the ἔργα (16) and the life: ἀπὸ τῆς ζωῆς δοκιμάζετε (7); similarly Irenaeus, Frag. 23 (ed. Harvey).

[40] And conversely the false prophets themselves have at all times been the recipients of flattery: Lk. 6:26.

to hear, and that they also allow enquiries to be put to them: 'For no Spirit given of God needs to be consulted; but having the power of deity, speaks all things of itself.'[41] Naturally there is also the criterion whether or not the predictions made come true;[42] but on the other hand it is recognised that occasionally even demons and the Devil himself speak the truth in the hope of thereby 'breaking down some of the righteous'.[43]

Despite such uncertainties the proud sense of being in fact able to test and distinguish the spirits remains very much alive in the Church. It is the duty of a true congregation to unmask the 'false apostles'.[44] Hence one very important criterion is that a prophet be prepared to submit to their judgment. The fraudulent man of the Spirit always evades such a test if he can, and displays his powers only 'in a corner', before weak and doubting Christians. In such circumstances the 'empty vessel', banging together with others equally empty, will of course make a satisfying noise;[45] but in the assembly of righteous men filled with the Spirit its nothingness becomes immediately apparent. The earthy spirit which filled the false prophet nervously makes its escape, leaving its medium in the lurch, with the result that the latter stands dumb and helpless. By contrast it is precisely at the worship of the faithful that the true prophet is filled with the Spirit of God through the agency of the angel who attends him, and speaks to the company 'as God wishes him to speak'.[46]

In what has just been said evidence has been drawn from very varied, more or less popular writings. The question takes on a more serious aspect, and is to some extent raised on to a loftier plane, when defence against gnostic teachers and prophets becomes the immediate problem, for then attention has to be paid to matters of content, to the 'dogmatic' significance of what is said. Thus, one should not pay heed to a spirit which does not acknowledge that Jesus Christ was truly born, died, and rose again; such a one is from the Devil.[47] Equally indispensable, however, is loyalty to the traditional moral commands, which the

[41] Hermas, Mand. XI, 5; cf. XI, 8; Irenaeus, Adv. haer. I, 13, 4; for the contrast with the heathen μάντις cf. again Frag. 23 (ed. Harvey), and Plutarch, De def. or. 51.

[42] Like those of Agabus, Acts 11:28; 21:10ff.

[43] Hermas, Mand. XI, 3; cf. Justin, I Apol. XXVI, 2 and 4.

[44] Rev. 2:2.

[45] Hermas, Mand. XI, 13; 'emptiness' as the opposite of being filled with the Spirit occurs also in Irenaeus, Frag. 24 (ed. Harvey).

[46] Hermas, Mand. XI, 9; XI, 14f. The sense of the 'Church' as a corporate body is clearly prominent here; and in face of it the special individual gift of testing spirits begins to disappear.

[47] I Joh. 2:22f.; 4:2f.; II Joh. 7; Polycarp, Phil. 7:1; Ignatius, Eph. 7:1; Trall. 7:1; 9; Smyrn. 6:1, etc.

docetist gnostics frequently despise. On this basis the author of I John once more combines the dogmatic and the ethical standpoint and approach in a remarkable theological unity, which though essentially akin to Paul yet goes beyond him in the direct and decisive attitude which it adopts toward an opponent who is only now fully recognisable for what he is. 'Beloved, do not believe every spirit, but test the spirits to see whether they are of God.'[48] There is in fact a standard by which the false prophets who are now coming into the world can be measured and condemned: 'Every spirit which confesses that Jesus Christ has come in the flesh is of God,' and any one who will not confess this, the real Jesus Christ, is from the Antichrist.[49] The man, however, who believes in Christ is begotten of God, and therefore also loves the old divine commandment of love to the brethren.[50] In the writer's characteristic spiral style the motifs of divine love, the confession of Christ, obedience, and brotherhood are intertwined, and understood as a unity which is made real in the Spirit. It is within this pattern that the light of faith becomes distinct from the powers of darkness. Not only are the spirits of the false prophets tested, but such prophets are themselves expelled, and this expulsion too is now seen as the work of the Spirit, the bringer of truth.[51] The concern here is as little with particular types of spirit-filled individual as with particular kinds of official, which John likewise either disregards or does not wish to acknowledge.[52]

In the consciousness of the average Christian, however, matters were undoubtedly very different. Here the effect of the fight against the gnosis was to intensify conservative trends and, as already mentioned, the authority of the church officials. This is especially clear in the Pastoral Epistles.[53] The task of defending the Church and refuting the seducers, who are characterised less as demonic tempters than as empty, futile, and morally unprincipled babblers, to whom the congregation should pay no attention, is here thought of as belonging primarily to the official leadership. Prophets, even true ones, are now hardly in evidence at all.[54] This, however, is not the case everywhere,[55] and in any

[48] I Joh. 4:1a.   [49] I Joh. 4:b1–3.   [50] I Joh. 2:7f.; 5:1–3; II Joh. 5.
[51] I Joh. 2:18f.; 3:10; cf. Joh. 6:60–65; 16:7–11; Rev. 2:2, 20.
[52] Cf. pp. 121f. above.
[53] For this reason they are at once pressed into service not only in the fight against the gnostic heretics but also in that against the Montanists: Hippolytus, Comm. Dan. III, 20; Origen, De princ. II, 7, 3; Comm. Matt. XV, 30. Polycarp and II Peter display the same tendency as the Pastorals; and the stress on office, though in the context of a different general attitude, is also to be found in Ignatius.   [54] Cf. pp. 110ff., above.
[55] *Pap. Oxyr.* I, 5 combines a quotation from Hermas, Mand. XI, 9f., with a statement which, according to A. von Harnack, 'Über zwei von Grenfell und Hunt entdeckte und publizierte Fragmente,' *SBA* 1898, p. 520, may derive from Melito (cf. p. 189f. below): τὸ γὰρ προφητικὸν πνεῦμα τὸ σωματεῖόν ἐστιν τῆς προφητικῆς τάξεως, ὅ ἐστιν τὸ σῶμα τῆς σαρκὸς Ἰησοῦ χριστοῦ . . .

event the possibility of their existence in principle is still taken seriously, and their testimony, where it has the authentic ring, is regarded as a divine command to which the whole congregation, including their clergy, must then submit.[56] It is into this kind of situation that the Montanist 'Prophecy' bursts with its new eruption of enthusiasm.

In many respects Montanist prophecy exhibits an entirely new phenomenon. The prophets with whom men were familiar in the second century possessed in general only local significance, or in what they had to say accorded more or less without friction with the general sense of the Church. Here, however, was a claim to a new outpouring of the Spirit, asserted to have been promised by Christ himself,[57] and demanding universal attention with its message of the imminent end of the world.[58] Montanism aimed at a total renewal of the life of the Church, and in support of this appealed to the inspired authority of its prophets, unequivocal and unique. 'Hearken not to me but to Christ', runs an utterance of the prophetess Maximilla.[59] 'The Lord has sent me as partisan, revealer, and interpreter of this distress, this covenant, this promise. I am compelled, will I nill I, to make known the knowledge of God.'[60] On the distinctive character and the justifiability of this prophetic claim to authority focuses at once the zeal of polemist and of apologist alike.[61]

The subjective genuineness of the ecstatic experience undergone by Montanus and the 'women', and after them by other lesser Montanist prophets, was not in itself challenged. The only question was whether here a divine or a demonic power was at work. The later polemical writers assert that the Montanist 'hypocrites' would not allow their spirit to be tested by exorcism; but this statement presupposes a stage at which a breach, indeed a separation of the two parties, had already taken place.[62] The customary dogmatic criteria, as these had been

[56] This can be seen in the way that Hermas, for example, takes for granted his right to lay a charge on the leading members of his church (Vis. II, 4, 3), and also in the 'hostile, but sharply observed' (H. Lietzmann, *History of the Early Church* II, 1950, p. 55) picture of prophetic pretensions drawn by Celsus (Origen, Contra Celsum VII, 9). Whether in the latter instance, however, Catholic Christians are referred to is open to question.

[57] So, on the basis of Matt. 23:34, in the Anti-Montanist (Eusebius, *HE* V, 16, 12); cf. p. 182 n. 18 above.

[58] The claims of the prophetess Philoumene, on which the Marcionite Apelles relied (Rhodon in Eusebius, *HE* V, 13, 2; Tertullian, *carn.* 6; *praescr.* 6, 30), were perhaps just as extreme; but the success of her adherents can hardly be compared with that of the Montanist movement.

[59] Epiphanius, Pan. 48, 18, 4.   [60] Epiphanius, Pan. 48,13,1.

[61] Cf. Schepelern, *op. cit.,* pp. 19ff.

[62] The Anti-Montanist in Eusebius, *HE* V, 16, 16; Apollonius, *ibid.* V, 18, 10; Aelius Publius Julius, *ibid.* V, 19, 3. At what stage the Montanists were first formally examined, condemned, and excommunicated (cf. the Anti-Montanist, *ibid.* V, 16, 10) we can no longer say with precision.

developed for use against the gnosis, could not be applied in the case of the Montanists; for the Montanists were not heretics. Hippolytus,[63] and even Epiphanius, state frankly that on questions of dogma they were in entire agreement with the Catholic Church;[64] and the fact that Tertullian went over to them and his position after becoming a Montanist simply confirm this.[65] It is only later controversialists who at a more advanced stage try hard to stigmatise the 'Kataphrygians' as also trinitarian heretics.[66] Even with regard to morals calumny was hesitant to venture near the leader of the movement;[67] and it was precisely by the strictness of their moral behaviour and of their ascetic rule that the Montanists first made an impression. Their radical attitude on the questions of repentance, martyrdom, and numerous details of the Christian way of life might seem at least arguable; and one might therefore have to accept that they were directed by the Spirit of God.[68] At this point it might have been possible to develop instead a more profound theological refutation, and to press forward to a general critique of legalism, by which the Montanist movement, for all its emphasis on enthusiasm, is characterised from the very first. But this the spokesmen of the majority were manifestly not in a position to do.[69] Hence they turned to consideration of the ecstatic phenomena as such— phenomena which, though given great importance by the Montanists themselves, had never before been made the object of theological reflection. This meant that the methods of testing the spirits were shifted, with momentous consequences, from the realm of the moral

[63] Elench. VIII, 19, 2; 19, 3; X, 26.

[64] Pan. 48,1. Nevertheless, they are possessed: λέγοντες, ὅτι δεῖ ἡμᾶς, φησί, καὶ τὰ χαρίσματα δέχεσθαι (48, 1, 3f.).

[65] In his view the Paraclete brings absolutely no dogmatic but only ethical advance (ieiun, 1; monog. 2), and for his doctrine of the Trinity he appeals explicitly to the Paraclete as a confirmatory witness (Adv. Prax. 2, 8, 13, 30).

[66] Hippolytus is the first to take this step (Philos, VIII, 19; X, 26), when he points out that τινὲς αὐτῶν went over to the heresy of Noëtus. The same type of vacuous non sequitur occurs in Cyprian, Ep. 55, 7, with reference to Firmilian of Caesarea.

[67] The Anti-Montanist still does not dare to relate the legends about the bad end of Montanus, Maximilla, etc. as certain truth. Eusebius, HE V, 16, 14f. He is content to assert that the seducing spirit was cunning: ὅσθ᾽ ἔπη δὲ καὶ κατακρίνοντος στοχαστικῶς καὶ ἀξιοπίστως αὐτοὺς ἄντικρυς ἵνα καὶ ἐλεγκτικὸν εἶναι δοκῇ (V, 16, 9). Apollonius, however, provides enough slander to satisfy anyone: ibid. V, 18.

[68] The non-fulfilment of their prophetic predictions could not, of course, affect the argument until a later stage: cf. the Anti-Montanist in Eusebius, HE V, 16, 19.

[69] By contrast Tertullian, from his legalist standpoint as a Montanist, was able to develop a magnificent panorama of salvation history: H. Von Campenhausen, 'Urchristentum und Tradition bei Tertullian,' Theol. Blätter 8, 1929, pp. 198ff. For the relevant texts cf. de Labriolle, Sources, pp. 12ff.

and theological to that of the psychological and parapsychological. The primitive Christian concept of prophecy had certainly not excluded the element of ecstasy;[70] but equally it did not make use of this element to prove its superhuman, spiritual nature. For Paul prophecy always means the power of moving and convincing speech, which as such is inevitably practised with the aid of 'reason', and likewise makes its appeal to the lively rational judgment of the audience. The element of 'rapture', the silencing of the 'natural' consciousness, and the use of a correspondingly miraculous, supernatural mode of speech, quite unintelligible to the natural man, do indeed also belong in his view to the sphere of the miraculous operations of the Holy Spirit; nevertheless, they are to be regarded not as prophecy but as the expression of another gift distinguishable from this. Concerning the value of this other gift it was possible to hold various opinions. Paul himself possessed the ability to speak in supernatural languages (or 'tongues'), but made it clear that he considered this one of the least important gifts, since—without special interpreters—it remained valueless for the Christian congregation.[71] In the second century this gift seems to have fallen into almost complete desuetude; it had to all intents and purposes died out, and even prophetic enthusiasm was in decline.[72] For this very reason the 'new Prophecy' stresses precisely this aspect of the matter, and sees in the spasmodic ecstasy which suspends consciousness, and on occasion causes outbursts of strange, incomprehensible cries and sounds, the hallmark of genuine prophecy. ' "Behold, Man is like a lyre," says the Spirit, "and I strike it like a plectrum.[73] Man sleeps and I wake. Behold, it is the Lord, who takes the hearts of men out of them, and gives them a new heart." '[74] It was precisely these surprising and alien features which could be regarded by the opponents of Montanism as 'innovation', and used to explain or justify the condemnation of the 'new Prophecy'.

This view may have been expressed as early as the work which Melito

[70] This is true pre-eminently of Revelation, on which, as a matter of history, Montanism may be dependent: cf. p. 181 n. 16 above.

[71] I Cor. 14; cf. Schepelern, op. cit., pp. 153ff.

[72] Despite the remarks of Schepelern, op. cit., p. 157, the texts dependent on Paul hardly suggest the opposite conclusion: Irenaeus, Adv. haer. V, 6, 1; Tertullian, Adv. Marc. V, 8; cf. de Labriolle, Crise, pp. 168ff. Even the account of the inspiration of the gnostic Mark (Irenaeus, Adv. haer. I, 13, 2) seems to me (as against H. Weinel, Die Wirkungen des Geistes und der Geister im nachapostolischen Zeitalter bis auf Irenäus, 1899, p. 125) not entirely unambiguous. R. A. Knox, Enthusiasm. A chapter in the history of Religion, 1951, p. 34, would see the ecstatic element as on the whole a Montanist innovation.

[73] The same image to describe inspiration is used also by Hippolytus, De Antichristo 2; Ps-Justin, Cohortatio 8; and a very similar one in Athenagoras, Suppl. 9, 1.

[74] Epiphanius, Pan. 48, 4.

of Sardis, who was himself a prophet, wrote on the subject of this gift.[75] The 'philosopher' Miltiades then offered in a work of his own a proof that a prophet definitely ought not to speak in a state of ecstasy,[76] and the Anti-Montanist sees in the strange and irrational manner of speech of Montanus proof that his must be a case of a false spirit inducing a state of *parekstasis*, in which the 'tradition and succession' of the Church of previous generations are contradicted.[77] He also adduces an argument from Scripture to the effect that no prophet either of the Old or of the New Covenant ever prophesied in this manner.[78] In Clement of Alexandria the anti-Montanist sections are still headed, 'Concerning the Prophecy'.[79] Naturally the Montanists for their part give as good as they get. In Rome their spokesman draws the opposite conclusion from the existence of prophets in the Church's early days,[80] and from their unbroken line stretching down through the Apologist Quadratus to the Philadelphian prophetess Ammia and the Montanist prophets.[81] And no less a man than Tertullian writes a work, unfortunately no longer extant, first in six then in seven volumes, 'On Ecstasy', in which he defends Montanist prophecy.[82] For this, he maintains, is the precise point at issue in the controversy with the 'psychics' of the Great Church. It is essential to grasp that a man who really experiences and perceives God's glory is bound to lose the use of his mind and reason, because he is eclipsed by the power of God.[83] Paul, the expert on spiritual gifts, is regarded by Montanists in general as Queen's Evidence for their view.[84]

In the later period the 'ancient folly' of the 'bacchantic' Montanist ravings is but seldom mentioned,[85] and no longer plays an important part in the controversy.[86] Montanism, once condemned, became an

[75] Eusebius, *HE* IV, 26, 2.
[76] Eusebius, *HE* V, 17, 1.
[77] Eusebius, *HE* V, 16, 7; 16, 9; cf. p. 162 n. 74 above.
[78] Eusebius, *HE* V, 17, 2f.; Epiphanius, Pan. 48, 3–8. By contrast Athenagoras, Suppl. 9, 1, explicitly states that the O.T. prophets gave their testimony (ἐξεφώνησαν) in the Spirit κατ' ἔκστασιν τῶν ἐν αὐτοῖς λογισμῶν; and Theophilus of Antioch expresses the same view: Ad Aut. II, 9.
[79] Strom. I, 158, 1; IV, 2, 2; IV, 93, 1; (V, 88, 4).
[80] Cf. Proclus in Eusebius, *HE* III, 31, 4.
[81] Eusebius, *HE* V, 17, 4.
[82] Jerome, *vir. ill.* 40.
[83] Adv. Marc. IV, 22; cf. V, 8 (ed. Kroymann, 600; 22): *in ecstasi, id est: in amentia;* Adv. Prax. 15.
[84] Cf. the introduction to the Μοντανιστοῦ καὶ ὀρθοδόξου διάλεξις, *ZKG* 26, 1905, pp. 446ff.; de Labriolle, *Sources*, p. 93; and p. 186 n. 53 above.
[85] Greg. Naz., Or. 22,12.
[86] Nevertheless, the assertion of the Anti-Montanist (Eusebius, *HE* V, 17, 4; also Epiphanius, Pan. 48, 2) that with the death of Maximilla prophecy died out among the Montanists is rebutted by Tertullian, *De anima* 9, 4, and the *Passio Perpetuae* (cf. Tertullian, *De anima* 55, 4).

obscure rigorist sect, in which as a rule the decisive factor was no longer the Spirit but office. A curious extension of the catholic hierarchy by two higher ranks[87] is perhaps a last trace of earlier, spiritual positions of authority which in the course of time have become petrified into clerical grades. Later the adherents of the 'New Prophecy' merged to some extent with the reactionary Novatianists. Their importance for world history lies not in their straitened later career but in the revolutionary enthusiasm of the original movement, that is to say, in the continuing repercussions which their expulsion and condemnation had on the mainstream of Christianity. From this time dates the 'ecclesiastical', and later also 'official' mistrust of all the cruder forms of religious enthusiasm and ecstasy. If Montanism (in this respect going beyond primitive Christianity) saw in this the surest criterion of divine inspiration, the tendency within the Church was now fixed firmly in the opposite direction, namely to condemn it as a mark of demonic possession. Enthusiastic promptings, raptures, and visions are in general forced out on to the periphery of the Church and into heresy, until monasticism creates a new home for them and new, organised opportunities for development. Moreover, the increasing hellenisation of the Church, with its emphasis on the spirituality and rationality of the faith, restricts understanding of the very different nature of earlier 'prophecy'. In vain did Irenaeus warn his contemporaries against driving the true prophecy out of the Church from anxiety over the false.[88] In opposition to the 'boastful parading of revelations'[89] the tendency is to rely more and more on rational and didactic forms of spiritual utterance. The era of the prophets draws to a close[90]—indeed,

[87] Jerome, Ep. 41,3.

[88] Irenaeus, Adv. haer. III, 9, 9; in I, 13, 4 θεόσδοτος προφητεία is mentioned in contrast to the magical prophecy of the gnostic Mark. Akin to this is the advice of Clem. Alex., Strom. VI, 66, 5, that mistrust of a suspect person should not lead one to reject his statements out of hand.

[89] Ps-Cyprian, sing. cler.: nec nos esse adulterantes verbum domini aut volentes iactanter de revelationibus gloriari. . . .

[90] That the line of prophets has come to an end, and is not to continue any further, would seem to be the explicit meaning of the Muratorian Canon (77f.); and Origen (Comm. Matt. 28: ed. Klostermann, p. 52), like Hippolytus (antichr. 31), emphasises the same point, directly applying it against the falsos Phrygiae prophetas. In a controversialist dialogue of the fourth century (cf. p. 190 n. 84 above) the orthodox spokesman is not prepared to concede the Montanist accusation that he acknowledges no further prophets after Christ, but in practice he restricts himself—in an almost Ebionite fashion (cf. p. 179f. above)—to the argument that the apostles had possessed τῆς προφητείας τὸ χάρισμα. On the whole subject cf. de Labriolle, Crise, pp. 285ff., and, in reply to the view of A. von Harnack, Die Lehre der zwölf Apostel, 1884, p. 124 n. 38, that 'henceforward prophecy was non-ecstatic', the same author's pertinent comment (Crise, p. 547): 'to be precise, prophecy was virtually non-existent.'

the very word slowly falls out of use[91]—and their place as witnesses to the living truth is taken by the 'teachers' of both the free and the official Church, that is, by their catechists, preachers, and 'philosophers'.

Both the form and the concept of the teaching body unquestionably underwent a marked change in the course of the second century.[92] The teachers in primitive Christianity were enumerated in a fixed order immediately after the apostles and prophets, and in their activities were frequently hard to distinguish from the latter.[93] We may conjecture that they were especially active as catechists in the congregation, and preserved and passed on in their instruction the oral or written tradition.[94] This same characteristic is crucial for the period that follows. The gift or art of teaching continues to be something present in particular individuals; but both it and its authority are based not on any revelation directly received but on the exposition of existing traditions, and very particularly of the Scriptures—a term which includes at first simply those of the Old Covenant, then those of the New and of the apostles. At the same time from the very beginning there is no resting content with imparting merely the simplest, most essential knowledge, such as must be indispensable to every Christian. The pride of a good teacher is to reveal to his pupils in addition to these things deeper and higher mysteries, as, for example, the author of the Epistle of Barnabas attempts to do.[95] In Hebrews too we find the complaint about lack of maturity in listeners to whom the preacher ought really to be declaring more difficult and more important truths.[96] Teachers of a gnostic tendency often make it very emphatically their object to gather about them only those truly elect souls whose faith comes solely 'through the Spirit and from the Spirit'.[97] Here the concept of the Spirit is

[91] As early as Hippolytus the term 'prophet' is restricted entirely to the canonical prophets: A. Hamel, *Kirche bei Hippolyt von Rom*, 1951, p. 122. It may be that the disappearance of the loan-word *charisma*, which is still used by Novatian, is also linked with rejection of that *charisma prophetiae* which the Montanists demanded (cf. p. 188 n. 64 above): C. Mohrmann, 'Les origines de la latinité chrétienne', *VC* 3, 1949, p. 172.

[92] On what follows cf. A. von Harnack, *Die Mission und Ausbreitung des Christentums*[4], 1924, pp. 332ff.; also G. Bardy, 'Les écoles romaines au second siècle,' *RHE* 28, 1932, pp. 501ff.

[93] The two groups are mostly mentioned in conjunction: Acts 13:1; Did. 13:1f.; 15:1f.; also Eph. 4:11. According to the *Martyrdom* (16,2) Polycarp is a διδάσκαλος ἀποστολικὸς καὶ προφητικός; and both Quadratus, who is certainly to be identified with the Apologist of that name (Eusebius, *HE* V, 17,3) and Melito of Sardis (Jerome, *vir. ill.* 24) are described as prophets. According to Justin, *Dial.* LXXXII, 1, prophetic *charismata* are to be found in the Church 'to this very day'.

[94] Cf. pp. 61f. above.

[95] Barn. 6:10.

[96] Heb. 5:11ff.

[97] Heracleon, cited in Origen, Comm. Joh. XIII, 31:187, 191.

understood in a way different from that of the Montanists, whose doughtiest opponents are to be found precisely among the professional teachers.[98] The teachers of the second century are not enthusiasts. They are biblical scholars and theologians, and as such the first conscious champions of an individualist and personal spirituality within the Church. In this connection contact with the philosophical spirit of the pagan world becomes continually closer. If in primitive Christianity the teachers were conditioned primarily by the inheritance of Judaism and by the conflict with Jewish scribal learning, in the succeeding period it is the controversy with paganism which becomes increasingly important. Justin exhibits the transition. Like the whole Church of his day he is fighting a war on two fronts; but his *Dialogue with Trypho* in part, and his *Apology* completely, reveal the effort to do as much justice as possible to the style of heathen philosophers and orators, and to some extent to meet them on the common ground of the same 'enlightened' intellectual approach. Undoubtedly hellenistic Judaism had already paved the way for this new ideal of the teacher's role.[99] Justin and numerous of his contemporaries themselves came from the circles of popular philosophers and men of letters, and did not wish as Christians to disown their previous training. Thus Justin after becoming a Christian retains the outward sign of his profession, the philosopher's cloak,[100] and even the harsh Tertullian copied him in this.[101] Christianity becomes the true philosophy—indeed, something more than a philosophy[102]—and the Christian teacher the true philosopher, because it is he who has now at last discovered the whole divine truth. The link with earlier Christian teaching is seen chiefly in the fact that exegesis of the Scriptures, now as in the past, is regarded as the noblest task of a Christian philosopher.[103] It is for this that Justin declares he has received divine 'grace'[104]—this emphasis on higher assistance being, of course, conditioned in his case by Christianity. A good deal in the philosophical manner of Christian teachers is certainly to be put down

[98] Miltiades, Apollonius(?), Caius, Clement, and, on the opposite side, Proclus and Tertullian, were certainly not clerics.

[99] Mention of Philo will suffice to make the point.

[100] Justin, Dial. I, 2; Eusebius, *HE* IV, 11, 8.

[101] De pallio 6; in his case this does not exclude a fierce opposition to all philosophy as alien to Christianity: A. Labhardt, 'Tertullien et la philosophie,' *Mus. Helv.* 7, 1950, pp. 176f. Origen relates that Heraclas first adopted the philosopher's cloak when he became a Christian: Eusebius, *HE* VI, 19, 4.

[102] Cf. Harnack, *Mission,* pp. 270f.; W. Kamlah, *Christentum und Geschichtlichkeit. Untersuchungen zur Entstehung des Christentums und zu Augustins "Bürgerschaft Gottes",*[2] 1951, pp. 97ff., 191ff.

[103] Aristides, Apol. 2; Diognetus, Ep. 1; and even so early a work as the Kerygma Petri, cited in Clem. Alex., Strom. VI, 128,3: οὐδὲν ἄτερ γραφῆς λέγομεν.

[104] Dial. IX, 1; LVIII, 1.

to nothing more than missionary and propagandist adaptation; but at the same time the confession of the revelation in Christ is combined in these circles with an appeal to the God-given Reason of the philosophers. And with the adoption of current conventions, methods, and concepts the inner shape of Christian teaching is also radically altered.

In the later second century the teacher no longer operates exclusively within the congregation. Circumstances permitting, he rents his own premises,[105] and like the heathen philosophers gathers round him a group of any pupils who may be interested.[106] He holds to his own scholastic traditions, which he receives and passes on in the way already discussed in the preceding chapter.[107] At the same time he begins literary activity in his own name.[108] In this way arises a new and, so to speak, academic attitude to Christian education on the part of teachers and their 'schools',[109] against which the ordinary Church member often reacts with understandable suspicion.[110] The accusation of arrogance on the part of the sages and philosophers goes hand in hand chiefly with the constant reproach that they are the prime authors of dangerous errors and heresies.[111] And indeed it is true that the leaders of the gnosis mostly operate as heads of circles and conventicles modelled on the philosophical schools. Nevertheless there are also orthodox teachers. Between the orthodox and the heretical, those within the common tradition of the Church and the separatists, it is as little possible, at a time when instruction is uncontrolled, to draw a sharp dividing-line as between the theological and the philosophical teacher, the rationalist and the pneumatic, the traditionalist and the innovator or individualist. Moreover, what immense differences of intellectual level exist, for

---

[105] Eusebius, *HE* IV, 11, 11; Act. Just. 3; cf. the much too cautious study of H. R. Nelz, *Die theologischen Schulen der morgenländischen Kirche während der ersten sieben christlichen Jahrhunderten* (Diss. theol. Bonn 1916), pp. 20ff.

[106] Likewise those who are anxious to learn look out for the right teacher: Clem. Alex., Strom. I, 11.

[107] Cf. pp. 158ff. above.

[108] It must have been in some such way as this that Papias began his activity as the 'first Christian man of letters': M. Dibelius, *RGG* 3, 1930, p. 892.

[109] In this connection cf. especially the charges brought against the Roman Theodotians by an unknown controversialist: Eusebius, *HE* V, 28, 13–19; cf. H. Schöne, 'Der Einbruch der antiken Logik und Textkritik in die altchristliche Theologie,' *Pisciculi* (Dölger-Festschrift), 1939, pp. 252ff.

[110] Cf. J. Lebreton, 'Le désaccord de la foi populaire et de la théologie savante dans l'Église chrétienne de IIIe siècle', *RHE* 19, 1923, pp. 489ff.; M. Hirschberg, *Studien zur Geschichte der simplices in der alten Kirche* (unpubl. Diss. theol. Heidelberg 1946).

[111] Hermas, Vis. III, 7, 1; VIII, 6, 5; Sim. IX, 19, 2f.; and Irenaeus, Adv. haer. I, 28, 1 (Eusebius, *HE* IV, 29, 3) on the subject of Tatian, who: ἀποστὰς τῆς ἐκκλησίας οἰήματι διδασκάλου ἐπαρθεὶς καὶ τυφωθεὶς ὡς διαφέρων τῶν λοιπῶν, ἴδιον χαρακτῆρα διδασκαλείου συνεστήσατο. Further examples in Harnack, *Mission*, pp. 367ff.

example, between the followers of Simon Magus or of a 'prophet' such as Elchasai on the one hand, and gentlemanly, educated thinkers such as Justin, and a Ptolemaeus or Heracleon on the other![112] On the whole one ought neither to generalise too much from the impression of deviation and phantasmagoria given by a few thaumaturges nor to underrate the level of philosophical education of the more significant Christian teachers of this period. It is true that they were not figures of the standing of a Nicomachus or Numenius, but a man like Justin has no reason to fear comparison with the average pagan popular orator and preacher.[113]

The intellectual prestige of teachers had been high from of old. It is an expression of modesty when 'Barnabas' declines to speak 'as a teacher'.[114] Christ himself is teacher of his Church,[115] and in retrospect the teachers of the early period are classed with the apostles.[116] Even so outstanding a personality as Polycarp, Bishop of Smyrna, is celebrated—next to his martyrdom—principally for the fact that he had been an 'apostolic and prophetic teacher',[117] a teacher for the whole of Asia.[118] This example indicates at the same time that a combination of teacher and cleric in one person struck men as perfectly natural. Moreover, many of the old men or Elders to whose testimony Irenaeus appeals presided over their congregations as bishops or presbyters.[119] A contrast between freelance teachers and those in official positions, so long at any rate as the former were orthodox, is nowhere discernible in the second century. If, however, we wish to enquire what was the distinctive sense of authority which animated the teacher as such, then

---

[112] Quite in a class by himself is the revolutionary reformer Marcion, who rejects philosophy and wishes to act not at all in his own name but simply as an exegete of Paul: A. von Harnack, *Marcion: Das Evangelium vom fremden Gott*, 1924, pp. 2, 93f., 162 n. 2.

[113] Cf. the comment of Harnack, *Mission*, p. 373 n. 2 in reply to J. Geffcken, *Zwei griechische Apologeten*, 1907; and esp. W. Schmid, 'Die Textüberlieferung der Apologie des Justin', *ZNW* 40, 1941, pp. 128ff. ('Der Bildungsgrad des Justin und seine "Irrtümer" '), and: 'Frühe Apologetik und Platonismus', *Festschrift Otto Regenbogen*, 1952, pp. 163ff. esp. p. 178.

[114] Barn. I, 8; IV, 9; cf. A. Von Ungern-Sternberg, *Der traditionelle alt-testamentliche Schriftbeweis "de Christo" und "de evangelio" in der alten Kirche*, 1913, pp. 235f.

[115] Ignatius, Eph. 15:1; Magn. 9:1; Trall. 9:2; also Mart. Polyc. 17:3, and Justin—under the influence of philosophical terminology—*passim*.

[116] In I Tim. 2:7; II Tim. 1:11, Paul figures as both apostle and διδάσκαλος, John in Polycrates of Ephesus (Eusebius, *HE* III, 31, 3) as μάρτυς καὶ διδάσκαλος. Hermas mentions the apostles and teachers in the same breath: Sim. IX, 16, 5; 25, 2.

[117] Mart. Polyc. 16:2; 19:1.

[118] Mart. Polyc. 12:2.

[119] Cf. p. 171 above; further examples may be found in H. Koch, 'Tertullianisches II, 5', *Theol. Stud. u. Krit.* 103, 1931, p. 97 n. 1.

naturally it is no good starting from the teaching bishops. Unfortunately the material available on this point as regards the freelance teacher is sparse. The Apologists, in those writings which are extant, did not express themselves on the subject of their special commission or the prerogatives of their profession; even Justin is in this respect strikingly reticent. Pronouncements by the gnostics are almost always transmitted only in fragmentary form and distorted by the polemical misrepresentations of their opponents. Bar-Daisan is the easiest one of whom to sketch some kind of picture;[120] but this Syrian poet and teacher from outside the bounds of the Roman Empire is undoubtedly an exceptional case. When we come down to it, therefore, there is only one man left, Clement of Alexandria. In their intensity and abundance his many theological essays on the nature and task of the spiritual teacher are both unusual and highly personal. But this does not mean that they are a wholly new creation. Clement acknowledges that he stands in a teaching tradition on which he draws repeatedly. Much in the views which he expresses is therefore the current opinion in other teaching circles. In the absence of other sources it is worth giving a rather a fuller account of Clement the teacher. His ideas on theological education and hermeneutics are among the most interesting productions of the Early Church on these subjects. But it was not till the fourth century, in the so-called 'Macarius', Simeon of Mesopotamia, that Clement found a worthy, if at the same time heretical, successor.[121] Later tradition made Clement[122] an Athenian by birth—whether with historical or only symbolic truth we do not know. But in his innermost being Clement was certainly a Hellene. His was an intellectual nature in the sense that everything with which he came into contact provided him with an occasion for conscious intellectual appropriation and understanding. At the same time it was a moral nature, which took the real task of all education to be that of enabling a man constantly to deepen and train his own moral sense. And above all it was a religious nature, for which all human life was seen in terms of the God–Man relationship, of the

[120] Cf. esp. the dialogue in the 'Book of the Laws of the Lands', and on this the good summary by L. Cerfaux, *RAC* I, 1950, pp. 1180ff.

[121] Even Clement himself, according to an edict of Pope Benedict XIV in 1718, is not to be considered a saint.

[122] There is no need here to detail the immense literature on Clement. Fundamental to modern Clement studies is the edition of his Works by O. Stählin in the *GCS* (1905–1909), together with the important Index volume (1936). In what follows references are to the *GCS* paragraphs. The last major complete survey of the subject (E. de Faye, *Clément d'Alexandrie. Étude sur les rapports du christianisme et de la philosophie grecque au IIe siècle*[2], 1902, is no longer adequate. On the recent work of W. Völker (*Der wahre Gnostiker nach Clemens Alexandrinus*, 1952), which touches on just those questions of interest to us here, cf. my review in *TZ* 9, 1953.

approach to the life of God, and of union with him. Here alone Clement finds ultimate meaning and fulfilment. His astonishing familiarity with the literature and philosophy of the ancient world is for the most part an inheritance from his pagan days. As a religious seeker he may have been initiated into many mystery cults, on which later he shows himself better informed than other writers.[123] It is certain that as a Christian he passed through a fairly lengthy period of development.[124] It is significant that Clement himself later came to regard these years of teaching and wandering as a time of searching for a sufficient, truly 'gnostic' teacher. He only hints at the various great spiritual figures who taught him and helped him in Greece, Italy, and Palestine. Of decisive importance, however, was one in particular, a 'Sicilian bee', who understood how to suck the honey of perfect knowledge from the prophetic and apostolic testimonies, and to communicate it. The reference is to Pantaenus, who came from Sicily, whom Clement finally 'tracked down' in Egypt, and with whom he 'came to rest'.[125] It was due to him that Clement made his home for a long period in Alexandria, and entered fully into the rich intellectual life of that cosmopolitan city in which philosophy and the sciences, theosophy and the mysteries flourished simultaneously, and pagans, Jews, and Christians had long been in polemical and apologetic contact and controversy.[126] Here Clement himself became a teacher of wisdom. As such he was hardly invested with an official position. We cannot accept that, as tradition would have it, he was appointed head of the Alexandrian 'catechetical school'.[127] Instead we must think of him as an independent teacher and 'philosopher', like Justin, who was able to gather his disciples around him from all sides, and not merely from the church camp. Clement's life is entirely one of personal intercourse and instruction, investigation and discussion, and of the free pursuit, praise, and purveyance of truth. He

[123] Eusebius, Praep. evang. II, 2, 64; cf. L. Fruchtel, *Philol. Wochenschrift* 59, 1939, p. 1047. It is suspicious, nevertheless, that the hints which Clement gives are expressed almost entirely in phrases borrowed from Plato, Euripides, and similar writers: P. T. Camelot, *Foi et gnose. Introduction à l'étude de la connaissance mystique chez Clément d'Alexandrie*, 1945, p. 85.

[124] Nevertheless, it is not really possible, despite the arguments of W. Bousset, *Jüdisch-christlicher Schulbetrieb in Alexandria und Rom*, 1915, pp. 248ff.; J. Lebreton, 'La théorie de la connaissance religieuse chez Clément d'Alexandrie', *RSR* 18, 1928, pp. 457ff., *et al.*, to arrange the extant works in such a way as to exhibit the course of this development: cf. G. Bardy, 'Aux origines de l'école d'Alexandrie', *RSR* 27, 1937, pp. 76f. The marked differences between them are to be explained in terms of the elastic temperament of Clement, which delighted to adapt itself to the varying purposes and areas with which his writings are from time to time concerned.

[125] Strom. I, 11, 2; Eusebius, *HE* V, 11, 3f.

[126] Cf. W. Schubart, art. 'Alexandrien,' *RAC* I, 1950, pp. 271ff.

[127] Cf. J. Munck, *Untersuchungen über Klemens von Alexandria*, 1933, pp. 273ff.; Bardy, *op. cit.*, pp. 82f., 86.

tells us very little directly about the professional and organisational aspect of his work; but his entire literary output is rooted in his teaching activity, and is thus indirectly a source of major importance for the Alexandrian educational system of the time, with its controversies, scholastic traditions, and didactic writing.[128]

Our main question here is, in what way did Clement himself think in principle of his calling and spiritual authority?—and the answer is to be found by considering his Christian purpose and his religio-philosophical attitude as a whole. After the start made by Justin and the earlier Apologists Clement is the first to detach Christian doctrine completely from the salvation-history setting of the Early Church, and to proclaim it to the pagan world public as a new religion. Christianity is a religious world-view, combining in one entity both dogma and a way of life,[129] and this implies that its content and meaning can be appropriated more or less thoroughly by the individual. With conversion and the first unformed 'faith' in Christ the process of seeking and learning is still far from its consummation. The Christian, or at any rate the more mature Christian who has the necessary capacity, is at this stage only beginning his daring ascent into the heights of spiritual 'knowledge' which faith in Christ has opened up to him. By Christ Clement normally understands not the earthly man Jesus; of him, his birth, crucifixion, and resurrection he has less and less to say. Instead 'Christ' connotes pre-eminently the eternal Logos of God,[130] the Son as teacher and revealer of truth, as cosmic Mind, and as the hidden goal of all the intellectual striving of mankind. This determines also the meaning of Christianity for the Christian. In principle, according to Clement, the way to God is here open to every man; for in contrast to the radical gnostics Clement will have nothing to do with the idea that certain classes of men may by their nature be excluded from salvation, and that only gnostic knowledge and not simply the faith of the Church makes it possible to attain to Christ and eternal life. Moses and the prophets, Plato and the philosophers—all were already on the way to him; and therefore the teaching of Christ must constantly be elucidated and confirmed from these two sides, prophecy and philosophy.[131] On the other hand, even bare faith in Christ has the

[128] On this subject, in addition to Stählin, Bousset, and Munck, cf. esp. G. Lazzati, *Introduzione allo studio di Clemente Alessandrino*, 1939, pp. 1ff.

[129] This unity of theory and practice is constantly emphasised: Strom. III, 35, 1; 44; IV, 13f.; V, 15, 2; VI, 91, 2f.; 108, 3; 111, 3; 122, 4; 152, 2; VII, 3, 6; 54, 1; Eclog. proph. 37.

[130] Though Clement uses numerous figurative terms and descriptions, 'Logos' is the name which he prefers: cf. G. Kretschmar, *Jesus Christus in der Theologie des Klemens von Alexandrien* (unpubl. Diss. theol. Heidelberg 1950).

[131] The 'ecclesiastical canon'—which is the crucial point at issue against the gnostics who reject the O.T.—is the principle of the homogeneity of the Old

advantage over both Jews and pagans, and is sufficient, if need be, of itself for salvation; for it stands on the one foundation which is of decisive importance for everyone. If, however, one wishes to understand the real truth of the matter, one should not remain static at this stage. The 'disciples of the Lord' gain access to new and unheard-of treasures of knowledge, they acquire a new vision, a new ear, a new heart,[132] and in this way become truly alike and akin to Christ their model.[133] Thus the presentation of Christianity in Clement regularly reaches its climax in the portrait of the perfect Christian, who has become like Christ, or, in Clement's own idiom, the true 'gnostic'.[134] Such a one has passed beyond all passions and desires. To do the good is for him no longer something imposed but something natural; he is perfected in love,[135] and thus becomes 'elect of the elect'.[136] The gnostic is the true Christian, and therefore he is also the true guide to Christ the Logos, the teacher of Christianity for every man and above all for Christians themselves.

This does not mean that every gnostic is to be pronounced a teacher in the narrower sense. Nevertheless, gnosis and teaching of their very nature go together. Faith and love, the beginning and the consummation of what it is to be a Christian, can neither of them be taught; but between them stands the gift of knowledge, which God commits to such as are worthy of it,[137] so that they radiate spiritual power to all around them.[138] For the gnostic himself, to give thus to his fellow-men, to foster and train them in this way whenever there is the slightest hint of an opportunity, is a natural and obvious expression of the love which is alive in him.[139] He, the one endowed by God, becomes richer only if he in turn endows others, communicates fellowship with God to others, and,

---

and New Testaments: cf. Strom. VI, 125, 3; VII, 94, 1; 94, 5; 97, 4; 100, 5; 105, 5; also F. Kattenbusch, *Das apostolische Symbol* 2, 1900, pp. 121ff.; H. Kutter, *Clemens Alexandrinus und das Neue Testament*, 1897, pp. 110ff.; W. C. Van Unnik, 'Opmerkingen over het karakter van het verloren werk von Clemens Alexandrinus "Canon Ecclesiasticus"', *Nederl. Arch. v. Kerkgesch.* 33, 1942, pp. 49ff. In his systematic exegesis of the whole of Scripture, which survives only in the exoteric works, we have the finest demonstration of Clement as a teacher. On the subject of Clement and pagan philosophy studies are continually appearing which for the most part have nothing new of importance to offer; I shall therefore content myself here with a reference to the thorough discussion of the problem in E. Molland, *The conception of the Gospel in the Alexandrian theology*, 1938, pp. 40ff.

[132] Strom. II, 15, 3.   [133] Strom. VI, 114, 4ff.

[134] It is from Clement that the technical concept of the 'gnostic' derives in the first place.

[135] For Clement it is in love that the fullness of spiritual perfection is to be found: cf., e.g., Strom. II, 55; IV, 53f.; 113; VII, 46, 3; 55ff.; 84f., and even as early as Paed. III, 3.

[136] Quis dives 36, 1.   [137] Strom. VII, 55, 6.   [138] Strom. VI, 158, 2.

[139] Cf. Strom. IV, 139, 1; VII, 3, 4f.; 4, 2; 13, 2; 16, 1; 35, 4; 49, 5; 53, 5; 101, 4.

as the redeemed, himself redeems.[140] Thus, in his own person he becomes like God,[141] an 'instrument of the divine voice' like the prophets of old,[142] and a living copy of Christ himself.[143] The fusion of his own moral and religious striving and living with his educational task is therefore the characteristic mark of the nature of the true gnostic.[144] Other Christians are, however, exhorted to take real advantage of the helping hand thus proffered to them. With compelling seriousness Clement in one sermon calls on everyone to look for a mature Christian of this kind to be their spiritual instructor. For there is no effective progress without instruction; and there can be no instruction without a teacher.[145] Each man needs his own, as a ship needs a pilot or an athlete a trainer. The teacher is not to be a mere purveyor of information, but should form and guide us so that we ourselves increase in power, and should be vigilant to bar us from the ways that would lead us backward once more. 'Tremble before one man at least, fear one at least, make an effort to listen at least to one man who tells you the truth plainly, and who at one and the same time treats you with firmness and makes you healthy. . . . There is nothing more terrible for the soul than that state of uninterrupted comfort which is the result of being pampered and no longer exposed to the forthright word of criticism.' The director so chosen will, for his part, spare no effort to ensure that his care, sympathy, and intercession are wholly available to his ward.[146]

We here catch a glimpse of the beginnings of a conscious practice of individual pastoral care which the gnostic must undertake toward his pupils and those Christians less mature than himself. It is a perpetual astonishment to the reader how little is said in this context about the Church as a social reality and organisation, its official superstructure, its worship, and its public methods of discipline. That all these things were already present in Clement's environment cannot be doubted; and he himself has no thought of polemising against them. The gnostic is not to avoid the normal forms of public worship, but for him himself they are dispensable;[147] they are of no significance to him—at least of

---

[140] Strom. II, 102, 2; VI, 161, 1; VII, 3, 4f.; 52, 1.

[141] Strom. II, 97.   [142] Strom. VI, 168, 3.

[143] Strom. VII, 52, 2f., cf. VI, 115; frag. 33 (GCS III, pp. 217-18, cited by Nicephorus Constant., Antirrhesis, as from a work περὶ τοῦ νομικοῦ πάσχα).

[144] Strom. II, 46, 1; cf. 73, 4.   [145] Strom. VI, 57, 2.

[146] Quis dives 41; cf. 34f., 42, 13ff. The novel element in this admonition is the individual relationship, and the voluntary submission of the 'penitent' to a director of his own choice. The general requirement of consideration for one's Christian brother, whatever inconveniences may threaten to stand in the way, is on the other hand an old one: cf. pp. 127ff. above; also esp. Ep. Apost. 39 (47); 50 (61); and J. Hoh, Die kirchliche Busse im zweiten Jahrhundert, 1932, pp. 69ff.

[147] Strom. VII, 49, 2f.

no essential and decisive significance.[148] Moreover, just as Clement himself and his own teachers are outside the ranks of the professional clergy, and remain laymen,[149] so too in his spiritual instructions he hardly ever finds occasion to speak of the 'shepherds'[150] belonging to his church.[151] If he does refer to the offices of the old or the new covenant, then they almost automatically serve him as allegories; the pattern of the 'priestly' man is for him not the bishop or priest of the official hierarchy but the gnostic and the gnostic teacher.[152] The authority, therefore, which the gnostic teacher exercises has virtually nothing to do with an ecclesiastical call or authorisation. Together with the capacity for spiritual things it is the product of the tradition of spiritual knowledge as this has come down from the apostles through a chain of living witnesses right to the present day, like some hidden treasure which son takes over from father, or like a light which again and again bursts into flame at the light of the gnostic love and glory.[153] Although Clement knows Irenaeus, the latter's combination of the argument from tradition with the concept of episcopal succession[154] is never mentioned by him.[155] His language is almost entirely like that of Ptolemaeus or any other gnostic teacher outside the organised Church who relies solely on the secret, oral tradition of his teachers and on his own direct experience.

Yet in fact it is precisely at this point that Clement remains absolutely distinct from the heretical gnosis; for he takes over in his own work, with full conviction, the most important product of the anti-gnostic struggle, something for which he is indebted to his own teachers, namely unqualified loyalty to the Scriptures, an attachment to the documents

---

[148] Strom. VII, 35, 3; 40, 3; 43, 1; 57, 2; cf. 56, 4 and the corresponding liberty with regard to fasts (VII, 75) and feasts (VII, 35, 3; 76, 4).

[149] Cf. H. Koch, 'War Klemens von Alexandrien Priester?' *ZNW* 20, 1921, pp. 43ff.

[150] Paed. I, 37, 3; Strom. II, 69, 2.

[151] In his extant writings Clement never mentions his own bishop. Conversely, the Alexandrian church seems hardly to have preserved any memory of Clement himself. Origen (Eusebius, *HE* VI, 19, 13) appeals to the example of Pantaenus and Heraclas, but not to Clement: cf. Bardy, *op. cit.*, pp. 82f. n. 63.

[152] Strom. V, 39, 4; 40, 1; VII, 36, 2; also IV, 158f.; V, 19, 4; VI, 105ff. This does not, of course, exclude the possibility that someone holding an official position in the Church may also be included among the gnostics, if he rightly practises the θεραπεία βελτιωτική committed to him: Strom. VII, 3, 3.

[153] Strom. I, 11, 3; V, 63, 2; VI, 61, 3; VII, 55, 6.

[154] Cf. pp. 170ff. above.

[155] In general Clement appeals only to the teachers and Elders of the past: Protrept. XI, 113, 1; Strom. I, 11, 3; Eclog. proph. 11, 1; 27,1; 27,4; 50,1; fragments from the *Hypotyposes*: GCS, pp. 197; from the *Adumbrationes*, GCS, pp. 210–11; from the treatise *On the Pasch*: frag. 25, GCS, p. 216. By contrast, Origen *is* acquainted with the official διαδοχή τῶν ἀποστόλων: De princ. I, 2; IV, 2, 2 (9).

not only of the Old but also of the only recently defined New Testament.[156] Clement is a scriptural theologian.[157] Only the Scripture is capable of giving real certainty,[158] something more than uncertain human opinion.[159] Furthermore, Scripture alone can provide decisive refutation in the fight against heresy,[160]—and let no one imagine he has found the truth until he discovers it here,[161] and has based it on this independent ground.[162] It is this fundamental attitude which explains the distinctive style of Clement's didactic writing, constantly permeated with biblical quotations and allusions. Clement almost apologises for the fact that regard for his listeners, and the overall plan of his work, oblige him to reduce the amount of biblical evidence presented; but in fact, if not in the precise words, what he is expressing is wholly founded on Scripture, and derives its 'breath and life' solely from the Bible.[163] At the same time, however, Clement knows that nothing of importance is achieved simply by proclaiming the principle of loyalty to the Scriptures; in opposition to the heretical perversions of Scripture there has to be a clarification of the principles on which Scripture is to be understood. Thus it comes about that, a generation before Origen, Clement appears as the first Christian theologian to grasp the full extent of the problem of hermeneutics. He does not imagine that it can be solved purely externally by appealing to particular ecclesiastical rulings or norms—a method which in fact simply destroys Scripture and denies it real influence. He is fully familiar with the inevitable circle in which all understanding of biblical truth, by its very nature, must move.[164] The word of the Holy Spirit can be known only with the

[156] According to the Anti-Montanist (Eusebius, *HE* V, 16, 3) Clement is the first to use this expression (cf. W. C. Van Unnik, *art. cit.*, *VC* 3, 1949, p. 36). It should be pointed out, however, that even for him the N.T. canon is not definitively closed, and, more important still, he does not regard its various parts as being on the same level or as possessing an equal measure of authority: cf. p. 198 n. 131 above. Cf. on this subject Kutter, *op. cit.*, and the exact, if somewhat too cautiously selected evidence in J. Ruwet, 'Clément d'Alexandrie: Canon des Écritures et Apocryphes', *Biblica* 29, 1948, pp. 77ff., 240ff., 391ff.

[157] For a general survey of Clement's understanding and use of the Scriptures cf. C. Mondésert, *Clément d'Alexandrie. Introduction à l'étude de sa pensée religieuse à partir de l'écriture*, 1944.

[158] Strom. II, 48, 3; V, 40, 1; VI, 128, 3; VII, 93, 1; cf. the similar language of Ptolemaeus, *Letter to Flora* (cited in Epiphanius, Pan. XXXIII, 3, 8) concerning the words of Jesus.

[159] Strom. VII, 92, 2ff.; 93, 3.

[160] Strom. VII, 92–106; it is equally necessary to provide proofs for the educated Greek: Strom. VI, 91, 5.

[161] Strom. VII, 93, 1.   [162] Strom. VII, 95, 4.   [163] Strom. VII, 1, 3f.

[164] It is in this fact that, for him, the problem of faith and reason takes its rise, and once raised never lets him go. Clement feels that somehow both these things must be combined in Christianity (Strom. VII, 102, 1; cf. 94, 4), but he never achieves complete clarity on the questions that flow from this. The

help of that Spirit;[165] it is essential that we should have received the 'Church's guideline', the guideline of truth, or the truth itself, that is, the Logos of God,[166] who speaks to us in the Scripture.[167] The will and mind of Christ must be known if a man wishes to understand[168] the 'clarity' of the Bible.[169] Faith precedes knowledge of the Scriptures, and only there, in the word of the Lord, finds its confirmation.[170] By contrast, men in themselves are 'not trustworthy teachers, when the question is one to do with God'.[171] Christ is the only teacher,[172] and he makes it possible for anyone to find him. For the man who has realised his own lack of knowledge, 'who begins to seek, and, having sought, then finds the teacher, and having found him, then believes on him, and having believed on him, then loves him, and having become deeply attached to him, then becomes like the Beloved, may be himself that very thing which formerly he learned to love'.[173]

The surprising point for us in this train of thought is the curious role which, despite what has been said, the person of the human, 'gnostic' teacher is to play in any real appropriation of spiritual truth. For Clement he is virtually indispensable, and neither the stress on the authority of Scripture nor the polemic (borrowed from Paul) against human wisdom and direction counterbalance this. *In concreto* the circle of the spiritual understanding of revelation proves always to include the person of the spiritual teacher.[174] One cannot hope to find God and his

---

fullest discussions on faith and knowledge are to be found in the material in Strom. VIII, where an attempt is made to overcome scepticism by means of Stoic logic: cf. A. Schmekel, *Die positive Philosophie I. Forschungen zur Geschichte des Hellenismus*, 1938, pp. 549ff.; also K. Prümm, 'Glaube und Erkenntnis im zweiten Buck der Stromata des Klemens von Alexandrien,' *Scholastik* 12, 1937, pp. 17ff.; and on the question in general, T. Camelot, *Foi et gnose. Introduction à l'étude de la connaissance mystique chez Clément d'Alexandrie*, 1945; J. Moingt, 'La gnose de Clément d'Alexandrie dans ses rapports avec la foi et la philosophie,' *RSR* 37, 1950, pp. 195ff.

[165] Strom. VI, 166, 3, where appeal is made to I Cor. 2:10, 14.

[166] Strom. VII, 94, 5.

[167] Strom. III, 5, 4; V, 178, 6; VI, 59; 78, 6; VII, 98f. The original words of Christ himself have for Clement by that very fact especial value. But the principle applies in all cases, that only God can give complete knowledge of God, and that when he does so it is always through his Word: Strom. V, 82, 4; cf. VI, 68, 3; 70, 2f., 78, 5; 166, 4.

[168] Strom. VII, 96, 4; Quis dives 5, 4.

[169] Strom. VI, 59, 3: πεισθέντες . . . τῇ τῶν γραφῶν σαφηνείᾳ; but cf. 131, 3.

[170] Strom. VII, 95, 5f. Naturally Scripture also reinforces Scripture: Strom. VII, 96, 4; 104, 1.

[171] Strom. VI, 165, 5; cf. 57–59; 167, 5; VII, 95, 7f.; similarly Heracleon, *frag.* 39, quoted in Origen, Comm. Joh. XIII, 53.

[172] Strom. I, 12, 3.   [173] Strom. V, 17, 1; cf. 57f.

[174] Strom. I, 5, 2; 16, 3; IV, 97, 5. Elsewhere too emphasis is again laid on the idea of the teacher as model. In this, Clement is following the ancient philosophical tradition, though with more in mind than a mere illustration of

covenant simply in scriptural documents; he himself is the true
'Testament'.[175] The believer must be guided to the life of God by the
teaching and example of one who is himself living that life. 'There is
no faith without teaching.'[176] 'Out of instruction grow both understanding and knowledge.'[177] Such statements might be taken in a flat,
rationalistic sense; but when used by Clement in accordance with his
habit of speaking and thinking in an elastic way, with many levels of
meaning, seeking points of contact on every side, their import changes
with every shift of light and of the observer's position. What he really
means is most clearly discernible when he comes to treat of the essential
precedence of oral over written tradition, and of the unavoidably personal
and direct nature of teaching.[178]

It is well known that the Stromata begin with a discussion of the
question whether it is entirely permissible to set down the teaching of
the truth in writing. There are many arguments in favour;[179] but
nevertheless, the consideration that finally decides Clement to give
his expositions is that he is deliberately choosing a difficult, badly
arranged, and indeed confusing form in which to record them. Vital
points will be mixed up with peripheral ones; and this will hinder
anyone except the 'initiated' from really learning anything from the
gay complexity of what is offered, or from being able to grasp the full
meaning of what is said in this fashion.[180] These statements are seriously
meant. It is quite inadequate to explain them as referring to nothing

doctrine by life; for him it is a question of the mediation of actual fellowship
with God.

[175] Strom. I, 182, 2: Μοῦσῆς δὲ φαίνεται τὸν κύριον διαθήκην καλῶν, »ἰδοὺ
ἐγώ«, λέγων, »ἡ διαθήκη μου μετά σοῦ.« (Gen. 17:2) ἐπεὶ καὶ πρότερον εἶπεν
»διαθήκην« ,<ἐπιφέρει.> μὴ ζητεῖ αὐτὴν ἐν γραφῇ. ἔστι γὰρ διαθήκη αὐτὸς ὁ
αἴτιος τοῦ παντὸς θεός <ὃς> τίθεται (θεὸς δὲ παρὰ τὴν θέσιν εἴρηται καὶ τάξιν)
τὴν δικαιοσύνην. The reconstruction of the text is taken from GCS. Cf. Kutter,
op. cit., p. 105: 'For Clement . . all writings, even the Holy Scriptures, are,
qua writings, on an equality.'   [176] Eclog. proph. 28, 3.   [177] Strom. VI, 57, 2.

[178] Even the concept of 'secret' tradition is connected with this, and must not
simply be dismissed as an isolated 'gnostic' peculiarity: cf. Camelot, op. cit.,
p. 94: 'In this preoccupation—strongly present, it should be noted, even in the
First Book of the Stromata—with his being himself linked to a secret tradition,
to a succession of teachers, we find the same concern to justify his esotericism
which inspired in Clement his reflections on allegory and the hidden sense of
Scripture. It is the same intellectual and spiritual conception, but now transferred, if we may put it this way, to the social, collective, and institutional plane.'

[179] Clement refers (Strom. I, 1, 1) to the Holy Scripture itself, and (Strom.
I, 11f.; 14, 2f.; cf. Eclog. proph. 27, 4) to the obligation of preserving the
tradition of the Fathers from oblivion. He seems to have said something similar
in his work On the Pasch: Eusebius, HE VI, 13, 9 (GCS frag. 25, o. 216).

[180] Perhaps the phrase οὐ γραφὴ εἰς ἐπίδειξιν τετεχνασμένη (Strom. I,
11, 1) may be understood, with Lazzati, op. cit., pp. 14f., in the sense that the
purpose of publishing the material in this guise is simply to avoid the form of a
textbook accessible to everyone.

more than the novelty and boldness of his literary undertaking,[181] or to understand the words wherever possible as simply a kind of author's coquetry, designed to win forbearance for the lack of organisation and discipline of thought in the Stromata.[182] Clement really means what he says, and in the course of his expositions he frequently returns to the points of view expressed in the introduction.[183] Fundamentally, his objection is that 'things so mysterious as the truth about God ought to be entrusted only to word of mouth and not to writing'.[184] It is no accident that the teachers of old time were satisfied to use this one method only.[185] Compared with the direct, enthusiastic force of speech,[186] dissemination of the word in writing can never be more than a secondary measure,[187] and, if used entirely by itself, is always dangerous or at any rate in need of supplementation by word of mouth. A fixed text is an excellent thing when what is required is to consolidate that which has been said earlier, and to 'remember' it;[188] but of itself it can never kindle dialogue nor answer a single question—for these things the pupil needs an expositor, the skilful and understanding teacher.[189] The teacher is the guardian of the mystery of spiritual truth, and woe to him if from ambition or self-assertion, or, it may be, from a kind of affectionate weakness, he betrays to the curious listener more than the latter can endure![190] That which is holy is not to be given to dogs,[191] nor do we put knives into the hands of children.[192]

In substantiation Clement likes to appeal to the example of the ancient mysteries and to the *disciplina arcani* in all its forms.[193] Every-

---

[181] The well known comments of F. Overbeck, 'Über die Anfänge der patristischen Literatur', *Hist. Zeitschr.* 48, 1882, pp. 416ff., esp. pp. 465ff., tend in this direction.

[182] By contrast, the Anti-Montanist (Eusebius, *HE* V, 16, 3) really does exhibit such coquetry; here, however, the reluctance to write is based on quite different reasons in virtually diametric opposition to those of Clement. The writer is afraid of arousing the suspicion that he may be intending to add something to the written corpus of the N.T.; cf. Van Unnik, *op. cit.*, pp. 1ff., 9 n. 33.

[183] Cf. esp. Strom. IV, 4ff.; VI, 1ff.; VII, 111; Eclog. proph. 27.

[184] Strom. I, 13, 2; V, 64, 5; similar views, though on the much less original lines of the customary *disciplina arcani* are also expressed by Origen: Comme Rom. I, 4: de 'libris vitae' quamvis periculosum videntur cartulis committer. sermonem, tamen non otiose praetereunda sunt dicta sapientium et aenigmata. . . .   [185] Eclog. proph. 27, 1f.   [186] Eclog. proph. 27, 3.

[187] Strom. I, 4, 1f.; IV, 111, 1; VI, 91, 5; Eclog. proph. 27, 3.

[188] Strom. I, 14, 1f.; VI, 91, 3; Eclog. proph. 27, 3.

[189] Strom. I, 14, 4; 16, 3; V, 56, 4.

[190] Strom. I, 5f.; V, 54; Eclog. proph. 27, 7.

[191] Strom. I, 55, 3; V, 7, 3.

[192] Strom. I, 14, 3; cf. 13, 3; 15, 1; 56, 3; IV, 4, 4-7; VI, 2; 129, 4; Eclog. proph. 27, 5. In such contexts I Cor. 3:2 is, of course, a favourite quotation.

[193] Cf., e.g., Strom. V, 58, 4; in addition there are repeated references to the Pythagoreans, the ancient poets, the Egyptians, and so on.

where he finds this principle recognised—in the prophets, the poets, and the philosophers, among Jews, Greeks, and barbarians. In this he is a child of his time, and takes a child's delight in secrets and mysteries of all kinds. In his view even Jesus and the Apostles obviously operated on this venerable,[194] divine, and quite indispensable method of concealment and step-by-step revelation. The highest truths of all they passed on only allusively.[195] Consequently Holy Scripture too has very many different levels, and is full of hidden riddles,[196] which only the gnostic can make plain.[197] But at bottom more is implied by such remarks than a mere *disciplina arcani*. What Clement is aiming at is rather the living, educational responsibility of a spiritual teacher in view of the trans-rational and supraterrestrial character of Christian truth, which can be 'known' and tested only in personal, existential appropriation.[198] It is true that to a certain extent the gnostic exegete is also superior to the tyro simply by virtue of his erudition; his relationship to the novice is like that of the expert to the layman,[199] and therefore he is naturally in a position to answer his pupil's questions, himself to raise objections, and then to choose the right words with which to refute them.[200] But the point of crucial importance is that he himself lives by the thing of which he speaks, and that he can impart in personal intercourse that which he proclaims in words—communion with God, that living knowledge of his nature which transfigures human action and is one with love. Because he possesses this love, he can make the dead coals of sacred learning once more glow with heat.[201] In this intercourse between man and man 'mountains are moved'.[202] Nevertheless, it is always important to keep in mind the listener's actual capacity for comprehension, to adapt oneself to him—though with absolute veracity—and only to say what is beneficial for him at his stage.[203] It is not whim or vanity which lays this task upon the teacher, but the living mystery of the truth itself, which it is his duty

[194] Strom. V, 65, 4.

[195] Strom. V, 19, 3; 63f.; VI, 127, 3f.

[196] There is no need to demonstrate in detail the presence of this idea in Clement: cf., e.g., Strom. V, 25; 26, 3; 32, 1; 51ff.; VI, 131, 3ff.; VII, 94, 1; Eclog. proph. 32, 2.

[197] Strom. V, 57, 1; 58, 5; VI., 116; 126, 1; 132, 5; Eclog. proph. 28, 1.

[198] Strom. V, 56, 3 (the writings of the 'barbarian philosophy'): τῶν γὰρ πολλάκις αὐταῖς πλησιαζόντων καὶ δοκιμασίαν δεδωκότων κατά τε τὴν πίστιν κατά τε τὸν βίον ἅπαντα μόνων ἐθέλουσιν ὑπάρχειν τὴν ὄντως οὖσαν φιλοσοφίαν καὶ τὴν ἀληθῆ θεολογίαν. Cf. VI, 149, 5.

[199] Strom. VII, 95, 9.

[200] Strom. III, 38, 5; VI, 1, 4; 65, 1; 65, 6; 81, 4; 82, 4; VIII, 44, 8.

[201] Strom. VI, 116, 2.

[202] Strom. VII, 77, 4.

[203] Strom. I, 9, 1; 45, 1; 55f.; V, 18, 6f.; 57, 2; 66, 1; VI, 3, 3; 116, 3; 127, 4; 129, 4; VII, 2, 3; 6; 29, 7; 53.

to champion.[204] However much in the formulation of these ideas may be traditional or conventional, we are here in touch with a genuine experience of an insight into the seriousness of spiritual authority and responsibility astonishing in its profundity and vitality.

In this connection Clement refers to Plato, his favourite philosopher and 'prophet'.[205] He cites not only the Phaedrus but also the Second Epistle,[206] in which Plato refuses to write textbooks of his own teaching, and explicitly commends the oral form of instruction.[207] This is more than a case of mere external and accidental coincidence. For all that their intellectual worlds are so far apart,[208] both these men, the great dialectician and the Christian theologian, are yet convinced in a closely comparable sense that knowledge and appropriation of truth are no mere theoretical processes, forming one sector only of human life, but an event of comprehensive human, nay religious significance, making the whole of life new. And from this unique personal event the person of the teacher cannot conceivably be excluded. Furthermore, Clement likes to emphasise the Socratic truth that the teacher can be no more than a helper, that he merely points the way which each man has to traverse by his own efforts.[209] For Clement, however, the teacher signifies even more than he does in Plato, in accordance with the different nature of the religious message of which he is an advocate. Whereas in Plato the philosopher's work is developed in the clear setting of logical and dialectical reason, Clement's divine Logos encounters the inquirer as the messenger of a different world, one which without his aid is unattainable—in other words, as revealer. In this work of revelation he takes on personal, divine-in-human form, bestowing direct knowledge and expressing love, and demanding personal surrender and love from men in return. This change in the nature of reason is reflected also in the person of the teacher. He is no longer solely partner

---

[204] H. U. Von Balthasar, *Origenes. Geist und Feuer—ein Aufbau aus seinen Schriften*, 1938, p. 35, coins, with reference to Origen, the felicitous concept of 'existentieller Wahrheits-Relativismus' (= existentially controlled relativism in the treatment of truth).

[205] Strom. V, 106, 2; cf. VI, 42, 3.

[206] Plato, Phaedrus 276D ff.; Ep. II 314; Ep. VII, which is also relevant (341) is quoted by Origen (Contra Celsum VI, 6).

[207] Strom. I, 9, 1; 11, 1; 13, 2; 14, 3f.; V, 65, 1; Protrept. 68, 1.

[208] This aspect, the dissimilarity, is the only one emphasised in J. Meifort, *Der Platonismus bei Clemens Alexandrinus*, 1928.

[209] Strom. IV, 4, 4; 5, 1; V, 24, 2; VI, 2, 2f.; 126, 1. As a believing Christian the pupil already possesses the Spirit (Strom. V, 25, 5); all that he lacks is the higher knowledge. God has already shown in the course of the salvation-history that he wishes to to stimulate men to independence in their knowledge of God (Strom. VI, 111, 1); and this same purpose, namely of encouraging each man's own exertions, is also served by the difficult nature of written communication in the style of the Stromata (I, 10).

and helper, but is seen also as in the full sense a messenger and mediator of salvation, because he for his part is already in communion with Christ the Logos. By virtue of this fact he can through word and example draw his listeners into the same communion, a fellowship which God reveals through his own Word, and which without this revelation would be unattainable to mere natural knowledge. As preacher and pastor the teacher brings his pupil into the sphere of the divine Spirit, and by so doing at the same time discloses to him the depths of the divine Word.

More difficult to define is the relationship in which Clement's ideal of the teacher stands to the pattern exhibited by Jesus and by the apostle Paul, to both of whom he continually appeals in this connection.[210] It is plain that the method which he ascribes to them, namely that of concealing the mystery, accommodating to the hearer, and allegoric instruction, will not in fact fit them. Nevertheless, Clement is right when he protests against the practice of taking the simple truth of Jesus's words as sheer platitude,[211] and of no longer having an ear for the hidden question which the words contain.[212] His interpretation in terms of the category of mystery wrestles with the same riddle that Mark had resolved, hardly less violently, with his theory of hardening. Out of the open secret, which children are able to grasp but which the wise never discern, Clement makes a secret teaching only to be understood in the course of a long religious training and development. His exegesis of Jesus's words, which he gives in fragments scattered throughout his work, is therefore nearly always wrongheaded. None the less, he really does know something of the unfathomable depth in the content of these words which, as he on one occasion remarks, give birth to truth for all the world and yet remain eternally virgin.[213]

Closer still are his connections with the apostle Paul, though here too it is not hard to make out the profound differences between their systematisations and worlds of thought.[214] In his understanding of the Gospel, of freedom, and of the Spirit, Clement has absolutely nothing in common with the historical Paul, and, quite unintentionally, ascribes to him meanings very different from those originally in his mind. Nevertheless, better than many later expositors with dogmatic axes to grind, he grasps the significance of the activity of preaching in Paul. For Paul too knew something of the difficulties of communication, of the need to preach among those who are perfect a wisdom which not every Christian would understand without further ado; and above all

---

[210] Strom. I, 13, 1f.; V, 26, 3; 60ff.; VI, 124, 6; 125, 1; 126, 4; VII, 2, 3; Quis dives 5, 2ff.

[211] Quis dives 5, 4.   [212] Quis dives 6.   [213] Strom. VII, 94, 1.

[214] Cf., in addition to Molland, op. cit., H. Seesemann, 'Das Paulusverständnis des Clemens Alexandrinus', Theol. Stud. u. Krit. 107, 1936, pp. 312ff.; F. Buri, Clemens Alexandrinus und der paulinische Freiheitsbegriff, 1939.

Paul too emphasised the immense responsibility of the preacher, who must really become one with the cause which he represents. For these reasons Clement compares the authority and function of the gnostic teacher directly with the apostolate.[215] What misleads him into doing so is the abundance of Paul's statements about his own spiritual ministry and his authority in the Church. It would have been more appropriate for Clement to link his teacher with the Pauline teachers or prophets or other persons endowed with a particular spiritual gift; for the teacher lacks precisely that thing which, on Paul's view, distinguishes the apostle from other ministries within the Church, namely the unambiguous call and the public authority which he claims by virtue of this. But this distinction is of no importance for Clement. He can dispense with any extraordinary authority because he has confidence in the power of direct contact with the truth, which bears witness to itself in the very person of the spiritual man. At this point, despite the gnostic and religious tinge to the idea, he displays once more a certain approximation to philosophical idealism. For Paul, between the wisdom of the world and the foolishness of faith yawned an abyss which only God's word and God's authority could bridge; Clement sees everywhere points of contact with and preparations for the truth of Christianity, which need only to be cultivated and developed. The stages and progressions within the spiritual life, which in Paul are additional—but only additional, and therefore subsidiary—subjects for consideration, in Clement acquire a universal and essential significance which attracts reflective thought, and thus makes the professional preacher into a 'teacher' and educator.

And it is this which in turn makes his responsibilities so abundant and so complex. His art has to have as many levels and aspects as the Word itself, if he is to bring men near to that Word and to convince them of its truth. The Pauline maxim, 'all things to all men', is made into an all-embracing principle for the communication of truth in general. The message no longer hurls the messenger into battle like a standard-bearer, nor does it trample its opponents in triumph in the dust. Instead, through the art of the teacher it woos men to a free decision by approaching them in friendship, attracting and instructing them. For the Son of God compels no one, but leaves each man to lay hold of salvation for himself.[216] It is true that Paul too can lay stress on this idea, and, in accordance with Jesus's example, renounce any sort of domination; but he does so within the Christian congregation, which has already taken the paradoxal step of faith, and whose freedom therefore is both based upon and limited by the 'word of the Cross'. Of this word Clement has almost nothing to say; it is extremely rare for

[215] Strom. VI, 105, 1; 106, 1; VII, 77, 4.
[216] Strom. VII, 6, 3.

him even to mention the Cross of Christ, and so the power of freedom, bringing inner enlightenment and conviction, to which he appeals, becomes a basic quality of human nature and of Man's religious capacity.

Hence the importance of the teacher as mediator of knowledge is in the last resort circumscribed and restricted once more in a peculiarly philosophical way. The teacher, as we have seen, is by definition not concerned simply with bare, theoretical instruction; he reveals to the novice a higher way of life, he is his personal pastor, his pattern, his counsellor, his intercessor with God, and his friend. The whole of Christian life is seen in terms of pastoral fellowship of this kind,[217] which only the enlightened gnostic teacher can provide. Not everyone is qualified for this task.[218] But however close the teacher may come to being so for his pupil, however near to him he may bring the world of God and of the divine Logos, yet he never in the strict sense speaks to him 'in Christ's place'; his authority is not that of a representative, but only that of a teacher and of an enlightened example. Clement himself certainly does not feel this as in any way a deficiency; he is simply unacquainted with any form of communication other than that which invites the hearer to worthy comprehension and imitation of the teacher's own opinions, knowledge and experience. The aim is not faith as an act of free acceptance and surrender; faith, for Clement, never means anything more than a rather stupid form of knowledge and understanding based on trust in authority. As such it is characteristic of the uneducated mass of church members, in whom therefore he personally takes little interest. In the higher world of the spiritual life, where he is at home, each man has to lay hold on truth for himself, in whatever way and to whatever extent this is disclosed to him by the help of a mature Christian teacher. Clement plainly knows nothing of those desperate situations where a man longs for the concrete and authoritative word of God to which he can submit in freedom, transcending the limitations of his own understanding, and even, it may be, against the resistance of his own heart. Clement has never met the Word in pure encounter, impervious to psychological interpretation, in the almost sacramental givenness of a pronouncement made on the authority of Christ alone.[219] For him the significance of the pastor lies simply in

---

[217] Even the offices of the Church are symbolic of grades of spiritual perfection (Strom. VI, 107, 2f.), and those who have attained these grades have no need of office (Strom. VI, 106, 2).

[218] Strom. V, 12, 3f.

[219] It is clear that Clement attaches no crucial value to the sacrament in the narrower sense either, and that whenever he comes to speak of it he quickly evaporates it into a spiritual 'image'. Most significant of all, however, is his doctrine of penance, in which in fact self-purification takes the place of forgiveness, even though it is a self-purification within the fellowship of the Church and of pastoral intercession; cf. the remarks of B. Poschmann, *Paenitentia*

what he personally can convey on the subject of spirit and life; and the pupil accordingly acquires only so much as he himself can appropriate from this by observation, imitation, and sympathy. This pedagogic and imitative Christianity consequently has no serious interest in the intrusions of an alleged authority. Ultimately it acknowledges no professional 'office' in this sense—or rather, acknowledges it only as a pedagogic aid for a Christianity which spiritually has not yet become genuinely free and alive.

It is therefore certainly no accident that Clement shows no more than a superficial interest in the 'official' and 'sacramental' Church in general. But, it must be said once more, this does not in his case as yet imply conscious rejection or hostility. And it seems, conversely, as though the Church herself never felt any special difficulties with regard to him.[220] Only with certain anxious one-track minds within the Church did he occasionally come into conflict, because they took exception on general grounds to his preoccupation with pagan philosophy and education. Other Church fathers of this period, after all, display a similar interest.[221] But there is no reason to suppose that these reactionary pietists had rightly interpreted and understood the weakness of Clement's concept of authority, and the extremely subtle reasons why his standpoint was in the end incompatible with that of the Church— even though this incompatibility was in fact connected with pagan philosophy and philosophical idealism. To assume that they had discerned this would be to pay too much respect to their limited intelligence. In the next generation, with Origen, the problem emerges much more clearly; but even then, as we shall see, it is neither fully comprehended in theory nor effectively resolved in practice.

We may assume that the attitude which Clement adopted toward Church office and his own calling was also, with individual variations, widespread among other teachers in the East. But it will be enough to recall the Western counter-instance, Tertullian, to keep us from mistaken generalisations. Tertullian too is a 'teacher' without an official position in the Church;[222] he too wears the philosopher's cloak, and

secunda, 1940, pp. 229ff., who emphasises the official element rather too strongly, and the, on this point, rather more correct assessment of the texts by J. Hoh, *Die kirchliche Busse im II. Jahrhundert*, 1932, pp. 115ff. (= *ZKT* 56, 1932, pp. 175ff.); also H. Karpp, 'Die Busslehre des Klemens von Alexandrien,' *ZNW* 43, 1950/51, pp. 224ff., esp. p. 235.

[220] Clement was entrusted with missions on behalf of the Church, and acquired the reputation of an able and respected man in such affairs (Eusebius, *HE* VI, 11, 6). After his death Bishop Alexander of Jerusalem called him 'the holy Clement, who was my master and benefactor' (ibid., VI, 14, 9).

[221] Cf. p. 194 n. 110 above.

[222] Cf. H. Koch, 'Tertullianisches II, 6,' *Theol. Stud. u. Krit.* 103, 1931, pp. 108ff. On the fact that Tertullian was a layman cf. also the cautious comments

emphasises his own superiority to the *simplices* and *idiotae*—even if these happen to occupy the highest episcopal thrones.[223] But at the same time how totally different is the frame of mind in which he approaches the Church and her message! His passionate temperament positively welcomes the end of free, unfettered discussion and speculation, and the saving absolutism of an authority which is able not merely to commend faith and obedience but to demand them.[224] It is—or at least so he would have us believe—only the vexatious meddling of the gnostic false teachers, and the inability of the stupid catholic congregations to defend themselves, which compel him as teacher and author to take up his pen and use his skill in logic and rhetoric to do battle for the truth that has been revealed.[225] For Tertullian too this truth is to be found above all in the Holy Scripture; but what Scripture contains is first and foremost not higher knowledge and mysteries, but sacred norms and commandments to which every man must submit, and the Church is the community in which this *nova lex* of the Christian faith is observed. Hence Tertullian also respects its governing and teaching authorities, the bishops, who are placed at its head in accordance with the will of the apostles as their successors.[226] At least, he wants to respect them; and if in the end he comes into conflict with them all the same, this at any rate does not imply to his mind that external authority as such should not in any circumstances be normative within the Church. It is only against the truth that such authority has no rights.

Nevertheless, this contrast between liberal gnosis on the one hand and an official nomism on the other is not enough to enable the Church to grasp the real problem of office. A decision on the question of the authority attaching to spiritual office is reached only when this question also becomes one of salvation in the strict and immediate sense. Clement was never acquainted with such an authority; but already in his day it was an inescapable requirement in the context of the Church's discipline of penance. For here what is at stake is no longer merely a matter of education and knowledge, but the justification and authority for the pardon and remission of guilt in God's name.

---

of G. F. Diercks, *Q. Septimius Florens Tertullianus de oratione. Critische uitgave met prolegomena, vertaling en philologisch-exegetisch-liturgische commentaar,* 1947, pp. 207ff.

[223] Adv. Prax. 3, 1; for mockery of the moral failings of bishops cf. also cor. mil. 1.

[224] Cf. scorp. 2: auctoritas divina praecedit, an tale quid voluerit atque mandaverit deus, ut qui negant bonum non suadeantur accommodum, nisi cum subacti fuerint.

[225] Cf. K. Holl, 'Tertullian als Schriftsteller,' *Gesammelte Aufsätze zur Kirchengeschichte* 3, 1928, pp. 1ff., esp. pp. 11f.

[226] Cf. K. Adam, *Der Kirchenbegriff Tertullians. Eine dogmengeschichtliche Studie,* 1907, pp. 56ff.

CHAPTER IX

The Church in the West: the Conflict over Repentance

IT IS no accident that the problem of the Christian sinner should force itself on the attention of the Church so late and so hesitantly. The starting-point of the Church's preaching did not lie here, but in the confession of complete redemption, of a real and present salvation, and of the new, miraculous holiness which had been bestowed on all believers: Christ had made their life a new thing. Nevertheless this faith was built from the start on the concept of repentance, of total 'conversion', and this had everywhere released powerful moral forces. Demands, exhortations, and an all the more urgent summons to amendment naturally followed; the new life in holiness and piety is Man's response to the gift of redemption. No Christian, as Paul in particular emphasises, can or ought to evade this consequence; each person is to confirm, demonstrate, and maintain his calling by a corresponding change in his way of life. 'Become what you are,' that is to say, 'Continue to be what you have been made', may in this sense be called virtually the guiding principle of Christian paraenesis. Now the result of thus relating moral conduct back to the object of faith, the reality of the new being, may very well be to sharpen perception of what contradicts this reality, and to awaken and encourage the conscious struggle against it. At the same time, however, it does not allow the sin of Christians to be treated as a natural, constantly recurring, and possibly even permanent phenomenon of life. Such an assessment of the self would deny the very essence of Christian redemption, and would mean a final abandonment of the new, supramundane nature which Christians have received and in which they must stand before God at the Last Day. It is this contradiction which the dialectic of I John expresses very clearly when it simultaneously requires both sinlessness and confession of sin, and thus allows real and present holiness to achieve continuance in constantly renewed 'repentance'.[1] Nevertheless the author of the Epistle is unique for his time in this clearly defined understanding and description of the situation. The other writers of the apostolic and sub-apostolic era have

---

[1] Cf. pp. 136ff. above.

as yet not even noticed the problem at issue as such. They are content with asserting the holiness of Christians, with fighting sin where it appears, and also indeed with summoning men to humble penitence and confession of sin;[2] but how this paradox is to be understood in theological theory and evaluated in principle remains undiscussed and unexplained.

The next stage in development results from the necessities of Church practice and not from theological reflection. Congregational discipline insists on its rights; gross sinners cannot be tolerated within the Church; she neither can nor will give them her protection in dealing with the outside world, nor will she allow them to be regarded as Christians. 'No Christian is an evildoer,' assert the Apologists; 'if he were, his membership would be mere sham.'[3] The alleged evildoers among Christians are simply false apostates, already expelled and condemned, who were never genuinely Christians, or at any rate are so now no longer.[4] In reality, however, it is not so simple to spot these 'so-called brethren',[5] and to separate oneself from them unequivocally. The Church has ramified into countless groups and congregations and in countless directions. The borderlines between orthodoxy and heresy are fluid; there are no valid guidelines, nor, what is more, any unified organisation. The simple rules in accordance with which the primitive Christian congregations may have dealt with their sinful brethren, and preserved good order,[6] are no longer applicable; unquestionably there is a widespread danger of a dissolution of unity and discipline. It is only from the middle of the second century onwards that a basic change in the situation begins. In the struggle against the gnosis the 'catholic' Church had achieved closer cohesion and a more settled structure in its congregations, and this provided the necessary conditions for an effective development of discipline. We have now reached the beginnings of an organised practice of penance.

But this means that we have also reached a crucial point in the wider history of the concept of office. Tangible supremacy over sin is of decisive importance for the nature and definition of all spiritual authority within the Church, and this includes the authority of the organised ecclesiastical offices. The question is now asked what rights and what power within the Church pertain to the bishop in the judicial process of penance and of the 'binding' and 'loosing' of sin; in what sense these

[2] So with particular impressiveness in the so-called II Clement, whose author describes himself forthrightly as πανθαμαρτωλός (18, 2): ὡς οὖν ἐσμὲν ἐπὶ γῆς, μετανοήσωμεν (8, 1); cf. Poschmann, *Paenitentia secunda*, 1940, pp. 124ff.

[3] Athenagoras, *Suppl.* 2, 3.

[4] Justin, I Apol. 7, 2; 16, 8; Dial. XXXV; Tertullian, Apol. 44, 3; 46, 17; Ad nat. I, 5; Minucius Felix, Oct. 35, 5; cf. from the N.T. period, I Pet. 4:15.

[5] I Cor. 5:11.

[6] Cf. pp. 126ff. above.

belong to him by virtue of his office; and whether he alone can lay claim to authority of this kind. For the period under discussion, however, these questions must not be considered in isolation. In the controversies over penance in the second and third centuries the formal juristic problem of official rights and 'competence' is at first neither particularly prominent nor of decisive importance. The dispute between official and non-official authority in the matter of penance is but one element in the more vital struggle concerning the mediation of salvation through the Church and the objective appropriation and certainty of salvation, which are the principal questions in debate and the ones to which answers must be found. The disaster, both for this period and for the whole future development of Christianity, is that these ultimate and critical theological questions are never really clarified. Hence the more 'canonistic' consequences for the theory of office, which the Church has inherited, are still to a great extent full of contradictions, and have never been thought through as to their ultimate meaning. The Church, as so often, has become more clearly conscious of what she rejects and excludes than of what she wishes to retain and affirm. In this context the first practical decisions, which we are to discuss in the present chapter, are of great importance and far-reaching effect. But first a short review of the beginnings of the Church's penitential practice may be in order.

The origin of penance as an ecclesiastical institution is to be found neither in the general hortatory and penitential sermon in the style of Hermas nor in the acts of voluntary humiliation and expiation, commended in that work and elsewhere—prayer, fasting, almsgiving—by means of which any Christian with a sense of guilt can purge his spirit and repair his failures. Such voluntary measures can give scope at most to private pastoral care, such as we find in the East in the case of Clement of Alexandria, and ought perhaps to assume here and there at an even earlier date.[7] Public penance in the congregation has other roots: first of all, the act of excommunication, as this was used again and again in the second century against gross sinners;[8] and secondly, the Church's own internal procedure for judgment and arbitration, such

[7] Cf. pp. 197ff., 136ff. above. Pastoral care of this kind may of course also have been exercised by such officials as had the gift for it, bringing the wandering sheep back on to the right path, and 'strengthening those who have grown weak': Strom. II, 69, 2f.

[8] I do not include here the expulsion of false teachers, for this can hardly be regarded as a 'disciplinary' problem, and falls under a different law: cf. pp. 142ff. above. E. F. Mackenzie, *The delict of heresy in its commission, penalization, absolution* (Diss. Washington 1932), p. 4, gives unwilling assent to this: 'The writings of the Fathers show a preoccupation with the making of converts and the repelling of false teachings, rather than any attempt to formulate legal and punitive codes.'

as had long been applied to deal with civil disputes and with charges and accusations of all kinds. This is of special importance, inasmuch as Paul had already been reluctant to see the congregation as a whole attend to such matters, and had recommended the choice of particular persons, suited to this work, who were to be appointed as arbitrators.[9] It could be that at first they were chosen *ad hoc* as the need arose, or even that they were chosen by the contending parties themselves. In the course of time, however, it came about—no doubt spontaneously —that the leading personalities of the congregation were also regarded as its appointed judges, and that their services were regularly called upon in this connection. In the Pastorals and in Polycarp the judicial function of the church president is taken for granted without comment. Polycarp works into his picture of the ideal presbyter the significant warning not to be harsh in judgment,[10] nor to act recklessly. In the Pastorals the bishop as the monarchical head of the presbyterate must have been thought of as especially the judge for the whole congregation.

Naturally the bishop and his presbyters play an outstanding part in the excommunication of a church member, a judicial act which takes place before a full assembly of the whole congregation as the court of last instance. The work of an arbitrator or judge in sorting out civil disputes, which is to some extent a merely 'human' activity, here passes without any sharp dividing line into a sacral authority to decide on behalf of God and of his Church what can be tolerated within the community and what can not. Nevertheless, final expulsion is still not an act of 'penitential discipline'. The specific requirement for this is met only where a gross sinner is excluded from participation in worship, and in particular from the Eucharist, and his full communion with the congregation and thus with Christ declared at an end, but where there is notwithstanding readiness to receive him back, should he be converted and amend his life,[11] or alternatively, where this possibility is envisaged throughout, and the expulsion is from the start understood as no more than a temporary measure. In this way expulsion is changed from a sentence of damnation to a term of punishment, giving an opportunity for expiation and purgation, or to a period of probation which leaves the door open for a return to the community. Such a procedure, however, is never regarded as devoid of religious significance, as, so to speak, a purely practical measure of legal coercion or precaution; there is none of the mental background necessary to enable them to think in this way. The Church from which the sinner is separated

[9] I Cor. 6:5; cf. p. 135 above.
[10] Polycarp, Phil. 6:1: . . . ἀπεχόμενοι πάσης ὀργῆς, προσωποληψίας, κρίσεως ἀδίκου, μακρὰν ὄντες πάσης φιλαργυρίας, μὴ ταχέως πιστεύοντες κατά τινος, μὴ ἀπότομοι ἐν κρίσει, εἰδότες, ὅτι πάντες ὀφειλέται ἐσμὲν ἁμαρτίας.
[11] II Thess. 3:6 already points in this direction.

is the very Body of Christ, and the sentence which is passed on him as a sick member of that body comes with the full spiritual power of a divine judgment or 'provisional judgment',[12] pregnant with the most serious consequences, and therefore demanding from the judges the highest degree of responsibility.

We can no longer trace in detail the emergence of the institution of penance from these beginnings. In essentials it must have been complete sometime during the second half of the second century. There seems to be some possibility of detecting the first indications of a formal act of reconciliation—which is the point of special significance—in the Pastoral Epistles.[13] On the other hand, no trace of such is to be discerned either in Irenaeus or in Clement of Alexandria.[14] In Tertullian, at the turn of the second and third centuries, the institution of penance is already firmly developed in Africa, and is known to all Christians as a standard piece of ecclesiastical machinery. For the crucial period before this date, however, we must rest content with a few uncertain hints and conjectures. Moreover, local differences in the development of the institution may at first have been very great. In the early stages there can hardly have been fixed, generally binding rules as to whether and when a penitent could be received back into the community.[15] It is obvious that the monarchical bishop, where there was one, must have had an important say in the matter. It was he who was primarily responsible for the conduct of the Eucharist, and therefore in the last resort it was he, in conjunction with his presbyters, in whose hands rested the decision to exclude or to admit the sinner. But equally obviously for the same reason he could not act unilaterally or arbitrarily. He was bound to keep in touch with his congregation, to respect their feelings and demands, and to pay due attention to the opinion of other respected and influential members of the Church. For both expulsion and the giving of the 'Pax' are in principle always a matter for a decision by the whole Church, in whose various members Christ is at work,[16] not for an exercise of episcopal or clerical privilege.

Gradually, however, norms of customary law began to develop. There is a general mistrust of recidivist sinners.[17] Men doubt the possibility

---

[12] Tertullian, Apol. 39,4.   [13] Cf. pp. 147ff. above.

[14] J. Hoh, Die kirchliche Busse, pp. 94ff., and Poschmann, op. cit., pp. 224f., agree as regards Irenaeus. Poschmann, p. 256 (cf. also p. 259), however, thinks that Clement's familiarity with an act of ecclesiastical reconciliation cannot be doubted; in my view, Hoh, op. cit., pp. 123ff., has assessed the relevant evidence more correctly, and in any case more prudently; cf. also Karpp. op. cit., pp. 235ff.

[15] Cf. Poschmann, op. cit., p. 261: 'There was no universal Church law of penance.'

[16] So Tertullian, paen. 9,6; cf. pudic. 22,6.

[17] This can already be seen in the NT period: cf. Matt. 12:45 par.; Heb. 6:4ff.; also p. 220 nn. 30, 31; p. 222 n. 41 below.

of repeated repentance, and in this connection appeal *inter alia* to the prophecy of Hermas. The once for all, final repentance which this writer had originally preached,[18] is quickly taken to mean that the possibility of repentance is open to any Christian only once in his life.[19] The prophetic preaching is thus given a new interpretation which removes it from the category of the apocalyptic and universal to that of the casuistic and individual.[20] In the case of very serious crimes such as, for example, apostasy or murder, and also heresy or adultery, re-admission of the sinner by the Church is frequently regarded as out of the question.[21] Should anyone in such case be admitted to penance at all, they must perform it all their life long, and at best receive the Church's forgiveness on their deathbed.[22] For the present, however, it

[18] In reality, however, even this time-limit in Hermas is not intended so radically as the actual words suggest; the deadline beyond which there is no repentance is arbitrary and constantly postponed: M. Dibelius, *Die apostolischen Väter IV: Der Hirte des Hermas*, 1923, p. 512. Hermas is simply concerned to provide a final and decisive deterrent, which will keep the heedless sinner permanently on the path of virtue, by proclaiming a last chance, soon to pass and never to return. This is 'on the same principle of pastoral pedagogy' as that which in other contexts 'conceals from the catechumen and neophyte the prospect of any repentance at all for Christians, and from Christian sinners the prospect of a second or even more frequent repentance': Poschmann, *op. cit.*, p. 170. Poschmann's argument decisively refutes the idea that in Hermas repentance means final repentance; and he should at last have put an end to the so-called 'post-baptismal theory', which since H. Windisch, *Taufe und Sünde im ältesten Christentum bis auf Origenes*, 1908, has dominated almost all Protestant scholarship, especially H. Koch, and even Dibelius. These scholars wrongly consider that any Christian who after baptism fell into serious sin was originally expelled irrevocably and on principle. Hence they see Hermas as daring for the first time to proclaim a possibility of repentance, though to begin with only on one occasion and that only in exceptional circumstances. On the whole subject cf. further p. 222 n. 41 below.

[19] Clem. Alex., Strom. II, 55ff. (cf. Hoh. *op. cit.*, pp. 118ff.; Poschmann, *op. cit.*, pp. 230ff.); Tertullian, *paen.* 7,10; 9, 1; *pudic.* 10, 11; 20, 2 (cf. Poschmann, *op. cit.*, pp. 171, 285). Even Origen expresses himself on this question with caution: K. Rahner, 'La doctrine d'Origène sur la pénitence', *RSR* 37, 1950, p. 77 n. 122, pp. 435f.

[20] Cf. Dibelius, *op. cit.*, p. 512: 'The ecclesiastical element has replaced the apocalyptic'; Poschmann, *op. cit.*, p. 171: 'The doctrine has shifted from the psychological to the dogmatic.'

[21] That murder and apostasy were never forgiven is constantly asserted by Tertullian in *De pudicitia*, esp. 12, 11. I do not think that one should try to reconcile this evidence with the supposedly fundamental principle that all sins can be forgiven, by saying that on the deathbed even these offences were regularly pardoned: cf. n. 22 below. According to Tertullian, until his day adultery and fornication were also unforgivable, and constituted a third deadly sin; but it may be questioned whether his statement is correct in this universal form. In other of his writings there are already hints of a different enumeration in terms of seven *capitalia delicta*: cf. Poschmann, *op. cit.*, pp. 321ff.

[22] This is the conjecture of Poschmann, *op. cit.*, pp. 321ff.; cf. also H. Koch,

is not to be thought that such principles were rigidly implemented. The efforts of rigorists to move in this direction are constantly rebuffed. Thus, around 170 Bishop Dionysius of Corinth in one of his 'catholic' epistles[23] warns the churches of Amastris and Pontus against excessive strictness,[24] and explicitly recommends them to receive all penitents,[25] including returned heretics.[26] The case of the Martyrs of Lyons a few years later points in the same direction. During their imprisonment they win back to the faith the brethren who had previously apostatised, so that afterwards they all go to their deaths together. It is not, however, simply by witnessing unto death that the apostates regain membership of the Church; the martyrs have already resumed full fellowship with them in prison,[27] and by so doing have, 'to the joy of the virgin church', given back life to those who before were dead. 'They had an excuse for all, and accused none; all they loosed, none they bound.'[28] Here it is implied that the mild attitude of the

---

Kallist und Tertullian, 1920, p. 45. For murder and apostasy, however, if not for the other two, the matter is not quite so simple. It is more probable that 'because they occurred only exceptionally, they were never discussed': so H. Von Soden, *TLZ* 41, 1916, p. 174, in a review of G. Esser, *Der Adressat der Schrift Tertullians "De pudicitia"*, 1914. Tertullian takes advantage of this state of affairs to put forward his own view as the one universally obtaining.

[23] Eusebius, *HE* IV, 23, 1.

[24] He has in mind not only the question of penance, but also requirements concerning 'marriage and chastity'; he also reproves the Bishop of Knossos for pitching the latter too high: Eusebius, *HE* IV, 23, 7f. There is no need to detect Montanist influences in this case. If the beginnings of Montanism are placed in the year 172/3, as in my view they must be, then influences from that quarter are in fact excluded for chronological reasons. On this once much disputed question of dating cf. A. Ehrhard, *Die Kirche der Märtyrer*, 1932, pp. 231ff.

[25] The unusual term δεξιοῦσθαι must here be understood to mean full reception back into the Church, not merely admission to penance: cf. Hoh, *op. cit.*, p. 88; Poschmann, *op. cit.*, pp. 267f.

[26] Eusebius, *HE* IV, 23, 6. Dionysius's letter is, significantly, directed to the congregation as a whole, and was requested not, it would seem, by Bishop Palmas but by two otherwise unknown church members, Bacchylides and Elpistos.

[27] It is purely arbitrary to say, as Poschmann, *op. cit.*, pp. 271f., does, that this resumption of fellowship, which is explicitly described as 'loosing' in contrast to 'binding', is to be distinguished from true priestly reconciliation, and to seek to deny it on these grounds a fully 'ecclesiastical and sacramental' character. To begin with, absolutely nowhere is there any mention of a special priestly authority in matters of penance, and, as Poschmann himself admits (*op. cit.*, p. 238 n. 4), specifically none in the case of Irenaeus, who is working in Lyons about this time, and even calls for consideration as a possible author of the document in question. Furthermore, Tertullian's evidence is precisely (Ad mart. 1) and most emphatically (De pud. 22, 1f.) to the same effect. The view which Poschmann (*op. cit.*, pp. 272ff.) would like to maintain in opposition to de Labriolle, *La crise montaniste*, 1913, p. 449, and K. Müller, *RGG* 3², 1929, p. 972, has no basis whatever in the sources.

[28] Ep. Lugd. in Eusebius, *HE* V, 1, 45f.; 2, 5f.

martyrs stands in marked contrast to a less compassionate and 'humble' judgment, and for this reason is deliberately stressed. The target here is Montanism, which had found adherents but also opponents in Lyons. We do in fact know of the Montanists that they expressly rejected any readmission of apostates.[29] In the decades that follow it is primarily Montanism which keeps the discussion about the possibility or impossibility of ecclesiastical forgiveness going; and in the course of this debate the basic points of view, and the practical consequences of the decisions they involve, slowly emerge, and acquire great significance for the question of office and its authority to absolve.

Neither did Montanism, however, at its first appearance possess a developed doctrine of penance.[30] Its eschatological preaching looked to the imminent end and not to the permanent organisation of the Church; but the energetic fight against moral and ascetic laxity which it initiated led very quickly to a critical dispute with the dominant penitential practice, which seemed to Montanists far too mild and sloppy. No one dares to deny to the Church the right in principle to forgive sins; but the Montanist 'Paraclete' demonstrates the seriousness and greatness of the new epoch in salvation history which he has inaugurated, precisely by the fact that he will not allow this right to be exercised any more, and thus puts an end on his own authority to both the use and misuse of absolution. 'The Church can forgive sins; but I will not do so, lest even more should sin,' runs a prophetic oracle which has come down to us.[31] The meaning is that the 'Spirit' will no longer intercede in the accustomed way for pardon and reinstatement for grievous sinners.[32]

---

[29] Eusebius, *HE* V, 3. Opposition on the penitential issue is not, however, expressly emphasised here, and may have been overcome in practice by the special authority of the martyrs, which is not bound by any rules or regulations. Nevertheless the refusal of any καύχημα κατὰ τῶν πεπτωκότων (V, 2, 6) without doubt has the Montanists primarily in mind.

[30] The anti-Montanist polemical writer Apollonius poses (Eusebius, *HE* V, 18, 7) the ironic question whether the prophet forgives the martyr his robberies or whether the martyr forgives the prophet his deeds of covetousness. This question takes for granted that the Montanists just as much as the Catholics have a practice for the forgiveness of sins. In fact, however, it seems doubtful whether genuine Asia Minor Montanism was in general familiar with penitential discipline and forgiveness after repentance: cf. de Labriolle, *Crise*, pp. 404ff., and W. Schepelern, *Der Montanismus und die phrygischen Kulte*, 1929, pp. 76ff.

[31] Tertullian, De pud. 21, 7: potest ecclesia donare delicta, sed non faciam, ne et alii delinquant. The MS tradition (preserved in but one printed edition) reads not *alii* but *alia*. If this reading is retained, then the danger envisaged would be that not of bad example but of recidivism. The future, *non faciam*, does not, in my view, allow one to conclude with Poschmann, *op. cit.*, p. 262 n. 4, that even the Paraclete himself had originally adopted a different attitude. He simply declares that he is not prepared to tolerate any longer what has been customary in the Church prior to his coming.

[32] The words used presuppose penance and the possibility of forgiveness in

On the contrary, the man who now still dares to sin is lost. The strictest rigorism is seen as an appropriate expression of heightened sanctity in the Spirit; and against the terrifying effects of such an implacable attitude is set, as the reason given shows, nothing more than an unrealistic optimism.

The consequences of this critique are quick to show themselves. Where its implications are put into practice, the earlier debate about the standards and limits of penitential procedure flares up once more. Even where there is no desire to support the 'New Prophecy', the rigorists now intensify their demands, and force a decision.[33] Penitential discipline now takes in sins which hitherto had passed unnoticed or had been left to the individual to expiate.[34] Penance for especially abominable or 'monstrous' offences, among which unnatural vice is particularly included, strikes the Montanist as hopeless; in such cases the sinner is to be avoided altogether and never again admitted to penance.[35] An attempt is made to define exactly the number of mortal sins which call for lifelong penance but which may not be pardoned; and for this purpose reference is made to earlier practice and tradition. Above all, efforts are made to base the penitential systems of both sides on Scripture;[36] and in the struggle to establish detailed standards and decisions attention is also paid to the meaning of the institution as a whole, and to supplying a more or less complete exposition and definition of it.

Our own understanding of these controversies is conditioned principally by the polemic of Tertullian, the Catholic who became a Montanist—which means that the voice we hear is first and foremost that of the rigorist party.[37] In Rome Hippolytus, despite his rejection of the

the Church, but tell us nothing further about the form these take or the authority involved. It is therefore inadmissible, with Poschmann, to link this with the 'church under the bishop', on which the 'power to forgive sins' is thus conferred as a matter of principle. Even in later Montanism there is very little mention of episcopal authority, and in the anti-Montanist satire of Apollonius (cf. n. 30 above) the reference is precisely not to forgiveness by the bishop but by the pneumatics: cf. also Rahner, op. cit., p. 167 n. 24.

[33] This can be seen in Hippolytus, even though his controversy with Callistus is not really centred on the question of penitential discipline: cf. Hoh, op. cit., pp. 58ff.; Poschmann, op. cit., pp. 348ff. On Hippolytus's attitude to Montanism cf. also A. Hamel, Kirche bei Hippolyt von Rom, 1951, pp. 120ff.

[34] Cf. the list in Tertullian, De pud. 7, 15f.; 20.

[35] Tertullian, De pud. 4, 5.

[36] This may be seen clearly in Tertullian, De paen. 8, and most of all in his polemical Montanist work, the De pudicitia, the main section of which (cc. 6–20) consists of a single, systematically developed proof from Scripture, with a detailed refutation of the perverse exegeses of his opponents.

[37] Tertullian's doctrine of penance is treated accurately, but from a modern dogmatic standpoint wholly unlike that of Tertullian himself, by K. Rahner, 'Zur Theologie der Busse beim Tertullian', Abhandlungen über Theologie und Kirche (Festschrift Karl Adam), 1952, pp. 139ff.

Montanist Prophecy, is in this respect close to him; and in the East too the old (or new) finds champions. Nowhere, however, does it win a complete victory. By Tertullian's time the Montanist movement itself has already lost its first tempestuous power, and is on the point of sinking into a mere sect or party. Plainly it has already proved impossible on practical grounds to implement the demands of the rigorists on any large scale. That nevertheless their position at first strikes us as the clearer, the more precisely thought out, and the better argued, is due to the intellectual superiority of their brilliant African spokesman. In reality this position is but a half-truth for which there could never be any theological future. For its legalist solution of the problem of sin is an enforced compromise between the demand for complete sinlessness, which it cannot meet, and the readiness to forgive on principle, which it cannot accept. Once, however, one adopts Tertullian's standpoint, and takes this hybrid formation, as he does, as an ordinance commanded and justified in the Scriptures, then in fact everything which he says about repentance and the limits of forgiveness follows entirely logically, and is, moreover, in no way lacking in spiritual greatness and objective passion.

The Bible, says Tertullian, is familiar with the concept of a sin unto death, the unforgivable sin against God, precisely in the case of Christians; and the commands and actions of the apostles show us what this means—Ananias and Sapphira are killed,[38] the incestuous man in Corinth is thrust out of the congregation,[39] and, according to John, one should not even pray for a lost brother, since Christ himself no longer intercedes for him.[40] These examples are to be our guide. Everything which the Bible contains by way of exhortation or threat or reference to an ultimate line which even the Christian cannot cross with impunity is applied by Tertullian to the question whether forgiveness is permitted or forbidden, and then, having been transformed into fixed standards of penitential discipline, is set up for ever as a strict divine and apostolic command.[41] 'For what else does God require but that we should walk

[38] De pud. 21, 4; 21, 13f. [39] Ibid., 13f. [40] Ibid., 2, 14; 19, 25ff.
[41] The principal passages relevant here (Mk. 3:28f. par.; I Joh. 5:16f.; and Heb. 6:4–6) are not intended to answer the concrete problem of later penitential discipline, namely whether and, if so, in what cases absolution is to be refused to the contrite sinner who is ready to do penance. The controlling viewpoint is read into the text by Tertullian, and therefore inevitably leads in his formal legalist exposition to distorted exegesis which does violence to the passages in question. These emphasise in various ways the seriousness of an actual, irrevocable perdition which is a real possibility even for Christians, indeed precisely for them; but in so doing they are thinking hardly at all of individual moral offences, but of the fundamentally different possibility of apostasy. The sin against the Holy Spirit, which Mark still speaks of in connection with a particular situation in the life of Jesus, seems already to have been interpreted in this general sense in Matt. 12:32 and Lk. 12:10: blasphemy against the Son of Man

is regarded as the sin of pagans, and is forgivable; blasphemy against the Holy Spirit, on the other hand, is possible only to those who have already experienced him but, this experience notwithstanding, have then betrayed him and can no longer be forgiven: cf. C. K. Barrett, *The Holy Spirit in the Gospel Tradition*, 1947, pp. 105ff. Another, more limited exegesis seems to be put forward in Acts 5:3 and especially in Did. 11:7: here it is a matter of blaspheming the Spirit who is speaking through the pneumatics in the congregation: cf. p. 131f. above. In I John too the 'sin unto death', as is today fairly generally agreed, refers to the sin of apostasy. The brotherly duty of intercession is expressly suspended in this particular case; for the apostate is no longer a brother, and the man who has abandoned the faith and plunged back into heathenism is truly lost. Hence it is here and here alone that the promise that prayer will be heard (I Joh. 5:14), which within Christianity itself is valid without restriction of any kind, finds its limit. Hebrews speaks explicitly of those who have tasted the heavenly gift, been made partakers of the Holy Spirit, and then have nevertheless fallen away: it is impossible to 'renew' such people again to repentance. This means what it says: it is impossible to bring them back to repentance, not, it is impermissible, if they should come to repentance, then to pronounce their forgiveness. The meaning of ἀνακαινίζειν here is attested especially in Hermas, Sim. IX, 14, 3. Hebrews too, therefore, considers that there is no prospect of the conversion of those who have once apostatised. Our own view of these passages is much too strongly conditioned by a mental picture of the *lapsi* as we find them in the great persecutions of the third century—hordes of Christians who under the acute pressure of severe threats and tortures have temporarily weakened, striving to get back into the Church, confessing their sin, and greatly concerned about penance and reinstatement. But apostasy in the earlier period wears a very different appearance. Here the persecutions affect only individual, occasional confessors (or renegades), and in general apostasy is much more markedly the exception, the individual, personal, and often more or less voluntary abandonment of the faith. In these circumstances it was not normally necessary in practice to reckon with a subsequent return of the apostatising traitor.

Exegesis must be in accord with these facts. Poschmann, *Handbuch der Dogmengeschichte IV*, 3: Busse und letzte Ölung, 1951, pp. 6ff., has rightly emphasised, in opposition to Windisch and the other champions of the 'post-baptismal' theory (cf. p. ooo n. oo above), that none of these texts, not even the one from Hebrews, directly prohibits readmission; for, in our view, they do not consider the repentance of lost brethren a real possibility. For this very reason, however, it is perverse to apply these statements directly to the question of penance and then be forced to claim 'normative' and 'regular' validity in ordinary cases for the text understood in this sense. Once Hebrews is viewed from the standpoint of later penitential discipline, then it is *bound* to be understood in a rigorist and Montanist sense; Heb. 10:26f.; 12:16f. in particular resist all Poschmann's efforts to soften them down. In fact, however, they are not legal and disciplinary in intention but paraenetic, and they must be taken as such. The preacher wants to give his hearers the most impressive warning possible against apostasy, and he therefore depicts the situation of the man who has once given into this temptation, and turned his back on the Church, as absolutely desperate; in such a case there is no hope of retracing the steps taken along the road to destruction. For all this, however, the Epistle is as ignorant as 'Q' or 'John' of any external restriction on the Gospel power of absolution, in the sense of a legal requirement that any apostate or mortal sinner who may repent should be rejected. Such an idea is impossible in primitive Christianity, and is certainly nowhere attested in the N.T. This applies also to the strict

according to his ordinance?'[42] In the problem of penance, therefore, it is not a question whether we should be prepared to forgive our adversaries—of course we must, since Jesus's commandment is as much in force as ever.[43] Nor is it a matter whether God is kindly and compassionate—obviously he is, since in baptism he once freely and unconditionally remitted all our guilt. The real issue is that we should learn to distinguish between what concerns us and what concerns God, and that we should respect God's clearly formulated will exactly as it is laid down.[44] For God is not only gracious, but also strict and righteous.[45] Every day he is tolerant enough of those lesser sins from which we can never, alas! entirely refrain.[46] He also allows more serious offences to be expiated by the regular procedures of penance, and to be forgiven through the Church.[47] But in the case of really grievous sins this permission is withdrawn. These come under his own judgment, and in this matter no earthly tribunal may obstruct him.[48] Even in cases such as these the sinner may still do penance, and it may be that on the strength of this God will in fact grant him forgiveness; but from the Church he has absolutely nothing more to hope for on earth. If he approaches her, the best he can expect is sympathy,[49] and apart from that merely the public exposure of his ignominy and shame.[50] There

---

measures taken by Paul, for whom anyway the circumstances of the problem are very different: cf. pp. 133ff. above. (Apostasy, in the sense of a conscious rejection of Christian belief, is something which Paul does not even envisage, but he accords a basically similar significance to moral failure: I Cor. 5:1ff.; I Thess. 4:8; also Eph. 4:30.)

A thorough discussion of all the relevant N.T. texts may be found in A. Kirchgässner, *Erlösung und Sünde im N.T.*, 1950. His main concern, however, is to prove that the N.T. never envisages the possibility of complete sinlessness on the part of Christians. Consequently he fails to grasp the dialectical relation in which the reality of forgiveness stands to the demand for holiness (cf. p. 137 n. 60 above). On this point cf. W. Joest, *Gesetz und Freiheit. Das Problem des Tertius usus Legis bei Luther und die neutestamentliche Parainese*, 1951.

[42] Tertullian, De orat. 4, 3: quid autem deus vult quam incedere nos secundum suam disciplinam. Further passages in K. Adam, *Der Kirchenbegriff Tertullians*, 1907, pp. 50f.

[43] De pud. 2, 10; 21, 15.

[44] De pud. 2, 10; 2, 11: porro et auctoritas scripturae in suis terminis stabit sine alterutra oppositione.

[45] De pud. 2, 3f.

[46] De paen. 12, 9; De orat. 7, 1; De pud. 19, 23.

[47] De pud. 18, 18.

[48] De pud. 3, 3f.; 18, 18; 19, 6; 19, 16; 21, 17; 22,3. The basic principle, that only God can forgive sins, is found—though not as yet used against Christian penitential discipline – in the earlier *De baptismo* (10, 3) with reference to the penitential baptism of John.

[49] De pud. 3, 5; 13, 11.

[50] De pud. 1, 20; 13, 9.

is no longer the slightest possibility of his 'peace' with God and the Church, that is, of formal pardon and readmission to the congregation.[51] There the matter must rest; for this is God's command and the expression of his holiness. In reply to the distorted accusations of their opponents, however, it must be explicitly stated that this strictness is not cruelty.[52] It is simply a practical necessity; for where forgiveness begins, fear is at an end.[53]

From this, Tertullian's judgment on Catholic practice follows automatically. To the Montanists Catholics are simply 'psychics', that is, earthy natures who just are not qualified to understand the holiness of the divine Spirit.[54] The forgiveness which, against God's command, they grant to grievous sinners is not only pernicious and of none effect,[55] but is based from the start on the arrogation of an authority which does not in fact belong to them. They trespass on God's preserves, for here he has pronounced his strict sentence, and has himself withheld pardon.[56] Tertullian perceives exactly what the controversy is ultimately about: the problem of actual forgiveness cannot be decided by general reflections on the nature of God and goodwill among men, but concerns (if we leave aside the casuistic and biblicist exegetical arguments) the concrete authority which God either has or has not given to his Church and to her ministers. The question of apostolic authority had once occupied Paul, but with a view to establishing his apostolic independence;[57] now, when it emerges once more after a century and a half, its bearing is rather different. But it still turns on the nature and rights of a quite specific calling—in this case the absolving power of the episcopate, deriving from the apostles and now established in the Church.

In his pre-Montanist period Tertullian had had no inducement to pursue any very precise reflections on this subject. Forgiveness, which he had once regarded as a 'fruit' of repentance,[58] seemed to him at that stage not a difficult and closely restricted possibility, but the natural outcome, once the Church's processes of expiation had been carried

[51] In contrast to Cyprian Tertullian in this context is still not thinking in particular of exclusion from the Eucharist.
[52] De pud. 3, 6.
[53] De pud. 16, 14: non enim timebitur (sc. fornicatio), quae ignoscetur; similarly Adv. Marc. I, 26. Elsewhere too Tertullian uses the importance of frightening people (De pud. 13, 21ff.) and the need for protection against infection (De pud. 14, 16) as arguments.
[54] De pud. 1, 10; 21, 16; Adv. Prax. 1; De mon. 1; De ieiun. 1; Adv. Marc. IV, 22.
[55] De pud. 3, 3; 3,6.
[56] Cf. p. 224 n. 48 above.
[57] Both in respect of his equal status with the other apostles (cf. chap. 3 above) and of his relationship with his own congregations (cf. chap. 4 above).
[58] De pud. 10, 14.

out.[59] To pronounce forgiveness no extraordinary divine commission was required, since the penitent had virtually earned it by his considerable exertions,[60] and on the matter of guidelines for giving absolution there is as yet no dispute. The intercession of the Church is additional to the mortifications and self-abasement of the penitent,[61] and is concerned simply with securing assured remission of punishment for the offence. Hence the penitent must do anything, go on his knees if necessary, to win the favour of the elders, the widows, and above all the 'beloved of God', that is, the martyrs.[62] For the Church is Christ, and Christ himself lives in each individual believer.[63] Where these intercede for a sinner, it is a certainty that Christ too will intercede for him with his Father, and will obtain pardon.[64] Readmission into the congregation therefore constitutes an expression and assurance of God's own forgiveness;[65] but the relationship between the Church's

[59] De paen. 9, 5; De pud. 1, 13; cf. De bapt. 10, 2 . . . paenitentiae . . ., quae est in hominis voluntate (not: potestate); on this reading and its meaning cf. J. W. P. Borleffs, 'La valeur du codex Trecensis de Tertullien pour la critique de texte dans le traité De baptismo', VC 2, 1948, pp. 191ff.

[60] Herein lies the emphatic distinction between penance and baptism: cf., e.g., De paen. 7, 10: . . . deus, clausa licet ignoscentiae ianua et intinctionis sera obstructa, aliquid adhuc permisit patere. Clement of Alexandria too draws a distinction in principle between the ἄφεσις of the first and the mere συγγνώμη of the 'second baptism', that is, penance, which is a process of purification in which the penitent has to strain every nerve, and put his own efforts into making it effective: cf. Poschmann, Paenitentia secunda, pp. 239ff. In Clement medical imagery predominates in his discussion of this subject, whereas in Tertullian it is only peripheral (cf. De paen. 10, 1; 10, 10; 12, 1; 12, 6), and in the De pudicitia has disappeared altogether. Neither for Tertullian, however, is there any possibility of venia sine cessatione delicti (De pud. 10, 14), that is, without a thoroughgoing purification and resanctification of the penitent.

[61] The latter are described in De paen. 9–11.

[62] De paen. 9, 1; Ad mart. 1; De pud. 13, 7; 22, 1.

[63] So also Origen, Sel. in Psalm: hom. 3, 12 (on Ps. 37); cf. A. Von Harnack, Der kirchengeschichtliche Ertrag der exegetischen Arbeiten des Origenes 2, 1919, p. 135 n. 2.

[64] De paen. 10, 6f.: in uno et altero ecclesia est, ecclesia vero Christus; ergo cum te ad fratrum genua protendis, Christum contrectas, Christum exoras. aeque illi cum super te lacrimas agunt, Christus patitur, Christus patrem deprecatur; facile inpetratur semper, quod filius postulat; cf. De fuga 12 (ed. Oehler, I, p. 484). As the rest of the passage confirms, the phrase in uno et altero obviously refers only to particular holy members of the congregation, not to both these and the penitent: Rahner, op. cit., p. 164, however, disagrees.

[65] This is an element which is determinative for the whole penitential practice of the Early Church, and which Poschmann therefore rightly regards as fundamental also to any dogmatic assessment: 'Moreover, in the fact that the act of readmission into the Church coincides with restoration to the interior communion of grace in the Holy Spirit lies the sacramental character of ecclesiastical penance. Understood in this way we find the sacrament of penance, despite all the emphasis on the fact that God alone can forgive sins, abundantly attested in the sources, while the assumption that the Church directly forgives sins in God's name is very difficult to prove from the Fathers . . .' (op. cit., p. 486).

action and God's is not more precisely defined. The congregation carries out the readmission whenever it is convinced that the penitent has done enough, and is now ready for God's pardon; and the penitent for his part receives and experiences the practical reality of this pardon when he is taken back into the community. In effect, Christ 'is' the Church; the Church is the sphere of his 'peace', and acts and takes decisions in his place.

The question, which particular individuals have the task of speaking for the 'Church', and of carrying out its sentence, is not discussed. Tertullian at this period is thinking purely in terms of a unified Catholic congregation, which has the power to act with Christ's own authority either through its official agents or directly as a whole. There is therefore no need for any particular definition of the rights and jurisdictions involved at one time or another. Plainly the *honorati* within the Church, who have already been mentioned, have an important say in the re-admission of sinners. Remarkably enough there is absolutely no explicit mention of the bishop himself.[66] Only in his later, Montanist writings does Tertullian mention him as the judicial authority by whom for-giveness is granted to the penitent when occasion arises.[67] This, however, cannot possibly be a Montanist innovation; it is undoubtedly an in-stance of general Catholic usage which is already traditional, and which at most is now somewhat more precisely formulated. On one occasion, when writing for pagans, Tertullian also mentions the 'elders', that is, the presbyterate under the presidency of the bishop, as the members of the church court which gives judgment 'in the sight of God'. This is done, as he stresses, with special seriousness; for such a judgment constitutes an anticipation of the coming judgment of God himself.[68]

The situation changes radically, so far as Tertullian is concerned, when he is converted to Montanism. The Catholics reject the Prophecy not least on account of the rigorist stringency of its penitential require-ments, and in so doing they rely on the opinion of their bishops. It is obvious that very few indeed of the latter were won over to the new movement; the Montanist leaders must—like Tertullian himself—have been at first predominantly laymen. Hence it is now a question not only of justifying the stricter practice but also of demonstrating the pre-sumptuous effrontery of an office which does not accept the Paraclete

[66] On the other hand, in the matter of the right to baptise, the precedence which the bishop has not only over the laity but also over the presbyters and deacons (De bapt. 17) is expressly emphasised (cf. n. 69 below).

[67] De pud. 18, 18; cf. 14, 16.

[68] Apol. 39, 4: nam et iudicatur magno cum pondere, ut apud certos de dei conspectu, summumque futuri iudicii praeiudicium est, si quis ita deliquerit, ut a communicatione orationis et conventus et omnis sancti commercii relegetur. praesident probati quique seniores, honorem istum non pretio, sed testimonio adepti. . . .

and yet proposes to forgive sins even where the Holy Scripture has expressly forbidden it. Even before this time Tertullian knew nothing of a sacral priestly office, holy in itself. For him, office is an institution, indispensable indeed to the order and dignity of the Church,[69] and therefore to be respected by the laity; but the mediation of salvation is not essentially bound up with the office. Moreover, the laity too are priests, and can if need be exercise all priestly functions, such as baptism or the administration of the Eucharist, by themselves.[70] Even the teaching office is not *a priori* a clerical preserve, nor is it subject to episcopal supervision, but only to the rule of faith.[71] These ideas may not be of Montanist origin;[72] but Tertullian, fighting on a new front, now accentuates them more sharply than before. Tertullian is the first Christian theologian to play off the idea of 'the priesthood of all believers' against the 'usurped'[73] rights of a particular office, when he protests against unspiritual 'lordship', the tyranny of the clerics.[74] Themselves self-indulgent and immoral,[75] the bishops, it is asserted, try to entice their congregations into sin by leniency in penitential discipline.[76]

The main source here is Tertullian's polemical work on the unforgivable nature of sins against chastity. In this document he has one particular bishop, unnamed, in mind, who had publicly declared for

[69] De exh. cast. 7 (cf. n. 70 below); De bapt. 17, 1: after the *summus episcopus* the priests and deacons also have the right to baptise, non tamen sine episcopi auctoritate propter ecclesiae honorem, quo salvo salva pax est; cf. H. Koch, 'Tertullianisches II, 5: Priestertum und Lehrbefugnis bei Tertullian,' *Theol. Stud. u. Krit.* 103, 1931, pp. 103f.; cf. p. 211 n. 222 above.

[70] De exh. cast. 7: nonne et laici sacerdotes sumus? . . . differentiam inter ordinem et plebem constituit ecclesiae auctoritas et honor per ordinis consessum sanctificatus, adeo ubi ecclesiastici ordinis non est consessus, et offers et tinguis et sacerdos es tibi solus; cf. De virg. vel. 9 (ed. Oehler, I, p. 895).

[71] Cf. H. Koch, *op. cit.*, pp. 95ff.

[72] Cf. de Labriolle, *Sources*, pp. 318ff.; K. Adam, *op. cit.*, pp. 190ff., had already cited De bapt. 7 in this connection.

[73] De pud. 21, 9: unde hoc ius ecclesiae usurpes? *Ecclesiae* here, however, is to be taken not as a genitive but as a dative. The question at issue in the rest of the passage is 'not how the bishop can usurp to himself this right which belongs to the Church, but rather how he can usurp for the Church the right given to Peter alone': Poschmann, *op. cit.*, p. 344 n. 1. Nevertheless, since only a little previously Tertullian has been talking about the *potestas delicta donandi* which the Church possesses, the question cannot be decided quite so definitely.

[74] De pud. 21, 6 (*imperio;* cf. p. 230 n. 94 below), and similarly De fuga 13. Tertullian is here attacking the practice of buying off Christians *en masse* from the hands of the police: hanc episcopatui formam apostoli providentius condiderunt, ut regno suo securi frui possent sub obtentu procurandi.

[75] De ieiun. 17.

[76] De fuga 13; De pud. 13, 7: . . . et in parabola ovis captas tuas quaeris, tua ovis ne rursus de grege exiliat, . . . ceteras etiam metu comples cum maxime indulgens.

the milder practice,[77] and he overwhelms him with biting scorn. Probably Agrippinus of Carthage is meant, the bishop, that is, of Tertullian's own city. The remote figure of the Bishop of Rome, who has also frequently been suggested, is hardly a probable candidate.[78] Tertullian's polemic is in any case not directed against the occupant of any particular *cathedra*, but concerns the penitential authority of the episcopal office as such.[79] The dignitary in question, who is addressed as 'bishop of bishops' and *pontifex maximus*,[80] has now, according to Tertullian, in his exalted majesty 'as good shepherd and blessed father (*papa*)'[81] issued a ukase[82] which really deserves to be posted on the doors of every brothel;[83] he states that, being fully conscious of his 'apostolic' power,[84] he is prepared to grant his pardon to adulterers and fornicators, if they will only do penance.[85] The affected style of the titles, half devotional, half official and imperial,[86] and the lack of reserve with which the bishop emphasises the absolute character of his own power, are of course to be attributed to Tertullian. But the real point of disagreement, the one crucial in practice, is none the less clear enough: it lies in the different evaluation of the bishop's penitential powers. Plainly the Catholic had appealed in support of his absolving power to the Gospel promise to Peter of the power of the keys.[87] Now Tertullian too regards Peter as the patriarch, so to speak, of all clerics,[88]

[77] In what 'official' form this was done can no longer be discovered owing to the element of caricature and distortion in Tertullian's account. The bishop in question may, for example, have made his position clear in the course of a public sermon.

[78] For the Agrippinus theory, first propounded by G. Esser, *Der Adressat der Schrift Tertullians De pudicitia und der Verfasser des römischen Bussedikts*, 1914, and K. Adam, *Das sogenannte Bussedikt des Papstes Kallistus*, 1917 cf. the, in my view, conclusive arguments of B. Altaner, 'Omnis ecclesia Petri propinqua (Tertullian, Pud. 21,9)', *TR* 38, 1939, pp. 129ff., and Poschmann, *op. cit.*, pp. 348ff.

[79] Cf. Koch, *Kallist*, pp. 94 ff. and *Cathedra Petri. Neue Untersuchungen über die Anfänge der Primatslehre*, 1930, pp. 18ff. Koch still considers Callistus of Rome to be the bishop meant.

[80] At this period this title still retains some of its pagan overtones.

[81] De pud. 13, 7: bonus pastor et benedictus papa.

[82] E. Caspar, *Primatus Petri*, 1927, p. 14, suggests this rendering for the ironically exaggerated phrase *edictum peremptorium*.   [83] De pud. 1, 7.

[84] De pud. 21, 5: apostolice (cf. p. 230 n. 96 below); 21, 9: Petrus.

[85] De pud. 1,6: Ego et moechiae et fornicationis delicta paenitentiae functis dimitto.

[86] Cf. Adam, *op. cit.*, pp. 12ff.; A. Beck, *Römisches Recht bei Tertullian und Cyprian*, 1930, pp. 128f.

[87] De pud. 21, 9. This is not an instance of an idea which Tertullian has simply invented and put into the mouth of his opponent: Koch, *Cathedra*, pp. 5ff.; Altaner, *art. cit.*, p. 138, and *TR* 39, 1940, p. 200.

[88] De monog. 8: Petrum solum invenio maritum, per socrum: monogamum praesumo per ecclesiam, quae super illum aedificata omnem gradum ordinis sui de monogamis erat collocatura.

and by the keys which open up the kingdom of heaven he understands the saving confession of the Church and of her martyrs.[89] He seems, however, never to have connected them with the power of the Church or of her bishops to forgive sins. At any rate he decisively rejects the exegesis in support of Catholic penitential practice; the Petrine authority never had this meaning. But even if the power of the keys really did justify the forgiving of grievous sins, and even if Peter, the preacher of repentance and the judge of the primitive Church, had at some time used it in this sense, this would imply nothing whatever with regard to the official position of the present Catholic bishops.[90] By the un-equivocal statement of the text Peter the apostle, Peter the prophet, received his authority exclusively for his own personal use.[91] No church can take it over in this form from him—or, even if some church could, then it would certainly not be the church of the psychics, which does not possess the Spirit, but the church which does have the Spirit, which is the Spirit, and in which Christ himself speaks through Spirit-filled men—not a church which consists of a handful of bishops, that is, not one which is merely an official and hierarchical organisation.[92]

Office as such has absolutely no spiritual authority,[93] and therefore has of itself no right to forgive sins in God's name. The bishop is authorised to administer penance solely in accordance with the valid biblical norms, which have been made even more strict under the direction of the Paraclete; that is, it is the bishop's job to serve and not to command.[94] Should he dare to speak directly in God's name, then let him first prove that he has the Spirit; let him like Peter raise the dead,[95] and give us instances of his prophetic powers![96] As a Montanist

[89] Scorp. 10: nam etsi adhuc clausum putes caelum, memento claves eius his dominum Petro et per eum ecclesiae reliquisse, quas hic unusquisque interrogatus atque confessus feret secum. The passage is martyrological, but has in mind only the confession, not in any sense the absolving power of the martyrs: cf. p. 231 n. 98 below.

[90] De pud. 12, 11–15.

[91] De pud. 21, 10.

[92] De pud. 21, 16f.: et ideo ecclesia quidem delicta donabit, sed ecclesia spiritus per spiritalem hominem, non ecclesia numerus episcoporum.

[93] Tertullian distinguishes (De pud. 21, 1) inter doctrinam et potestatem. disciplina hominem gubernat. potestas adsignat; that is, 'disciplina authorises a man to govern, to teach the faithful, to exercise the episcopal office, while potestas stamps a man with a seal which marks him as spiritalis, spirit-filled' (Poschmann, op. cit., p. 341).

[94] De pud. 21, 6: quod si disciplinae solius officia sortitus es nec imperio praesidere sed ministerio – quis aut quantus es indulgere, qui neque prophetam nec apostolum exhibens cares ea virtute cuius est indulgere.

[95] De pud. 21, 3f.

[96] De pud. 21, 5: exhibe igitur et nunc mihi, apostolice, prophetica exempla, ut agnoscam divinitatem, et vindica tibi delictorum eiusmodi remittendorum potestatem.

Tertullian will no longer admit as valid even the favourite appeal to the power of the martyrs. Their merits, he now thinks, are in fact often extremely doubtful,[97] and in no case do they achieve more than the expiation of the martyrs' own sins. If the martyr wishes also to be a genuine man of the Spirit, and as such to pardon others by his spiritual authority, he must first prove that authority by supernaturally revealing the hidden secrets of men's hearts, and then he may indeed be Christ, and like Christ forgive sins directly.[98] There can therefore be no possessing the Spirit, and no spiritual claims, without prior demonstration;[99] and without this demonstration the situation remains that the prerogative of pardon belongs to the Lord alone and not to his servant, to God and not to a priest.[100]

It is not altogether an easy matter to establish Tertullian's real meaning at any point in his argument. He is always proving too much, because he wants to be one hundred per cent right all the time and on every possible assumption. Whether Peter had the power to forgive sins or not, whether he exercised it or not, whether he bequeathed it to the Church of Christ or not—the outcome is always the same, namely that the lenient policy of the Catholic bishops and their adherents is an outrage and a piece of effrontery. This is the point at issue. Tertullian, the man of order and rule, is not really fighting for the freedom of the laity for freedom's sake; he is fighting for the rigour and sanctity of God's law, and he enlists 'laicist' feelings on his side in this extreme way only because the clergy themselves have abandoned this law. The appeal to the Montanist spirit of prophecy serves the same purpose. Like his laicism, subjectively it is entirely honourably meant, but it does not contain the real motive for his fight. At a time when the concept of the spiritual is already being weakened to a merely devotional sense Tertullian recalls the exceptional and radical nature of this phenomenon in the early days. He also quite definitely strikes at the formal character of spiritual authority, when he demands that before this—in contrast to the authority of mere official position—is conceded there should be factual evidence of spiritual power; for in primitive Christianity this

[97] De ieiun. 12. Hippolytus too seeks to discredit the alleged martyr status of Callistus, his milder rival in the dispute over penitential discipline: Elench. IX, 11, 4; 12.

[98] De pud. 22, 6f. In his Catholic period Tertullian had also acknowledged the power of the martyrs to forgive sins, without, however, explicitly approving of it: Ad mart. 1; cf. Adam, op. cit., pp. 65ff.

[99] In Adv. Marc. V, 8, the same argument is used to demand from the Marcionites proof of their prophetic authority—proof which they are unable to provide: sub illa praescriptione, iustissima opinor, qua non alterius credenda sit exhibitio, quam cuius probata fuerit repromissio.

[100] De pud. 21, 17: domini enim, non famuli est ius et arbitrium, dei ipsius, non sacerdotis.

was an essential mark of its special quality.[101] But Tertullian's concept of Spirit has not now become one-sidedly parapsychological;[102] fundamentally he brings this aspect of it to bear simply in order to exclude from the start any other form of power or authority which might be able to claim the right to forgive sins. What is at stake is the strict and unqualified character of Christian *disciplina*—a favourite concept of Tertullian's, which for him includes significantly not just the moral law of the Church, but also its faith, indeed the whole of Christianity.[103] To restore this to its original purity Tertullian turns against even an institution so important to him as spiritual authority, and bases everything on the Spirit itself in a seemingly fanatical and enthusiastic manner. For this at any rate he knows about his Montanist Spirit, that it is in truth a Spirit of holiness and discipline, as he understands these things. The Spirit will never relax its rigour, will at all times judge without partiality or leniency, and will never forgive one in mortal sin. It is this which makes Tertullian confident that it cannot be a false, demonic spirit, but only the true genuine Spirit of God.[104]

Laicism and prophetism thus combine to bring about the nomism and moral rigorism in which Tertullian sees the backbone and essence of Christianity. Hence he has no interest in an authority which might acquire an importance of its own alongside that of the valid law of God. This becomes apparent, quite involuntarily, in his fight against the episcopal power of the keys. The strongly evocative language in which Tertullian inveighs against human presumption and tyranny has something of a 'Protestant' ring; but it is in fact anything but 'Evangelical'. Tertullian is not fighting for freedom to forgive sins; he is attacking office precisely because, amid the growing legalism of church life, it is the last element which still possesses this freedom. This is why he always contests freedom of spiritual action. If the Church does still possess the authority of the apostles,[105] nevertheless, as Tertullian sees it, it is

[101] Cf. esp. pp. 62ff., 69f. above.

[102] If it were, he would be no more than an ordinary Montanist: cf. pp. 187f. above.

[103] Cf. V. Morel, 'Le développement de la "disciplina" sous l'action du saint-esprit chez Tertullien,' *RHE* 35, 1939, pp. 243ff.; and 'Disciplina—le mot et l'idée représentée par lui dans les oeuvres de Tertullien,' *RHE* 40, 1944/45, pp. 5ff.   [104] De pud. 21, 17.

[105] In De pud. 21, 7 Tertullian is compelled—by an appeal to the Paraclete (cf. p. 220 n. 31 above)—to admit this. But the exception which he thus makes is most unwelcome to him. Poschmann, *op. cit.*, p. 342, rightly concludes that in Tertullian's day the idea of the Church's power to forgive sins was taken for granted, and could no longer be set aside. But this certainly does not mean that in the 'traditional conception' the 'ecclesiastical and the episcopal power' were also already identified (cf. p. 220 n. 32 above). It is precisely at this point that development is still in progress, and it is because the episcopal and catholic party is promoting this new conception that Tertullian, even if one-sidedly for the opposite view, feels himself led to make his protest.

not the bishop who has inherited it,[106] nor is the true and abiding task of the Church to be found in the forgiveness of sins. This makes Jesus, who did bestow forgiveness, a non-normative figure for his ministers; he, it is now asserted, belonged to a different epoch of salvation-history, before the sending of the Spirit of Pentecost, related by the apostles, and so he is at bottom an exception and a disruptive element in the story of the divine work of education, which leads progressively to greater and greater rigorism.[107] In this way Tertullian subjects his own concept of the Church to a *reductio ad absurdum*. His doctrine of repentance must in any event be labelled Judaistic;[108] it is certainly no longer Christian, for the concept of law has devoured the Gospel.

If we now turn to Tertullian's opponents, we must take care not to see them because of their opposition to him simply as champions of a New Testament doctrine of repentance. If this had been what they were, they would have been quite incapable of continuing to uphold the current penitential arrangements, with their system of works, expiation, and verification, directed simultaneously toward God and the Church. But it is precisely in the period under discussion that this system undergoes even greater extension and more rigid elaboration. Indeed, the difficulty of the anti-rigorist, 'catholic' party consists instead in the fact that, despite their willingness to make forgiveness possible, they still fundamentally think of it in legalist terms. There is

[106] De pud. 21, 17. The concept of a *potestas* of absolution is juristic in character, and used equally in connection with the Church and with the pneumatics. 'It is, however, of fundamental importance to state that *potestas* in the sense of official authority is never used by Tertullian with reference to the official ecclesiastical positions of the clergy, especially of the episcopate' (Beck, *op. cit.*, pp. 66f.).

[107] De pud. 11; cf. H. Von Campenhausen, 'Urchristentum und Tradition bei Tertullian,' *Theol.Bl.* 8, 1929, pp. 198f.

[108] If one compares the individual classes and sub-classes of sins, the reflections on God's righteousness and lovingkindness, etc., with the corresponding Jewish views, the similarity is immediately obvious: cf. the material in E. Sjöberg, *Gott und die Sünder im palästinensischen Judentum*, 1938, and the work, inaccessible to me, by H. Ljungman, *Guds barmhärtighet och dom. Fariséernas lära om de twa "matten"*, 1950 (reviewed by H. H. Schrey, *TLZ* 76, 1950, pp. 290f.). As in other fields, the question of Jewish influence, precisely during this period, cannot be burked, and is certainly not confined to Tertullian. K. Rahner, 'Busslehre und Busspraxis der Didascalia apostolorum', *ZKT* 72, 1950, pp. 278ff., has established it for the Didascalia Apostolorum. In any event the distinctions, for example, between *peccata in Deum* and *peccata in hominem* (I Sam. 2:25) cannot be ascribed purely to the 'sophism of the African', as Poschmann, *op. cit.*, p.338, does, for they are already to be found in Origen as a current, traditional concept, as the examination in K. Rahner, 'La doctrine d'Origène sur la pénitence', *RSR* 37, 1950, p. 70 n. 98, shows. It may be added that a comparison of Judaism with Christianity on this point would, for all the inner uncertainty and contradictions of the patristic doctrine of penance, hardly turn out, at any rate to begin with, to the advantage of Judaism.

not the slightest inclination to extend the divine forgiveness freely to the penitent sinner; and the readmission of a grievous offender without a lengthy period of penance and atonement is never even envisaged.[109] Moreover, the concept of the 'unforgivable sin' is still too strong to be merely abandoned. Tertullian's fight against the forgiveness of sins of unchastity is thus able to rely again and again on the argument that it is illogical to exercise leniency in one case but in other cases, namely apostasy or murder, to cling as before to the requirement of lifelong penance, where there is no readmission.[110] In such circumstances any 'evangelical' ideas which may be brought to bear prove ineffectual. There are, it is true, references to the universal sinfulness of mankind, including Christians, and to the consequent obligation and necessity of forgiveness;[111] but because these are not regarded as absolute, not enough is said to give them a decisive influence in concrete instances. There are references too to the mercifulness of God, who does not wish the death of the sinner, but rather that he should be converted and live;[112] but the righteousness and holiness of God, stressed by Tertullian, cannot so easily be dismissed. There is an inability to grasp the dialectic of law and gospel, which is the heart of the matter, and so both subside into the indeterminate concept of a divine lovingkindness or gentleness,[113] which in serious cases is always more or less flexible, and permits of no really unambiguous decision.

This is just the kind of situation in which the authority of an office acquires paramount importance. Amid the general uncertainty concerning the meaning and correct administration of the rules of penance the bishop is seen as the existing, proven, and legitimate judicial authority which can give judgment in the name of God. The bishops themselves did not shirk what was expected of them; as responsible shepherds of the congregation they felt themselves in duty bound to be their pastors and judges. The system of penance was no simple automatic procedure; it called for supervision, experience, and firmness. Assailed continually by Montanist polemic it was essential to evaluate

[109] These penances are never regarded simply as efforts to provide the congregation with satisfactory proofs and assurances, but are also always treated as expiatory and as meritorious works having an influence upon God.

[110] Cf. p. 218 n. 21 above.

[111] De pud. 2,2; De orat. 7; cf. the earlier instance in Polycarp, Phil. 6:1. According to Hippolytus, Elench. IX, 12, 22, Callistus also cited Rom. 14:14 to support his case.

[112] De pud. 1, 1; 7, 1; 7, 4. Similarly, with reference to Christ, Callistus in Hippolytus, Elench. IX, 12, 24.

[113] The concept of *clementia*, which Tertullian uses for this in the De pudicitia, corresponds exactly to the *clementia* with which, for example, Caesar treats his conquered enemies: cf. E. Stauffer, 'Clementia Caesaris', *Schrift und Bekenntnis* (Zeugnisse lutherischer Theologie, herausgeg. von V. Herntrich und T. Knolle), 1950, pp. 174ff.

rightly the traditional practice, the moral and religious feelings of the churches, the attitude of the martyrs, the political situation, and the settlement of the individual cases, and to move toward a solution that was both tactically and morally viable. We know that the African bishops were not entirely in agreement even among themselves in their assessment of the various sins; yet they must have done their best to maintain peace in the Church.[114] Dissensions and difficulties might arise anywhere, and did in fact lead constantly to schisms and conflicts until well into the fourth century. In these circumstances the bishops took good care not to boost their own demands and pretensions so crudely and one-sidedly as Tertullian implies that they did. But on the crucial point he saw the issue correctly: the claim to decide whether a sinner should be excommunicated or readmitted was from now on based essentially not on the concrete authority of spiritual power or direct illumination, but simply on the possession of a spiritual office to which one had been regularly appointed. The stress is on the office as such.[115] 'By the holy spirit of priesthood', as the ordination formula has it, the bishop has received both authority and power to forgive sins as God commands;[116] for he is the holder of an apostolic office, and thus vested with apostolic authority.[117] The idea of apostolic succession, which had once been established with quite other purposes in mind, is thus given a new significance, and develops a motive power of much wider relevance. It is only now that the promise of the keys in Matthew acquires its fundamental importance for the self-awareness of the clergy.[118] It is no longer the right to remit or retain sins which is justified as the 'power of the keys'. The authority which Peter received has become, by way of the official succession, the official jurisdiction of the bishops, and thus the right of every church united with Peter by its possession of this office.[119] It is still a matter of a church right, one belonging to the whole

[114] Cyprian, Ep. 55, 21. Later, even within the Catholic Church, a whole series of bishops acted in accordance with Tertullian's demand, and refused readmission indefinitely to adulterers.

[115] Hence even a bishop in mortal sin is no longer automatically to lose his office: Hippolytus, Elench. IX, 12, 21; instead he must first be formally deprived of it by judicial process. His rights are based not on his personal possession of the Spirit but on his official status, and 'just as the bishops alone could give him in God's name both the office and the charisma needed for it, so they alone can deprive him of it in God's name': K. Müller, *Kirchengeschichte* I, 1³, 1941, p. 271.

[116] So in the Church Order of Hippolytus (I, 7); on its genuineness cf. the literature mentioned in p. 175 n. 157 above.

[117] Cf. pp. 174ff. above; Hippolytus, Elench. Pref. 6; and the Prologue and Epilogue to the Church Order; cf. Hamel, *op. cit.*, pp. 99ff.

[118] The promise makes its first appearance in this sense in Tertullian's polemic; on later developments cf. J. Ludwig, *Die Primatworte Matth. 16, 18.19 in der altkirchlichen Exegese*, 1952.

[119] De pud. 21, 9: de tua nunc sententia quaero, unde hoc ius ecclesiae

congregation,[120] which the bishop is to attend to responsibly on behalf of all the 'saints'.[121] But it is only as the authorised, appointed, and officially ordained bishop that he is in a position to do this. To this extent authority is already acquiring the character of a privilege which is even now in principle directed against the laity, and one day will be explicitly so.

At first, however, Tertullian is the only man to make a great deal polemically of these dangerous possibilities, and to suspect them as an expression of clerical lust for power. But the more profound reason for the new development is to be sought, as we have seen, in another quarter: the authority of the bishop makes it possible for the institution of penance to go ahead and develop organically in the direction of an increasingly effective forgiveness. It answers the urgent longing for salvation of a church which has known the experience of sin, and can no longer evade this in a sectarian way by mere punishment and expulsion. A hint of the evangelical meaning of all Christian authority thus exerts its continuing influence through the outward form of the official system and of the privileges of the bishop in particular. And this influence continues despite all the heterogeneous moralistic, practical, tactical, and professional motives which at once both obscure and support the sense of penitence within the life of the catholic congregation. It is precisely in these terms that we are to understand the enormous upsurge in the importance of the episcopal office everywhere in the course of the third century.

We have been able to follow the beginnings of this development in some detail only in Africa. But we know that about the same time the Bishop of Rome, likewise against the opposition of a dissenting minority,

usurpes. si quia dixerit Petro dominus: "super hanc petram aedificabo ecclesiam meam, tibi dedi claves regni caelestis" vel "quaecumque alligaveris vel solveris in terra, erunt alligata vel soluta in caelis"—idcirco praesumis et ad te derivasse solvendi et alligandi potestatem, id est ad omnem ecclesiam Petri propinquam. The correct explanation of the last, much disputed phrase is given, in my view, by H. Koch, *Cathedra Petri,* pp. 18ff. His proof that the point at issue here cannot be a specifically Roman theory, applying only to the successors of Peter, is confirmed beyond question if the addressee of the De pudicitia, as in my opinion cannot be doubted (cf. p. 229 n. 78 above), was in fact not the Roman bishop. This also disposes of the brilliant conjecture (*Romanam* for *omnem*) with which Von Harnack, *Ecclesia Petri propinqua. Zur Geschichte der Anfänge des Primats des römischen Bischofs,* 1927, sought to emend the text. The 'religio-historical' interpretation in terms of possession of Peter's grave, as further elaborated by W. Köhler, *Omnis ecclesia Petri propinqua. Versuch einer religions-geschichtlichen Deutung,* 1938, and 'Zum Toleranzedikt des römischen Bischofs Calixt', *ZKG* 61, 1942, pp. 124ff., is also hard to combine with the conception of a traditional *ius.*

[120] De pud. 21, 9; cf. p. 228 n. 73 above.

[121] This description of Christians is still absolutely normal usage in Hippolytus: cf. Hamel, *op. cit.,* p. 52.

also decides on a similar procedure. The regulations for penance are relaxed, and the authority of the episcopal office is correspondingly strengthened.[122] And even in the East, where the resistance of the Montanists and later of the Novatianists and other schismatics lasts longer, finally passing into the history of the mediaeval sects, the milder tendency—which is at the same time the more 'clerical'—triumphs. But here influences of a different kind, already discernible at an earlier stage, continue to work powerfully in the Church, and once more, this time from within, call in question an excessively one-sided emphasis on episcopal power.

[122] Hippolytus, Elench. IX, 12, 20f. That Bishop Agrippinus of Carthage for his part modelled himself on Callistus, as Ludwig, *op. cit.*, pp. 17f., would have it, is unsupported by any evidence. Even more rash is his assumption that the reason why Callistus did not cite Mt. 16:18f. in support of his milder penitential practice is that in Rome these words were already used at that time exclusively to uphold the doctrine of the Roman primacy.

CHAPTER X

Church Office and Authority in the
Time of Origen

THE GREAT strides made by ecclesiastical office in the period of the
penitential controversies may also be detected in the East during the
third century. Ecclesiastical development is undoubtedly more advanced
in the East than in the West. The Greek churches are by and large more
numerous, more powerful, and spiritually more alive than the congregations in the West, and also evince a strongly developed awareness of
themselves as churches with their own distinctive law. The 'nation'
of the Christians feels itself to be a great, independent, and morally
superior community within the world, a strong corporate body reveren-
cing and upholding God's holy ordinances; and the bishops with their
clergy are the 'princes' of this people. If the Church is the world's inn,
to which Christ as the merciful Samaritan brings grievously wounded
mankind, then the bishops are the innkeepers to whom the manage-
ment of the inn is entrusted.[1] They proclaim the will of God in accordance with the Scriptures, and are the priests of the new tabernacle.[2]
Above all, they are also the 'judges' of the people placed under them.
This claim is now generally recognised in the East, and forms the focal
point of the respect paid to the bishop, though this is also reinforced
by his more ancient rights of control over teaching and of leading
liturgical worship. The sonorous pronouncements about the Church as
God's vineyard,[3] as Bride of Christ and Mother of the faithful,[4] acquire
a fixed and definite meaning as a result of this legal development. They

[1] Origen, Hom. Luc. 34 (ed. Rauer, pp. 201f.), where this interpretation is
given as that of an ealier exegete: aiebat quidam de presbyteris . . . pandochium,
id est stabulum, quod universos volentes introire suscipiat, ecclesiam inter-
pretari; porro duos denarios patrem et filium intelligi, stabularium ecclesiae
praesidem, cui dispensatio credita est . . .; cf. A. Von Harnack, *Kirchengeschichtliche Ertrag* 2, 1919, pp. 27f.

[2] Didasc. apost. II, 25, 7; cf. p. 239 n. 7 below.

[3] Didasc. I Inscr.

[4] The concept of 'Mother' Church may derive from Asia Minor. At first it
has the character of a gnostic hypostasis or personification. It attains its full
significance for ecclesiastical law only in the West in the time of Cyprian: cf.
J. C. Plumpe, *Mater Ecclesia. An inquiry into the concept of the Church as Mother
in early Christianity*, 1943; also C. Mohrmann, *VC* 2, 1948, pp. 57f.

are much more than just a reflection in rhetoric of allegorical exegesis and theological speculation. This outlook derives from a living social reality, from the experience of a new community structure of which the bishops are the rulers and guardians. Even the judiciary of the pagan government begins to understand the significance of this fact, and to take account of it in decisions, whether friendly or hostile, relating to the Church.[5]

On the subject of the interior life and theological evaluation of office the East has left us two major sources which admirably complement one another. One is the Didascalia, of which a complete version exists only in Syriac—a long-winded, in parts almost homiletic[6] Church Order, which is attributed to the apostles, and probably derives from Syria. It cannot be dated with precision, and by its very nature reflects first and foremost the average clerical conception of the nature and function of office. Our second source is the writings, and especially the sermons, of the great Origen. Here the holders of spiritual office are less characterised in terms of their rights and practical functions than set up against a definite theological ideal, by which they are measured and on the basis of which they are criticised. Most of the evidence of this kind which Origen has left us comes from his later period, and thus also belongs to the world of Syria and Palestine. It is, of course, not unimportant to bear in mind that our field of view is limited by this geographical standpoint. But we are already in an era when ideas and conditions within the Church are much more strongly unified than they were in the second century; and both detailed fragments of information from other sources and the uniformity of later developments show that we are in general justified in taking the picture which we can form of Syria as typical of a wider area. First then, let us consider the Didascalia![7]

[5] Even as early as the persecution under Maximin the Thracian (235–328) the clergy are the particular objects of attack (Eusebius, *HE* VI, 28), and Aurelian gives judgment in the dispute concerning the church at Antioch that the church building should be assigned οἷς ἂν κατὰ τὴν Ἰταλίαν καὶ τὴν Ῥωμαίων πόλιν ἐπίσκοποι τοῦ δόγματος ἐπιστέλλοιεν (Eusebius, *HE* VII, 30, 19).

[6] Cf. Didasc. I, 10, 4: καὶ εἰ δι' ὀλίγων νουθετήσαντες ἐπαιδεύσαμεν ὑμᾶς, ἀδελφαὶ καὶ θυγατέρες καὶ μέλη ἡμῶν, and the liturgical conclusion, VI, 8.

[7] References are to the edition of F. X. Funk, *Didascalia et constitutiones apostolorum* I, 1905, where the text of the *Apostolic Constitutions*, printed in parallel, often allows the original Greek to be reconstructed with certainty; cf. also H. Achelis and J. Flemming, *Die syrische Didaskalia, übersetzt und erklärt*, 1904; and R. H. Conolly, *Didascalia Apostolorum*, 1929. For the understanding of the Latin version cf. E. Tidner, *Sprachlicher Kommentar zur lateinischen Didascalia apostolorum*, 1938. It is not possible to say with certainty whether the *Didascalia* should be placed in the first or the second half of the third century. Lately the earlier date has gained ground: cf. B. Altaner, *Patrologie*[2], 1950, p. 42; Rahner, *ZKT* 72, 1950; but in fact we have not advanced

The author of the Didascalia is no precise systematic thinker, and in his badly arranged work views from earlier and more recent times peacefully co-exist. He is conscious above all of the fact that he is a bishop. He is concerned not only to take seriously the many different tasks pertaining to his office in the Church but also to safeguard the special interests of the episcopate against the laity and the inferior clergy.[8] He begins his remarks about the 'shepherd'[9] with a sober list of virtues in the style of the Pastoral Epistles, with regulations about the age and way of life of the bishop, and with various instructions about the right way for him to fulfil his tasks as teacher, judge, and example to the flock. For 'as the priest is, so will the people be' (Hos. 4:9).[10] Stress is laid on the need for knowledge of the Scriptures and for the ability to distinguish correctly in preaching between the commandments of the Old and of the New Testaments;[11] the bishop ought therefore as far as possible to be an educated man.[12] But most important of all is his work as the judge who must reprove and punish sins by the exercise of his power to bind and to loose within the framework of the penitential system.[13] To him alone has Christ committed[14] this 'great, heavenly, and divine power'.[15] 'Therefore see to it, O bishop, that you are pure in your works, and know well what a high position you occupy, for you stand invested with divine authority, and represent God the almighty.'[16] As soon as the author comes to deal with the episcopal office his style changes and takes on a heightened tone of a solemn and sacral kind. To be a bishop is a high and heavy burden, not easy to bear.[17] The bishop is 'God's mouth',[18] and his decisions have 'an authority like that of God'.[19] On the other hand, the right to pass judgment has been

one step beyond the prudent discussion of the problem by Achelis, *op. cit.*, pp. 369ff. P. Galtier, 'La date de la Didascalia des apôtres', *RHE* 42, 1947, pp. 315ff., has done no more than rebut effectively arguments from penitential discipline which were supposed to tell against the earlier date: cf. p. 245 n. 54 below.

[8] Cf. Achelis, *op. cit.*, pp. 268ff., 378.

[9] Didasc. II, 1 (4,1); ποιμήν and ἐπίσκοπος begin to be synonymous: cf. Tidner, *op. cit.*, pp. 97ff.

[10] Didasc. II, 6,5.

[11] On the evaluation of the Law in the Didascalia cf. W. C. Van Unnik, 'De beteekenis van de mozaische wet voor de kerk van Christus volgens de Syrische Didascalie', *Nederl. Arch. v. Kerkgesch.* N.S. 31, 1940, pp. 65ff.

[12] Didasc. II, 1,2.

[13] On this point cf. the special study by K. Rahner, 'Busslehre und Busspraxis der Didascalia apostolorum', *ZKT* 72, 1950, pp. 257ff.

[14] Didasc. II, 17, 2; 33, 3; 37; 38, 1.

[15] Didasc. II, 34, 4.

[16] Didasc. II, 11, 1.

[17] Didasc. II, 25, 12: . . . ne putetis facile ac leve onus esse episcopatum.

[18] Didasc. II, 28, 9.

[19] Didasc. II, 12, 1.

completely withheld from the laity by Christ, particularly where judgment on the bishop is concerned.[20] To him, as to the apostles in earlier
days, the dominical saying applies: 'He who hears you hears me, and
he who rejects you rejects me . . . and him who sent me' (Lk. 10:16).[21]
Just as Christ is the model for the bishop, so the bishop is, like Christ,
to govern his people and bear their sins.[22] This train of thought invites
further elaboration; if the bishop represents God, then the deacons
are like Christ through whom we gain access to God;[23] the presbyters
correspond to the apostles,[24] and the deaconesses to the Holy Spirit.[25]

These kaleidoscopic comparisons with the divine order[26] immediately
recall Ignatius, 'the bishop of Syria', with whom the work also has
literary affinities.[27] As in Ignatius, so in the Didascalia there is no
concept of an apostolic succession.[28] Taking the work as a whole, however, the spirit of this Church Order is no longer simply Ignatian;
new and different elements have been added, and have become determinative. The 'archives' of the primitive Christian, which Ignatius had
despised,[29] and especially the Old Testament tradition, are continually
cited and regarded as indispensable. The enthusiasm of the Epistles is
replaced by the precisions of validly formulated canon law, the pattern
of the Old Testament priesthood,[30] the 'noble words' of Jesus, and the
'instructions' of the apostles who took these words as their guide.[31]

[20] Didasc. II, 36, 7; 36, 9.
[21] Didasc. II, 20, 1; similarly II, 36, 7–37, 3.   [22] Didasc.II, 25, 12.
[23] Didasc. II, 28, 6. The comparison (which appears again at II, 44, 3) is in
this context singularly inept, since the task allotted to the deacons here is precisely that of keeping unwanted visitors away from the bishop. The bishop himself may also, of course, be compared to Christ, especially when as penitential
judge he pronounces absolution (II, 20, 9: Christi vultum portans). As dis-
penser of the sacraments he is the mediator of the Holy Spirit: II, 32, 3. On the
τύπος–concept in this context cf. Tidner, *op. cit.,* pp. 164f.
[24] Didasc. II, 28, 4: nam et ipsi tamquam apostoli et consiliarii honorentur
episcopi et corona ecclesiae; sunt enim consilium et curia ecclesiae. The image
of ἀξιοπλόκου πνευματικοῦ στεφάνου ὑμῶν occurs first in Ignatius, Magn. 13:1.
[25] Didasc. II, 26, 4ff.; 31, 3.
[26] Didasc. 31, 3 points out that in Exod. 22:28 the rulers of the congregation
are even called 'gods'.
[27] Cf. the comparison in C. Holzhey, 'Die beiden Rezensionen der Ignatius-
Briefe und die "apostolische Didaskalia"', *TQ* 80, 1898, pp. 380ff.; also H.
Lietzmann, 'Zur altchristlichen Verfassungsgeschichte,' *ZWT* 55, 1914, pp.
141f.; Achelis, *op. cit.,* p. 272; Galtier, *op. cit.,* pp. 344f.
[28] Cf. Achelis, *op. cit.,* p. 270. This can hardly be an accidental omission, at
any rate in the concluding section, where there is a warning against seducers
who work their way into the Church *falso sub nomine apostolorum,* or in VI 7, 2,
where there is mention of the laying-on of hands.
[29] Ignatius, Philad. 8, 2; cf. p. 103 n. 200 above.
[30] Cf. esp. Didasc. II, 25, 7ff.; in II, 30 the deacons are equated with the
O.T. prophets.
[31] Didasc. I Inscr.; II, 55, 2: et nos apostoli quoque, qui digni habiti sumus

Despite the occasional extravagance of the language the purpose of the remarks is practical and juristic. With this goes the further innovation of a marked formalisation of the concept of office, and a stress on the rights and jurisdiction which attach to the office as such and are no longer simply based on the functions which the bishop performs as administrator, judiciary, and spiritual focus of the church's life. The old Ignatian requirement to 'do nothing without the bishop'[32] is now given a strong anti-laical emphasis; it is explicitly stated that without the bishop their actions at the altar are 'null and void'.[33] Again and again the laity are harangued directly in order to remind them of their place and to draw their attention to the special privileges which are granted only to the bishop.[34] He is their High Priest and Levite; 'he it is who dispenses the Word to you and is your mediator; he is the teacher and, next to God, your father, who through water brings you back to life; he is your prince and governor, he is your mighty king. Let him'—the conclusion follows naturally enough—'who rules in God's place be given by you like honour with God'.[35] It is clear that these uninhibited propositions occasion not the smallest theological scruple; instead they seem to the writer, using the sermon form to teach and to train his church, genuinely edifying statements to be taken entirely seriously. The man who submits to the orders of his shepherd, the one responsible for the congregation, may be sure that he remains blameless in the eyes of God.[36] On the other hand, it is always 'dangerous' to speak against the bishop, even when he is in error. Only the 'shameless man' fails to consider this, and stirs up trouble in the congregation.[37] What hope is left to a man who despises a bishop

---

testes esse adventus eius et praedicatores verbi eius divini, ex ore domini Jesu Christi audivimus et probe scientes dicimus, quae sit voluntas eius et voluntas patris ipsius, ne quis intereat, sed omnes homines credant et vivant.

[32] Ignatius, Trall. 2:2; Smyrn. 8:1; Philad. 7:2; cf. pp. 101f. above.

[33] Didasc. II, 27, 2, and with O.T. backing II, 28, 7. Here the reference is primarily to the work of caring for the poor, which is to be unified under the control of the bishop; cf. II, 33, 2; III, 3f.; 10, 5; 10, 8f.; V, 1, 3. II, 31, 1 provides a formula summing up the situation, which while reminiscent of Ignatius yet goes beyond him: propterea ergo quasi in honorem episcopi omnia, quae facitis, ei indicetis et per eum perficiantur.

[34] So e.g. Didasc. II, 26, 1. Any principles which might restrict the freedom of the bishop are left unformulated: Galtier, op. cit., p. 343. It is asserted merely that he is governed by God's word and the Scriptures: II, 14, 12; 15, 8; 20, 7.

[35] Didasc. II, 26, 4; for similarly exaggerated passages cf. II, 17, 6; 25, 7; reverence equal to that paid to God is mentioned also in II, 20, 1 (if, with Conolly, we insert Deum before secundum; cf. Tidner, pp. 137f.); II, 30; 31, 3; 34, 5.   [36] Didasc. III, 8, 4.

[37] Didasc. II, 17, 3: . . . nescit enim periculum esse, si quis adversus episcopum loquitur et in vico illo toto scandalum oritur; nam peccator tenui mente est nec parcit animae suae.

or a deacon?—when anyone who calls an ordinary layman 'fool' or 'Raca' is already damned![38] The person who harms the bishop by word or deed sins against almighty God.[39]

The extent and responsibility of the bishop's work is described from every angle. The liturgical importance of the office is already beginning to outstrip the general function of government, and to concentrate attention on his specifically sacramental prerogatives, especially in the matter of baptism. It is through the laying-on of the bishop's hands that every Christian at his baptism receives the Spirit; hence the Holy Spirit of God dwells, filled with all wisdom, in the bishop.[40] His practical work and administration of business matters is also given prominence; the whole task of caring for the poor is apparently centralised under his control.[41] His highest prerogative, however, remains the power of the keys exercised in the institution of penance. There is no longer any suggestion that the congregation or the martyrs have a right to intercede.[42] It is now no longer the church[43] but in effect the bishop, the official appointed by God, who has to make the decision independently.[44] He is the head of the congregation, and must not be guided by the

[38] Didasc. II, 32, 2f.

[39] Didasc. II, 31, 3.

[40] Didasc. II, 32, 3 (cf. VII, 7, 2); Baptism and Eucharist: II, 33, 2.

[41] Cf. p. 242 n. 33 above; Achelis, *op. cit.*, pp. 294ff.

[42] Even the intercessory prayer, which the martyrs—together with the bishop —offer for the sinner is almost ignored: Didasc. II, 18, 7; 41, 2; intercession by widows, III, 6, 9. Everything is left to the pastoral care and intercession of the bishop: II, 16, 1. The congregation does indeed see the tears of the penitent, but they serve only to exhort its members to amend their own lives, not to take any active part in the sinner's restoration: II, 10, 5 (cf. II, 39, 7). The martyrs win forgiveness for themselves alone: V, 9. In the final periods of persecution, however, the influence of the martyrs did revive, as the surviving fragments of the writings of Peter of Alexandria show—at any rate for Egypt. For the role of the martyrs under Cyprian cf. pp. 282f. below.

[43] Didasc. II, 50, 4 is the only passage in which the Church is still mentioned in this connection, and even here it is in conjunction with the bishop: ... donec paenitentiam egerit et episcopum vel ecclesiam deprecatus ac confessus fuerit se peccasse et paenitentiam acturum esse. In II, 56, 4, the laity are said to be worthy of praise if they pacify quarrelsome people and bring them back to the Church. On the other hand, in III, 8, 5, there is a severe condemnation of anyone who, in disobedience to the bishop, remains in fellowship with an excommunicated person; and conversely, the man who instigates slander against a fellow-Christian, and tries to secure his expulsion, is himself threatened with excommunication: II, 37f.; 42f.; 46; 49f.

[44] Even Matt. 18: 15ff. is now explicitly interpreted as referring to the bishop, the 'two or three witnesses' being the Three Persons of the Trinity: Didasc. II, 38; cf. 11, 18. Rahner, *art. cit.*, p. 274, rightly comments: 'In the *Didascalia* the authoritative forgiveness of sins is to a greater degree detached from incorporation into the Church as the means of salvation.' Rahner's further remarks, about a clearer emphasis on the 'sacramental character' of the forgiveness, however, seem to me somewhat overstated.

rebellious 'tail';[45] 'for this burden lies,' as the text expressly states, 'not on the laity but on the bishops'.[46] Hence bishops 'are to be honoured with all conceivable honour; for they have received from God power over life and death'.[47] But this power signifies above all an immense responsibility for the bishops themselves. It is true that the laity are not to seek to dictate to any bishop;[48] but this does not mean that the bishop is free—on the contrary, he is subject to an even more stringent law. Woe to him, if as a judge he shows partiality, if he is vindictive and violent, or allows himself to be corrupted, and if he can no longer find the courage to follow the straight path of God's word in punishing and pardoning as a faithful shepherd and physician.[49]

These passages are not concerned with merely theoretical possibilities; such cases of failure in office do really occur, and may become acute in either of two directions. First, it is possible that the bishop may be all too slack in carrying out his duty to exhort and to reprimand, and may give way to resistance within his church. Especially is the vigour of his judicial activity crippled when he himself suffers from a bad conscience. Such a bishop becomes a severe temptation to a congregation which has to put up with a situation in which members who are dead in the sight of God nevertheless suffer no hurt before men, but continue in honour. The bishop is to blame if the congregation, together with its neophytes, catechumens, and young people, then becomes more and more demoralised and finally completely ruined;[50] and God will call him to account for each individual soul.[51] The opposite danger, however, is envisaged as the more frequent. The bishop must not tire of going after his wandering sheep and lovingly calling them back. Otherwise, once outside the Church, they fall into the toils of the heathen and the heretics.[52] The man who greets repentant sinners with a relentless lack of compassion is himself barring against them the way of amendment. God and the 'Saviour' Jesus Christ will to forgive, and it is by the bishop's mouth that the redemption of forgiveness should be pronounced to the lost.[53] An abundant store of biblical quotations, considerably increased since Tertullian's day, serves to justify this requirement. Here we find the expression of

[45] Didasc. II, 14, 11; on the text cf. Tidner, op. cit., p. 118.
[46] Didasc. II, 37, 2: nam pondus huis oneris non laicorum est, sed episcorum; cf. II 18, 6.
[47] Didasc, II, 33, 3; cf. 47, 3.
[48] Didasc. II, 9; 35, 3f.
[49] Didasc. II, 17, 2; 20, 2ff.; 21, 1; 41; 43, 5.
[50] Didasc. II, 10; 43, 5; 50, 4.
[51] Didasc. II, 21, 3f.; 37, 3.
[52] Didasc. II, 2f.; 5; 21, 2f.
[53] Didasc. II, 20, 9: διὰ σοῦ ὁ σωτὴρ λέγει τῷ παρειμένῳ ἐν ἁμαρτίαις· ἀφέωνταί σου αἱ ἁμαρτίαι . . .

a contemporary concern vis-à-vis the rigoristic tendencies within the Church, the Montanists, and later the Novatianists.[54] In the East too the emphasis on episcopal prerogatives went hand in hand with a penitential practice oriented in principle toward forgiveness and the seeking out and education of the repentant sinner; and on this basis greater importance than before is now attached to the bishop's obligation to be individually responsible, and to enquire pastorally into the specific case of the individual sinner. The bishop must know how to exhort and to threaten the sinner, before he excommunicates him; he must be able to estimate the appropriate periods of time which should be allowed to elapse before the sinner is readmitted.[55] He is to be not merely the teacher and judge of the penitent, but also his helper and physician, his 'fatherly' friend and counsellor.[56] Freelance pastoral care in accordance with the ideal of the 'gnostic' teacher may have prepared the way for this attitude, and had an influence on it;[57] but there is no necessity to make it the only source of this development— the practical problems involved in a graduated system of penance, where rehabilitation was left to subjective judgment, would inevitably exert pressure in the direction of pastoral care and individual responsibility.[58]

It is striking how little importance is attached to the problem of faulty rulings by the bishop himself. The guidelines for right decisions are clearly laid down in God's word and revelation; and it would seem that the only factor entertained as possibly giving rise to a wrong sentence is malice on the part of the judge. Accordingly the bishop is threatened with the deterrent of God's wrath; but what such an eventuality might mean for the penitent is hardly discussed at all. On the one hand, there is a desire to maintain the obedience of church members,

---

[54] Cf. in this connection the repeated denunciations of troublemakers and slanderers in the congregation: II, 37; 38; 42, 5f.; 56, 2f. The rigorists against whom the Didascalia is immediately directed are to be found within the Church. The view that the text has undergone an anti-Donatist revision, first put forward as a conjecture by A. Von Harnack, *Chronologie der altchristlichen Literatur bis Eusebius* 2, 1904, pp. 490, 499. and later definitely asserted by E. Schwartz, *Bussstufen und Katechumenatsklassen,* 1911, cannot be maintained in that form, as Galtier has shown. Generally speaking, the text appears to be a unity: Achelis, *op. cit.,* pp. 261ff.; Conolly, *op. cit.,* p. XXXVI. Nevertheless, a fresh examination of the Didascalia from the point of view of its structure and of the strata within the material is much to be desired.

[55] Didasc. II, 13, 4; 24, 2.

[56] Didasc. II, 16–20. The image of the physician is developed in especial detail in II, 41. Achelis, *op. cit.,* pp. 381ff., suggests that the writer may have been a practising doctor.

[57] It has not proved possible to demonstrate any influence from Clement or Origen on the Didascalia.

[58] This is shown by the parallel development in the West.

and for this reason to stress the objective, religious significance of acting through the hierarchy: the bishop does effectively bring 'healing' to the sinner whom he receives back into the Church,[59] and the man who is excommunicated by him is equally effectually lost.[60] On the other hand, there is no desire that a superstitious value should be set on this authority at the cost of moral sensitivity. If the decision is unjust, then the 'human' judgment will be automatically cancelled by the judgment of God,[61] who alone will pronounce the ultimate and decisive verdict.[62] Hence the false decision can, it is asserted, harm only the judge and not the person condemned.[63] Equally, the fact that a bad Christian is to be found within the church without doing penance does not alter the fact that he is nothing more than a diseased member of the body, and can win no permanent advantage by it.[64]

This whole outlook would be incomprehensible if the power of the keys were indeed understood here as primarily a pastoral office for mediating and ensuring salvation, as it seemed to be at first sight. In reality, however, penance is now less an aid to pastoral care, in the manner of I John, than to the maintenance of moral and social life, of good order in the Church, and as such it is envisaged instead in disciplinary and moralistic terms. What is at stake is not so much the consolation of a troubled conscience, or the actual acceptance or rejection of eternal salvation, as first and foremost discipline and righteousness in the congregation, and only then, as a result of this, the moral development of each individual belonging to it. Often enough, indeed, the judicial power of the episcopate is concerned merely with civil disputes which call for a decision, and with moral offences arising from these, which are not denied by the guilty party but which only as an afterthought are held to call for some sort of expiation or punishment.[65] This is now carried out in the name of God. The intention is that the legalistic method of punishment and the pedagogic method of training and purgation shall between them slowly make the excluded sinner once more 'worthy' of the Church's fellowship.[66] One method

[59] Didasc. II, 24, 2.
[60] Didasc. II, 47, 3; cf. 21, 8.
[61] Didasc. II, 48, 2.
[62] Didasc. II, 19.
[63] Didasc. II, 42, 4; 48, 2f.; 51; 52, 3.
[64] Didasc. II, 43, 2f.; 50, 4. For the congregation there is, it is true, the danger of moral contamination and, if the bishop does not intervene, there is the threat of general demoralisation (cf. p. 244 n. 50 above); but there is no magical pollution of the Church from the presence of the sinner—not even if Judas himself were to worship with her: II, 14. N.b. the urgent exhortation not to be slack in attending divine worship: II, 59ff.
[65] For this civil law approach cf. esp. II, 46ff. The need for deterrent punishments is emphasised in II, 39, 6; 49, 5. Further cf. Achelis, *op. cit.*, pp. 307ff.
[66] Didasc. II, 16, 2.

merges into the other, and everything is done on divine authority and thus acquires a sacred and sacral importance. At bottom the penitential sentence of the bishop is no different in inner structure from any just, morally serious sentence of a secular court.[67] The just decision calls for much care, conscientiousness, and personal understanding of the case —this is stressed again and again—but of the Holy Spirit there is absolutely no mention. Only at the very end does he appear in a purely sacramental and liturgical context: the laying-on of the bishop's hands in the act of reconciliation infuses him afresh into the forgiven penitent.[68] The episcopal office is holy, and the bishop mediates holiness; for he is, as we have heard, the spiritual prince and monarch of a holy and spiritual community.[69]

Thus it is a strangely sublimated form of the social and moral concept of government which bestows upon the bishops in the Church both their prerogatives and their responsibility. Analogies from Old Testament and even general political sovereignty are boldly adduced in explanation; and yet, as we are at the same time reminded, the case in question is of course one of a far greater and more sacred authority than that found in the secular powers.[70] For the bishops are the rulers of the holy 'people',[71] the ones who proclaim divine teachings and laws, and the possessors of God's supreme judicial authority, which gives them a right to honour, obedience, and material support.[72] By being intent on the peace of all[73] they themselves become the light and the peace of their congregations.[74] We need not doubt that such ideals were not merely preached but acted upon, and that they released moral resources of a high order within the clerical ruling class.[75]

The complementary picture to that of the Didascalia is to be found in the Homilies of Origen. If the Didascalia shows us the official hierarchy

[67] Didasc. II, 52, 1; 60, 2; 60, 4.
[68] Didasc. II, 41, 2; cf. Rahner, art. cit., pp. 268ff.
[69] Didasc. II, 34, 1; 34, 4.
[70] Didasc. II, 27, 7f.; 34, 4; 52, 1. The bishops are not to behave like 'tyrants': II, 57, 1. Significant too are the more generalised comments on non-Christian piety: II, 28, 8; 60, 2; 60, 4.
[71] Didasc. II, 21, 1: . . . noli inludere populo, qui sub te ligatus est. In the Latin version *populus* and *plebs* are used indiscriminately for the congregation: cf. Tidner, pp. 167f.
[72] The widows are instructed to offer special intercessions for the righteous bishop: Didasc. III, 10, 5.
[73] Didasc. II, 46, 2.
[74] Didasc. II, 54, 4.
[75] On the other hand, there is absolutely no trace of any opposition on principle to this understanding of the hierarchy. The polemic against the teaching activity of the laity, and especially of women (widows): Didasc. III, 5, 4–6, and the occasional hostile comment on visionaries and prophets: IV, 6, 3; VI, 20, is certainly significant, but it still does not permit us to deduce the existence of any radical opposition: cf. Achelis, *op. cit.*, pp. 274ff.

of the Church proud and venerable in the multiplicity of its tasks and duties, Origen is concerned much more with its spiritual potentialities and limitations, and makes clear the difficulties which stand in the way of a complete fulfilment of the ideal. The shadow-side and the dangers of the clerical calling, which the warnings in the Didascalia rather hint at than expound in detail, Origen both sees clearly and describes without reserve. Origen is no radical opponent of 'clericalism', like Tertullian; but he is the first penitential preacher of the clerical profession, and it is to the conscience of the members of that profession in his audience that he is often particularly concerned to speak.[76] For all that he is a churchman by temperament Origen is not really interested in practical affairs or ecclesiastical politics. He is above all an exegete and a systematic theologian, and if, from a sense of moral responsibility, he does from time to time come down to the lower levels of the Church's everyday problems, yet he is always glad when he can leave them behind, and deal only with the true 'mysteries' of spiritual and allegorical exegesis.[77] Nevertheless, whenever Origen does decide to speak in this way about the realities of the Church and the life of her officials, what he has to say is impressive and serious. We hear nothing of the emphatic praise of episcopal dignity and authority to which the ordinary Christian must submit 'as to God himself', but we hear far more complaints and accusations concerning the spiritual failure of the clergy in their proper calling. More than half the relevant passages strike this note of bitter criticism and concern.[78]

In part this difference of attitude is certainly due to Origen's personal position and to the course of his career within the Church. Origen did not start as a cleric but as a teacher. As such he had become famous; and this gave him, even when a presbyter at Caesarea, an inner independence of his fellow officials as great as that of the episcopal author of the Didascalia. Moreover, the painful conflict in which, despite all

[76] Cf., e.g., Hom. I Reg. 1, 7. This purpose of Origen's must be borne in mind if his critical remarks are to be rightly assessed. The warnings against a false confidence in priestly holiness and indefectibility apply less to the people than to his fellow-presbyters and other clerics and to those who wish to be ordained: οἳ δοκοῦμεν εἶναι ἀπὸ κλήρου τινὲς προκαθεζόμενοι ὑμῶν, ὥστε τινας θέλειν ἥκειν ἐπὶ τὸν κλῆρον τοῦτον. ἴστε δὲ ὅτι οὐ πάντως ὁ κλῆρος σῴζει: Hom. Jer. 11, 3; 12, 3. In saying this Origen includes himself as a 'sinner' with them: Hom. Lev. 3, 7; Hom. Ezech. 2, 1; 7, 3. It is significant that Origen's great commentaries, extant in the original Greek, have almost nothing to offer on the questions of interest to us here; in what follows we have to rely overwhelmingly on the Homilies, which have survived in Latin translation. There is, however, no reason to doubt that the relevant portions are the work of Origen; in this connection there were no dogmatic reasons for Rufinus either to abbreviate or to 'supplement'.

[77] Cf., e.g., Hom. Num. 22, 4.

[78] Cf. Harnack, Kirchengeschichtliche Ertrag 2, p. 129.

his efforts to be loyal, he was engaged with his home bishop could only intensify his critical appraisal of clerical virtues. Yet in no sense was he championing the rights of the laity against the clergy; for Origen had himself plainly made great efforts to obtain ordination as a presbyter, and had finally received it abroad after it had been refused him in Alexandria.[79] The point at issue was simply the special difficulties which he as an ecclesiastically appointed[80] school or university teacher experienced with regard to the centralising efforts of the Patriarch.[81] In later years Origen never said much about these matters,[82] and for his part entered wholeheartedly into clerical life, preached to the congregation, attended synods, disputed with heretics, and generally proved himself the churchman that he wished to be.[83] This practical attitude is entirely in accord with his theological conception of the Church. It is true that in his idea of the Church Origen does not start from an official constitution, but understands the Christian community as Irenaeus and Paul had done, that is, primarily as a living, free cosmos of spiritual gifts in which every Christian can have his share even without the help of official mediators.[84] Nevertheless, the normal and desir-

[79] It is less probable that the ordination of Origen the Alexandrian was performed in Caesarea quite innocently and unwittingly. The very fact that 'Demetrius had stubbornly and jealously refused him this dignity' (Harnack, *Chronologie* 2, p. 31 n. 4) must have meant that a deliberate decision was made to take this unusual step. Demetrius for his part justified his protest against the ordination by referring to the fact that Origen was a eunuch: Eusebius, *HE* VI, 8, 5; 23, 4.

[80] Eusebius, *HE* VI, 8, 1–3; cf. G. Bardy, 'Aux origines de l'école d'Alexandrie', *RSR* 27, 1937, pp. 87f.

[81] Cf. W. Bauer, *Rechtgläubigkeit und Ketzerei im ältesten Christentum*, 1934, pp. 57ff.; H. Koch, art. 'Origenes' 5, *Pauly-Wissowa* 18, 1, 1939, 1039f. On the other hand Origen had been the first to organise the catechetical school as a two-level institute of 'higher' education: Eusebius, *HE* VI, 15; cf. R. Cadiou, *La jeunesse d'Origène*, 1935, pp. 68ff.; Bardy, *art. cit.*, pp. 53ff.; J. Daniélou, *Origène*, 1948, pp. 28ff.

[82] In the extant writings Origen touches on the 'Alexandrian storm' only once, and that discreetly, in the Preface to the *Commentary on John* (VI, 2, 8f.) in order to excuse the interruption of his work.

[83] Cf. the very full collection of autobiographical references from Origen's works in H. de Lubac, *Histoire et esprit. L'intelligence de l'Écriture d'après Origène*, 1950, pp. 56ff.

[84] Cf., e.g., Comm. Rom. IX, 2; Contra Cels. VI, 48; for the special value of the gift of teaching cf., e.g., Hom. Exod. 13, 4; Hom. Lev. 3, 7; 7, 2. K. Rahner, 'La doctrine d'Origène sur la pénitence', *RSR* 37, 1950, p. 279, makes the following pertinent comment: '. . . thus the bestowal of a function of remission of sins on the pneumatics cannot be regarded, in Origen's view, as a transfer or unjustified extension to the laity of a power attaching to the duties of a bishop; quite the contrary, it is in his capacity as the pneumatic which he ought to be that the bishop shares in a function belonging primarily and inalienably to the saints of the Body of Christ by virtue of the place which they occupy in the Body'. The idea of the *corpus mysticum* itself, however, is not, so

able thing in his view is that the one who is endowed with spiritual gifts should also be appointed to the corresponding position in the Church, so that he may be able to work for the benefit of the whole. Consequently, Origen nowhere envisages an independent 'teaching profession' distinct from the clergy.[85] Unlike Clement, Origen, the ordained 'professor', normally prefers to group the teachers with the holders of church offices. There is hardly one passage where they can be clearly distinguished from the clergy, and any number where they are only to be understood as such.[86]

If we compare the general picture of clerical duties and tasks in Origen with that in the Didascalia, we find that the evidence of the two is basically in agreement. Origen gives greater prominence to the work of biblical 'instruction'; this is his own special field, all the way through from the simple instruction of catechumens to the higher education of mature Christians, and not least the constant refutation of heresy. The author of the Didascalia had shown relatively little interest in this aspect of his calling—though he too takes it for granted; Origen, on the other hand, is himself an outstanding teacher, and his whole conception of Christianity is consequently framed in terms of teaching and education. Secondly, Origen sees the work of the bishop as involving the government and administration of every aspect of the church's life,[87] especially the giving of judicial decisions, and the regulating of peniten-

---

far as I can see, developed any further by Origen. The really agonised remarks of H. U. Von Balthasar, 'Le Mystérion d'Origène', *RSR* 27, 1937, pp. 38ff., on this point may confirm this.

[85] Among the 'saints' of the Church who have a right to special maintenance and respect, namely widows, martyrs, and ascetics, teachers are not mentioned. One should therefore be chary of seeing them automatically in the *servi dei* of Hom. Is. 10,3, as Harnack, *Ertrag* I, 1918, p. 84 n. 1, tries to do. Significant is Origen's contrast (Comm. Matt. XV, 1, 25) between the proud bishops and the 'little ones', the 'simple', devout Christians. When Demetrius declared that it was unheard of for laity to preach in the presence of bishops, this exaggerated assertion was not so 'obviously untrue' as Origen's friends imagined. In reply they themselves could collect only three far-fetched examples, and even in these instances the lay sermon had on each occasion been sanctioned by the bishop himself: εἰκὸς δὲ καὶ ἐν ἄλλοις τόποις τοῦτο γίνεσθαι, ἡμᾶς δὲ μὴ εἰδέναι (Eusebius, *HE* VI, 19, 17f.).

[86] E.g., Hom. Lev. 6, 6; 12, 7; Comm. Matt. Ser. 14. *Principes* and *doctores* occur in conjunction, e.g., Hom. Num. 20, 4; Comm. Cant. III. Only once, in Hom. Ezech. 3, 7, does Origen explicitly distinguish between *presbyteri* and *magistri*, and that because the biblical text compels him to do so.

[87] Hom Lev. 6, 6: haec duo sunt pontificis opera, ut aut a deo discat legendo scripturas divinas et saepius meditando aut populum doceat; Hom. Num. 12, 2: . . . si enim reges a regendo dicuntur, omnes utique, qui ecclesias dei regunt reges merito appellabuntur multo autem illi rectius, qui et illos ipsos dictis atque scriptis suis regunt, a quibus reguntur ecclesiae.

tial discipline.[88] That which is really important—and, when compared with the Didascalia, novel—in the description of the clerical vocation which Origen has to offer is not to be found in the concrete activities which he assigns to it but in the fundamental conception and the ideal interpretation of its religious meaning. From this derive the profound tensions and the serious doubts concerning the practical reality of the way in which the work of the Church is in fact carried on. It is a similar difference of outlook and mood to that between Polycarp and Ignatius, or Hippolytus and Clement of Alexandria.

However highly the Didascalia may regard the bishop's position, and however greatly it may desire reverence and obedience in the congregation for the bishop's orders, personally the holder of this office is just a purer and more mature Christian, who observes the universally valid rules of Christian morality, and understands the ins and outs of teaching his church. To that extent he evinces quite prosaic and almost homely characteristics. Origen too sees in the good bishop the incarnation of the true Christian; but intellectually Origen comes from a different world, and for him the requirement of perfection is very different in scope, and has a very different and far higher, indeed boundless, significance. It may be that he himself was never a pupil of Clement, despite Eusebius's assertion that he was.[89] But the ideal picture of the perfect gnostic, with which we have become acquainted in Clement's writings, dominates Origen's thoughts and feelings as well; this is the ideal which he himself, both as a teacher and as a priest, sought to satisfy. The cleric is to be a 'spiritual'; only so can he really fulfil his calling as bishop, presbyter, or deacon. For the true Christian life is 'spiritual', and the man who presides over the Christian congregation has the task of displaying directly for all to see this higher life, this heavenly conduct, and of bringing them step by step to the same level by unwearying education. In contrast to the Didascalia[90] Origen therefore takes it for granted from the start that the cleric will be an ascetic. He must not be attached to earthly possessions, and inwardly is to be as little as possible occupied with the common affairs

[88] The relevant texts are very fully cited in Poschmann, *Paenitentia secunda,* 1940, pp. 427ff., and Rahner, 'La doctrine d'Origène sur la pénitence, *RSR* 37, 1950.

[89] Eusebius, *HE* VI, 14, 8f. Origen would have had to receive instruction from Clement very early in life; and Clement is not known to have bothered with children or young people in any other instance. Moreover, Origen himself mentions Pantaenus, but not Clement, as his predecessor (*ibid.* VI, 19, 13). It is precisely in the concept of the Church that the differences between Origen and Clement are considerable. Cf. on this question J. Munck, *Untersuchungen zu Klemens von Alexandria,* 1933, pp. 224ff.; Cadiou, *La jeunesse d'Origène,* 1935; and Bardy, 'Aux origines de l'école d'Alexandrie,' *RSR* 27, 1937.

[90] Which in general attitude is astonishingly little ascetic: cf. Achelis, *op. cit.* pp. 313ff.

of everyday earthly life. He must be able to devote himself wholly to the study of God's word, and to ensure that the light of his spiritual knowledge burns brightly. For this very reason Origen presses repeatedly for the conscientious payment of the prescribed tithes, for this means that the priest who receives them will 'be free' for God.[91] The tension, already emphasised by Clement, between the interior longing for God and the duties which the friend of God has toward his neighbour, is something that must be endured. It is precisely the truly devout man who would like to withdraw from human society, and, best of all, flee to complete solitude. But in this 'monastic' idea Origen always sees a temptation, indeed a 'sin', to which the man of the Spirit will not give way.[92] He remains at his post as teacher and educator, and fights for his fellow-men by warding off through prayer the demons that everywhere besiege their souls.[93]

This should be the real task of Christians in authority. But how do the Church's clergy appear in reality when measured against such an ideal? Most of the bishops, says Origen, are completely lacking in understanding of their proper vocation. Instead of acting as religious examples and sympathetic physicians of the soul to their congregations, they are worldly minded, pursue earthly occupations and affairs, long for wealth and land, are haughty, quarrelsome, and self-assertive, allow themselves to be flattered and corrupted, and are often less particular in the conduct of their business than secular officials.[94] As the men in charge of penance they are alternately harsh and impermissibly complaisant, and if anyone tries to bring them to book for their sins, they form cliques, and if need be anti-churches, which keep them in office.[95] None asks what is his true spiritual calling. A real cleric would refuse ecclesiastical honours,[96] or accept them only when, after prayer and supplication, God had made it unmistakably clear to him

[91] Hom. Gen. 16, 6; Hom. Num. 11, 1f.; Hom. Is. 17, 3; on the question of the dues and their administration cf. also Hom. Lev. 3, 6; Comm. Matt. IX, 9.

[92] Hom. Jer. 20, 8; cf. Harnack, Ertrag 2, pp. 133f. Yet Origen has a great deal to do with the historical beginnings of monasticism: cf. W. Seston, 'Remarque sur le rôle de la pensée d'Origène dans les origines du monachisme', RevHR 108, 1933, pp. 197ff., and—though perhaps not decisive enough—K. Heussi, Der Ursprung des Mönchtums, 1936, pp. 45ff.

[93] Hom. Lev. 16, 7: fugant enim fideles doctores innumeros daemones, ne animas credentium antiqua fraude decipiant. An abundance of material on this idea, and especially on Origen's ideal of a teacher may be found in W. Völker, Das Vollkommenheitsideal des Origenes. Eine Untersuchung zur Geschichte der Frömmigkeit und zu den Anfängen christlicher Mystik, 1931, esp. pp. 168ff.

[94] Hom. Gen. 16, 5; Comm. Matt. XI, 15; XVI, 8; 22; Comm. Matt. Ser. 12; 14; further comprehensive examples in Harnack, Ertrag 1, pp. 69ff.; 2, pp. 129ff.

[95] Hom. Is. 7, 6; Hom. Ezech. 10, 1.

[96] Contra Cels. VIII, 75; Hom. Num. 20, 4.

that this was his will.[97] But as things are, the most sordid methods of intrigue and demagogy are brought into play as soon as there is a chance of snatching an office, especially the highest and most lucrative office, that of bishop.[98] Clergy brag about their seniority,[99] and try to ensure that their children or relatives will succeed them.[100] Such clergy are in fact serving Pharaoh rather than God.[101] These 'tyrants'[102] will not take advice even from their equals, much less from a layman or a pagan.[103] The only things they take seriously are their advantages and privileges, just like the Pharisees of old—it is in Origen's writings that this comparison appears for the first time in Church history.[104]

The picture thus unrolled of the moral condition of the clergy is a gloomy one. Origen knows that he may give offence with his accusations; but he takes nothing back, he waters nothing down.[105] It is the sacred duty of the Church's teachers to secure a hearing for God's word in all the fierceness of its condemnation, and not to shrink from the trials and sufferings which may result from so doing.[106] In evaluating his charges, of course, it is important not to lose sight of the hortatory nature of a penitential sermon, and generalise too hastily. Origen is not writing a Church Order, but giving a practical exegesis of the Scriptures, intended to improve and instruct. Nor at bottom does he himself regard the mournful examples which he censures as the rule but as the exception, even if a very frequent one.[107] If we compare his concrete details with the more cautious and reticent warnings of the Didascalia, then here and there we see the same fundamental dangers and temptations. The decisive factor which makes Origen's overall assessment markedly the more pessimistic is not so much his own external circumstances or the difference in temperament between the two writers, but the basically different standard by which Origen measures his churchmen. The gnostic ideal of 'perfection' was not originally thought of in the context of 'office'. By exalting it into the norm for the clerical

[97] Hom. Num. 22, 4: . . . vel ex ipsis etiam sacerdotibus quis erit, qui se ad hoc idoneum iudcet, nisi si cui oranti et petenti a domino reveletur?

[98] Hom Num. 9, 1; 22, 4; Comm. Matt. XI, 15; the correct form of election is described in Hom. Lev. 6, 3.

[99] Hom. Gen. 3, 3.

[100] Hom. Num. 22, 4: it is common to boast of one's episcopal relatives and ancestors: Comm. Matt. XV, 26; cf. Polycrates of Ephesus, p. 169 n. 101 above.

[101] Hom. Gen. 16, 5.

[102] Comm. Matt. XVI, 22; Comm. Matt. Ser. 14.

[103] Hom. Exod. 11, 6. In Didasc. II, 45, 2, it is forbidden on principle to admit evidence from a pagan in legal proceedings.

[104] Comm. Matt. XI, 9; similarly XVI, 25; Hom. Ezech. 2, 1: pseudoprophetae.

[105] Hom. Jud. 4, 3; Comm. Matt. IX, 15.

[106] Hom. Jer. 20, 8.

[107] Hom. Jud. 3, 2; Hom. I Reg. 1, 7.

way of life Origen now subjects the Church's officials to a demand which as a body they can never meet. Hence he is compelled to develop his critique along accusatory and pietistic lines. Typically pietistic is his unargued assumption that there has been a serious 'degeneration' of church life, and his nostaligic yearning for the ideal age of the 'first love', when Christianity and its leaders had not yet become worldly. What miracles, says Origen, might not the priests among us accomplish, if they were that which they ought to be—that which indeed they actually were in the days of the small, persecuted Church![108] The present state of the Church can be understood only in terms of a serious discrepancy between the true, binding ideal and its hardly even approximate, often quite inadequate realisation.

But what does all this signify for our assessment of the actual value of the clergy as they are, and for the practical application of their ecclesiastical authority? The hierarchical structure of the Church is by now something so long established that Origen would never dream of questioning it.[109] It is for him a sacred datum based on divine revelation; but it also corresponds to a universal and necessary cosmic law of moral and religious growth. All spiritual natures on their way upward toward God are bound by the law of gradual development through various stages each of which brings them closer to their goal; in the course of this progression they are constantly in need of governance and guidance and the helpful co-operation of other beings already at a higher stage.[110] Just as, among spirits in general, the more mature lend their assistance to those below them, so also the holders of spiritual office in the Church are significantly organised in ranks and grades, and are to stand alongside the simple and helpless members of the congregation as their guides and helpers. They must instruct them, and by intercession take their sins upon themselves and make atonement for them.[111] This spiritual order was already foreshadowed in the structure

[108] Hom. Is. 4, 2: et quis hodie in sacerdotibus tantus ac talis est, qui in illo ordine mereatur adscribi? si enim sit aliquis talis, cedet ei fluenta Iordanis et ipsa elementa verebuntur. Despite the great number of Christians, there is a lack (Hom. Jer. 4, 3) of believers such as characterised the age of the martyrs: cf. also p. 262 n. 144 below.

[109] A nice example of his emphatically 'correct' attitude occurs in the recently discovered *Discussion with Heraclides* (*Entretien d'Origène avec Héraclide*, ed. J. Scherer, 1949, sec. 4, p. 128): ἐπιτρέποντος οὖν τοῦ θεοῦ, δεύτερον κὰι τῶν ἐπισκόπων, τρίτον τῶν πρεσβυτέρων καὶ τοῦ λαοῦ δέ, τὸ κινοῦν με πάλιν εἰς τὸν τόπον ἐρῶ.

[110] Cf. A. Miura-Stange, *Celsus und Origenes. Das Gemeinsame ihrer Weltanschauung*, 1926, pp. 84ff.; H. Koch, *Pronoia und Paideusis. Studien über Origenes und sein Verhältnis zum Platonismus*, 1932, pp. 78ff.

[111] Hom. Num. 10, 1: qui meliores sunt, inferiorum semper culpas et peccata suscipiunt . . . Israhelita si peccet, id est laicus, ipse suum non potest aufferre peccatum, sed requirit levitam, indiget sacerdote, immo potius et adhuc horum

of the Old Testament people of God; it is also continued in the world above, in the choirs of angels who fill the heavenly realms. Again and again Origen brings out these ideas in his allegorical exegesis of the prescriptions of the Mosaic Law; only quite occasionally, as, for example, in connection with the Ten Commandments, do we find a direct, 'literal' interpretation, such as the Didascalia, and earlier I Clement, had employed in order to confirm the rights of the clergy. The Christian Church is not simply a continuation of the old people of God on the same level. Instead it has fulfilled Israel's law in a higher, 'spiritual' manner, and thus for the first time revealed the true, 'mystical' meaning of the earlier regulations, so that now the laws relating to government and sovereignty are also to be seen in an altered, spiritual light. This is the point at which the charismatic general concept of the Church, already touched upon, becomes of vital importance in Origen's exposition. That which the Old Testament hierarchy was meant to foreshadow is not simply and directly the visible hierarchy of the Church's clergy but the new invisible hierarchy of the Spirit and of the Spirit's gifts, which Paul describes, and which at most is only manifested in the hierarchy of church officials. Everywhere where the Spirit of God begins to work, where human faith is open to his revelation, there spontaneously arises a fellowship of leading and being led in the power of his gifts, distributed in many different ways and on the various levels of his modes of operation. The advanced, spiritually enlightened Christians are the true 'priests' and 'Levites' of the new people of God,[112] which is itself a priestly race. This spiritual exegesis, which is not primarily intended in any 'official' sense, is crucial for understanding Origen, and often enough seems as though it held the field alone.[113] But at the same time it also indicates to Origen what is the task of the priestly calling in the narrower sense; the churchman is to be the spiritual leader of his congregation, the mediator to other Christians of higher gifts and knowledge. He displays the higher stage of perfection for the benefit of all.[114]

---

aliquid eminentius quaerit: pontifice opus est, ut peccatorum remissionem possit accipere.

[112] Hom. Is. 17, 2: . . . in qua re quid aliud sentiendum est, nisi quod sint in ecclesia domini quidam, qui virtute animi et meritorum gratia ceteros omnes praecedunt, quibus ipse dominus esse haereditas dicitur . . . pauci vero sunt et valde rari, qui sapientiae et scientiae operam dantes et mentem suam mundam puramque servantes atque omnibus praeclaris virtutibus suas animas excolentes ceteris simplicioribus per doctrinae gratiam illuminant iter, quo gradiuntur et veniunt ad salutem. hi fortassis nunc sub levitarum et sacerdotum nomine designantur . . .

[113] Cf. e.g., Hom. Lev. 5, 3; 6, 6; Hom. Num. 5, 1; 11, 1.

[114] Comm. Matt. XIV, 22: οὐδένα γὰρ τῶν ἀπὸ τῆς ἐκκλησίας ὑπεροχήν τινα παρὰ τοὺς πολλοὺς ὡς ἐν συμβόλοις ἀνειληφότα βούλεται ὁ Παῦλος δευτέρου

In principle, therefore, one might think in terms of, so to speak, a double hierarchy. Where the bishop does not in fact fulfil his spiritual duties, he stands spiritually among the laity whom he ought to lead,[115] and often the layman is a bishop in the eyes of God, even though he has never been made a bishop by any human consecration.[116] This is not, however, a normative situation, but rather a contradiction of the proper spiritual norm,[117] and a consequence either of failure on the bishop's part or of general human inadequacy in the appointment of the Church's ministers. Consequently Origen never contemplates drawing any sort of general legal conclusions from such situations. Apart from the visible hierarchy of the bishops the only hierarchy he knows is the invisible one of ministering spirits. In view of the short-comings of the clergy it may have been a comfort to him that in addition to each earthly bishop a heavenly bishop from the angelic world was watching over the congregation, an infallible guardian with whom it was the duty of the visible bishop to co-operate.[118] The idea of a special ecclesiastical 'order of teachers', with a status of their own independent of the clergy, is a modern misunderstanding which changes Origen's criticism, intended by him in the moral and personal sense appropriate to a pietistic preacher of repentance, into a political proposal.[119] In such contexts Origen never thinks in terms of canonistic consequences and possibilities. The goal of his efforts is simply and solely the personal instruction, improvement, and education of Christians; and he therefore applies himself to achieve this in the case both of those who hold office in the Church, and of those who have to live with and endure these officials as their spiritual governors.

From what has been said certain consequences follow automatically for the bishops and clergy. Origen is concerned to educate them in a more spiritual conception of their authority and calling, and to awaken in them a personal spiritual life and a deeper sense of responsibility. To celebrate a solemn liturgy before the assembled people—in the last

---

πεπειρᾶσθαι γάμου. And yet we see how the δίγαμοι are often better than many μονόγαμοι.

[115] Hom. Num. 2, 1 (cf. n. 117 below); Hom. Jer. 11, 3; Hom. Luc. 20.

[116] Comm. Matt. Ser. 12.

[117] Hom. Num. 2, 1: . . . saepe accidit, ut is, qui humilem sensum gerit et abiectum et qui terrena sapit, excelsum sacerdotii gradum vel cathedram doctoris obsideat et ille, qui spiritalis est et a terrena conversatione tam liber, ut possit 'examinare omnia et ipse a nemine iudicari', vel inferioris ministerii ordinem teneat vel etiam in plebeia multitudine relinquatur. sed hoc est et legis et evangelii statuta contemnere et nihil 'secundum ordinem gerere' (I Cor. 14:40).

[118] Cf. esp. Hom. Luc. 13, and also Harnack, Ertrag 2, pp. 134f. n. 2.

[119] Even Daniélou, op. cit., pp. 56, 62, is, in my view, still being too tentative when he sees in Origen only the beginnings of a fusion of the 'visible hierarchy of the presbyters' with the 'invisible hierarchy of the doctors'.

resort anyone can do that. What matters much more is the real possession of virtue, the knowledge of Christian doctrine and of the hidden, spiritual wisdom of the heart, without which all external spiritual dignities remain dead and worthless.[120] There is no point in asking Origen the question what value can office in itself, leaving aside the personal qualities of the incumbent, have for the Church, or does it possess any spiritual significance at all? Such canonistic and dogmatic questions are of no interest to him. In his writings there are not even intimations of the later doctrine of priestly 'character'. Office 'as such' is as little guaranteed by an objective sacramental principle as it is overthrown in favour of the rights of 'freedom' in the Spirit or for the laity. It is not possible, therefore, either to supplement or to restrict his conception in accordance with any modern view, be it 'catholic' or 'protestant', for it remains entirely within the sphere of the private, pietistic, and pastoral. It is clear, however, that the idea of a 'universal priesthood', in the sense of an ultimate individual freedom even of the laity vis-à-vis all human teachers and examples[121] is always and absolutely maintained. Of course Origen exhorts all Christians to humility and patience even when confronted with the unjust and 'tyrannical' decisions of churchmen;[122] pride, quarrelsomeness, and arrogance have at the very least a foothold in the Church. But this does not mean that in the real world of religion Christians are necessarily tied to the often very inadequate person who happens to be their ecclesiastical superior for the moment. Instead the Christian is subject to Christ, who is his true bishop; the patriarchs and apostles are his presbyters, and the archangels his deacons.[123] Moreover, 'teaching' is no preserve of the clergy. Origen has no qualms about calling on his hearers to criticise his own sermons, to engage in responsible theological 'testing' of that which he has conscientiously delivered to the best of his knowledge.[124] But nowhere is the ultimate spiritual independence of the Christian to be more clearly seen than in connection with that institution in which office finds its supreme task and authority, namely penance with its sacred power to bind or to loose the sinner.

Origen sets a high value on penance.[125] Its moral significance for the life of the individual and of the whole congregation could remain hidden

[120] Hom. Lev. 6, 6.

[121] Hom. Lev. 4, 6; 6, 5; 9, 1.

[122] Hom. Ezech. 10, 1; Comm. Matt. Ser. 14.

[123] Comm. Matt. Ser. 10; Hom. Ezech. 7, 3; cf. also Greg. Thaum., Euch. XV, 173.

[124] Hom. Is. 7, 6; 21, 2; Hom. Ezech. 2, 2; 2, 5; cf. Hom. Is. 7, 3: volo ego ipse, qui doceo vos. vobiscum pariter discere; also Greg. Thaum., Euch. XV, 179.

[125] On what follows cf. the very fully documented comments of Poschmann and Rahner.

least of all from a soul so emphatically moral and pedagogic as his. Again and again in his sermons he finds occasion to speak of its purifying and healing power, and he likes to take up earlier ideas expressed on the subject by others in order to develop them impressively and, to some extent, along new lines. Origen is one of the outstanding penitential theologians of the Early Church; his influence can be detected right down into the refinements of the penitential methods of later monasticism. Now the practice which Origen's teaching presupposes is that found in the Didascalia. Like the author of that work Origen constantly stresses the unique responsibility which the priest has to shoulder before God for each individual member of his flock, warns against loveless rigorism in excommunication and irresponsible indulgence in readmission, and emphasises the dangers of moral contagion and the necessity of deterrents for the congregation; and for him too the exercise of the power of the keys to bind and to loose is in practice extremely closely associated with the episcopal courts of arbitration and moral discipline. In their decisions and in the penalties they inflict the bishops have an obligation to act righteously and with the most painstaking care. In principle, however, there are no limits to their power of absolution;[126] like the apostles of old they have received it from Christ and from God himself.[127]

In all this Origen's thinking is entirely that of a churchman and a 'catholic'. To question the existing penitential system simply never occurs to him. Nevertheless, his attitude toward it is different from that of the author of the Didascalia. In penance as in everything else Origen constantly bears in mind the distinction between the ideal norm and definition on the one hand and the practice which dictates what is actually done on the other; and he states openly what this gap implies for the religious life. A problem which in the Early Church with its solid confidence in the unfailing presence of God's Spirit in judgment and forgiveness had not as yet come to light, and which even in the Didascalia is only just emerging, without, however, provoking any very deep reflection, is now definitively formulated by Origen, and more than once discussed by him in detail. That this should be so is the automatic and inevitable result of his pietistic and critical appraisal of the professional clergy, for the question is this: which of all the many 'judges' in the Church is the one who is in truth so filled with God's

---

[126] This has been conclusively demonstrated by Poschmann, and there is no need to prove it once again here in order to refute the earlier exponents of the 'post-baptismal' theory.

[127] Hom. Jud. 2, 5; Hom. Pss. XXXVII, 1, 1; Comm. Rom. 2, 2; Orat. 28, 8f. The idea of succession, however, is not emphasised in Origen; at Comm. Matt. Ser. 46 it has, as the Greek parallels show, been imported into the text by Rufinus.

Spirit that he cannot err, and can really secure peace for God's people?[128] The fact that someone sits on the proud throne of a bishop in no way answers this question. There is both the possibility and the fact of unjust judgment, of excommunication which, though outwardly valid and given in proper form, is in fact a miscarriage of justice.

What are we to say about the inner meaning and religious effect of such an act? For Origen as for others the Church is the people of God's devout elect, the fellowship of salvation which possesses within itself the gifts of God's grace; hence expulsion from the Church is not merely a disgrace but a serious misfortune for the person affected, and an ominous threat to his salvation.[129] But this whole approach is valid only so long as the sentence of excommunication is justly imposed. In the case of an unjust sentence these considerations have no further force, and the position is quite the reverse. If a bishop, from personal dislike or selfish motives, or, it may be, simply from error and human weakness, turns an innocent Christian out of the Church, such a decision is null and void in the eyes of God and can do no harm to the person on whom it is passed.[130] This view is explicitly emphasised in opposition to a radical hierarchical theory. Those who claim episcopal jurisdiction, it is asserted, appeal in their proceedings to the promise of the keys to Peter, and explain 'that they have received the keys of the kingdom of heaven from the Saviour, and that for this reason everything which is bound, that is, condemned, by them is also bound in heaven, and everything which is loosed, that is, forgiven, by them is also loosed in heaven'. This, Origen goes on, is correct only in so far as the bishop himself is like Peter in his life, and can in fact pass judgment with the same degree of authority. But if he himself is 'entangled in the snares of his own sin', then he binds and looses 'to no effect'. It would be a risible delusion to assume that anyone could exclude his fellow-men from salvation simply 'because he enjoyed the title of bishop'.[131] The converse is also true. No one should regard himself as safe just because he attends church regularly and is seemingly at home there, bows low before the priests, offers them his services, and makes charitable provision for the pious and widows of the congregation.[132] A sinner who fails to complete the appropriate period of penance 'outside the Church' does not return into the spiritual community of the heavenly Jerusalem even when he is released from excommunication by 'men', that is, by irresponsible bishops.[133] The decision of such

[128] Hom. Jud. 3, 3.
[129] Hom. Pss. XXXVI, 4, 2; XXXVII, 1, 6; Hom. Jer. frag. 48; cf. Poschmann, op. cit., pp. 468f.
[130] Hom. Lev. 14, 3; Comm. Matt. Ser. 14.
[131] Comm. Matt. XII, 14.
[132] Hom. Is. 10, 3.   [133] Hom. Jer. frag. 48; Hom. Lev. 12, 6; 14, 4.

bishops, who merely 'feign' the virtues of their office'[134] therefore has
no effectual power to save.[135] Thus it comes about that many who
appear to be in the Church, and are generally regarded as brethren,
are in reality 'outside', and many who seem to be outside are in fact
'inside'.[136]

The inevitable consequences for the concept of the Church, if this
position is adopted, are explored by Origen no more than they are by
the author of the Didascalia,[137] or by Hippolytus, who is indeed the
first to make observations of this kind.[138] The consequences for the
concrete authority of office are obvious. Indeed, it is hard to think of
any genuinely moral standpoint from which, when faced in practice
with a miscarriage of justice, one would not be driven to make some
such statements; and it is only the fact that Origen puts his finger on
the problem so firmly and emphatically that is really distinctive. The
relativisation of official authority, however, goes even further than this.
The power of the bishop in penance is not solely concerned with judgment, excommunication, and readmission. In Origen more than anyone
penance as a means to salvation is a coherent moral process of gradual
spiritual purification, expiation, and amendment, which as such calls
for expert pastoral guidance. The bishop who is appointed to do this
work must therefore also be an effective man of the Spirit; and if he is
not, then he is no longer capable of administering penance in a meaningful and spiritually productive manner. It is at this point that Origen,
faced with the shortcomings of the bishops, draws certain practical
conclusions. Even though the formal and sacramental acts of penance
may still be left to the official holders of the power of the keys,[139]

[134] Comm. Matt. Ser. 24.
[135] This applies even to 'the act of reconciliation, which only the bishop
can perform'. Unlike Poschmann, *op. cit.*, pp. 469f., I can discover virtually
no 'sacramental' element in the efficacy of bishops in Origen.
[136] Hom. Lev. 14, 3; Hom. Jud. 2, 5.
[137] Those separated sinners who remain in the bosom of the Church are
merely 'church members who are thought to be believers': πιστεύειν νομιζόμενοι
ἐκκλησιαστικοί (Comm. Matt. XII, 12), and the 'so-called brother', the
ἀδελφὸς ὀνομαζόμενος (*ibid.* XIII, 30), is therefore also in reality no longer such.
Rahner, *op. cit.*, p. 253, goes beyond Origen, however, when he writes: 'To
"treat-as-part-of-the-Church" in this way is not a simple mistake made by men,
whose earthly empiricism, incapable of distinguishing the chaff from the wheat,
is misled by appearances. . . . For both chaff and wheat are in fact contained
within the single Church of the present age. . . .'
[138] Hippolytus, Comm. Dan. IV, 38, 2: εἰ γάρ τις δοκεῖ νῦν καὶ ἐν ἐκκλησίᾳ
πολιτεύεσθαι, φόβον δὲ θεοῦ μὴ ἔχει, οὐδὲν τοῦτον ὠφελεῖ ἡ πρὸς τοὺς ἁγίους
σύνοδος τὴν δύναμιν τοῦ πνεύματος ἐν ἑαυτῷ μὴ κεκτημένος.
Cf. A. Hamel, *Kirche bei Hippolyt von Rom*, 1951, pp. 54f.; also Comm. Dan.
I, 22, 5.
[139] Formal ecclesiastical reconciliation or absolution can never be given by
laymen. A power of the keys vested in the laity, which K. Holl. *Enthusiasmus*

yet as regards the pastoral care which must accompany them, and by which alone they can be made meaningful in a deeper sense, the person in need of help cannot be expected to confine himself to the officials of the Church alone. After all, Peter too was not the only one to receive the keys. Christ entrusted them to all the apostles, which, in the spiritual interpretation, means to all the believers in general; and in so far as they believe in Christ, and show the same virtue and knowledge as Peter in their lives, they share in Peter's authority, and themselves become 'rocks' on which Christ builds his Church.[140] The penitent is not lightly to rest content with the formality of an ecclesiastical reconciliation, with which any episcopal official can provide him. If he is in earnest about his salvation, he must assiduously seek out the right spiritual director, and 'test' the physician to whom he entrusts his soul.[141] For in the last analysis it is his 'virtues', his own spiritual progress, which open heaven to him, just as it is his vices which create his real hell.[142] Everything here depends on the personal moral life, and in comparison with this little or no importance is attached to official order; what matters most is actual spiritual development, and the only man who deserves the rank of bishop is the 'spiritual' man who possesses in himself the capacity to forward such development.

It now becomes clear that Origen both has no feeling and can have no feeling for the distinctive character of the element of office within the Church, and why this is so. What makes spiritual office a living thing is the dignity of its commission and the importance of that which, in the power of that commission, is to be done for the people who are subject to the officeholder. Origen, however, does not pay much attention to this authority or the promise which stands behind it, nor does he really make everything depend on the 'word' of forgiveness with which the minister encounters the penitent in Jesus's name. That which he does heed, and in which he places his confidence, is the moral and religious progress which the penitent actually makes under the minister's guidance. This progress achieves salvation for the penitent, and the officeholder can help him on the way to this; but in the last resort he can neither detract from that achievement, nor can he by his words add anything which goes beyond the scope of the penitent's own spiritual maturity. From this point of view everything is perpetually in a state of flux. The life of the penitent, like the moral and religious life of Christians in general, is a single, never-ending movement, which is to

---

und Bussgewalt beim griechischen Mönchtum, 1898, pp. 234 ff., following Daillé, attempted to prove, and which even Völker, *op. cit.*, pp. 172ff., detects in Origen, is no longer a tenable hypothesis since the remarks of Poschmann, *op. cit.*, pp. 462ff.

[140] Comm. Matt. XVI, 11,   [141] Hom. Pss. XXXVII, 2.
[142] Comm. Matt. XII, 13f.

lead out of the depths into the height, out of the darkness and loss of this world into the ever nearer presence of God and of his salvation. In this process there must be no standing still; but equally there can be no unqualified, once for all decision. Sin is never totally overcome here on earth; there is only an approximation to (or recession from) the ideal of Christian perfection. At the same time there is no final perdition for men; in the end there will be the restoration of all.

The same principles determine the function of the spiritual office, which at bottom, spiritually considered, is indeed no longer an 'office' at all. All that is necessary, and in a certain sense indispensable, for the Christian is a teacher, a guide, a friend to educate him. For Origen as for Clement there is no moral progress without the person of the spiritual helper, without the living example and the loving participation of someone who is perfect. Hence in detail the whole question is treated in his writings in a much more two-dimensional and schematic way,[143] and above all the conception of the 'gnostic' teacher and educator is now radically ecclesiasticised, and projected, at least in the ordinary way, on to the holder of church office. For this very reason, however, at the crucial point, office is no longer important; in the end the office-holder always counts for just so much and no more than he as a man of the Spirit can bring to his official task. It is the pedagogic authority of the gnostic which gives meaning to the authority of the office; the latter has no independent value, and everything which the commissioned cleric of the Church undertakes by virtue of that office is at once relativised, and made dependent on the greater or lesser degree of his own spiritual capacity. Even the sacraments which he dispenses acquire a higher or lower value in accordance with his personal qualities;[144] and the power to bind and loose is also all the more or less effective in proportion to the higher or lower rank in the spiritual order of the man who lays claim to it.[145] There is absolutely no one who can speak the ultimate word of an unconditional Either–Or. Hence even penance and absolution lack the ultimate authority of both assuring and themselves being salvation. But it is indicative of Origen's

[143] In particular Origen shows less profundity than Clement in his demand for oral teaching and in his treatment of the practical problems of the association. The differentiation between types of instruction is the result of taking into account the various groups within the congregation; thus, e.g., Hom. Lev. 1, 4. Furthermore the problem of the canon, which Clement handled with such originality, Origen's biblicism leads him to approach with an arid rigidity of principle.

[144] Baptism too has lost in virtue as a result of the secularisation of churchmen. Now it is no more than a *typus mysteriorum,* whereas during the time of the apostles it also mediated *virtus ac ratio*: tamquam scientibus et edoctis (Comm. Rom. V, 8). Further details in K. Rahner, *art. cit.,* pp. 53f., and H. Rahner, 'Taufe und geistliches Leben bei Origenes', *ZAM* 7, 1932, pp. 205ff.

[145] Comm. Matt. XIII, 31.

'pedagogic idealism'[146] that no more than Clement does he feel this to be a deficiency.

Just as little does such an attitude afford any basis for a serious practical threat to the institution of office. The liberty of personal religious development which the individual enjoys in his relations with it is one more reason for allowing it to retain undiminished its external governing position in the Church. This Origen did with complete conviction. For all his emphasis on the Church's spiritual and supra-terrestrial nature he too regards the Church as a sacred sociological entity of an admittedly quasi-political importance. It is as such an entity that the Church has to have its own princes and 'kings',[147] and Origen insists with pride, in the course of his dispute with Celsus, that they govern their congregations far better than the corresponding state or communal officials.[148] Their position is of course infinitely higher and holier, since they administer spiritual things, but their status is none the less analogous to that of secular judges and rulers.[149] This explains the fact that Origen still calls for reverence and obedience even toward inadequate and evil bishops. Origen's attitude toward the representatives of the spiritual government is roughly the same as that of Plato or Socrates toward those of the state. In his struggle for virtue and righteousness Origen's temper is never revolutionary but peace-able, and to this extent his pietistically detached attitude toward those in office is in practice very close to the outwardly much more exaggerated and authoritarian demand for obedience found in the Didascalia. How easily Origen's critical assessment of bishops and his idealistic demand for the religious independence of the individual was compatible with an explicitly monarchical concept of office, or could at any rate be held in equilibrium with it, becomes apparent early on in the number of Origen's episcopal disciples, and is unmistakable in many later Origenists.[150]

[146] The phrase used by H. Koch, *Pronoia*, pp. 32ff., to characterise the essence of Origen's piety, in which the central Christian concept of forgiveness no longer has 'any meaning at all' (pp. 82, 135ff.).

[147] Cf., e.g., p. 250 n. 87 above.

[148] Contra Cels. III, 30.

[149] Hom. Num. 12, 2; Contra Cels. VIII, 75; for the conjunction of spiritual and secular dignitaries cf. also Comm. Joh. XXXII, 12.

[150] Cf., e.g., the Ep. Canon. of Gregory Thaumaturgus. That Methodius of Olympus was a bishop seems to me, in view of the contradictory evidence and, even more, of the style of his writings, highly problematic. He has repeated the views of Origen on the task of the episcopate, the deficiencies of its representatives, and the consequences of a miscarriage of justice in penance, virtually unaltered: cf. G. N. Bonwetsch, 'Über die Schrift des Methodius von Olympus "Vom Aussatz"', *Oettingen Festschrift*, 1898, pp. 29ff.; L. Fendt, 'Sünde und Busse nach den Schriften des Methodius von Olympus,' *Der Katholik* 31, 1905, pp. 24ff. The only error in these presentations is that of Bonwetsch

The succeeding period once more combines the cultic, typological, and above all sacramental characterisation of office with the 'political'. The ground for this development was also prepared by Origen. His unrestrained allegorising of the biblical sacrifices and priesthoods is, as we have seen, not really meant to refer to the officials of the Church, and he has no sort of inclination for an objectivist doctrine of the sacraments in the sense of an *opus operatum* performed by the priest. But by using such comparisons he gives the offices of the Church and their functions the feel of something sacral and mysterious without effectively protecting them against more exaggerated interpretations, since all the reservations which he makes are one-sidedly moralist and individualist, and lack an ecclesiastical or dogmatic reference. The exaltation of office as an objective means of salvation, the spiritual 'character' imparted to it by ordination, and finally the incorporation of the whole clerical machinery into a fixed 'hierarchy' embracing heaven above and the Church below, which we find in Pseudo-Dionysius, are certainly not Origenist in feeling.[151] But dogmatically they fall in a sector in which Origen took hardly any interest, and it is for this very reason that such theories have fitted so well into the Origenist tradition. In the framework of a theory which provides such solid backing for the institution of office a pietistic critique of clerical abuses becomes completely harmless. It may have a stimulating or liberating effect in detail, but it can no longer shake the total structure of the hierarchical system—and this, after all, is entirely as Origen would have wished.

(pp. 51f.), who assumes in the usual way that Origen was setting clergy and teachers over against one another as leaders of separate groups within the congregation. Peter of Alexandria also stands in the Origenist tradition. In his case too the relationship between clergy and charisma is quite different from that given in the account by E. Schwartz, 'Zur Geschichte des Athanasios II', *Nachr. Ges. Wiss. Gött. (Phil.–hist. Kl.)* 1904, p. 177; also *ibid.* 1905, p. 173.

[151] This is a point which modern Catholic interpretation has failed to recognise: cf. Balthasar, *op. cit.,* p. 49; K. Rahner, *art. cit.,* p. 278. In my own view Origen's typologism, despite Harnack, *Lehrbuch der Dogmengeschichte* I⁴, 1909, p. 476, is not to be interpreted in the ecclesiological and sacramentalist spirit of the Pseudo-Dionysius.

CHAPTER XI

Cyprian and the Episcopate

CYPRIAN IS a younger contemporary of Origen. At the same time, however, he is a Westerner, and for this reason the Church as a visible organisation plays from the start a much larger part in his thinking. Secondly, he is himself a bishop, the highest representative of the clerical class, and this position is ideally suited to both his inclinations and his character. Origen too, indeed, had been ordained presbyter, and served in the ministry of the Church; but in so doing he remained the freelance 'teacher' and theologian, and the aim which he commended in his preaching was always the completely personal one of spiritual perfection. By contrast Cyprian, the discreet ruler of his congregation, who also wishes to train his people and to instruct them to their edification, never for one moment forgets that this can only be done in the context of an organised Church, and must result in what is best for the catholic world-community as a whole. In everything he does he is at all times the bishop, and it is from this standpoint that he understands and interprets all the work which is carried on in the Church. Office and the gift, or duty, of teaching, between which Origen had already attempted to establish a relation, are in Cyprian absolutely impossible to separate. Moreover, in his environment free charismatic gifts which might set themselves up in rivalry to office are now almost unknown. Differences in principle, therefore, seemingly no longer exist. But under cover of the dominant ecclesiastical consensus Origen and Cyprian, the theologians of the Eastern and the Western Church, still represent two divergent trends in Christian thinking, both of which were very much alive from the beginning—the authority of the spiritual and the authority of office, the 'gnostic' and the hierarchical self-consciousness, the former associated with the Greek, the latter with the Roman tradition. Each of these from its own starting-point constantly seeks to interpret, to organise, and to shape the reality of the Church in its own way. Each feels itself to be the heir to the unabridged tradition, and each affirms the unity of the Church. Cyprian is no more rigidly hierarchical in attitude than Origen is an anti-clerical reformer; neither of them wishes to tear up and destroy the opposing elements but to combine and harmonise them with his own position.

In each case, however, the synthesis is only half successful. The old tensions between spirit and office are not to be resolved in this way; they are overcome more on the level of feeling and practice than by arguments on theological principle.

This becomes even clearer when the two men are seen in the context of their predecessors. Origen did not acknowledge Clement of Alexandria as his teacher;[1] but the unsystematic, liberal character of the latter's 'academic' approach, with its gnostic strivings and its complete indifference to everything which goes to make up ecclesiastical organisation and the normal life of a congregation, nevertheless reveals ultimate concerns and motives which also dominate Origen, even while the latter is combining them with the existing cultic and official structures of his church. Cyprian treads consciously in the footsteps of his 'master' Tertullian;[2] he copies him and plagiarises him in his writings, and tacitly tones him down and corrects him. Tertullian had died a schismatic, in passionate protest against the dilution of the strict Christian standard in mainstream Christianity, and it was precisely the bishops whom he as a layman had made the targets of his most savage mockery and scorn. But, for all that, the message which emerged from his unbridled rigorism was still one of radical order, of rigid organisation, and even to a certain extent of official government of the people of God to protect them from all the temptations and diversions of the world around them. The flexible and tactically clever Cyprian is much more circumspect and sensible; but at bottom he is striving for the same goal. He is less abrupt and exclusive, he does not kick against the ineluctable facts of life. Energetic and definite in his official decisions, he also knows how to catch with a sure touch the mild and solemn tones of the pastor and the edifying preacher; he values humility, and moderates his demands when this is unavoidable. It was because of these characteristics that he was able to handle the ecclesiastical problems which destiny brought his way; his decisions proved effective beyond the immediate moment. Intellectually and religiously much less richly endowed than Tertullian, dominated by a few, easily comprehensible basic ideas, he formulated and championed the determinative principles of his concept of the Church, of office, and of the practical bases for the direction and government of the church with such force that it proved impossible for men ever to forget them. The image of Cyprian, the holy bishop and martyr, controls—despite some lapses in dogmatic taste—the ecclesiological thinking of Roman Catholicism to this day.

Cyprian came from high social circles. Scion of a family as rich as it was respected, he was educated in Carthage, and achieved success as a

---

[1] Cf. p. 251 n. 89 above.   [2] Jerome, vir. ill. 53.

rhetorician. About the year 246 he became a Christian, was ordained presbyter not long afterwards, and no more than two or three years after his conversion was promoted to be Bishop of Carthage. He thus found himself at the head of the greatest and most influential church in all Africa. As their bishop and as spokesman for the whole of African Christianity he had found the appropriate setting for the work which he was to carry on for the next decade, right to the very end of his life. These were uncommonly stormy years for the whole Church, and throughout his episcopate struggles and crises came thick and fast. The Decian persecution of 250 inaugurated a new era in the relationship between Church and State. For the first time the proceedings against Christians took on the character of a comprehensive and systematic persecution, aimed at the total extermination of the faith. This convulsion also brought with it serious repercussions in the internal life of the churches. The question of the readmission of the numerous apostates led in Carthage to divisions and the election of an anti-bishop, and in Rome to the radical Novatianist schism. During this period Cyprian was fighting not only for himself, but also for his great sister-church, and for the maintenance of catholic order throughout the world. There followed the years of the great plague, with their extraordinary demands on the powers of resistance and the readiness for sacrifice of congregations who had had only the briefest respite after the persecutions; and hardly had they surmounted these troubles than a political controversy flared up within the Church on the subject of heretic baptism, in which the previously friendly relations with the Roman see turned to bitter hostility. In order to maintain and carry his point against Rome Cyprian established diplomatic relations with his fellow-bishops right across to the far East. Yet even these anxieties quickly died away before the outbreak of a new storm of persecution. Now, however, it became apparent that Cyprian had not fought, struggled, and preached in vain for all these years; his church 'stood firm', and all the bishops of Africa rallied around his person. There was no need now for Cyprian to avoid martyrdom, as he had once done.[3] Steadfastly and calmly he let the danger come, and on the 14th of September 258 he went to his death like a Christian and a Roman, upheld by the certainty that the Church which he had served would not perish, but could look with confidence for the imminent day when Christ the Judge would appear on the clouds to lead his own in triumph.[4] All these events are reflected in his varied writings, most of

[3] Cf. p. 290 n. 118 below.
[4] As regards guidance on the immense Cyprian literature it will be sufficient here to direct the reader to the following works of reference: O. Bardenhewer, *Geschichte der altkirchlichen Literatur II*[2], 1914, pp. 442ff.; B. Altaner, *Patrologie*[2], 1950, pp. 142ff. H. Koch, *Cyprianische Untersuchungen*, 1926, is still indispens-

which are of a practical and edifying nature, and especially in his voluminous correspondence with his church, his clergy, and the numerous colleagues who turn to him for advice, and whom he in turn seeks to guide and to direct along the way that seems to him the one commanded by God. These letters are our most important source when it comes to describing Cyprian's view on the calling and the privileges of his office.[5]

The episcopate is an office of the Church. It represents the Church, it exists for the sake of the Church, and it can be rightly understood only in the context of the totality of the Church's living community. As a theologian of the Early Church Cyprian's thinking on the subject of office is not done in the absolute terms of abstract capacities and detached privileges which belong to the office holder by virtue of his position and as an individual, but everything connected with office is still directly and palpably linked with the holiness of life of the congregation and with its manifold needs. Here, in the midst of the Church, Cyprian finds his intellectual and social home. The Church is the society for which he lives, works, and fights, and she supports and surrounds him in these endeavours with her ordinances and her gifts. Cyprian is the first theologian to give the Church a thematic treatment of his own,[6] as Bride of Christ[7] and mother of the faithful—'Mother Church' as with special emphasis he loves to speak of her.[8] She is the mediatrix of all salvation, and can never be the true Church except— schismatics please note!—as the one, undivided, catholic Church.[9] Only in association with her, therefore, can Christians have life; her commands point the right way, and outside her holy fellowship there is nothing but falsehood, error, and darkness. Even the sacraments and episcopal ordination,[10] even the Christian confession of faith and the

---

able. The numerous disputed problems of dating in Cyprian's life are of no importance for our present purposes, and may be ignored.

[5] References are to the edition of Hartel, CSEL 1868–71, though this is not in itself satisfactory. The Sententiae LXXXVII episcoporum are cited from the edition of H. Von Soden, Nachr. Ges. Wiss. Gött. (phil.-hist. Kl.) 1909, pp. 247ff.; cf. also the same author's Die cyprianische Briefsammlung, 1904.

[6] Ep. 59, 1; 73, 11; 74, 6.

[7] It is true, however, that the De ecclesiae unitate too was written in response to a particular need, namely the refutation of the schismatics. The borderline between letters and treatises in Cyprian's works is a fluid one: cf. Bardenhewer, op. cit., p. 452. [8] Cf. J. C. Plumpe, Mater Ecclesia, 1943, pp. 81ff.

[9] The concept of the 'catholic' Church occurs in Cyprian for the first time in the period of the Novatianist schism, but from then on he uses it with great regularity: cf. Koch, op. cit., pp. 102ff.; less to the point are the comments of H. Janssen, Kultur und Sprache. Zur Geschichte der alten Kirche im Spiegel der Sprachentwicklung von Tertullian bis Cyprian, 1938, pp. 18ff.

[10] Ep. 55, 8: . . . nec habeat ecclesiasticam ordinationem, qui ecclesiae non tenet unitatem; cf. 55, 24.

Bible itself, no longer have any meaning so soon as they are sought and used outside the true Church.[11]

Cyprian's picture of this holy Church is conceived in concrete sociological terms. Without prejudice to her spiritual nature as Tertullian had already described it, she is above all a visible, human community, and is found—here Cyprian goes further than Tertullian—exclusively in this form, as the one, fully articulated, stratified, and comprehensive organisation of the Christian people. The Church is not simply the aggregate of all Christians in every place, united by their participation in God's Spirit. She is a corporate body with a clear structure and constitution, and with an organised hierarchy of classes at once spiritual and social: first, the brethren and sisters as a whole, then the holy virgins and ascetics, then the martyrs and confessors proved in the persecutions, and highest of all the clergy of various grades, headed in each congregation by the bishop.[12] At all times a sharp distinction is drawn between clergy and laity; the clergy are the picked officials of the Church, and the bishop is the leader and head who sets their standard.[13] They hold this position in accordance with the will of God on the basis of and within a definite system, established by Christ, which already obtained in the time of the apostles.[14] This system is not only in practice but also in principle a necessity, of fundamental importance for the very existence of the Church. Every Christian must be clear on this point, namely that not only is the bishop in the Church, but the Church is in the bishop. That is to say: without the office of bishop there is no Church.[15] Cyprian is never tired of stressing this idea again and again in his struggles against rebellious schismatics, arrogant martyrs, and refractory laymen. To this extent it also has its importance for ecclesiastical politics, since it supports and justifies him in his fight to maintain his position as bishop. Cyprian is not particu-

[11] Cf. E. Altendorf, *Einheit und Heiligkeit der Kirche,* 1932, pp. 92ff.

[12] Cyprian lays stress on these organised divisions especially when he wishes to emphasise the sacral order and dignity of the Church in argument against the disobedient and apostate: cf., e.g., Ep. 30, 5; 33, 1; 59, 13. The virgins form an *inlustrior portio gregis Christi* (hab. virg. 3), but even so are inferior to the martyrs (*ibid.* 21).

[13] He is in authority over the presbyters and deacons, and they are in duty bound to submit to him: cf. Ep. 3, 1; 3, 3; 14, 3 (*regi*); 16, 1.

[14] Ep. 3, 3; 66, 4 (75, 16); cf. Sent. 79; on this and what follows cf. Altendorf, *op. cit.,* pp. 53ff.

[15] Ep. 66, 8: . . . et illi sunt ecclesia plebs sacerdoti adunata et pastori suo grex adhaerens. unde scire debes episcopum in ecclesia esse et ecclesiam in episcopo, et si qui cum episcopo non sit, in ecclesia non esse et frustra sibi blandiri eos, qui pacem cum sacerdotibus dei non habentes obrepunt et latenter apud quosdam communicare se credunt, quando ecclesia [quae catholica] una est, scissa non sit neque divisa, sed sit utique connexa et cohaerentium sibi invicem sacerdotum glutino copulata.

larly fastidious in his choice of effective arguments with which to intimidate the congregation and reduce it to submission.[16] But this does not mean that he himself did not regard the cause at stake as sacred, serious, and certain, or that he merely asserted his claims without himself believing in them. On the contrary, he commits himself to it without scruple or reservation precisely because he has no doubts that he is right to exercise absolute control, and because experience only convinces him again and again of the necessity of such episcopal authority. There is no order, and therefore no unity and sanctity of the Church, without an office responsible for her governance. That is why the office was established, and therein lie its inalienable rights and its divine and theological nature.

Cyprian's ecclesiological thinking is thus at bottom sacral-juristic and sacral-political in character. The high value which he sets on the episcopal office is the direct expression of his desire for order, understood in religious terms. Cyprian thus fits into that tradition of Christian thinking on the subject of office which we saw begin in I Clement.[17] Now, however, the concept of office has been given a much fuller and more complex development. Above all the liturgical and sacramental element has been greatly intensified; and the underlying juristic conceptions have been interwoven and interfused with this at all points. When we compare Cyprian with Tertullian in this respect, it is clear that a very appreciable step forward has been taken. The justification for official position is no longer a matter of simple 'competence', valid in accordance with apostolic ordinance for the conduct of liturgical worship. In addition to the correct mode of election, carried out by the appointed bodies in the prescribed manner, clerical authority is now always confirmed by the special act of sacramental ordination. This is added to the legal proceedings as a further element with its own increasing importance, and for the first time makes the priest truly a priest. Henceforward he can pass on special spiritual gifts by the laying on of his hands in baptism or penance, and as bishop he can by himself ordain new clergy. He can consecrate the baptismal water, offer the eucharistic sacrifice,[18] and make especially effectual intercession for

[16] Cf. the horror story (laps. 26), telling how God himself punished little children who tried to deceive their bishop in the reception of the Eucharist. God avenges his priests, as both Old and New Testaments show: Ep. 3, 1f.; 73, 8f. Divine 'inspirations' too come to Cyprian at very convenient moments; cf. A. Von Harnack, 'Cyprian als Enthusiast', *ZNW* 3, 1902, p. 190. Harnack rightly warns against describing Cyprian *tout court* as a 'hypocritical cleric' because of these things, but it would seem that doubts about his miraculous spiritual experiences had already been expressed in ancient times: cf. R. Reitzenstein, *Die Nachrichten über den Tod Cyprians*, 1913, pp. 64f.

[17] Cf. pp. 91f. above.

[18] Instance sin B. Poschmann, *Die Sichtbarkeit der Kirche nach der Lehre des heiligen Cyprians*, 1908, pp. 105ff.; 166ff.

others.[19] No layman is competent to do anything of the sort. The capabilities which ordination bestows are by definition spiritual, but they now consist in a particular transferable spirit specific to the office, which is not simply to be equated with the endowment of the Spirit granted to all devout Christians. In the earlier period a confessor, who had by that very fact demonstrated beyond all doubt that he was endued with the Spirit, was received without further ado into the ranks of the clergy;[20] in Cyprian's view he has merely the expectation of a spiritual office, but still requires to be ordained before actually receiving it.[21] Purely as a matter of edification, without any legal force, the older idea still persists that in the case of such a man human decisions have been by-passed, and that he has been chosen directly by God and included in the clergy.[22] The rigid legal system which divides the clergy from the laity may no longer be disturbed even by the Spirit himself. This has the further effect of once more marking out the distinctive sacramental position of the clergy. For Cyprian, priesthood as such has no effectual power independent of its official position and function within the congregation as a whole; in this his conception is different from the formalised one of an indestructible sacramental 'character', which at a later period was the only valid one. The man who by apostasy, disobedience, or other offences proves himself unworthy of his office, has lost his spiritual capacities. He must be deprived, and, once this is done, no trace of his earlier distinction remains.[23] This conclusion sounds very 'Donatist'; but Cyprian, unlike the later Donatists, does not make everything depend on the element of personal 'holiness' in the individual officeholder. His concern is rather to see the man's position as a unity rooted both spiritually and politically in the Church; and the task and function of the Church is the only thing which gives

[19] Ep. 18, 2; laps. 36.
[20] Cf. p. 177 n. 169 above; also Tertullian, Adv. Valent. 4. On the whole problem cf. V. Fuchs, *Der Ordinationstitel von seiner Entstehung bis auf Innozenz III* (Diss. Würzburg, 1930), pp. 41ff.
[21] Ep. 49, 2; 40.
[22] Ep. 39, 1: . . . nec fas fuerat nec decebat sine honore ecclesiastico esse, quem sic dominus honoravit caelestis gloriae dignitate. In Cyprian martyrdom is constantly presented as the highest state of glorious perfection; cf. p. 269 n. 12 above. Hence the noblest sight of all is that of a bishop or cleric who also becomes a martyr or confessor. Cyprian begins the glorification of such men which was to become typical of later periods: cf. Ep. 38, 1; 61, 1; 69, 3; 81; also Vit. Cypr. 1; and H. Von Campenhausen, *Die Idee des Martyriums in der alten Kirche,* 1936, pp. 136f.; A. Kiesgen, 'Der Typus des Konfessor-Pontifex nach den Communenmessen', *LZ* 4, 1931–2, pp. 363ff.
[23] Ep. 65, 2; 66, 1; 67, 3; 67, 9; 70, 2. On this point the Donatists followed Cyprian and the African tradition; the development of the concept of character in the strict sense was, in the West, the result of the anti-Donatist struggle: cf. E. Altendorf, *op. cit.,* pp. 117ff.; H. Von Campenhausen, 'Prästbegreppets uppkomst i den gamla kyrkan', *SEÅ* 4, 1939, pp. 93ff.

the office both its holiness and its legal status. Office, therefore, must be treated as a single whole, and no distinction made in evaluating it between the objective and subjective prerequisites, nor must there be any compartmentalising of its juristic or sacramental rights and powers.

In this way Cyprian seeks to combine all the demands and requirements for the spiritual man in the one figure of the officeholder; and conversely, the man who satisfies these requirements is the one who has been called and who is to be received into the sacred college.[24] The bishop must be the model for the members of his church,[25] and naturally he is also their preacher and teacher, the conscience and the judge of his flock. Occasionally Cyprian also lays claim to supernatural illuminations in order still further to enhance the respect due to his episcopal decision.[26] The general principle, however, remains at all times fundamentally the same, namely that the bishop is the appointed president and director of his church, and that through him therefore 'all ecclesiastical measures whatsoever must be carried out'.[27] It is as such that he possesses his authority. Every man is to honour his bishop for the sake of his office. When he—or his presbyter—enters the church, the congregation must rise;[28] for he is their head, who has received *potestas* over them,[29] and even robbers and wild beasts are obedient to their leaders.[30] Naturally Cyprian also deplores all failures on the part of bishops to meet the demands of their job—when, for example, they exploit their office as if it were a benefice, or become involved in secular business affairs, or break in times of persecution.[31] But this note is struck far less often than in Origen, and is quite irrelevant to the basic demand for obedience laid upon the laity. Confidence in God's priests must not be undermined.[32] It would mean that divine Providence was not to be taken seriously, if those who have been appointed bishops by God's will were lightly to be regarded as unworthy sinners.[33] Christ has taught us by

---

[24] Ep. 39, 1; cf. n. 22 above.

[25] Ep. 4, 3; 9, 1; 38, 1; 72, 2; laps. 6. Nevertheless the idea of the model or pattern in this context is on the whole not especially frequent in Cyprian.

[26] Ep. 15, 3; 16, 4; 63, 1; 66, 10; cf. p. 270 n. 16 above.

[27] Ep. 33, 1: . . . ut ecclesia super episcopos constituatur et omnis actus ecclesiae per eosdem praepositos gubernetur.

[28] Test. III, 85.

[29] Ep 59, 2: actum est de episcopatus vigore et de ecclesiae gubernandae sublima et divina potestate; cf. Ep. 3, 1; unit. 4.

[30] Ep. 66, 6.   [31] Ep. 1, 1f.; 4, 3; laps. 6.   [32] Ep. 45, 2.

[33] Ep. 66, 1: . . . mores nostros diligenter inquirere et post deum iudicem, qui sacerdotes facit, te velle non dicam de me—quantus enim ego sum?—, sed de dei et Christi iudicio iudicare. hoc est in deum non credere, hoc est rebellem adversus Christum et adversus evangelium eius existere, ut cum ille dicat: 'nonne duo passeres asse veneunt et neuter eorum cadit in terram sine patris voluntate', et probet maiestas eius et veritas sine conscientia et permissu dei etiam minora non fieri, tu existimes sacerdotes dei sine conscientia eius in

his example not to despise even godless priests.[34] The man who rebels against his bishop will therefore be cut off by the sword of the Spirit and the wrath of God, like the company of Korah in the Old Testament.[35] Failure to obey the bishop is the source of the heinous schisms that rend the Church.[36]

The appointment of a bishop is consequently an act of the highest significance. It is the basis of law and authority, and must be proof against any objections that may be raised. The right of the congregation to take part in the election of the bishop is not disputed in principle;[37] in practice, however, it is suppressed in favour of that of the presbyters, and, above all, of the neighbouring bishops, who also carry out the consecration.[38] The people are merely present at the act of election, and can give voice to their wishes and their approval.[39] When a deposition becomes necessary, the same *mutatis mutandis* is true. The congregation cannot simply proceed of their own accord against their unfaithful pastor. This is a matter for the other bishops of the province, and especially for the relevant metropolitan.[40] The congregation is brought into the matter, and the part it plays is not completely passive; but equally it is not legally competent to act directly and independently. It is still the 'flock' which has to be 'pastured' by the bishops,[41] the 'churchpeople' who step down in favour of their leaders. On the latter,

---

ecclesia ordinari. nam credere, quod indigni et incesti sint, qui ordinantur, quid aliud est quam contendere, quod non a deo nec per deum sacerdotes eius in ecclesia constituantur? Ep. 48, 4: ... dominus, qui sacerdotes sibi in ecclesia sua eligere et constituere dignatur, electos quoque et constitutos sua voluntate atque opitulatione tueatur, gubernanter inspirans ac subministrans et ... vigorem et ... lenitatem. It does also happen, however, that bishops are elected *secundum humanam praesumptionem*—and that obviously is why they fail: Ep. 67, 4.

[34] Ep. 3, 2. In the same way Paul honoured *umbram ipsam inanem sacerdotalis nominis:* Ep. 66, 3.

[35] Ep. 4, 4; cf. 3, 1f.; 73, 8f.

[36] Ep. 3, 3; 59, 5.

[37] Ep 67, 3: plebs ... ipsa habeat potestatem vel eligendi dignos sacerdotes vel indignos recusandi. *'Dignus est'* is the customary shout of approval with which the elective assembly give their assent.

[38] Ep. 55, 8; 55, 24; cf. K. Müller, *Kirchengeschichte* I. 1³, 1941, pp. 270f. Consecration and installation in office is termed *ordinatio in* Ep. 1, 1; 38, 2; 66, 1; 67, 4, zel. et liv. 6.

[39] Ep. 19, 2; 55, 8; 67, 5; cf. n. 37 above.

[40] Ep. 16, 4; 34, 4; 68; cf. K. Müller, 'Die älteste Bischofswahl und -weihe in Rom und Alexandrien', *ZNW* 30, 1929, pp. 276f. (= *Kleine Beiträge zur Kirchengeschichte* 16); 'Rom, Arelate und die spanischen Kirchen', *ibid.,* pp. 296ff. (= *KBzK* 17); also G. Roethe, 'Zur Geschichte der römischen Synoden im 3. und 4. Jahrhundert', *Geistige Grundlagen römischer Kirchenpolitik 2,* 1937, pp. 27ff., on the subject of the *consensus episcoporum.*

[41] This image is extremely common in Cyprian: cf., e.g., Ep. 57, 5; 59, 14.

however, rests an unlimited liability.[42] The sense of office has now reached complete and self-contained development. The political self-awareness of the clergy, which in Origen was concerned more with the outward framework, has now become basic and definitive for the Church of God.

For all this, the power of the bishop is not 'absolute'. The genuinely responsible leader knows that he must keep in touch with his colleagues and his followers, because he is involved with them in a fixed, objective association. 'From the moment I received my episcopal office I made it my fundamental principle to undertake nothing simply on my personal decision without your counsel and the assent of the church'[43]—so writes Cyprian to the 'fellow-presbyters' over whom he presides.[44] Certainly the bishop must know what is owing to his position,[45] and what befits the *auctoritas* of his office.[46] This is reflected superbly in the quiet but decisive manner in which Cyprian rejects the 'insolent' and unreasonable suggestions put to him either within or from outside the congregation.[47] He does not, however, act irresponsibly; he fixes his requirements by the standard of God's law, in agreement with the sacred tradition of the Church, and on the principles which his predecessors in office followed of old.[48] When occasion demands, however,

[42] Ep. 16, 3: erunt autem rei, qui praesunt; 59, 13: viderint laici hoc quomodo curent. sacerdotibus labor maior incumbit in adserenda et procuranda dei maiestate. . . .   [43] Ep. 14, 4.

[44] The concept of the *compresbyter*, which is not found in Tertullian, occurs frequently in Cyprian: Ep. 1, 1; 7; 48, 1; cf. Janssen, *op. cit.*, pp. 78ff., and on the wider pre-history of the term p. 119 n. 304 above.

[45] Cf. the emphasis on the *loci honor*: Ep. 41, 2; 74, 8. Elsewhere in Cyprian *honor* and *potestas* are virtually equivalent concepts (though they are not for Pope Leo I, Ep. 14, 11): cf. de Labriolle, *Cyprien, De l'unité de l'église catholique. Introduction, traduction française et notes*, 1942, p. 52 n. 5.

[46] Ep. 45, 2: honoris etiam communis memores et gravitatis sacerdotalis ac sanctitatis respectum tenentes. . . . The episcopal office has the character of a magistracy. 'The civil law terminology used by Tertullian is now, so far as the ruling authorities in the Church are concerned, replaced deliberately by that of political law' (A. Beck, *Römisches Recht bei Tertullian und Cyprian*, 1930, pp. 159ff.); 'The language of Cyprian betrays clearly the skilled ecclesiastic, who has grown up in a political tradition. Potestas, honor, dignitas, maiestas, fas, ius, gravitas—terms like these from the life of the State now become the vital concepts of episcopal office in the Church' (U. Gmelin, 'Auctoritas. Römischer Princeps und päpstlicher Primat', *Geistige Grundlagen römischer Kirchenpolitik I*, 1937, p. 94).

[47] Cf. e.g., Ep. 33. There is no indication here who is addressed, since the *lapsi* did not form 'an entity for which there was any appropriate form of epistolary address'. Documents intended for them were presumably sent only to the clergy, who then either read them publicly or posted them up.

[48] The appeal to the *antecessores* is a typical feature of Cyprian's decisions in matters of church politics: Ep. 1; 15, 1, 16, 1; 55, 21; 63, 17; 68, 5; 70, 1; 71, 4. This expression of the sense of official tradition and authority also occurs elsewhere: cf. the document of the Roman clergy (Ep. 8, 1); of Firmilian of

the bishop must have the courage to act on his own responsibility, and even to infringe customary law if the need of the hour—as, for example, in times of persecution— calls for some such step;[49] but he must be able to justify his action subsequently to the Church.[50] It is, of course, precisely in times of crisis, such as periods of persecution and schism, that a strengthening of the episcopal office is proved to be generally indispensable in practice; but Cyprian is a master at calculating just what is possible and really necessary, and then not enforcing what is required in practice in an authoritarian or revolutionary manner, but rather explaining and implementing it step by step with continual appeals to order and tradition and keeping in constant touch with the loyal portion of his church. He takes care not to create new law arbitrarily.[51] He does not act like a dictator, but with high statesmanship, simultaneously respecting the community of the Church which he rules, and, when he does lead it into new paths, seeking to protect and preserve its essential nature.

In this context even more important than his close relationship with his presbyterate and with the congregation as a whole is his collaboration with his fellow-bishops in the neighbouring churches and with the catholic Church throughout the world. It is a fundamental principle with Cyprian that the bishop never stands alone, and the universal interrelationship of the one catholic Church is crucial for the whole of his ecclesiological thought. Here again we are dealing with an immemorial traditional concept; what is distinctively Cyprianic is simply the way in which this primitive Christian belief in the unity and spiritual cohesion of the Church is given a strictly and exclusively official form, and thus defined in concrete terms. The unity of the whole Church springs from the firm covenant between the 'bishops bound together in mutual association',[52] just as the unity of each congregation is actualised in its common subjection to a single bishop. There is only 'one episcopate', a single office of bishop with its representatives every-

---

Caesarea (Ep. 75, 6); and the saying of Victor of Octavu(?) in the Sententiae (78).

[49] Ep. 55, 7; 64, 1.

[50] Thus, during the persecution Cyprian in his hiding-place ordained extra clergy without the assent of the Church, and later applied for ratification of what he had done: Ep. 29; 39, 1; 40, 1; cf. Harnack, op. cit., pp. 183f.

[51] Ep. 20, 3: . . . nec in hoc legem dedi aut me auctorem temere constitui; cf. also Ep. 63, 1, where Cyprian excuses himself for giving instruction on the ground that he is obeying God's special inspiration: nec hoc putes, frater carissime, nos nostra et humana conscribere aut ultronea voluntate hoc nobis audaciter adsumere, cum mediocritatem nostram semper humili et verecunda moderatione teneamus.

[52] Ep. 66, 8 (cf. p. 269 n. 15 above); similarly, 55, 1; 59, 14; 60, 1; 68, 3; 73, 26.

where.[53] In sign of this, Christ in the first instance committed the supremacy to one single man, Peter, and then only at a later stage entrusted it to all the apostles, who in their turn are the predecessors of the future fellowship of bishops.[54] Each individual bishop exercises the full episcopate; nevertheless, it does not belong to him alone, but he possesses it only in solidarity with all the other holders of the office, with whom he is on an equality 'in honour and power'.[55] This is particularly emphasised in the controversy over heretic baptism with the Bishop of Rome, who had boasted of his special succession from Peter, and on the grounds that he possessed a higher status than that of his episcopal colleagues had wished to dictate a decision on the question. This, however, is nothing more than insolent presumption, and a folly[56] against which Cyprian makes a solemn protest in a great council

[53] This conception accords with the remarkably oecumenical attitude of the time, by which men were frequently called and elected from far distant provinces to be bishops: cf. G. Bardy, 'Sur la patrie des Évêques dans les premiers siècles', *RHE* 35, 1939, pp. 217ff.

[54] De unit. 4; Ep. 43, 5; 59, 14; cf. H. Koch, *Cathedra Petri*, 1930, pp. 33ff., 91ff. The crucial chapter of the *De unitate ecclesiae* has also been transmitted in a second version, which explicitly promises the *primatus* to Peter, and founds the whole Church on his *cathedra*. The overwhelming majority of scholars now consider that this second version—whether it be earlier or later than the first, whether drafted in reply to Roman or to African heretics—is to be ascribed to Cyprian himself. J. Ludwig, *Der heilige Märtyrerbischof Cyprian von Karthago*, 1951, pp. 30ff., in fact is inclined to regard it as the original text and the only one written by Cyprian. I myself consider that the evidence to the contrary adduced by H. Koch in *Cyprian und der römische Primat*, 1910, and especially in *Cathedra Petri*, 1930, is still, despite all the ingenuity that has been devoted to rebutting it, both apposite and satisfying; so also H. E. Feine, *Kirchliche Rechtsgeschichte auf der Grundlage des Kirchenrechts von Ulrich Stutz I: Die katholische Kirche*, 1950, p. 53 n. 1. Further literature on the subject, mostly taking the opposite view, is listed in Altaner, *op. cit.*, p. 147. Confessional interests have caused this question to be much debated; but for our present purposes it is of subsidiary importance inasmuch as the 'Roman' version, to the extent that its meaning diverges from that of the standard version (and even on this point there is not a unanimous answer), can in any case not reflect Cyprian's true and permanent opinion. It must be understood as an occasional concession, dictated by tactical considerations, since it contradicts Cyprian's view as clearly formulated elsewhere, and given special emphasis precisely in his controversy with Rome. Thus far Koch's proof is correct; cf. esp. Ep. 71, 3; also Altendorf, *op. cit.*, pp. 44ff.

[55] De unit. 5: episcopatus unus est cuius a singulis in solidum pars tenetur. The exact juristic provenance and meaning of the concept employed here, *in solidum tenere*, is disputed. What Cyprian wants to say, however, is clear: cf. Beck, *op. cit.*, pp. 153ff. In the interests of this solidarity Cyprian dislikes taking important decisions on his own, and tries to bring them before a council: ut . . . figatur apud nos . . . firma sententia multorum sacerdotum consilio ponderata (Ep. 56, 3).

[56] Ep. 74, 1.8.10, and even earlier, 71, 3; cf. also Cyprian's comments in n. 59 below, and the echo of the remarks from his letters in the document by Firmilian

of the African church.[57] In fact, at this council Cyprian, as Bishop of Carthage, and by virtue of his intellectual superiority, played a commanding role throughout, and to this extent operated himself as an African 'Pope'.[58] Cyprian nevertheless attaches the greatest importance to the fact that the following which he acquired there was at all times entirely voluntary; it came about simply through unanimity on the question at issue, not as a result of pressure or demands from his side. As president of the council he underlines the fact that in the true catholic Church there is no tyrannical 'compulsion', no regulations laid down by an individual to which others must conform, and also no arriving at conciliar decisions by majority votes. Each bishop has equal rights and is free without hindrance to express his opinion and, so far as he individually is concerned, to act accordingly. Christ alone will be his judge.[59] The Church does not collapse just because here and there alternative practices are in use;[60] but she would disintegrate if the peace and cohesion of the epsiocopate were to be destroyed by this—or, to be more precise, the man who sought to do this would thereby place himself outside their holy covenant of love, and thus outside the one, indivisible Church.[61]

The flaws in the internal logic of this Cyprianic conception, and its

---

of Caesarea (Ep. 75, 2.6. 16f. 24f.), which may in translation have undergone a certain amount of revision to bring it into line with Cyprian's views: so Ludwig, *op. cit.*, p. 39; cf. further Roethe, *op. cit.*, pp. 43ff. As against the view of M. Bévenot, 'A Bishop is responsible to God alone (St. Cyprian)', *RSR* 39, 1951–2, pp. 397ff., there would then be no difference in principle between the polemic of Cyprian and of Firmilian.

[57] Cf. the text and discussion in Von Soden, *op. cit.* (p. 267 n. 4 above).

[58] The word *papa* occurs 'no fewer than five times as a title of the Bishop of Carthage in correspondence with Rome, and once in correspondence inside Africa. Cyprian himself, however, never uses it' (Janssen, *op. cit.*, p. 94). At this time, moreover, the word still had a more popular and familiar ring, and had not yet acquired emotional and hierarchical overtones. Cf. further p. 279 n. 66 below.

[59] Cf. the introductory remarks to the *Sententiae* of the council: superest, ut de hac ipsa re singuli quid sentiamus proferamus, neminem iudicantes aut a iure communionis aliquem, si diversum senserit, amoventes. neque enim quisquam nostrum episcopum se episcoporum constituit aut tyrannico terrore ad obsequendi necessitatem collegas suos adigit, quando habeat omnis episcopus pro licentia libertatis et potestatis suae arbitrium proprium tamque iudicari ab alio non possit quam nec ipsum possit alterum iudicare. sed expectemus universi iudicium domini nostri Iesu Christi, qui unus et solus habet potestatem et praeponendi nos in ecclesiae gubernatione et de actu nostro iudicandi; cf. Ep. 69, 17; 71, 3; 72, 3; 73, 26. M. Bévenot, *art. cit.*, has demonstrated the constantly recurring emphasis on this fundamental principle in Cyprian, but against all likelihood wishes to see it as a Roman principle, which Cyprian learned from a passing phrase of Novatian's (Ep. 30, 1), and never used with full logical rigour against the Pope.   [60] Ep. 55, 21, and Firmilian, Ep. 75, 6.

[61] Cf., e.g., Ep. 55, 3; De unit. 12; and also Altendorf, *op. cit.*, pp. 61ff.

supposed crudity, have often been pointed out. On the one hand the structure of the Church as a whole is based on the episcopate as a whole, and yet at the same time each individual bishop is declared to be sovereign—is this not a complete contradiction? Where is the final court of appeal which can put matters right in an emergency, if a monarchical-papalist constitution is explicitly rejected and an aristocratic and conciliar one proves impossible to work in practice? What in the last resort is to happen if the hoped-for unanimity between the bishops does not materialise, and the continuing dissension is concerned for once not merely with relatively peripheral matters (among which Cyprian is compelled to include heretic baptism) but touches the very substance and faith of the Church itself? But a critique of this kind fails to grasp the distinctive character and the nerve of living religion in Cyprian's thinking. Cyprian *believes* in the episcopate, just as he believes in the catholic Church. However much he may be conditioned by organisational and political considerations, and however important it may be to him to establish a clear juristic confirmation of his position, the Church itself, which he serves, and the office which supports and empowers him in this service, are for Cyprian no merely juristic entities. They are divine, sacred realities given to men, and in their vital power one not only must but ought to have complete confidence. In office holy Church is made manifest; it represents, as it were, the Spirit of God present in her, of whose action elsewhere it is significant that nothing much is now said. That the bishops throughout the world will be unanimous in their opinions is simply taken for granted;[62] other possibilities are just not worth discussing. It can and it will never happen that the bishops acting as a whole should fall into error.[63] It must therefore always be possible for them in concert to arrive at the truth without coercion by rational discussion in which one listens to another and no one condemns another.[64] In the liberty of the bishops we see the truth of the Church. Individual bishops may fall, and must then, as occasion requires, be corrected and converted or even deposed; but the totality, that is, the episcopate as a whole and thus the Church itself, remains on the right path and never falls prey to 'innovations' alien to its essential nature.[65] Seen in this light, the bishop's office is indeed for Cyprian 'indefectible', and he therefore has no need to look for a fixed organisational form with which to preserve the Church unity in which he believes. That Cyprian was no 'Papalist' is well known; the Roman claims with which he had to contend, but which unfortunately

[62] So, e.g., Ep. 55, 8.
[63] Ep. 67, 8.
[64] Ep. 71, 3, and the introduction to the *Sententiae* quoted in n. 59 above.
[65] Cf. from this point of view the strong expressions used in the passage quoted at p. 273 n. 34 above.

cannot be very precisely determined,[66] remain for this century anyhow completely isolated and without discernible effects. But Cyprian was also no 'conciliarist', in the constitutional sense of the word familiar in the later Middle Ages.[67]

We may say that in the Cyprianic conception of the relationship of mutual love between the bishops a definite element from the primitive Christian concept of the Church lives on. The belief in freedom, a belief based on faith in the power of that Christian truth in which Christians as members of Christ at all times have their being, and which yet has constantly to be triumphantly demonstrated afresh to be the truth, is no longer a real option for the mass of Christians; but it is still valid for the leaders of the Church, the group of bishops through whom the Holy Spirit works, and who in their proceedings continue to represent the totality of Church members. Nevertheless the effect of thus limiting freedom to an aristocratic official class is a profound alteration of the original conception, the decisive point being that truth itself, which is the thing that matters, is no longer understood in a christo-logical and 'evangelical' sense, that is to say, no longer as the truth of the gift of unconditional forgiveness. In practice this changes everything, and such formal analogues to the original concept as have been retained provide for freedom only in a purely formal sense, and cannot be carried to their logical conclusion. For freedom no longer springs directly from the assurance of God's continuous redemption, but is now imprisoned in the frame of a human system and community in which not faith but law and respectability and official discretion have the last word.

Naturally none of this is done with the conscious intention of making a radical break with the past. Cyprian is a Christian, and when he professes his loyalty to the tradition, this means that in his own opinion he is professing absolute loyalty to the unchangeable truth of Christ by which the Church has always lived. Cyprian is a biblical theologian

[66] This much at any rate is clear from the direct and indirect polemic, namely that Stephen had appealed to the rights of the Chair of St. Peter, called for his followers to rally behind him, and threatened the community with disruption. It is quite misleading to describe Cyprian himself as the 'first Pope', as von Harnack, op. cit., p. 186, wishes to do, simply because by appealing to direct inspiration and revelation (cf. p. 270 n. 16 above) he combined episcopalism and enthusiasm. The essential feature of the concept of papacy is precisely the one which is missing here, namely a theory which bases the illumination (and the resulting authority) on the office; the pronouncements are not ex cathedra.

[67] The beginnings of this kind of conciliarism are none the less to be found in the Early Church, and in fact in Africa. They appear particularly in Facundus and generally in the African opposition to Justinian and the Pope dependent on him during the stormy controversy of the Three Chapters: cf. W. Pewesin, 'Imperium, Ecclesia universalis, Rom', Geistige Grundlagen römischer Kirchen-politik III, 1937, pp. 67ff.

and feels himself—as Origen and Tertullian had done—controlled first and foremost by the Bible. The Bible possesses unqualified authority for everyone, and therefore also for those who hold office in the Church. Tertullian, however, had already expounded the Bible from both the practical and the dogmatic standpoints in a strictly legalistic manner, and thus misunderstood it. Cyprian follows his lead, but now in addition renounces even the heroic and enthusiastic radicalism of his master, and the unqualified character of the spiritual demand, which had to some extent still recalled the early days of Christianity. He interprets and distorts everything in accordance with the practical and pedagogic needs of contemporary Church life, justified as brotherly 'love' and respect, the whole picture being dominated by a gloomy moralism. This moralism is certainly not without considerable practical seriousness. Cyprian is truly concerned that there should be no relaxation of moral effort within the Church, and that the struggle against sin and against the challenge threatening the Church from without, and for obedience to God's commandment, should not be crippled but prosecuted with energy. But the relationship between the moral demand and the equally strictly emphasised kindness and forbearance of God is not explained, and is determined in practice from case to case in accordance with varying considerations. Christ is seen now as an austere judge and now again as a compassionate helper; the works of Christians are regarded in one passage as quite inadequate and in another as worthy of the highest praise; the salvation which is set before the eyes of all Christians is described at one moment as an assured possession and at the next as an urgent task, something to be won only by supreme efforts and achievements. The way in which Cyprian presents these demands and promises, heightens them or plays them down, gives them prominence or pushes them into the background, is neither valueless nor irresponsible, and always displays a high degree of pedagogic skill. It is also obvious that his exhortations were neither ineffective nor unsuccessful. But they are no longer spiritually straightforward, and have no value as theological statements; the only thing which is clear and unambiguous is the instruction to remain faithful to the Church and to obey her rules; this is the way to redemption. And of course, where men are thus pointed to 'the Church', then naturally it is the 'official' Church, the office and persons of the clergy, which occupies the foreground, and above all the person of the bishop, who gives the instructions and has received authority from God himself. How is this authority which he exercises to be defined in detail?

It has already been stressed that the bishop comes to his church vested in the authority of a teacher, and that it is this which distinguishes him; he teaches and preaches God's law to the people of God.

This duty of the clergy and very especially of the bishop to teach and exhort, Cyprian takes with the greatest seriousness. It is, however, hardly treated as an official 'privilege' which has to be justified as such, but rather as something to be taken for granted. In its theoretical aspect this task is seen as very simple and uncomplicated. The understanding of biblical truths, of the principles of doctrine and, above all, of practical morality is nowhere felt to be particularly difficult; basically these things are either known already or else they are plain for all to see. Cyprian nowhere requires that a Church teacher should possess a special gift of teaching or of higher spiritual knowledge, as Clement and Origen had done. The bishop has to keep to the traditional and attested truth of the Church and of the holy Scriptures—that is all. In so far as any special pedagogic task is laid upon him in his preaching, this is less a matter of skill in the individual direction of particular souls than of responsible consideration for the congregation as a whole, with its need to be rightly governed. Cyprian knows no freelance class of teachers against whom he might have to defend the special rights of the episcopal teaching office;[68] nor does he have any real trouble with the teaching of false doctrine outside the Church.[69] If he has any special difficulty, then it is the one which arises when what has been taught in principle has to be applied in everyday practice, adapted to the situation of the moment, and implemented in the face of possible resistance—that is to say, when the teacher becomes a 'pastor', who has to lead and take decisions. The clerical teaching office constitutes only one part of the general responsibility for governing the Church; it has no special value or authority of its own, and apart from this relevance to the practical conduct of Church affairs does not of itself create any radical division between the clergy and the laity.

The distinctive official position of the bishop comes out more clearly in the administration of the sacraments. He is authorised to baptise, to ordain, and to celebrate the Eucharist—functions which are of the highest importance for the spiritual life of Christians. This special province of the clergy and of the bishop is much more strongly emphasised in Cyprian than in the layman Tertullian. Nevertheless, the signi-

---

[68] This does not mean of course that the intellectual life of the laity had become completely passive and dependent. Cyprian himself had written the *Ad Donatum* while still a layman, and in this work (chap. 5) he speaks extravagantly of the rich gifts which the Spirit can bestow on any man. Cf. also A. von Harnack, *Über den privaten Gebrauch der heiligen Schriften in der alten Kirche*, 1912, pp. 46ff.

[69] It is in keeping with this that he regards the instruction of heretics as an extremely simple affair, Ep. 73, 3: neque enim difficile est doctori vera et legitima insinuare ei, qui haeretica pravitate damnata et ecclesiastica veritate comperta ad hoc venit, ut discat, ad hoc discit, ut vivat. nos non demus stuporem haereticis patrocinii et consensus nostri, et libenter ac prompte obtemperant veritati.

ficance of these 'priestly'[70] prerogatives of the bishop in the normal course of church life ought not to be overestimated. They appear in Cyprian less as the distinctive prerogatives of particular exalted personages, namely the priests, than as a part of the general order of the Church and of the functions that pertain to it. Outside the true Church there are no means of grace and no salvation—this is the one idea which Cyprian never tires of repeating. Within the Church access to the sacraments is open to everyone; their administration by the bishop appointed for this purpose normally calls for no responsible decision on his part. The whole community without distinction participates in worship, everything takes place in the bright glare of public life; there is hardly any private pastoral work, and especially no secret penance. The bishop, therefore, is indeed the focal point and revered president of his church; but precisely in this matter of the administration of the sacraments he is still much more their servant and functionary than in the Middle Ages. We must conclude that the sacramental privileges of the bishop are not especially prominent, but are in essence only a concomitant of his general episcopal position as leader.

There is just one point at which this episcopal status can acquire an absolutely unique personal importance for the individual Christian. If, as Cyprian maintains, 'outside the Church there is no salvation',[71] then membership of this Church, the right to join in her worship, to receive her sacraments, to enjoy her fellowship, and to share in her intercession and sanctity, is the one quite indispensable prerequisite and condition of salvation for everyone. The sentence which is passed on the apostate, the malefactor, or the penitent is likewise of vital importance for the community; for she can remain the immaculate Bride of Christ only if she does not tolerate the presence of evildoers in her midst.[72] But the importance of the sentence to the person on

[70] In Cyprian the regular usage of *sacerdos* as an official title is to refer to the bishop, whereas Tertullian had distinguished him from the presbyters as *summus sacerdos* (De bapt. 17). The exceptions which Janssens, *op. cit.*, p. 87, proposes to this rule are without justification. The passages in which Cyprian seems to regard the presbyters also as *sacerdotes* are either formulated differently, that is, the actual term is not used directly (Ep. 1, 1: *sacerdotio honorati*; 61, 3: *sacerdotali honore coniuncti*), or are dependent on the Old Testament (Ep. 72, 2) and have a more general sense (Ep. 40). It therefore remains true: '*Sacerdotes* . . . in Cyprian are always the bishops' (K. Müller, *Die älteste Bischofswahl* p. 277 n. 2.).

[71] Ep. 73, 21. The statement in itself says nothing new, but merely expresses the 'old primitive Christian view of the two worlds, one of God and the other of the demons'. What is new, however, is the interpretation and consolidation of this concept of the 'Church' in terms of officials and institutions; cf. K. Müller, *Kirchengeschichte I.* 1, p. 273.

[72] De unit. 17; 23; Ep. 53, 1.15. In Cyprian's writings against Novatian, however, there are already signs of a different view which was eventually to

whom it is passed, and of the penance which alone can purify and restore him, is of a wholly different order; for him it is, in the religious sense, literally a matter of life and death. The man whose task it is to pronounce this sentence of judgment and redemption 'in Christ's place'[73] is, according to Cyprian, the bishop and the bishop alone.[74] It is for this that he has received 'the power to forgive sins'.[75] Only through him can a man render satisfaction to the Lord,[76] and his decision stands.[77] The triumph of this idea of Cyprian's marks an epoch in the history of the Western Church. It is here that the official rights of the bishop, which he advocates, find their ultimate basis. Certainly it is precisely in the conduct of penance that these rights are without question immensely old. The Pastoral Epistles already refer to the laying-on of hands at readmission;[78] the ordination rite of Hippolytus mentions the power of the keys as an important prerogative of the highest clerical rank;[79] and the Syrian Didascalia too lays especial emphasis on this aspect of the bishop's authority.[80] But Cyprian is the first finally to set aside the competing claims of the congregation and its saints, that is, primarily the martyrs, and thus to bring to its culmination the process begun so long before. The share of these other church members is now limited to petition and consent;[81] Cyprian will have nothing more to do with their readmitting penitents on their own authority, as the martyrs had done at Lyons,[82] nor does he recognise, as even Tertullian still had, their right to intercede on behalf of the sinner;[83] and he now succeeds in forcing this policy through in the teeth of violent resistance and criticism.[84] The power of the keys, which was already

---

issue in the understanding of the Church as a *corpus permixtum*: cf. Altendorf, *op. cit.*, pp. 103ff.

[73] Ep. 59, 5: iudex vice Christi.

[74] Ep. 59, 4; 66, 3.

[75] Ep. 73, 16; cf. 3, 1.

[76] Ep. 19, 1; 43, 3; *laps.* 29.

[77] Even if a man has managed to receive the 'pax' when he has no right to it, yet if this has been given him, 'as always', by the bishop then Cyprian will not have it withdrawn: Ep. 64, 1; similarly laps. 36 (cf. p. 287 n. 102 below.).

[78] Cf. pp. 147f. above.

[79] Cf. pp. 234f. above.

[80] Cf. pp. 243ff. above.

[81] Ep. 64, 1: readmission is not to take place *sine petitu et conscientia plebis*; cf. 18, 2; 49, 2.

[82] Cf. pp. 219f. above.

[83] Cf. p. 231 n. 98 above.

[84] Theologically this resistance is not to be taken too seriously. It is indeed concerned with the claims of the confessors, and thus, as has often rightly been emphasised, from the historical point of view, with the last offshoots of an authority which had once been claimed by the martyrs as men and women endowed with the Spirit. Plainly, however, no one was still aware what this meant. The only question which was really at issue in the controversy was

central and indispensable in the spiritual life of primitive Christianity, is thus shown once again to be the most important pre-requisite of all concrete spiritual authority. But just as its inner meaning is changed in Cyprian's writings from the evangelical to the moralistic, so too its outward form is no longer understood as directly spiritual, but is consciously regarded as an organisational and 'official' matter. It is based now on a sacral law. The objectivity of a legal ordinance replaces the Christ-centredness of the original word of forgiveness. In addition to the idea of official competence, the penitential prerogatives of the bishop are also given a sacramental basis: the readmission is sealed by the sacrifice of the Mass and by the mediation of the Spirit through the laying-on of the bishop's hands—*sacrificio et manu sacerdotis*.[85] The decisive factor, however, is the importance of the bishop's official position and appointment. It is as the guardian of God's order that the bishop becomes lord of penance; special priestly qualities, such as might be inferred from the fact of his ordination, very much take second place.[86]

Cyprian's significance for the history of the concept of authority and of penance can be discussed in detail only in the context of the actual controversies through which he had to fight his way.[87] Progress was not the result of theoretical speculations, but arose directly from the situations and conflicts of those years of crisis. The mass apostasy which the Decian persecution brought with it was something new for the Church.[88] The problem whether this type of sinner could be forgiven, which had been discussed earlier, was now posed with extreme urgency. Cyprian himself had, while the persecution raged, kept away from his church and in hiding. At first he handled the matter of the

---

whether or not it was possible safely and quickly to readmit the *lapsi*. The merits of the martyrs, who to some extent made common cause against Cyprian in this matter with the refractory presbyters, provided useful ammunition in the controversy. So soon, however, as this was settled by the concessions on the part of the bishops, no more was said about the so-called 'privilege of the martyrs'.

[85] Laps. 16; cf. Poschmann, *Paenitentia,* pp. 421f. Significantly, this laying-on of hands can also be undertaken by a presbyter, and if need be by a deacon with the bishop's commission: Ep. 18, 2.

[86] By contrast, in the East from the time of the Didascalia onwards the authority of the bishop is based primarily on his consecration: cf. G. Dix, 'The Ministry in the Early Church', *The Apostolic Ministry* (ed. Kirk), 1946, p. 212.

[87] On what follows, in addition to the discussion by H. Koch on the 'penitential question in Cyprian' (*Cyprianische Untersuchungen,* pp. 211ff.), cf. esp. the presentation by Poschmann (*Paenitentia,* pp. 370ff.; and *Handbuch der Dogmengeschichte IV. 3,* 1951, pp. 28ff.) which is in essentials the more correct; also K. Müller, *Kirchengeschichte I. 1,* pp. 259 ff.

[88] Most scholars fail to pay sufficient attention to this fact, or to see that it explains why in the new situation all the earlier practices and principles which dealt with individual cases were bound to prove inadequate.

lapsi in a rather dilatory manner, that is to say, he had rejected the idea of any hasty or immediate readmission, and had postponed his decision on the individual, widely varying cases, until careful investigation could be made at a later, more peaceful time.[89] But this position proved impossible to maintain. The 'martyrs', that is, the tried and tested confessors of the Church, accustomed from earlier days to come to decisions of their own accord in the name of the Spirit and of the Church,[90] gave way to the impatient pressure of those apostates who had wavered in face of the exceptional severity of the crisis, and did not wait for the bishop's decision. They brushed aside the policy set out in Cyprian's letters, and readmitted the *lapsi* on their own authority.[91] Cyprian, who could not in any way countenance such a proceeding, was compelled nevertheless to decide after his return, in consultation with his colleagues, to adopt a largely accommodating attitude. The bishops too now declare themselves ready in milder cases to grant the 'peace' of the Church at once, and those who had formally sacrificed to idols were, at least in cases of dangerous illness, to be able to receive reconciliation, as it were, on their deathbeds.[92] The situation, as regards both pastoral need and church politics, seemed to admit of no other solution. But events very quickly overtook even this approach, when the persecution after a brief pause threatened to break out once more, and it was now vital to rally and to arm the whole church, including mortal sinners still doing penance for their lapse, for the new conflict.[93] There was considerable fear that otherwise the latter would be lost altogether. A council presided over by Cyprian decided on an unconditional amnesty, and readmission for all who were by now ready to be put on probation. The document in which Cyprian justifies this sudden 'enforced'[94] change of position lays especial stress on the strengthening power of the Holy Communion, which ought not to be withheld from the penitent, if battle were once more to be joined.[95] He attempts, as well as he can, to give practical grounds for the decision, and declares

[89] Ep. 55, 6; 57, 1; 64, 1.

[90] That this tradition did exist cannot be doubted in spite of Poschmann's objections (*Paenitentia*, pp. 270ff.; *Handbuch*, pp. 39ff.); cf. pp. 219, 231 above. In Alexandria Bishop Dionysius was faced with a situation very similar to that of Cyprian: Eusebius, *HE* VI, 42, 5f. Here too the martyrs had readmitted the lapsed on their own authority, and Dionysius sought to avoid a conflict by accepting their decision and thus appearing to 'ratify' it officially. It seems that Cyprian at first attempted to find a settlement along similar lines (Ep. 15).

[91] Apparently no special importance was attached to providing a spiritual motive for this step. The martyrs simply felt themselves entitled to take it on the ground of their merits, and had no doubts about the power of their intercession with God: cf. H. von Campenhausen, *Die Idee des Martyriums in der alten Kirche*, 1936, p. 136.

[92] Ep. 55, 6.17; 57, 1.   [93] Ep. 57, 1.

[94] Ep. 57, 1: necessitate cogente.   [95] Ep. 57, 4.

that it has also been confirmed by miraculous indications and widely-attested revelations.[96] But this rapid and wholesale change of front continued, nevertheless, to present difficulty. For the sake of the community at large it was necessary to forgo altogether a conscientious examination and punishment of individuals, and Cyprian himself admits that he does not feel very happy about such a summary proceeding—he might now be granting forgiveness in excess, and thus be in danger of incurring guilt himself.[97] In answer to critics of sterner temper[98] he can only fall back on the general assurance that the decision was in no sense lightly taken by the bishops, but was given long and painstaking consideration.[99] But was it really possible on general principles and, so to speak, by categories to promise eternal salvation and peace with God and the Church to grievous sinners in this impetuous way? Could something which the situation on the large scale rendered unavoidable really be acknowledged and upheld in the congregation without reserve as an utterance of the Holy Spirit to each person involved? Thus Cyprian finally comes up against the question whether the judgement of the Church and the judgment of God can in fact always be identical. The broadmindedness of Church decisions taken for political reasons at last confronts him too with the same problem which had earlier arisen for Origen as a result of the latter's pastoral and critical examination of clerical practice.

It is clear that in the West penance was regarded as essentially a disciplinary system adequate only for the grossest cases, and that in the normal way little was done to regulate punishments, expulsions, and readmissions in the light of a more refined sense of responsibility. It is true that in administering penance Cyprian feels himself to be not merely a 'judge' but also a 'physician' of souls;[100] but the more profound difficulty inherent in his decisions has obviously never really dawned on him. In general he is automatically convinced of their correctness and saving efficacy. This is shown precisely by the twinges of conscience which he now feels in an extraordinary situation and as a result of novel decisions which, as he himself emphasises, have been

[96] Ep. 57, 1.2.5.

[97] Ep. 59, 16: remitto omnia, multa dissimulo studio et voto colligendae fraternitatis. etiam quae in deum commissa sunt, non pleno iudicio religionis examino. delictis plus quam oportet remittendis paene ipse delinquo.

[98] Ep. 59, 15: vix plebi persuadeo, immo extorqueo, ut tales patiantur admitti.

[99] Ep. 55, 3.

[100] Cyprian did not still accept the distinctively Western view emphasised by K. Holl, *Enthusiasmus und Bussgewalt*, 1898, p. 233 n. 1, that a sin 'can only be loosed or not loosed, forgiven or not forgiven'. Instead we find in his writings medical imagery, with its idea of gradual loosing from sin, alongside the juristic. In this respect, therefore, there is 'no difference in principle' between Cyprian and Origen: Poschmann, *Paenitentia*, p. 463 n. 1.

forced on him by circumstances. They are concessions the spiritual inadequacy and danger of which he himself perceives. But because he did not make up his mind to them lightly, but only under pressure and after conscientious consideration of all the data, he can quieten his doubts, convinced that he has always had in mind what is best for the Church as a whole and for her peace.[101] The real theological problem, namely what might be the significance of a possible incorrect decision of this kind for the individual sinner, appears as no more than a peripheral issue and one quite simply dealt with. In view of the universal possibility of human error, Cyprian adduces a kind of general proviso covering the readmission of sinners, which is to relieve the penitential judge where necessary. In the last analysis he cannot see into the heart of the sinner; but God's judgment at the Last Day will be infallible. If the bishop is double-crossed by a false penitent, this does not mean that the latter has escaped his punishment simply because of a 'human' promise.[102] On the other hand, because such errors may possibly occur, this is no reason for the responsible judge to refuse to exercise his power to pardon ever again, and to adopt the 'harsh' policy of the Novatianist rigorists.[103] Cyprian is in fact as convinced as ever that the man who is bound on earth by the official representative of the Church, and excluded from her fellowship, will also remain bound in heaven,[104] and indeed it is on this that he bases his demand not to be over-anxious in the use of the power to absolve.[105] But the positive, absolving decision of the Church does not have the same unconditional force to commit, so to speak, God himself; it provides only the necessary general prior condition for salvation, and makes it possible but not certain that pardon will ultimately be granted.[106] Here it is for the penitent himself

---

[101] Ep. 57, 7: salus multorum; similarly 59, 16 (cf. p. 286 n. 97 above): voto colligendae fraternitatis.

[102] Ep. 55, 18: neque enim praeiudicamus domino iudicaturo, quominus si paenitentiam plenam et iustam peccatoris invenerit, tunc ratum faciat, quod a nobis fuerit hic statutum. si vero nos aliquis paenitentiae simulatione deluserit, deus, qui non deridetur et qui cor hominis intuetur, de his quae minus perspeximus iudicet et servorum sententiam dominus emendet . . .; 57, 3: nos in quantum nobis et videre et iudicare conceditur, faciem singulorum videmus, cor scrutari et mentem perspicere non possumus. de his iudicat occultorum scrutator et cognitor cito venturus et de arcanis cordis atque abditis iudicaturus. obesse autem mali bonis non debent, sed magis mali a bonis adiuvari; laps. 18: neque enim statim videri potest divina maiestate concessum, quod fuerit humana pollicitatione promissum. Ibid., 16, it is virtually asserted that hasty readmission: nec communicationem tribuit, sed impedit ad salutem (of those responsible for carrying it out); but cf. ibid., 36: potest in acceptum referre, quidquid pro talibus et petierint martyres et fecerint, sacerdotes.

[103] Ep. 57, 3 (cf. n. 102 above); 68, 1.

[104] Ep. 55, 28.   [105] Ep. 57, 1; cf. 54, 3.25.

[106] Ep 55, 17.29; cf. 36, 2; 72, 2; also Poschmann, Paenitentia, pp. 403f.; 410f.; Handbuch p. 31.

to see to it that he is in earnest and is not disappointed at the Last Day.[107]

This Cyprianic answer to the problem of absolution apparently satisfied most people, and was regarded in other parts of the Church as the proper way out of the difficulty. At about the same period the Roman clergy came to exactly the same decision.[108] Apparently no one noticed the enormous implications in principle of this decision once it had ceased to be regarded as a general measure of discipline and church order for educational and political purposes, and was understood in the comprehensive sense which had belonged to the power of the keys in the early days. For while there were no qualifications attached to the condemnation of those outside the Church, the assurance of real here-and-now forgiveness was replaced by a mere likelihood and possibility of salvation. The yearning for immediate admission to the Church's fellowship, and the belief in the vital blessings which came with it, were apparently so obvious, clear, and compelling to every Christian[109] that the prudent reservations which had been introduced on this subject disturbed no one. A long process of development and painful experience were needed before men became fully aware of the dangers and temptations which here threatened the Christian conscience. It was mediaeval monasticism which provided the necessary conditions in the West for this harsh awakening, whereas development in the East was, as we have seen, directed along different lines from the first. Accordingly the proviso mentioned above was at first taken to apply only to the deliberate hypocrite—a case in which it will always be indispensable[110]—and Christians had in any case already become accustomed to look for the major assurance of their salvation in their own efforts after baptism,[111] and no longer in an act of confession, forgive-

---

[107] Laps. 17; only the martyrs are free from this anxiety: Ep. 55, 20.

[108] Cf. Novatian, Ep. 30, 8, on the possibility of readmitting the *lapsi* on their deathbeds: . . . deo ipso sciente, quid de talibus faciat et qualiter iudicii sui examinet pondera, nobis tamen anxie curantibus, ut nec pronam nostram inprobi homines laudent facilitatem nec vere paenitentes accusent nostram quasi duram crudelitatem: cf. Poschmann, *Paenitentia*, pp. 372f.

[109] It is on this pertinent observation that Poschmann bases his thesis that the 'sacramental' nature of penance in Cyprian (and in the early Church in general) is to be found in the act of readmission to the Church, while no emphasis is laid on the sinner's own confession, and there is still absolutely no evidence in Cyprian's case of a priestly absolution: *Paenitentia*, pp. 398ff.; *Handbuch*, pp. 31f.

[110] Unless one wishes to demand miraculous revelations and supernatural perception. But Cyprian is familiar with such things only as notable exceptions, and he cannot exalt the statement *sacerdotem dei nec occulta crimina fefellerunt* (*laps.* 25) into a general rule.

[111] On this point Cyprian, as is well known, is capable of the most astonishing exaggeration: cf. e.g., Ep. 59, 7: homo libertati suae relictus et in arbitrio proprio constitutus sibimet ipse vel mortem appetit vel salutem; *laps.* 35: oportet . . . iustis operibus incumbere, quibus peccata purgantur, eleemosynis fre-

ness, and acceptance, performed directly on Jesus's authority wherever there was faith in him.

Hence the spiritual problem of the personal appropriation and assurance of salvation, which Greek theology had at any rate perceived and, in its pietistic and idealist manner, also answered, nowhere receives serious treatment from Cyprian. His ideal bishop is content with demanding virtue (the moralistic meaning of sacrifice), the active fulfilment of religious obligations, and submission to God's will, and with strengthening earnest faith, discipline, and righteousness in the congregation generally. As the prize of this spiritual striving a noble reward and eternal glory and triumph beckon the Christian. For the bishop least of all is there any need to hesitate or waver on this course. If in his care for the whole church he has remained faithfully at his post, if he has not given way to the pressures of the faint-hearted majority but has unwearyingly encouraged and exhorted the steadfast, and reproved and punished those who fall, and if he has never 'flagged' in battle like a cowardly deserter but has always met the demands which his office makes upon him,[112] then he knows that he has a right to the honour paid to him,[113] and that his glory has become the glory of the Church;[114] for if she stays close to him, then she too will take her place with the Lord.[115] One is constantly astonished how nonchalantly Cyprian distributes praise and blame, and with measured pride claims due recognition for the leaders of the Church. He is confirmed in this attitude by his strict sense of official duty. It is a Roman, that is, a thoroughly political, self-consciousness which fills and sustains him, the leader of his 'people',[116] and his presbyteral 'senate'.[117] There is something imposing about the human greatness and intensity of this

---

quenter insistere, quibus a morte animae liberantur. 'Forgiveness' in the full, unqualified sense no longer has any place after baptism: cf. Poschmann, *Paenitentia*, pp. 398ff.

[112] Ep. 31, 6.   [113] Ep. 61, 4.

[114] Ep. 13, 1; 15, 1; 33, 1; 81.

[115] In Cyprian Christ, his Church, and his bishop are for practical purposes inseparable; *de unit.* 17: an esse sibi cum Christo videtur, qui adversum sacerdotes Christi facti, qui se a cleri eius et plebis societate secernit? Similarly *ibid.* 13, 21; Ep. 15, 1; 19, 1; 59, 13; 65, 5; 73, 26.

[116] For Christendom in this sense Cyprian mostly uses the word *populus*; by contrast *plebs* expresses the relationship of the rank and file to the bishop and clergy, and is Cyprian's favourite term for the total congregation of laity in a given place: cf. Janssen, *op. cit.,* pp. 60ff.

[117] This term, however, appears only in the pseudo-Cyprianic document *De singularitate clericorum,* which nevertheless derive from Cyprian's century and his tradition: cf. Koch, *Cyprianische Untersuchungen,* pp. 426ff. Important for understanding Cyprian is also Ep. 37, 2, where he places the *dignitas caelestis honoris* of the martyrs above the glory of the *magistratus consules* and *proconsules.* Cf. also p. 274 n. 46 above.

attitude; but it is clear that the spirit which animates the discharge of these professional duties, in whatever intellectual and spiritual terms its goals and tasks may be defined, is now, so far as its effect and its authority are concerned, exactly the same as that of secular officialdom. The distinctive dialectic between Spirit and ecclesiastical organisation, between the authority of Christ and that of his human representatives, between the spiritual authority of the authorised official and that of the Spirit-filled congregation as a whole, is now completely submerged. At the heart of this official thinking stands the Church as a sacro-social totality, a community of Christian ideas and of the Christian way of life, which lays down for its leaders an 'ecclesiastical', quasi-political pattern of conduct. In this way, for all its moral and pedagogic sense of responsibility, a strictly tactical and flexible element makes its appearance in the behaviour of the 'pastoral office', which—rigid as it may be in its legal claims and organisation—yet in detail proves to be thoroughly elastic and adaptable to whatever opportunities happen to be available at the moment.

At the crucial point, namely in the exercise of the power to judge and to pardon, this becomes completely clear, and is frankly stated by Cyprian.[118] Here Cyprian never acts other than conscientiously, but always in the light of circumstances and with due discretion. The primitive Christian instruction to forgive any penitent sinner has become, at least in this radical form, completely unacceptable to him—what would become of the 'fear' which God desires, if we were simply to extend forgiveness to everyone?[119] As a matter of principle, pardon is to be granted not to the sinner who merely is prepared to do penance, but only to one who has already shown amendment, has been purified by the performance of penance, and has undergone a suitably long period of waiting; and even then the favoured penitent is not to have all his spiritual rights restored automatically.[120] Such a standpoint is no doubt very understandable in an embattled social group like the Church of the third century, but it is not precisely that of primitive Christianity. Furthermore, it is clear that the moral problem of discretion, to which the bishop has to find an answer in the administration of penance, can no longer be kept clear of tactical and political considerations; if an apostate bishop is ready to return and to bring his entire following back into the Church with him, then special efforts must be made to accommodate him, since otherwise all those souls would be lost.[121]

[118] Ep. 55, 17; 57, 1; 59, 16 (cf. p. 286 n. 97 above). Cyprian had already explained his flight during the first persecution on similar lines as a step taken in view of the overall situation of the Church: Ep. 7; 20, 1.

[119] Ep. 31, 6.

[120] This is especially clear in the case of loss of clerical rank; cf. further Poschmann, *Paenitentia,* p. 444 n. 1.   [121] Ep. 55, 11; cf. also 64, 1.

Moreover, even the sacramental ordinances, on which Cyprian likes to lay such solemn emphasis, are in fact adjusted to meet the needs of church life, and in the process are unintentionally deprived of some of their own value and importance.[122] This is shown on the grand scale by his handling of the baptismal question during the controversy over heretic baptism. On the one hand Cyprian, in company with the whole theology of his time, asserts that all Christian salvation is rooted in baptism, and denies that baptism administered outside the legitimate Church has any effect whatever. It is an empty, demonic mimicry of that which is done within the Church, and can only defile those who receive it, but never make them Christians.[123] On the other hand, however, as an ecclesiastical statesman he cannot draw the obvious conclusion from this position, since opinions on the matter are far too conflicting. Cyprian praises 'harmony', and contents himself with tolerating recognition of heretic baptism where this recognition—which on his view is perverse—is customary, thus according it his own recognition as well.[124] Even as the fellowship of salvation the Church is still first and foremost the legally organised and self-contained organisation. Sacramental rites have to fit in with this basic conception, and by so doing can enrich and transfigure the whole; but they may not, in obedience to their own laws, disturb it or burst it asunder.

In Cyprian therefore the peculiar logic of political thinking is already beginning to show up the dangers of evacuating the concepts of Church and church office of their moral and religious content, and the 'tragic' possibilities of conflict which are implicit in so doing.[125] These are indeed only beginnings, and never become conscious even to Cyprian himself. Cyprian does not remotely contemplate replacing what for him is established Christian truth and righteousness with belief in the Church. He has never heard of a duty of obedience which sanctifies any means, nor does he desire any *sacrificium intellectus*. Even

[122] It might be claimed that this also results in the limiting of their 'magically' effectual character. But this limitation does not result, as it does in Paul, from their theological nature and their significance as Word of God, but only from the pressures of church practice, which is perfectly capable, should occasion require, of laying the very strongest emphasis on their magical associations: cf. p. 270 n. 16 above.

[123] There is no need to consider here the minor adjustments which Cyprian also makes in the doctrine of baptism in the course of the heretic baptism controversy; cf. H. von Soden, 'Der Streit zwischen Rom und Karthago über die Ketzertaufe', *Quellen und Forschungen ital. Arch. und Bibl.* 12, 1908–9, pp. 1ff., esp. pp. 28f.

[124] Ep. 55, 24; 68; and p. 277 n. 59 above.

[125] In this context one is reminded also of the common abuse to which Novatian is subjected the moment he finds himself in opposition to the bishop recognised by Cyprian: Ep. 60, 3.

Church unity is not something he will have 'at any price'.[126] But precisely because Christianity is essentially both rational and moral, this unity both can and must be realised and maintained in the holy Church without further ado. This is perfectly obvious; on this point there can manifestly be no difficulties whatsoever. This naïve ecclesiasticising of the Christian life is rooted in Cyprian's rationalistic moralism, which no longer has any feeling or comprehension for the infinite gulf between the events of the human and rational and those of the spiritual order. Nowhere, however, in the third century was there any serious resistance to this levelling procedure and its consequences, and that is why ecclesiastical development in the immediately succeeding period proceeds so smoothly and straightforwardly. It is, of course, true that there are still struggles to come over rights and jurisdictions, over differences of opinion on practical points and personal claims to independence; and the problems of office and of spiritual authority are as a result open to constant discussion. But the argument touches only superficial details, and does nothing to shake those foundations of ecclesiological thinking which were laid in the third century.

[126] So Ludwig, *op. cit.*, p. 67, with the comment, justified in itself, that Cyprian's 'demand for unity' almost overrides dogma. But this, leaving aside Cyprian's personal cast of mind, which is not really interested in doctrine, comes about almost against his will as the result of a faith which seeks to affirm the Church only in a particular, basically 'indefectible' legal form, and which therefore if necessary is bound to oppose doctrine as well.

CHAPTER XII

Retrospect

WHEN WE survey the development which the idea of ecclesiastical office underwent in the first three centuries, the impression which forces itself upon us above all others is that of historical movement, of the unceasing change and transformation of the available material. From the abundance of motifs already present in the first century the second century saw the selection of those which were to be fundamental for the future, and their combination in the fixed forms of developing church order and constitution. In the third century the theories of the nature and significance of office and official authority as elaborated in East and West part company. As they are given a theological basis, and worked out in terms of canon law, the doctrine and the formal law of ecclesiastical office which emerge become increasingly distinct. We have been able to trace this development only a little way past the middle of the century; but it does not seem that the remaining decades saw any important changes which might thus have escaped us. With Cyprian on the one hand and Origen on the other there is a kind of pause for breath; even in the fourth century the only advance is a measure of exchange and assimilation between the Greek and the Latin traditions under the outwardly very much altered circumstances of the unity of the Church and Empire. Relations with the Christian emperor and state, and the effort to absorb the monastic revival, present the Church and her officials in many ways with new tasks and problems which inevitably broaden and deepen the ideas hitherto held, but this does not have the effect of altering the foundations already laid. Even the great upsurge in biblical studies and in the science of theology in the second half of the fourth century evoked no sort of revolution in this context. The legal position and the meaning of ecclesiastical authority are not understood in any radically different or more profound way than heretofore.

It is, therefore, in antiquity that the abiding presuppositions of the whole succeeding development of office in the Church and of its spiritual authority are fashioned. The early Middle Ages in the West, with the irruption of the young barbarian nations, and the revival of missionary activity in markedly altered forms, do, it is true, bring with them new conditions and a profound change of mood in every department of life. One consequence is that East and West draw even further apart. Theologically, however, men continue to build on the old foundations, the ideas popularised by Augustine and reinterpreted by pseudo-Dionysius. Only in the golden age of scholasticism, with the systematic elaboration of clerical canon law, are essentially new viewpoints brought to bear; but even these at first cause no radical change in the existing structures. And even the Reformation, which intended change and to a great extent achieved it, in this particular field of the doctrine of ecclesiastical office remained relatively conservative, especially in Lutheran areas. Nevertheless it is here, we may say, that a real crisis in the early concept of office begins, and makes it increasingly impossible either to go back to earlier patterns or to persevere in traditional ways of thought.

This book has been concerned only with the foundations of the doctrine of office as these were laid in the Early Church. The central difficulty, which we have encountered at every turn, has been that of determining the right relationship between office organised on a legal basis and free spiritual authority. The two are not originally identical, and yet they have to be brought into a proper relationship if the office of the clergy is to retain its religious meaning and remain an office of the Church in the full sense of the word. A precise understanding of the beginnings of Christianity, in all their extraordinary historical and systematic complexity, is indispensable for a grasp of the problem, and also, precisely because of the difficulties which arise, instructive and essential in arriving at a solution. Church order does not begin with the 'founding' of a normative office by Jesus himself, to which faith would then be tied once for all; but just as little do we find in the beginning the chaotic freedom of the 'Spirit' and of individual spirit-endowed persons. Neither the authoritarian 'catholic' nor the liberal-protestant conception of the Church will stand in face of the actual facts about primitive Christianity. To understand these it is necessary to range theologically far wider. It is no use adopting office and charisma, or Spirit and Law, directly as the ultimate realities of the Church, which can then be used as the basis for a systematic treatment of the problem of the true exercise of authority. Instead the crucial factor is the firm correlation in which from the very first the 'Spirit' stands to the concept of the 'Word' or 'testimony', both of which go back to the person of Jesus himself. These are the determinative realities, and between them make it equally impossible either to give Spirit absolute value over tradition or tradition over the Spirit.[1] In relation to these primal

---

[1] I have already attempted to clarify this relationship in my essay 'Tradition und Geist im Urchristentum', *Stud. Gen.* 4, 1951, pp. 351ff., and will not repeat what has already been said there.

realities of the life of the Church the particular office and the special spiritual gift, the charisma, are both logically subordinate categories, by means of which the former become concrete and contemporary for the congregation at any given moment. Their relationship is analogous to that within the Church whereby Christ as the living Word is both attested and made effectively present. To exclude either reality, therefore, inevitably leads to an overthrow of Christ's sovereignty, and to an authoritarian or enthusiast distortion of the concept of the Church. The absorption of spiritual authority by office is thus just as senseless as the wholesale surrender of official authority to the charismatics who refuse to be tied to official forms. Naturally the two types of degeneration are at all times, and especially in the history of the Early Church, to a certain extent complementary. But 'ecclesiastical' thinking, in the narrower, sociological sense of the word, at all periods inclines in the direction of a one-sided preference for office, and thus it is predominantly toward that danger that the path of the Early Church also tends. It leads from primitive Christianity to 'catholicism'.

A perfect combination of official and charismatic authority is found, if we wish to describe it that way, only once, namely in the person of Jesus himself.[2] His unique consciousness of authority transcends, as we have seen, those alternatives which for all other men are unavoidable; and in this respect it is not continued in the Church. But neither are the 'Apostles' charismatics or officials in the customary sense of the word.[3] They are not charismatics; for their authority does not spring from any special spiritual 'gift', but is based on their historical encounter with the Risen Lord, and it is to bear witness to him throughout the world that they are appointed. But equally they are not officials; for they are appointed once for all, individually, and by the Lord of the Church himself, who thereby designates them as the source of all Church tradition in a way that can never be repeated. Later holders of church office have authority only to the extent that they in their turn take up this apostolic witness, and are in no respect on an equal footing with the apostles. Their individual identity as such is no longer important; they succeed one another simply as holders of a continuing commission, to which they are elected or appointed within the congregation. Moreover, the testimony which it is their duty to uphold in the presence of the Church is no longer committed to them alone; the whole of Christendom already possesses it, or is possessed by it, and it exists and continues to exist as a living reality in the whole Church through the Spirit. The apostles, therefore, in their personal vocation stand as it were half way between the person of Jesus, whose authority is based purely on himself and on his divine 'Name', and the later

---

[2] Cf. chap. 1 above.   [3] Cf. chap. 2 above.

holders of an 'office', who rather are themselves upheld by the office, and whose constantly changing names are now of no decisive importance. Hence it is only here, in the third generation, so to speak, that the really characteristic interplay of spiritual power and official authority begins. But such a systematic analysis of the situation was very far from being at once clearly and straightforwardly understood by the Church or manifested in her.

It cannot be denied that the apostle Paul developed for the benefit of his congregations a concept of the Church in which, generally speaking, there was no 'office' apart from the quasi-office of his own apostolate, the legal importance of which he moreover played down as far as possible.[4] There is no need to see in this any deliberate polemic; but it is clear, none the less, that the exclusive emphasis on the sovereignty of the Spirit, the 'freedom' of all Christians which came with this, the demand for the mutual submission of those endowed with the Spirit, and the abrupt rejection of all 'human' ordinances and authorities, accords very closely with the very heart of Pauline theology.[5] The theological meaning of this charismatic constitution of the Church is more clearly worked out than its sociological consequences. Paul is familiar with, and indeed mentions, particular 'helpers' and functionaries within the congregation, who at least have some affinity with later holders of ecclesiastical office; but Paul will not tolerate any sense of official authority. Even the regular everyday functions and ministries within the Church are seen as the operation of 'gifts', not of offices and prerogatives, and only as gifts are they known and freely acknowledged by the congregation.

Alongside the Pauline church grew up at the same time the opposite type of congregation, led by presbyters, which was Jewish Christian in origin and character.[6] Here from the very first the 'elders', even where their rights are understood in purely patriarchal terms, possess 'official' authority, that is to say, authority based on their position. The legal order is combined with the 'natural' order of age, experience, and personal ascendancy, and now tends, in a way quite alien to Paul, to enhance within the Church, as it does so often, the moral importance of natural, human attributes. Nevertheless, office is thought of as by definition spiritual. For it leads the Christian congregation, which is a spiritual community; and consequently the office too is spiritual in its origin and in its goals, and must be spiritual in the manner in which it is carried out.

The fusion of the two forms begins early. In Luke there is a conscious effort to achieve this, and the author of I Peter also strives to combine in the totality of the Church the rights both of order and of the full-

---

[4] Cf. chap. 3 above.   [5] Cf. chap. 4 above.   [6] Cf. chap. 5 above.

ness of the Spirit, regard for the elders and the cultivation of spiritual gifts. In fact, of course, any community with a history, which is concerned to preserve and practice a tradition, to bring others to it, to abide within it, and to educate all its members to do the same, cannot permanently dispense with the appointment of particular leaders and 'shepherds' to whom respect must be shown. Yet their position must not be absolute and sacral in character, nor on the other hand should it be purely secular and pragmatic. Office or offices have a particular spiritual commission within the Church—primarily to preach, and then, in close association with this, to exhort, to guide, to train, to exercise care and concern, and to represent the congregation in worship; and in the interests of this commission the officeholders possess a standing and rights of their own. Such rights, however, are in no sense absolute; they always exist in a dialectical relationship with the spiritual community as a whole, and with its gifts. Precisely because of its commission office is no self-sufficient entity; it is not valid 'as such', but constantly points beyond itself to its living Lord. Because it is in the authority of this Lord that he stands, the official is at all times confronted by the question how far his conduct is really true to his master and to the meaning of his commission, and how far he is justifying and measuring up to the 'rights' vested in him. This question is not merely one addressed to his own conscience, but one that concretely concerns the congregation in which he serves, and must be examined, answered, and approved as such; for the activity of the Church as a whole presupposes also the spiritual activity and responsibility of the congregation, and not just that of its leaders.

This equilibrium of forces could not be maintained for ever. The course of ecclesiastical development finally led everywhere to a strengthening and ever more marked preponderance of the official element and of its exclusive authority, in face of which the spiritual life of the congregation shrivelled up and lost its radical significance. This trend toward an unbalanced ascendancy of office is the one uniform feature in the otherwise widely varying concepts of power and authority in I Clement, the Epistles of Ignatius, and the Pastoral Epistles from Asia Minor; and in the course of the second century this development continued unchecked. That the charismatic church order of Paul, which was devoid of office, should have been unable to hold its own anywhere after the disappearance of the authority of the apostle himself is perfectly understandable, and can also be justified on theological grounds. But for all that, the repression of and lack of regard for free spiritual gifts on principle remains a dangerous shift in the general spiritual outlook of the Church, and one which could not fail to have profound consequences.

The overall position of the Church during the second century makes the increasing emphasis on office and its authority seem at first very understandable. The confusion of enthusiastic sects, proliferating and splitting off in all directions during the gnostic crisis, seemed to the Church to be threatening all her links with the past, and consequently to make the safeguarding of her original doctrine and tradition the matter of supreme importance. To this extent her position was the exact opposite of Paul's in his struggle against the Judaistic 'Law'. The result was not merely the formation of the 'apostolic' canon, but also the establishment of an apostolic office.[7] This office was, as we have seen, not maintained for its own sake, but was to serve primarily in the necessary function of upholding the original deposit of faith and of ensuring a legitimate continuity in preaching. This preaching itself, however, was no longer spiritually alive in the original sense. It has become predominantly something fixed, something to be preserved as valid rather than proved as viable; and as a result the office that serves it also breaks away from the dialectical authority of a spirit which simultaneously tests and guards, and acquires instead a direct, formal authority. This is made possible only by a profound change in faith itself. The original meaning of evangelical authority[8] begins to be obscured. The Church no longer lives in any radical sense by the forgiveness of Christ, and it understands its sanctity as a human task to be required of Christians and fulfilled by them. Hence the authority of office too is understood one-sidedly, and conceived predominantly in moral and pedagogic, juristic and political terms.

The point more than any other at which all this becomes clear is the understanding of penance, and the corresponding administration of the office of the keys.[9] It is remarkable that while the christological controversy was being pursued with passion in the field of objective dogma there should be such uncertainty and ambiguity in the confession of Christ on a point of such practical importance. The gospel proclamation of Christ, addressing men personally and determining and changing their lives, totally transcends the rationalistic, neutralising distinction between doctrine and ethics, and touches Man in his total reality. It is precisely in the work of office in the Church, therefore, that it is important that the word of forgiveness and of the new life in Christ should be not only heard, but also applied and given concrete force. Because penance is understood exclusively as education, discipline, and 'judgment', the bishops, as possessors of the power of the keys, become the lords of penance; and it is this which gives their sovereignty in the Church its ultimate sacral foundation. But this, as we have seen, is not in the first instance the product of a special priestly lust for arbitrary power. In contrast to the immoderate exaltation of the clerical

---

[7] Cf. chap. 7 above. [8] Cf. chap. 6 above. [9] Cf. chap. 9 above.

power of absolution and excommunication during the Middle Ages the episcopate of the Early Church displays far more the opposite weakness of a certain timidity and lack of decision in the exercise of its evangelical power of pardon. And yet it was for the sake of this power that bishops were sought out by their church and compelled to take action. The striving for forgiveness and the assurance of forgiveness can be seen to be the driving force behind this development, and also as a sign that the Church's power of the keys was now indeed tied to the institution of office.

In the course of the third century the exclusive authority of office attains its full stature. It is true that the right to co-operate and share in church decisions is nowhere absolutely denied to the congregation, and that in practice their influence shrank only gradually and step by step before the growing might of the clergy. But everywhere in governing circles we can see the effort to make the effectiveness of clerical authority as unrestricted, unqualified and exclusive as possible. These efforts were especially successful in the western Church, and Cyprian here marks the terminal point of the process.[10] He formulates for the first time quite unambiguously—and with terrifying precision and candour—the principle that authority resides uniquely with the bishops. Of a specially effective authority of the Bishop of Rome there is in this context hardly any indication. All we can say is that there are signs earlier in the capital than elsewhere that the bishop and his following think of themselves as enjoying a special pre-eminence in relations with other churches and bishops. Twice, in the Paschal controversy and in the dispute over heretic baptism, the 'Pope' demands with offensive lack of consideration that Roman decisions should be respected, without however being able to carry his point simply for this reason. In the second instance he also appeals in justification of his demand to the special status of the *cathedra Petri*; but it is not clear whether behind this move there is already a strongly developed theory.[11] The question which bulks so large in confessional disputes, how far the Roman bishop was at that time already acting on the basis of his distinctive 'primacy', is historically misconceived and anachronistic; and in any case these events play no part in the general development of the concepts of the Church and of office in the early period.

The reverse side to the coin of the authoritarian supremacy of office in the Church is that the spiritual life and its gifts become more and

10 Cf. chap. 11 above.

11 On the distinctive character of the Papal representation of Christ, which is curiously different from other possibilities developed earlier, cf. the brilliant, but in many respects also problematic, 'sketch of ecclesiastical history' by A. Von Harnack, 'Christus praesens—vicarius Christi', *Sitzungsber. Preuss. Akad.*, 1927, pp. 415ff.

more an individual and private matter. Where office exercises exclusive control they have no further functional part to play in the general scheme of church life, but become the specially cultivated preserve of the more highly 'endowed' Christians and their disciples.[12] This development took place predominantly within the Greek church, and finally issues significantly in the history of the monastic movement. The exclusion of the intractable Montanist 'Prophecy' took place early on. Those representatives of the gift of teaching who remained became hellenised in their understanding of their vocation, and no longer claimed, as they had once done, a general hearing in the Church. Clement of Alexandria's attitude to the Church and to its whole hierarchical and organisational 'machine' is almost one of indifference. It is only for the 'perfect' Christians that these Christian 'philosophers' develop ever higher capacities for theological instruction and for spiritual training and pastoral care.

In the long run, however, such a discrete co-existence of official and private education and direction of souls within the one Church could not be maintained. Origen already regards it as the normal and accepted thing for those endowed with gifts, and especially with the gift of teaching, to be incorporated into the clergy and to reinforce that body with their spirit.[13] But only when viewed externally does this solution of the problem seem to be a harmonious one. It means that the man of the Spirit is now set in the framework of an 'external' order, whose legitimacy he may indeed acknowledge, but which ultimately he can no longer in the deepest sense affirm as 'spiritual'. At the same time, however, the clergy now begin to be measured by an ideal standard which as a body they cannot hope to meet. The approach is thus half 'liberal' and half pietistic, and fundamentally there is still no reconciliation of the authority of office, understood in legal and political terms, with the power of the spiritual man, seen from an individualist standpoint.

In the succeeding period the result for both office and charisma remains the same just so long as there is no attempt to derive the commission and authority of each from the ultimate source of their meaning in Christ. Only on this basis is there any possibility of confirming them in their unqualified gospel freedom, and at the same time of seeing them as limited in their human transience, and thus combining them once more within the one Church. The difficulty, however, lies in the fact that a developed doctrine of office in this biblical sense has not yet been formulated within the New Testament itself. There are only the starting-points for such a doctrine, pointing in different directions, and neither unambiguous nor unified enough for a direct

[12] Cf. chap. 8 above.   [13] Cf. chap. 10 above.

'proof from Scripture'. One could hardly expect anything else, seeing that the New Testament documents reflect such an early stage in the development; for the doctrine of office was not a central concern of primitive Christian thinking. In looking for a rationale of authority, therefore, we come round to the fact that the answer and the direction are not to be found in the inadequate fragments, but must be elaborated on the basis of the biblical testimony as a whole. Only then do the individual pieces of evidence fall into place. On any other method all attempts at reform end up by setting the charismatic thought of Paul against the official thinking of the Pastoral Epistles, and giving exclusive rights either to the Spirit as opposed to office or to office instead of Spirit.

INDEX OF ANCIENT AUTHORS
AND SOURCES

INDEX OF MODERN AUTHORS